THE SOCIAL WORLD OF PUPIL CAREER

The Social World of Pupil Career

Strategic Biographies through Primary School

Andrew Pollard and Ann Filer

CASSELL

Cassell
Wellington House
125 Strand
London WC2R 0BB

Cassell and Continuum
370 Lexington Avenue
New York
NY 10017-6550

www.cassell.co.uk

First published 1999

British Library Cataloguing-in-Publication Data
A catalogue record for this book is available from the British Library.

ISBN 0-304-32640-2 (hardback)
    0-304-32642-9 (paperback)

372.24 POL

Primary education
Child development
Learning

EDU

Social aspects
Biographies
Peer groups

Typeset by Ensystems, Saffron Walden
Printed and bound in Great Britain by Redwood Books, Trowbridge, Wiltshire

This book is dedicated to Sarah, William, Robert, Harriet, Mary, Hazel, Daniel, Sally and James.

Contents

Acknowledgements

We are delighted to acknowledge the enormous contribution to this book made by the children, parents, teachers and governors of the school from which case-study data has been collected and analysed. The *Identity and Learning Programme* continues, and it remains a great pleasure to work with each young person as he or she grows up, and with their families and teachers. We are conscious of, and grateful for, the trust which has been placed in us and in this book we have done our best to represent the life of each child in appreciative but valid ways.

The fieldwork on which much of this book is based was funded by the Leverhulme Trust, and we are extremely grateful for their support.

Finally, we would like to thank Sarah Butler for her excellent administrative and secretarial work in relation to both the programme and the production of this book.

Bristol, January 1999   Andrew Pollard and Ann Filer

Figures, Tables, Documents and Matrices by Chapter

FIGURES

TABLES

DOCUMENTS

MATRICES

Introduction

THE FOCUS OF THE STUDY

This book reports a part of what has become the *Identity and Learning Programme*, a series of studies of two cohorts of primary school pupils throughout their years of compulsory primary and secondary schooling in England. It follows directly from a book entitled *The Social World of Children's Learning* (Pollard with Filer, 1996) and is based on research in the same location, Greenside Primary School.

The present book describes and analyses the experience of four pupils over the seven years in which they attended Greenside Primary School. In so doing, patterns of social processes and child experience are identified, and analytic models are generated.

The book addresses four core questions:

- How should we conceptualize, describe and analyse young children and their 'careers' as pupils in primary schools?
- How do young pupils cope with the experience of different teachers and class-rooms as they move through primary school?
- How do the strategies of young pupils interact with other influences, from family and peers, to effect their emergent identities?
- Is there a tension between national policies for the improvement of educational standards and concern with the intrinsic quality of pupil experience, commitment to lifelong learning, and the personal, social and moral development of our citizens of the future?

RESEARCH DESIGN AND METHOD

The Identity and Learning Programme is based on ethnography – a form of research which was initially developed by anthropologists for the study of traditional cultures and communities across the world. Since then, it has been considerably updated as an approach to qualitative research and is now used by social scientists in many fields of study. The primary goal of an ethnographer is to create an accurate description of the perspectives, social practices and behaviour of the people on whom he or she focuses. The main methods are likely to be discussion, interview, collection of documents and a great deal of 'participant observation', with copious fieldnotes describing events and a 'research notebook' to record analytic ideas and fieldwork experiences. The overall aim is to generate 'grounded theory' as an analytic representation of important patterns, processes, relationships and outcomes.

Ethnographic studies in education have often been focused on social processes in schools, and studies based on one or two years of fieldwork are common, since the timespan fits the registration period for a higher degree and also the conventional period for research funding bodies. The study reported in this book was started formally by Andrew Pollard in September 1987, though some work in the school had taken place previously. Using a degree of latitude afforded by his role as a Reader at Bristol Polytechnic (before it became the University of the West of England), Pollard was able to build good fieldwork relationships with the families, teachers and pupils and to establish a theoretically informed data-gathering schedule. Soon after, Ann Filer began to study for a PhD using a complementary design but in Albert Park Primary, a school on the other side of the city which we call Easthampton. At Greenside, Pollard continued data-gathering for four years up to June 1991, at which point the Leverhulme Trust's interest in pupil career enabled Filer to join the Greenside project and take on the major fieldwork role until the conclusion of that phase three years later. Meanwhile, a grant from the Economic and Social Research Council (ESRC) enabled an extension of Filer's longitudinal study at Albert Park (Filer, 1993c). This has led to a further book in this series, *The Social World of Pupil Assessment* (Filer and Pollard, forthcoming). The secondary school phase of the study has been funded by the ESRC from 1996 to 2001. In this project, pupils from both Greenside and Albert Park Primary schools are studied up to the age of 16, when they complete examinations at the end of their compulsory schooling.

Ethnography focuses on understandings, interpretations and subjective perceptions as well as on patterns in actions and behaviour. The researcher is part of the research process, and uses his or her empathy and rapport to develop close and trusting relationships with the people whom he or she is trying to understand. Often there is a dependence on a single ethnographic researcher, but in working together we have been able to discuss and refine our interpretations on a continuous basis.

A detailed account of the research design, methods for data-gathering, analysis, ethical framework and strategy for writing up the work at Greenside Primary School can be found in Chapter 10 of *The Social World of Children's Learning*. In relation to the fieldwork undertaken by Ann Filer and our collaborative analysis for the present book, see Filer with Pollard, 1998.

THEORETICAL FRAMEWORKS

The Identity and Learning Programme reflects something of our biographies and engagement in social science over many years. Thus, in contextualizing our account of pupil career and personal development through primary school, we offer a brief review of the major theoretical influences to which we have reacted in exploring the interface of sociology and psychology. We also suggest how some of the major concepts from sociology and psychology have become embedded in 'commonsense' thinking, and explain how we want to contest these ways of thinking.

Going back to the 1960s, a powerful juxtaposition of 'structural functionalist' sociology and behaviourist psychology provided something of a status quo. Both approaches reflected a sense of the postwar consensus – and were soon to be challenged by new developments.

Structural functionalist sociology conceptualized society as an organic social system made up of interdependent subsystems (e.g. Parsons, 1951). Thus the economy, political and legal systems, religion, the family and education 'functioned' together and, in so doing, embodied, produced and reproduced the central values of society. The 'roles' of children, as for others of particular status or social position, were delimited by the normative consensus which obtained: 'Is she a "good baby"?', 'What do you say to Mrs Jones?', 'How is he doing at school?'. Structural functionalism thus cast children as passive – they were to be socialized into ascribed roles – boy, girl, pupil, teenager, young man, young woman. The concept of 'socialization' is still perceived as being central to social integration, and has passed from the discourse of social science into commonsense thinking. Indeed, we will argue that it remains a key feature of taken-for-granted representations of childhood, and one which presents the child as passive and deficient. Indeed, the child must be 'civilized', controlled and integrated into established society.

Behaviourist psychology is concerned with the ways in which people or animals learn through interaction with their environment. Fundamentally, the proposition is that learning takes place through processes of positive or negative reinforcement. Thus when a given stimulus is reinforced, a learned association begins to form. As chains of association become established, learning becomes increasingly sophisticated. For the toddler, storytime becomes associated with the pleasure of being read to. The nursery nurse praises 'the good little girls who are sitting up straight'. The teacher awards 'stars' for 'doing neat work' or 'learning spellings'. As the child learns to fulfil particular behaviours, he or she is learning to respond to the external environment, most of which is created and controlled by adults. Once again, it can be argued that there has been a transfer from the core ideas of behaviourism into elements of commonsense thinking. In particular, the conceptualization of learning through stimulus and response resonates with such taken-for-granted representations of 'teaching' as the transmission of knowledge through instruction, practice and assessment of performance. The empty vessel must be filled; the pupil must be taught.

There were strong reactions against the deterministic and consensual assumptions which are embedded in these approaches.

Sociological reactions

Even as long ago as the early 1960s it was argued that sociologists held an 'over-socialized conception of man' (Wrong, 1961). Indeed, far from society being based on induction into norms, an alternative view suggested that it was based on the 'social construction' of a shared reality (Berger and Luckman, 1967). In recognizing the activity and autonomous action of individuals, the real task of sociologists was to describe and interpret the meanings which were developed in different social situations and among different social groups. Thus we have had many studies of social settings, such as schools (e.g. Hargreaves, 1967; Woods, 1979; Hartley, 1985) and classrooms (e.g. Sharp and Green, 1975; King, 1978); teachers (e.g. Lortie, 1975; Clandinin, 1986) and pupils (e.g. Davies, 1982; Willes, 1983). There were many forms of interpretive sociology, such as ethnomethodology, phenomenology and symbolic interactionism.

Symbolic interactionism has been a strong influence on our own research. Based in the work of Mead (1934), it is focused on the creation of meaning as people interact together using both verbal and non-verbal communication. For instance, *The Social World of the Primary School* (Pollard, 1985) demonstrated how classroom understandings and tacit rules are developed as teachers and pupils negotiate and cope with the challenges which each poses for the other. There is also an important symbolic interactionist model of the development of identity. In essence, it is postulated that the 'I' of the self is able to reflect on an objectified sense of the 'me' and, in so doing, represents social expectations. Identity develops as the person manages this sense of self within their particular social context. It follows that an individual is likely to be particularly influenced by 'significant others' (Shibutani, 1955), hence our attention to parents, siblings, peers and teachers in both *The Social World of Children's Learning* and in the present book.

Some, however, have argued that symbolic interactionism and other forms of interpretive sociology are unable to take adequate account of social positioning, of structural aspects of society, and of the impact of material forces. At an extreme are Marxist theorists such as Althusser (1971) who saw education as part of an 'ideological state apparatus', designed to reproduce the dominance of a ruling class. Similarly, Bowles and Gintis (1976) suggested that classroom practices exhibit a 'correspondence' with the workplace, and thus reproduce unequal labour relations. Such perspectives are at least as deterministic as functionalism.

Psychological reactions

In psychology, a sustained critique of behaviourism had come earlier, and Piaget's *developmental* constructivism become influential in the 1950s and 1960s. Here, the child was certainly seen as active as he or she worked to accommodate and assimilate new experiences. However, Piaget proposed a sequential model of 'stages' of development, and was interpreted as having established that the capacities of children were limited within each stage. In the late 1970s developmental psychologists such as Donaldson (1978) and Tizard and Hughes (1984) moved beyond this to demonstrate the considerably greater capacities of children when acting in meaningful and authentic contexts. The work of Walkerdine (1983) demonstrated how the discourse of developmentalism positioned pupils and conditioned adult perceptions of their capabilities. However, Piagetian ideas of 'readiness' and 'stages' have passed into the commonsense social representations of childhood development, and with them an underlying conception of incompleteness and dependency. Similarly, the common, and associated, belief in childhood 'innocence' suggests the need for protection, but it does not call for rights or for children's voices to be really heard beyond sentimentalized indulgence.

During the 1980s, the work of Vygotsky (1962, 1978), although written in the context of 1930s Russian society, became particularly influential as a new form of *social* constructivism. Two major arguments were established. First, that the socio-cultural context in which learning occurs is of considerable significance, because both the concepts to be learned and appropriate forms of cognition itself are embedded within the culture of a society. They are contextually 'situated', and children may be seen as being engaged in forms of 'apprenticeship' as they encounter and negotiate the culture of their society. As Rogoff (1990) put it:

> what children learn is a cultural curriculum. From their earliest days, they build on the skills and perspectives of their society with the aid of other people.
> (Rogoff, 1990, p. 190)

This statement also draws attention to the second major insight offered by Vygotsky – the role of others who are more knowledgeable in extending a learner's thinking beyond the point of understanding which they could reach alone. The argument rests on conceptualization of a 'zone of proximal development' which each learner can cross with appropriate support. Learning is thus 'scaffolded' (Bruner, 1986) and performance is 'assisted' (Tharp and Gallimore, 1988) beyond the level which would otherwise be possible.

In *The Social World of Children's Learning* we drew on both of these Vygotskian insights. Thus the socio-cultural context of the Greenside case study was documented – the social, political and economic context of the late 1980s; a middle-class suburb of a southern English city; the school, its teachers and its developmental history; the homes, with parents, siblings and family beyond; peers and friendship networks etc. We illustrated how significantly others influenced the children's approaches to new experiences, risk-taking and learning and we showed how important the support of more knowledgeable others could be – in learning how to read, for instance. When the children were very young, it was undoubtedly parents, particularly mothers, who played the most significant role in discussing, mediating, and helping to interpret new experiences and new challenges.

Social representations and childhood

Our interest in culturally embedded forms of perception has been illuminated by Muscovici's theory of 'social representations' (1976). He writes:

> By social representations we mean a set of concepts, statements and explanations originating in daily life in the course of communications. They are the equivalent, in our society, of the myths and belief systems in traditional societies. They might even be said to be the contemporary version of common sense.
> (Muscovici, 1981, p. 181)

This perspective is part of a French tradition which can be traced back to Durkheim (1956), for whom myths, legends and traditions were seen as part of a collective stock of consciousness, deeply rooted in the culture of a society as a whole, and not explicable at the level of the individual. However, in the case of modern societies, Muscovici argues that social representations are much more dynamic. Indeed, he believes they have a direct relationship to scientific knowledge as it evolves. This is communicated through the filters of the mass media and becomes transformed into new culturally embedded assumptions. As he puts it:

> What is most striking to the contemporary observer is the mobile and circulating character of social representations; in short, their plasticity. . . . And their importance continues to increase in direct proportion to the complexity of the unifying systems – official sciences, religions, ideologies – and to the changes which these must undergo in order to penetrate everyday life and become part of common reality.
> The mass media have accelerated this tendency, multiplied such changes and increased the need of a link between our purely abstract sciences and beliefs in general and our concrete activities as social individuals. In other words, there is a continual need to re-constitute 'common sense', without which no form of collectivity can operate.
> (Muscovici, 1984, pp. 18–19)

Muscovici emphasizes this way in which social representations *transform* special-ized knowledge, including scientific knowledge, into forms of common sense. He suggests that there are two stages in this. First, an unfamiliar concept is compared, classified, located and named within an existing stock of understandings. It is thus 'anchored' in relation to other ideas. 'Objectification' follows when the concept becomes taken-for-granted – as an 'element of reality rather than of thought' (Muscovici, 1984, p. 40).

In this book, a particular interest is in representations of children, childhood and pupils and, as we have seen, the social sciences have generated many relevant technical concepts, including 'socialization', 'reinforcement', 'needs' and 'develop-mental stages'. Despite their scientific origins, these ideas have became anchored and objectified within pre-existing conceptions of childhood. This has been very obvious in the professional discourse of primary school teachers, but the same could be said of the thinking of many parents, journalists and politicians. These key features of 'childhood' are now embedded in common sense, and are thus reflected in educa-tional policy and practice at every level.

From a sociological perspective, Moscovici's theory of social representations offers fascinating insights into the ways in which new concepts and ideas may become located in routine, everyday thinking within a culture. In some ways, it complements Gramsci's concept of 'hegemony' – the pervasive dominance of powerful ideas. These are legitimated by 'common sense' which ironically thus masks material interests. Indeed, while Moscovici tends to draw on examples of specialist knowledge arising from science, social representations may also receive significant impetus from power-ful interest groups. A good example would be that of monetarist economics, which started as an abstract, academic form of analysis, was promoted by Thatcherism and then became embedded in the thinking of most Western societies.

The past decade in the UK has seen an ideological struggle over the conceptuali-zation of the child and learning (Pollard *et al.*, 1994; Broadfoot and Pollard, forthcoming). While conservative politicians of both major political parties have asserted the need for more rigorous curriculum specification and *teaching* of 'pupils' (with implicit assumptions of passivity and deficiency), the defensive teaching profes-sion was loath to give up its developmental conceptions of 'children' (with implicit assumptions of innocence and dependency).

In our view, the assumptions of passivity, deficiency and dependency remain significantly embodied in the social representation of 'pupil' within much commonsense thinking. Indeed, they can be seen as having underpinned the subject-based, teacher-dominated emphasis of changes in curriculum and pedagogy of the 1990s. It is assumed that, if standards need to rise, the curriculum must be specified more clearly and pupils should be taught more effectively. There is little talk of trying to engage with pupil imagination or with empowering them as learners.

We see the *Identity and Learning Programme*, of which this book is a part, as a contribution to an emergent paradigm in studies of children and childhood (Prout and James, 1990). Two key features of this are, as Prout and James put it:

> 'Childhood' is understood as a social construction. As distinct from biological immaturity, it is neither a natural nor universal feature of human groups, but appears as a specific structural and cultural component of many societies.
>   Children are and must be seen as active in the construction and determination of their own social lives, the lives of those around them and of the societies in which they live. Children are not just the passive subjects of social structures and processes.
> (Prout and James, 1990, p. 8)

These points express the key sociological concern with the relationship of structure and agency. We certainly need to understand the social conditions, institutional arrangements, expectations, conceptualizations, forms of discourse and positioning which children experience. However, we also need to be able to complement this with study of the activity of children as they negotiate within these constraints and possibilities.

Our study of 'pupil career' and of 'strategic biographies' can be seen as an attempt, using detailed, ethnographic case studies, to track these factors being played out over time within the particular context of English primary schooling of the late 1980s and early 1990s.

THE STRUCTURE OF THE BOOK

Part One: Setting the Scene

Our first chapter offers a contextualizing review of the research programme from which this book derives. An initial study of 'coping strategies' and classroom relationships was published by Pollard in 1985 (*The Social World of the Primary School*) and this was followed by the immediate precursor of the present book, focused on children's learning (*The Social World of Children's Learning*).

Chapter 2 reviews the way in which we have conceptualized 'identity', 'pupil career' and 'strategic action'. In so doing, the chapter introduces the theoretical model which we have generated for our analysis. It also provides a conceptual orientation for the reader, prior to engaging in the detailed descriptive case studies of Part Two.

The social contexts affecting the case-study pupils are the subject of Chapter 3. We begin with a review of major changes at the level of national policy through the period (1987–94), the circumstances of Easthampton and its local education authority. The suburb of Greenside is then considered together with a more detailed account of developments in Greenside Primary School. The chapter concludes with brief vignettes of the classroom practices of each of the teachers encountered by the case-study children as they progressed though the school.

Part Two: Case Studies of Pupil Career

In Chapter 4 we introduce Sarah, competently fulfilling the expectations of family and teachers. Though somewhat in the shadow of a high-achieving older brother and some more confident friends, Sarah was often surprising in her underlying independence of action and strength of will. Readers of *The Social World of Children's Learning* will have encountered two of Sarah's friends, Mary and Sally, in that book. Chapter 5 brings us William, an able, confident and socially astute leader among the mainstream boys' groups. We see William successfully negotiating a series of social and learning contexts through most, though not all, of his primary school years. Robert, the subject of Chapter 6, was variously nicknamed the 'mad professor' and 'Einstein'. We see his creative self-directed approach to learning being variously evaluated and valued by teachers, with important implications for his social and academic well-being in school. Harriet's story in Chapter 7 is one of academic and social competence but also one of wry detachment from many aspects of school life. Her love of horses and capacity for imaginative expression combine in the development of a very close friendship with Hazel. Readers may also have encountered Hazel and her interest in dragons and dinosaurs in the earlier book.

Part Three: Reflecting

In Chapter 8, we stand back from the detail of these narratives to revisit the analytic issues. This is an important chapter, since it draws together our empirical findings, highlights key themes and presents our grounded theory of pupil career.

Finally, in Chapter 9 we provide a review of the *Identity and Learning Programme* as a whole, and attempt to relate its core arguments to the development of classroom practice and national policies. In so doing we reassert the significance of children's perspectives and argue that, if more account was taken of them, education systems would be both more effective in satisfying national priorities and more fulfilling for the teachers and pupils who experience them.

HOW TO USE THE BOOK

As in *The Social World of Children's Learning*, this book contains extensive narrative case studies of pupils' lives which are intended to provoke readers into reflection, comparison and discussion of their own biographies and experiences. Although posing important questions, the book does not seek to prescribe 'right answers' concerning specific ways in which children should be brought up or treated at school. At the same time though, readers are certainly invited to engage actively with the text and to consider the implications of issues which are generated by the unfolding stories or by the analysis itself.

Part One

Setting the Scene

Chapter 1

The Social World of Primary School Learning

1.1 INTRODUCTION

This chapter sets out the links between our previous work on the 'social world' of pupils and the analysis which is contained in this book. We highlight key issues from *The Social World of the Primary School* (Pollard, 1985) and *The Social World of Children's Learning* (Pollard with Filer, 1996). This provides a foundation for Chapter 2, in which we introduce the central analytic model of the present book.

A consistent theoretical influence on this work has been symbolic interactionism with its key focus on the ways in which meaning is developed through social processes. Individuals thus act on the basis of their interpretation of particular situations and 'self', or identity, is seen as a product of accumulated social experience.

A central focus of empirical work then becomes the relationship between action and context. In the case of our work on pupils, this has meant that we have been particularly concerned to try to identify patterns in the ways in which children interpret and then respond to classroom, playground and family contexts. Our early attempt to do this focused on schools and used the concept of 'coping strategy'.

1.2 COPING STRATEGIES IN PRIMARY SCHOOL CLASSROOMS

Development of the concept of coping strategies can be traced through Woods (1977), Hargreaves (1978), Pollard (1982, 1985) and Filer (1993a, 1993b). It is the central concept in what has been an explicit attempt by qualitative sociologists to analyse the relationships between society and individuals, history and biography.

One element of the analysis recognizes the extent of structural, material and ideological constraint in society. In the case of education, this highlights the subservient position of schools and teachers within state policy frameworks, the limited resources made available, and the existence of particular conceptions and concerns about education which dominate the mindset of much of the public and media. Children are also constrained, by legal restraints on their rights, dependence on parents or carers, media pressures, and by the existence of particular conceptions of what 'childhood' should be like and of how 'child' or 'pupil' roles should be fulfilled. Such pressures and constraints penetrate, and are mediated, through multiple levels of educational provision, until they have their effect in classroom contexts. We thus have particular curricular requirements, recommended pedagogies, prescribed forms of assessments, delineated resource frameworks, and management and accountability systems to which both teachers and pupils must respond. We can answer the question: 'What has to be "coped with"?'.

However, such an analysis cannot tell us what 'coping' will actually mean to any individual. To understand this, we need to know much more about each person. In particular, we need to understand the subjective interpretations which each individual makes of the contexts in which they find themselves. For symbolic interactionists, the key factor here is that of 'self'. How does each person think about himself or herself? What is their sense of identity? How do they present themselves? Who, in the context of their social group, do they think they are? Interviews, discussion and the study of biographies are essential ways of trying to understand such issues, and these methods lie at the core of the longitudinal ethnography which is reported in this book. Study of the perspectives and self of individual pupils and teachers will enable us to learn about their uniqueness, and about the ways in which they interpret their experiences. We can address the question: 'What does coping mean for any particular individual?'.

The Social World of the Primary School (Pollard, 1985) began with an analysis of teacher and pupil perspectives. The data derived from interviews and participant observation with teachers and pupils in three primary schools. It was collected while Andrew Pollard was a practising teacher and, in one school, with the direct assistance of pupils themselves.

Regarding teachers, a major disjunction was identified between the 'educationist context' and the 'teacher context'. While the former offered prescriptions on how teachers 'should' teach in line with educational theorizing and policy prescription, the latter spoke from the realities of classroom life. Thus teachers emphasized classroom management and the need to maintain discipline, together with the challenge of providing a stimulating and worthwhile curriculum. However, teachers also talked about how they coped with classroom life in much more personal ways. Starting from their own sense of 'self', they were concerned with retaining their dignity, with workload, health and stress issues, and with job satisfaction obtained through enjoyment of their work with children and the exercise of autonomous professional judgement in their classrooms.

Regarding pupils, a tension was identified between expectations of friends and peer culture, as developed in the informal contexts of the playground and beyond, and more formal requirements of teachers as a reflection of the school context. Normative prescriptions, both tacit and overt, delineated how pupils 'should' behave in school. Indeed, the teachers had clear ideas on the characteristics of their 'ideal pupil', to which some children were able to respond. On the other hand, the security and enjoyment of peer-group membership was very important for most children, reflecting shared experiences and a similar structural position of relative powerlessness in school. Underlying all this, more personal pupil concerns were detected, many of which were connected to the relative vulnerability of pupils in the evaluative setting of the school. Thus we have concerns with maintaining dignity and self-image,

	Teachers	**Pupils**
Primary	SELF	SELF
interests-at-hand	self-image	maintenance of self-image
	retention of dignity	retention of dignity
	workload	workload
	health and stress	control of stress
	enjoyment	enjoyment
	autonomy	autonomy
Enabling	ORDER	PEER-GROUP MEMBERSHIP
interests-at-hand	INSTRUCTION	LEARNING

Figure 1.1 *Primary and enabling interests of teachers and children (from Pollard, 1985, p. 35 and p. 82)*

particularly when being 'told off', with workload and avoiding stress, and, as with teachers, with deriving enjoyment and self-fulfilment from classroom life.

In *The Social World of the Primary School* it was suggested that the personal concerns of teachers and pupils could be seen as 'primary interests-at-hand' in classroom life. This means that they would be seen as being fundamental to each individual's attempt to cope, and in this respect it is interesting to note a degree of overlap in the primary interests of teachers and pupils. However, to actually succeed in coping – to 'survive' – teachers and pupils must also address the particular context and structural position in which they find themselves, as indeed they do when interviewed. Teacher concerns with 'order' and 'instruction' and pupil concerns with 'peer-group membership' and 'learning' were identified, and these were defined as 'enabling interests-at-hand'. What was suggested, then, was that both teachers and pupils, as people, have a fundamental and primary concern with maintaining and defending their sense of 'self', but that they have to try to do that in different ways. Teachers work to cope personally by maintaining order and by teaching effectively, while pupils cope by trying to achieve an appropriate balance between maintaining their peer-group status and satisfying school goals though learning.

Figure 1.1 sets out the key elements of this analysis.

Of course, one very important element of this story which we have not yet addressed is the fact that teachers and pupils have to cope with each other in classrooms. The fact is that both parties do have sufficient power to threaten the interests of the other. For teachers, this power is ascribed and backed by their socially sanctioned role. They can thus draw on support from other adults in school, at home and beyond, and the expectation is that they will initiate, lead and evaluate most classroom activities. Pupils largely accept this teacher authority and, on an individual basis, each may feel personally vulnerable. However, each class of pupils also has a considerable amount of power over their teacher, for collectively they can threaten classroom order and instruction and challenge the teacher's self-confidence. Further, as Waller (1932) demonstrated, there is latent conflict in all classrooms, since the basic yardstick of teacher success is to achieve some change in pupils' thinking to which they may, or may not, be receptive. The reality, however, is that only occasionally is life in primary school classrooms overtly conflictual. How is this achieved?

The Social World of the Primary School analysed teacher–pupil relationships as a process of negotiation through which tacit understanding and rules are evolved. A 'process of establishment' (Ball, 1980) at the start of each school year is a particularly active period during which teachers normally take the initiative. Pupils get to know their teacher's expectations but will also test her skill and resolve. Because both teachers and pupils do have sufficient power to threaten the interests of the other, there are genuine negotiations over issues such as noise levels, movement, behaviour, quality and quantity of work and routine procedures. Gradually the class becomes more 'settled' as understandings, conventions and taken-for-granted rules become established. Such a 'working consensus' reflects mutual acceptance by the teacher and pupils. While each could disturb the life of the other, negotiation produces sufficient understanding to enable them to 'get along together' in reasonably amicable ways. A type of moral order in the classroom is established.

However, not all pupils will interpret classroom rules and understandings in the same ways, nor do all pupils face similar circumstances in their lives. In *The Social World of the Primary School* three types of pupil friendship group were identified from detailed study of one year-group of 11-year-olds. 'Goodies' were relatively conformist but did not attain particularly highly. A significant proportion were girls' groups, but by no means all. Regarded as 'quiet but dull', they were not popular with their other peers and were sometimes overlooked by teachers. 'Gangs' on the other hand were quite prepared to be disruptive, particularly if they became bored or felt that they had been 'picked on'. They were generally less successful academically than most of the pupils but revelled in their reputations as 'rough and tough'. More, but not all, of the gang groups in the year-group were made up of boys and they tended to be from lower social class family backgrounds. The most successful type of group were termed 'Jokers'. Although of both sexes, Jokers in the year group often came from more middle-class families. These children were able to perform well academically and were also popular with their peers. They were active in sport and school events and took a disproportionate share of school responsibilities. Apart from their capabilities, they were distinguished by the close relationships which they established with their teachers and by their social awareness and skill. They could thus 'read' an evolving classroom situation, and 'have a laugh' *with* their teacher while also being alert to signals which might indicate a change of mood. For many teachers, these were seen as 'ideal' pupils.

Figure 1.2 below represents the analysis of differences between these three types of group in terms of their response to classroom rules. It was suggested that the central role in the negotiation of the working consensus is played by members of Joker groups, who use their skills, reputation and relationship to work with the teacher while also having a little mischief or light relief along the way. Teachers tend to indulge this within reason, for it also provides them with some amusement, diversion and enjoyment while not threatening their primary interests. 'Goodies' then conform to the teacher expectations, and may even remain nervous about 'doing something wrong'. Gang members, on the other hand, may not feel constrained by the working consensus. If they feel aggrieved, they may act unilaterally and challenge

	Actions within the understandings of the working consensus		Unilateral actions
	Conformity	Routine deviance	Rule-framed disorder
Goodies	>>>>>>>>		
Jokers	>>>>>>>>>>>>>>>>>>>>>>>>>>		
Gangs	>>		

Figure 1.2   *Parameters of child behaviour (from Pollard, 1979, p. 90)*

the teacher in disorderly ways. In so doing, their actions will be framed by the different set of rules which have been negotiated within the peer group.

The Social World of the Primary School thus provided a sociological analysis of teacher and pupil perspectives, of classroom relationships and of coping strategies. However, it did not directly face the question of children's learning itself, or of how children develop their perspectives and identities as learners over time.

1.3   SOCIAL RELATIONSHIPS, LEARNING AND DEVELOPMENT

The Social World of Children's Learning (Pollard with Filer, 1996) is the immediate precursor of the present book. As we saw in the Introduction, it is based on the early years of a longitudinal ethnography in one primary school tracking pupils from the age of four through to the age of seven.

The book was intended to make a contribution to a 'sociology of learning' (Pollard, 1990) and it explicitly attempts to link symbolic interactionist sociology with social constructivist psychology. As described in the introduction of the present book, social constructivism derives from the work of Vygotsky (1962, 1978), who suggested how language, conceptual tools and meanings are culturally embedded, and how social processes can extend or constrain the learner. From this perspective, the traditional concerns of psychology, such as 'ability', motivation, cognition, memory and attainment, are seen as providing only a partial account of influences on learning. Thus Bruner (1990), for instance, argues for a 'cultural psychology' which would unite social and psychological factors in an integrated and holistic analysis.

The Social World of Children's Learning was intended to provide an analysis of social influences on the learning of young children as they developed from year to year. We focused particularly on three clusters of influence: on the homes, parents and siblings; on the school playground and peer relations; and on the classrooms and interaction with each child's successive teachers. The book provided very detailed case studies of these influences on the learning of five children over the three years of Key Stage 1 (age 4/5, 5/6 and 6/7).

In terms of its research design, the longitudinal ethnography represents three

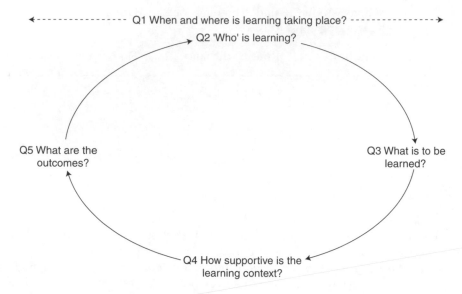

Figure 1.3 *A simple model of learning, identity and social setting (from Pollard with Filer, 1996, p. 14)*

crucial forms of development beyond that of *The Social World of the Primary School*. First, the focus is on individual children; second, they are studied longitudinally; and third, each of the most significant social contexts in their lives is included in the study. The result is an extremely holistic set of case-study accounts of young people growing up in their families and community. Unlike most sociological ethnography, based on cross-sectional studies at particular points in time, the longitudinal programme made it possible to construct detailed, contextualized and developmental accounts of new learning experiences, coping strategies, subjectivity and meaning. Using narrative approaches, biographical stories of development and change have been constructed. While *The Social World of Children's Learning* did this in respect of a three-year period and with particular reference to learning, the present book draws on the full seven years of primary education. It draws on a range of factors in children's strategic biographies to focus on 'pupil careers' in school.

Five deceptively simple questions were posed in the analysis of *The Social World of Children's Learning*, and these are represented in Figure 1.3.

The first question, 'When and where is learning taking place?', asserts the significance of the socio-historical context. In the present book, this is the focus of Chapter 3 in which social, cultural, economic and political circumstances of the country, region, city, community, families and school are set out in relation to the period of the study.

'"Who" is learning?' is a reference to the key issue of identity – of 'self'. In *The Social World of Children's Learning* each child's sense of self is seen primarily as a product of their relationships with significant others. However, the influences of biological endowment and social circumstances are also considerable. Thus interpersonal factors in the development of identity are conditioned by both intellectual and physical potential and by the opportunities or constraints afforded by the material, cultural and linguistic resources available to each family.

The third question, 'What is to be learned?', draws attention to the form and content of new learning challenges and to the learning stance and strategies which each child adopts. New learning challenges arrive in the form of experiences and relationships as well as in the form of curricular tasks. In each case, the content of the particular learning challenge will affect each child's motivation and self-confidence. In turn, this may affect the range of strategic resources on which they draw.

'How supportive is the learning context?' takes us back to *The Social World of the Primary School* and to questions about the quality of classroom relationships and the working consensus. Put another way, 'How is power used, and how does this affect children's willingness to take risks as they engage in learning?'. This issue is as apposite in homes as it is in schools. It is complemented by a further set of questions about adult provision: 'What is the quality of assistance in learning?', 'Is instruction well matched to the child's cognitive and motivational needs?', 'Does the adult have appropriate knowledge and skill to offer the child?'. The analysis of case-study children in *The Social World of Children's Learning* shows that children learn most in an atmosphere in which they feel secure and when they are offered appropriate instruction by others who are more knowledgeable.

Question five, 'What are the outcomes?', draws attention both to formal and informal outcomes. In formal terms, the learner achieves a new capability, attainment or standard, and may even be tested and certificated for it. In terms of identity formation, however, the informal processes which occur when friends, family and teachers affirm, mediate and interpret those achievements are perhaps even more significant. The consequence is that social status and self-esteem are both affected and their influence rolls round to contribute once more to the question, '"Who" is learning?'.

Interestingly, such overall processes can also be seen as socially embedded forms of assessment. Indeed, drawing on data gathered in a second primary school, we have constructed just such an analysis in *The Social World of Pupil Assessment* (Filer and Pollard, forthcoming).

The cyclical process which has been described above is dynamic and continuous, as is demonstrated through the narratives in *The Social World of Children's Learning*. Although developed through study of young children, we see it as a fundamental process which continues through life, with key questions and factors being played out through successive episodes and phases of experience. And so we become what we are, as we interpret past experiences and respond to new ones, and develop further. As Rowan Williams (cited in Maitland, 1991) put it: 'the self is, one might say, what the past is doing now'.

Figure 1.4 represents this spiral continuing through life, with positive, progressive imagery. Analytically, this is accurate, for the process will continue. However, as we all know, the outcomes of life experience vary considerably for different individuals, and sociologists attempt to trace patterns for richer and poorer, male and female, white and black, old and young, healthy and less healthy etc. Such issues will be particularly prominent in a further book from the *Identity and Learning Programme*, which will compare the secondary school trajectories and social identities of pupils

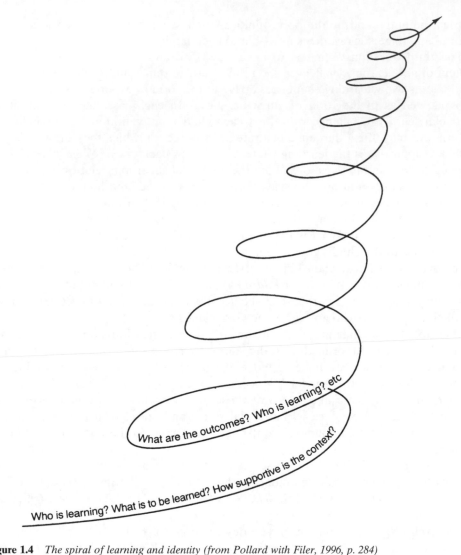

What are the outcomes? Who is learning? etc

Who is learning? What is to be learned? How supportive is the context?

Figure 1.4 *The spiral of learning and identity (from Pollard with Filer, 1996, p. 284)*

from the contrasting socio-economic communities of Greenside and Albert Park. Already, we know that these are beginning to diverge in very significant ways.

The present book is focused on the concepts of 'strategic biography' and 'pupil career' as they relate to pupil experiences in Greenside Primary School. We aim to track the cycles of learning which were experienced by four children, to trace them in detail over the seven years of their primary school careers, and to develop a grounded theoretical representation of the key processes, patterns and outcomes. In the final chapter we draw out the explicit implications for policy and practice.

1.4 CONCLUSION

This chapter has introduced the two previous studies of the 'social world' of primary school children on which the present book builds. Our initial interest centred on classroom relationships and coping strategies. Symbolic interactionism provided a theoretical framework, which we have sustained. However, as the study developed, we also began to engage with social constructivist psychology and to consider the influence of wider socio-cultural factors on learners and learning.

Chapter 2

Identity and Pupil Career

2.1 INTRODUCTION

In this chapter we review the ways in which we have conceptualized *identity*, *pupil career* and what we term *dimensions of strategic action*. We show how they have developed from our earlier work and also position them with reference to other related work.

The account is intended to further sensitize the reader to our theoretical interpretation, prior to engagement with the case-study stories of children's experience which form Part Two of this book. We have attempted to present the latter with minimal interruption of the narrative flow, and interested readers should thus be able to generate their *own* interpretation of them. However, our initial analysis here may help to inform and structure that reading.

In Chapter 8, following the presentation of the pupil stories, we return to these major themes for more detailed discussion and analysis.

2.2 IDENTITY

What is 'identity'? Breakwell (1986) suggests that the concept embodies three key principles of individuality, which people strive to sustain in their daily lives:

- distinctiveness and uniqueness;
- continuity across time and situation;
- self-esteem and a feeling of personal worth.

However, awareness and maintenance of individual differentiation are only part of the story, because a range of social factors also intrudes. For instance, structural position, cultural knowledge and particular forms of discourse represent social influences which make an impact on all individuals. Some therefore argue that, ultimately, we can only make sense of individuals in the context of their social relationships. Lloyd and Duveen, for instance, propose that:

individuals are so inextricably interwoven in the fabric of social relations within which their lives are lived, that a representation of the 'individual' divorced from the 'social' is theoretically inadequate. There is no pure 'individuality' which can be apprehended independently of social relations.
(Lloyd and Duveen, 1990: 20)

A satisfactory account of identity has therefore to synthesize the internal and personal concerns of individuals, and the external influences of cultures and expectations of appropriate social groups and the wider society.

In *The Social World of Children's Learning* we explored identity by posing the question: 'Who is learning?'. We focused on three contributing groups of factors: potential, resources and relationships (see Figure 2.1), and we showed how these were played out in respect of each case-study child (see, for instance, the detailed discussion of Mary, pp. 84–6 of *The Social World of Children's Learning*).

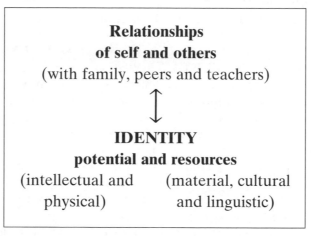

Figure 2.1 *Relationships, potential and resources: three factors in identity*

In identifying 'potential', we drew attention to the role of biological endowment. Neither physical and intellectual capacities nor affective dispositions are genetically fixed – but they do remain important factors in exploring capability. As Breakwell (1986, p. 14) suggested: 'the parameters of the biological organism, its physiological capacity, set the ultimate constraints upon the development of identity.'

By 'resources', we wanted to emphasize the role of material, cultural and linguistic factors. These are distributed in highly differentiated ways, reflecting politico-economic, socio-cultural circumstances and positions. The consequence, for individuals of particular social groups, is a differential flow of opportunities, living conditions, food, commodities, social experiences, cultural capital, concepts, vocabulary and linguistic skills.

'Relationships of self and others' is a direct reference to Mead (1934) and the symbolic interactionist conception of self. As Berger and Berger (1976, p. 73) put it:

identity ... is appropriated by the individual through a process of interaction with others. Only if an identity is confirmed by others is it possible for that identity to be real to the individual holding it. In other words, identity is the product of an interplay of identification and self-identification.

This is a very important element of the symbolic interactionist position and emphasizes the development of self-awareness and the construction of meaning through interpersonal relationships. With regard to young children, this is undoubtedly an extremely significant level of social awareness. However, wider and more diverse cultural forms of understanding will certainly be embedded in such interactions, and grow in significance. This leads to the concept of 'social identity', denoting definitions by self or others which are based on membership or identification with a social group, social category or social position within a particular socio-cultural context. In our study for instance, the social identities of 'boy', 'girl' and 'pupil' took a particular form in respect of the English, middle-class location of Greenside and were further modified by the positioning of the children in terms of attainment and participation in their school, families and the community.

Put concisely then, identity may be understood as 'an internal-external dialectic of identification' (Jenkins, 1996, p. 171) which, given the complexity, change and uncertainties of modern society, is likely to be played out continuously (Giddens, 1991).

As indicated in Chapter 1 of this book, in *The Social World of Children's Learning* we generated a model of one such process in relation to young children's engagement with learning. This took the form of a continuous spiral. 'Identity' was seen, to put it very simply, as a representation of the self-belief and self-confidence which learners bring to new learning challenges and contexts. However, it is also what they *become* through interaction with significant others, their experience of new learning opportunities and their engagement with dominant social representations within their culture. The case studies in *The Social World of Children's Learning* thus showed young children developing and incorporating aspects of the ways in which teachers, friends and family saw them as they began to shape and construct themselves as 'learners', 'pupils', 'boys' and 'girls'.

In the present book, analysis of data across the seven years of the children's primary schooling enabled *longitudinal* development of the learning and identity model. We were able to identify significant changes in children's approaches to learning as they encountered new experiences, but we also noted *patterns* of behaviour which were relatively consistent features of their relationships with parents and siblings, teachers and peers. Such developments and continuities can be represented as the 'strategic biography' of each child – their personal history of adaption, action and interaction regarding the important people, situations and events in their lives. 'Pupil career' can be seen as a particular social product deriving from children's strategic action in school contexts. However, it is also strongly influenced by cultural expectation.

2.3 PUPIL IDENTITY AND CAREER

We see children as active negotiators and decision-makers, but they are far from being free agents. As they negotiate their identities as pupils in the school setting, there are two particularly significant reference groups to whom they must attend – teachers and peers. However, as we suggested in the Introduction of this book, they cannot avoid the more pervasive influence of conceptions of the pupil role which are embedded in the wider culture. These may be reflected in the media and even through government policy.

Within English culture, children are exposed to many representations of the pupil role. This ranges, for instance, from traditional school-related children's stories such as 'Jennings and Darbishire', to the contemporary challenges of 'Grange Hill' portrayed on children's television. Such social representations strongly reflect social class, race and gender, and often contrast the sentimentalized quality and stability of traditionalism with the diversity and challenges of school life in the maintained sector.

An associated factor is the ambivalent view of school performance which is embedded in English culture. High attainment may be a goal of pupils, but in the child and youth cultures of many schools and communities there are considerable social pressures working against overt expression of such commitments. In such settings, peer status can be threatened by conformity to academic expectations, and pupil identity then becomes a product of the management of contradictory cultural forces. For instance, this has been a prominent argument in discussions about the 'underachievement' of boys, in which the 'conformity' of the pupil role is seen as being incompatible with the development of male identity in the youth culture of the 1990s, particularly for white, working-class and Afro-Caribbean boys. In a sense, such responses can be seen as assertions of independence, by particular groups of young people, from the conformity of ascribed pupil roles.

In recent years, successive UK governments have sustained relatively simple and unproblematic conceptions of 'the pupil' which, we would argue, stem from tacit assumptions of passivity and deficiency. Certainly, the nature of pupil learning or experience was never overtly addressed during the period covered by this research, despite the fact that the education system of England and Wales was fundamentally restructured. In 1989, the National Curriculum was introduced with English, Mathematics and Science among six other subjects to provide a 'broad and balanced' curriculum. It was then 'slimmed down' (Dearing, 1993) and then 'cut back to the core' (Blunkett, 1998). Assessment expectations changed as initial support for formative, ongoing assessment was replaced by the requirement to judge 'levels' of pupil attainment, and to administer standardized tests for reporting to parents and the production of league tables of schools. School inspectors, particularly through the Chief Inspector, maintained an unrelenting emphasis on 'standards' and asserted the pedagogic necessity of more 'direct, whole-class teaching' to replace 'old, child-centred orthodoxies'. Thus, both structural change and its associate discourse consistently emphasized teaching and the delivery of the curriculum, with relatively little attention to pupils as learners *per se*. A report of the Chief Inspector (OFSTED, 1997) provides an example in which 'children' and 'pupils' are mentioned solely as an adjunct of the dominant discourse about standards. The implicit representation of children is thus rather like that of industrial raw material awaiting processing and the addition of added value. Various strengths and weaknesses in the functioning of the educational machine are considered, but the assumed passivity of pupils is conveyed by the almost complete absence of any direct account of their perspectives, experiences or quality of life. Education, in this account, is something which is done *to* children, not *with* children, and still less *by* children.

We thus see how popular culture and national policies convey particular images or make assumptions concerning being a 'pupil'. However, at the level of the school and family, more specific factors come into play.

There is no doubt that teachers continue to have the power, authority and responsibility to control and structure classroom life. They also have immense influence over formal and informal processes of assessment, so that children have every reason to pay considerable attention to teacher perspectives and actions. We know (Hargreaves, 1972; Nash, 1976; Pollard, 1985; Cortazzi, 1990) that teachers' classroom knowledge of pupils tends to cluster around two issues: curriculum attainment and behaviour. However, extra-curricular activities outside the classroom can also be important in providing alternative opportunities for forging new identities. As significant influences on *pupil* identity, we thus have three key questions relating to curricular attainment, behaviour and extra-curricular activities:

• How is the child seen as a learner in terms of the school curriculum, and what is the child's own perception?
• How is the child seen in terms of school behaviour and social relationships, and what is the child's own perception?
• How is the child seen as a participant in extra-curricular activities, and what is the child's own perception?

For children, their friends at school are often a source of play and amusement, games and excitement, collaboration and defence (Davies, 1982). They are immensely valuable, and do much to enable pupils to cope with the challenges of school life. On the other hand, where friendships are not formed or bullying occurs, peers can be disdainful, cruel and aggressive (Tattum and Lane, 1989). We thus have a further question to pose:

• How is the child seen by his/her friends and by other pupils, and what is the child's own perception?

Parents, carers, siblings and other family members also exert influence over what it means to be a pupil, albeit indirectly. The interest shown by parents and grandparents of primary school children is frequently considerable, though the sources of information available to them may be weak. Nevertheless, using whatever scraps they can gather, concerned parents tend to maintain a constantly evolving image of their child as a pupil. This image forms as they both monitor and support the social, emotional and intellectual progress of their child. If concerns emerge, then further information will be sought and a visit to the school may take place to consult with the teacher. The image held in the family at any particular time offers the child a significant mirror back on themselves as a pupil. As we argued in *The Social World of Children's Learning*, parents are key mediators of children's experience. They assist in interpreting and making sense of new challenges – and this includes understanding oneself as a 'pupil'. A further important question is thus:

• How is the child seen as a pupil by parents, siblings and other family members, and what is the child's own perception?

These five questions and areas of influence highlight likely conceptions of the 'pupil', and one of the first challenges which any child faces on entry to his or her school is to learn the role as interpreted within that particular setting (e.g. Jackson,

1969; Willes, 1983). Initially, teacher guidance is likely to be very direct, with explicit attempts being made to induct new children into the established routines, procedures and rules. Individual children will respond to this in different ways. By drawing on their accumulated experience and biographical resources, they will act strategically in accommodating to the demands of the new situation. As we have seen, there are many sites of engagement as a pupil identity is developed. In relation to teachers, curricular activity, academic performance, social relationships and behaviour are likely to be particularly important. In relation to peers, participation within child culture and the development of appropriate friendships may well precede acceptance. Additionally, variations in the expectations and behaviour of both teachers and peers are likely in relation to gender, social class, ethnicity etc. The resulting positioning of each child as a 'pupil' will be mediated by wider cultural and political influences, and constantly evaluated by teachers, peers and parents. From the resulting understandings, children experience, shape and negotiate their status and sense of self as a pupil.

Our view of 'pupil career' develops from this initial construction of pupil identity. Indeed, it can be seen as a representation of patterns of coping strategies, learning and social outcomes as pupil identity and status are shaped through experiences in successive classrooms and other school contexts year on year. It is manifestation, in the school context, of each child's strategic biography. We have envisaged a spiral of learning and identity as children encountered new experiences through the years (Figures 1.3 and 1.4), and this model underpins our overall conception of 'career'.

At a more detailed level of analysis, we can thus identify three principal components of 'pupil career':

- *patterns of outcomes*, related to the learning and social contexts of successive classrooms, together with those of the wider school and playground;
- *patterns of strategic action* developed in coping with, and acting within, these contexts;
- the *evolving sense of self* which pupils bring to, and derive from, school settings and external contexts.

Our study showed that, as such factors are played out, there is both continuity and change. Indeed, some of the unfolding stories in our case studies might have been anticipated, for children in school do not behave randomly in response to school expectations and learning contexts. Rather, they build on existing biographies and experiences and act in ways which are often patterned. However, our longitudinal observations also showed us that year on year changes in contexts almost always produce some change in individuals' strategies for coping. Particular academic and social outcomes follow, with subsequent developments to each child's sense of self and the ways in which he or she is perceived by others.

To track such changes, we needed a secure way of conceptualizing and mapping strategic action.

2.4 DIMENSIONS OF STRATEGIC ACTION

Sociologists have studied pupil cultures and adaptions to school life for many years, with the result that we are not short of analytic models and representations. These

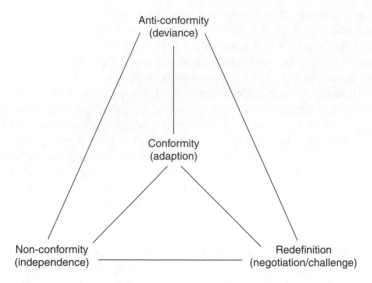

Figure 2.2 *Dimensions of strategic action*

range from the relatively simple bi-polar opposition of 'pro-school' and 'anti-school' (Hargreaves, 1967; Willis, 1977; Turner, 1985) to more sophisticated typologies of strategies (Woods, 1979; Ball, 1981). Such classifications are usually empirically derived and often take on local colour through the naming of groups. The 'Goodie, Joker and Gang' classification derived from *The Social World of the Primary School* (see Figure 1.2) is a case in point. Like many other typologies, it achieves its object in conveying something of the social organization of pupil groups at the time at which they were studied. The same occurs at the level of empirical illustration. Thus Mac an Ghaill (1988) offers us 'Black Sisters', the 'Rasta Heads' and the 'Black Brotherhood', Aggleton (1987) 'Rebels', and *The Social World of the Primary School* describes groups such as 'Janine's Terrors' and 'The Scorpion Gang'.

This rich accumulation of studies provides excellent resources for understanding pupil cultures, though almost all of it derives from relatively short, cross-sectional studies based on one or two years of fieldwork. A resulting strength is that such work is often thoroughly contextualized; but a concomitant weakness is that it has tended to yield relatively static analytic models. We found these to be relatively unsuitable for tracking processes of strategic adaption and change over seven years of primary school education, and on into the further five years of secondary education to which we are committed in the *Identity and Learning Programme*. In some cases, the focus on school life also underplays the significance of pupil experience in other settings, in particular, in the home and family.

We therefore attempted to develop an analytic structure which would be relatively timeless and more contextually portable than previous work on pupil cultures. We also wanted it to be conceptually parsimonious, while also, of course, being capable of representing the complexities and dynamics of strategic adaption as they occurred.

In Figure 2.2, 'dimensions of strategic action', we offer a simplified presentation of the model which we developed to represent our seven years of data. At its core is the concept of 'conformity' and, in the conventional contrast, the counterpoint to this is 'anti-conformity'. However, we have also introduced the dimensions of 'non-conformity' and 'redefinition'.

The 'dimensions' in Figure 2.2 represent ways in which pupils engage with and negotiate the structures and expectations which are embedded in schooling. As patterns of orientation and adaptive response to school, these dimensions can be described as follows.

Conformity is our starting-point; it represents the lowest-risk form of adaptive strategy. Through an often strategic compliance, pupils generally aim to satisfy teacher expectations. They generally show respect for teachers and accept the conventions of their peer group, including those associated with gender. They are in turn usually integrated into mainstream classroom life.

Anti-conformity is a rejection of conformity through deviance. It represents opposition to formal school expectations and rules, and it draws on alternative values, status systems and priorities. There is often conflict with teachers, and pupils derive solidarity from 'gangs' and stereotypically gendered behaviour (compare Pollard, 1985).

Non-conformity is characterized by a degree of independence in relation to formal school expectations. This is not deviance as such, for it does not reflect rejection so much as an absorption in alternative concerns. Integration and participative interaction occur very much on a pupil's own terms, being largely confined to those who share or respond to their interests. Friendship groups using this strategy thus operate on the margins of mainstream classroom and playground concerns, often being regarded fairly tolerantly as 'oddballs' within the class.

Redefining is associated with the same mainstream patterns of achievement and cultural norms as *conformity*. However, pupils using *redefining* strategies are not so much operating *within* norms and expectations as at the cutting edge of them. They are pushing at the boundaries of teachers' and peers' expectation, negotiating, challenging and leading their peers. This is a strategy which is only viable for pupils where their structural position in a class is high with regard to their academic and social status.

In Figure 2.3 we summarize these descriptions in terms of career orientation to school, strategic responses and overall patterns of adaption.

As patterns of adaptive response to school, there is a resonance between some of the strategies depicted in these dimensions and the more static analytic representations, described above, of 'Goodie', 'Joker' and 'Gang' groups (Pollard, 1985). It is important to stress however, that the 'dimensions of strategic action' do not describe *children*, nor do they represent psychological 'types'. Rather they describe typical and relatively coherent repertoires of strategic response. Thus, we will argue that particular pupils tend to use certain dimensions consistently, in so far as their interpretation of a context remains stable. However, pupils can and do change their orientation and patterned responses. This can happen, for example, where a pupil's

	Conformity	Anti-conformity	Non-conformity	Redefining
Career orientations	Reification	Rejection	Indifference	Identification
Strategic responses	Low risk strategies (conformity to others' agenda)	High risk strategies (trouble through oppositional agenda)	Little concern or awareness of risk (because own agenda)	High risk strategies (influencing the shared agenda)
Adaption	Adaption	Deviance	Independence	Negotiation/challenge

Figure 2.3 *Characteristic patterns of career orientation, strategies and adaption*

accustomed status, identity or preferred ways of working become subject to disruption or change, becoming no longer appropriate or viable.

The above model of the 'dimensions of strategic action' (Figure 2.2) can also be developed to plot the characteristic patterns of career adaption of particular children – their strategic biographies. In Chapter 8, we do this in relation to each of our case studies. We highlight both the continuities and dynamics of pupil strategy and identity as they negotiate their way through school. A pupil may, for example, move towards greater or lesser conformity in response to a particular pedagogic style or learning context. For similar reasons, a switch might occur from a redefining position of negotiation and challenge towards anti-conformity and deviance.

The model can also be used to highlight the potential tensions which exist between strategies of conformity and anti-conformity, non-conformity and redefining. Such tension may occur between an individual pupil and a teacher or between individual pupils and their peers as a result of, for instance, a learning stance or expression of identity which contravenes the structural norms or relationship expectations of classroom or playground.

With appropriate adaptions, this model can also be applied to home contexts, and social relationships within the families of the children studied, and to peer relations.

2.5 CONCLUSION

This chapter has reviewed our conceptualization of identity, a variety of influences on perceptions of 'pupil identity', and has introduced our particular analysis of pupil career and strategic action. It has also begun to demonstrate how our study articulates with previous sociological work on pupil strategies and responses to school life. The model of 'dimensions of strategic action' is of particular importance to this book as a whole, providing the analytic key for interrogation of our pupil case studies.

In Part Two of the book, we present four narrative case studies of children's strategic adaption and development through the seven years of their primary education. The longitudinal character of the study enables us to plot continuities and change in the children's strategies over time. We trace these developments in terms of our model of 'dimensions of strategic action' and attempt to identify the causes and consequences of such changes. In so doing, we will be able to chart pupil careers and then analyse factors which are associated with them in terms of personal, social and educational goals.

However, before introducing the children, it is important to understand the social and political circumstances of the era during which they were educated, the circumstances of the Greenside community, and more about the school and teachers whom they encountered in their primary school careers. This is the subject of Chapter 3.

Chapter 3

Layers of Social Context

3.1 INTRODUCTION

This chapter provides an account of some of the broader social contexts within which our case-study pupils developed their primary school careers. We focus the discussion at four interconnected levels: national political developments in relation to education; Easthampton and its local education authority; Greenside and its primary school; and the classroom teachers who worked with our case-study pupils. This narrative may be augmented by consideration of various summary tables which highlight the inter-relationships between key developments from 1984 to 1994 – a decade through which our case-study pupils developed from infancy, and completed their primary education.

The chapter can be seen as an illustration of Broadfoot and Pollard's (1996) analysis of government policy and other forms of external turbulence (media critique, economic forces, social change etc.) being absorbed through successive layers of professional mediation. This is represented in Figure 3.1 below.

This model was developed as part of the PACE project, a major study of the impact of policy changes on teacher and pupil experiences in primary schools during the 1990s (Pollard *et al.*, 1994; Croll, 1996; Osborn, McNess and Broadfoot, forthcoming; Pollard and Triggs, forthcoming). It represents the proposition that national policy and prescription is mediated, interpreted and applied by successive

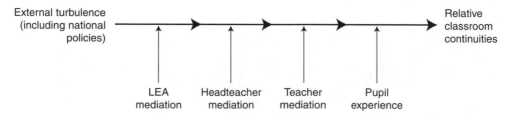

Figure 3.1 *Professional mediation: from external turbulence to relative classroom continuity*

professional groups in ways which reflect their own values and practices. There is thus a process of dilution, revision, or even distortion, as teachers act as 'policy-makers in practice'. Over the period of this study, PACE data suggested that teachers were particularly concerned to 'protect' children from what was seen as an over-loaded curriculum and a divisive assessment system. The result was that, despite the ambitions of policy-makers, classroom practice was relatively resistant to change during the late 1980s and early 1990s – a fact which may arguably have precipitated new forms of inspection and direct curriculum prescription for the teaching of literacy and numeracy.

Greenside Primary School was exposed to national policy developments, but it was also influenced by its local education authority (LEA) and its own particular community. Working with others, the biography, values and educational philosophy of its headteacher created a particular ethos in the school, and the individuality of each teacher was similarly reflected in the climate, routines and practices within their classrooms.

3.2 NATIONAL DEVELOPMENTS IN EDUCATION

The childhood years of the children in this study were lived exclusively under the Conservative governments of Margaret Thatcher and John Major. They were years which combined nationalism and materialistic individualism – a synergy which was underpinned by New Right arguments that Britain's strength was dependent on the existence of free market competition in every sphere of life. Teachers were among the professional groups which successive governments of the 1980s and early 1990s sought to challenge. Primary school teachers, steeped in 'child-centred' commitments, were particularly vulnerable to new demands for accountability and 'reform'.

We identify three phases in the development of education policy over the period:

- Gathering forces for change
- State control and the free market
- Pragmatism in the new hegemony

Gathering forces for change

The Government began the 1980s by taking forward the arguments for a national curriculum which previously had been advanced by Jim Callaghan. The postwar partnership of education professionals in schools and local education authorities was seen as having failed to produce an economically relevant education service of consistent quality. Government had been excluded from the 'secret garden' of the curriculum and, under the shield of teacher autonomy, both primary and secondary education were deemed to be suffering from various 'progressive' ideologies. The 1984 White Paper, *Better Schools*, rallied support behind a new conception of how curriculum, assessment, teacher effectiveness and school governance could be developed within a national system. For Secretary of State Keith Joseph, this showed how 'producer capture' of the education system by teachers could be challenged. In spite of rearguard recommendations on curriculum management by Her Majesty's Inspectorate in the *Curriculum Matters* series (e.g. HMI, 1986) and the 1986 House of Commons report on primary education, forces were gathering for a more radical approach to set up a new, national system for the education service as a whole.

State control and the free market

Kenneth Baker became Secretary of State following the 1987 General Election and began work on what was to become the Education Reform Act, 1988. The act was a curious beast, reflecting political divisions within the Conservative Party at the time. On the one hand, it offered schools a 'new freedom' from local education authorities based on the local management of schools (LMS), delegated budgets based on numbers of pupils on roll, and a policy of open enrolment. Schools were, in effect, to be placed in market competition with each other for pupil enrolments and would subsequently be encouraged to maximize this 'choice and diversity' by opting out of their local authorities by applying for grant maintained status (GMS). However, on the other hand, the Education Reform Act was also designed to introduce a standard national system for curriculum and assessment. Ten subjects plus religious education were specified, along with national tests to be held at age 7, 11, 14 and 16, and reporting to parents so that schools could be held accountable. This standardization of 'product' and the degree of central control exercised by ministers and new quangos for curriculum and assessment were unprecedented in English education. Meanwhile, the rights of the parental 'consumer' were set out in a new Parents' Charter (DES, 1992).

The introduction of a National Curriculum had a considerable effect on primary schools. Ignoring professional advice about the 'whole curriculum', the Government had decided that specialists should develop a curriculum for each subject and that these could be introduced over several years, with a different schedule for each Key Stage and follow-on arrangements for the assessment of each subject. While working towards an agreed notion of 'programmes of study', the working parties shared an even more powerful conviction in the importance of their subject, and did a great deal of work to ensure the completeness and subject-integrity of the curriculum which children were to be taught. Unfortunately, however, not only were they unaware of the effect of their subject on the National Curriculum as a whole, but they had different views on how their subject content should be specified. For instance, English required five 'attainment targets' while Science felt the need for no less than sixteen – with associated 'statements of attainment' to match. The net result was a National Curriculum of huge complexity, massive subject overload and inconsistent presentation. Teachers, many of whom had welcomed the concept of a National Curriculum on grounds of entitlement, began to wilt and protest under the strain.

Meanwhile the pace of Government policy had not slackened. A new system for regular school inspection, with publication of results to parents, was introduced in the 1992 Education Act. Additionally, Kenneth Clarke, by then Secretary of State, began a further challenge to primary school teachers by commissioning the report of the 'Three Wise Men' (Alexander, Rose and Woodhead, 1992). This questioned previously accepted forms of teaching and classroom organization and was a forceful attack on teachers' residual commitment to 'child-centred' methods.

However, the National Curriculum became increasingly unmanageable as further subjects were introduced and as pilot rounds of national assessment began. As they struggled to cope, many teachers drew the sympathy of parents. John Patten, who became Secretary of State for Education in April 1992, developed a unique approach to these circumstances. He refused to consider teacher concerns or to talk with teacher representatives. Indeed, he pressed ahead with his testing programme despite the difficulties which became increasingly apparent. In 1993, his insistence on introducing tests of secondary school English which the profession felt to be seriously flawed produced a national boycott of all testing. In 1993 the need for a review of the National Curriculum and assessment was finally accepted by the Government, and Sir Ron Dearing was given responsibility for its execution.

Pragmatism in the new hegemony

The Dearing Reports of August 1993 and January 1994 offered new hope to teachers. With effect from September 1995, the National Curriculum was to be simplified and reduced in form and content. There was to be a particular attempt to reduce overload at Key Stage 2, 20 per cent of time was to be 'discretionary' and standardized testing was to be limited to English, Mathematics and Science. In making these proposals, Dearing recognized the need to build on teacher professionalism, but he also reaffirmed the need for a complementary accountability. This, then, was the basis of a new conciliatory settlement on which Gillian Shephard was to build when she became Secretary of State in July 1994.

Whatever the concessions to teachers on overload and manageability, the fundamental framework and conceptualization of the National Curriculum, assessment, inspection and accountability remained. 'Producer control' had been removed, national requirements had been introduced, LEAs had been weakened and parental consumers were, in principle at least, able to exercise market choice among competing schools. Teachers and schools had become externally accountable in ways which were almost unimaginable before the provisions of the Education Reform Act and succeeding legislation started to take effect (see Pollard *et al.*, 1994). And yet, strangely, the very intensity of the experience seemed to lead many teachers to accept its apparent inevitability. For many, the initial attempts to assimilate new requirements into old practices and at 'creative mediation' gradually waned (Osborn, McNess and Broadfoot, forthcoming), and a significant number retreated from the fray to contribute to an exceptional number of early retirements. However, teachers in post gradually came to terms with the national requirements made of them and the accountability systems to which they were now subject. New teachers knew no other system. In the modern world of global competition, could there be any other way? The new 'reality' was simply that pupils had to be taught the prescribed curriculum, and their progress measured.

3.3 EASTHAMPTON AND ITS LOCAL EDUCATION AUTHORITY

As recorded in *The Social World of Children's Learning*, Easthampton in the south of England was a city with a population of about one million. It had a long history of manufacturing although, during the 1980s and 1990s, there was considerable diversification into new technologically based companies and finance. Additionally, many major international companies were attracted to the city over the period.

UK communications were excellent by road and rail and, because of its geographical location, the city was steadily increasing its international trade, particularly with European countries. It was a regional centre with extensive provision for shopping, exhibitions, libraries, sport, cinema, theatre, concerts and other forms of entertainment. During the period of study Easthampton and associated towns nearby grew steadily, with several major new housing developments and shopping centres.

The south of the city, in which Greenside was located, became increasingly affluent during the 1980s. There were some very fashionable residential areas in central Easthampton with Georgian and Victorian housing predominating. The between-wars expansion of suburbs such as Greenside also provided many attractive housing areas and these tended to be ringed on the outer boundaries of the city by large estates of council housing. On these, and in some specific inner-city areas, unemployment and poverty levels were high throughout the period of the study.

The local education authority had had a very good reputation for much of the 1970s but during the 1980s and 1990s it was rocked by successive rounds of financial cutbacks and a lack of stable political control. As a large authority, the leadership of the Chief Education Officer (CEO) and Principal Adviser was particularly important. Over the period of study, we identify four phases of LEA policy in relation to primary education in the city:

- Promoting 'good practice'
- Building a 'new professionalism'
- Mediation and incorporation of national policy
- Accommodation and resistance

Promoting 'good practice'

In the early 1980s the LEA was led by a genial chief officer of the 'old school'. Dr Jones had excellent relationships with CEOs in other parts of the country and took great pride in the achievements of Easthampton. The Schools Orchestra had been particularly successful nationally and the LEA had several 'show schools' which Dr Jones enjoyed showing visitors around. Within the LEA Dr Jones believed in working in partnership with the other professionals in his team. He thus gave his specialist advisers considerable independence and they worked on phase-specific initiatives across the LEA. The small team of primary advisers were led by Senior Advisers for 'early years' and 'junior years'. Dr Jones was not comfortable with the new challenges being posed by Mrs Thatcher's governments and he chose to retire in 1985. Mr Sutcliffe, the new CEO, perceived his role in two ways. He was to operate in the political world of the Easthampton parties and to secure the best terms for education, and he was to manage effectively the resources which he obtained. However, Mr Sutcliffe was not often seen among teachers and headteachers, and seemed uncomfortable in the company of children. He developed a reputation as an effective political operator and as a 'systems man', but he did not inspire Easthampton's teachers.

For most of the 1980s therefore, educational leadership in Easthampton primary schools was largely provided by the two Senior Advisers and their teams. There were strong commitments to particular forms of classroom practice, important networks within the LEA and elements of patronage in advancement. Two interconnected forms of practice were particularly promoted, both based on 'active learning'. First, for the younger children the principles of the High/Scope project were introduced. High/Scope is an early years 'cognitive curriculum' project which was first set up as part of the US Headstart Project. Based on 'key experiences' and a 'plan-do-review' planning sequence, children are encouraged to engage in classroom activities in aware and reflective ways. Second, addressing similar issues but for an older age group, the concept of the 'negotiated curriculum' was advanced.

Some elements of this approach are well illustrated by Rowland's book *The Enquiring Classroom* (1985). He provides examples of children controlling a process of progressive enquiry as topics of study are negotiated and understanding and capability are established. The adult is an active adviser, supporter and critical friend in this process. The approach thus constituted a move beyond the conceptions of 'good practice' which had been derived from Piagetian ideas. The teacher was expected to be active in instruction but to 'negotiate the curriculum', rather than to dominate as in traditional pedagogy, or to merely facilitate pupils' choice as in extreme forms of child-centredness. These approaches were promoted very effectively, with cross-LEA events, courses, national speakers, workshop and discussion groups, and advisory visits to schools.

At Greenside Primary School, the LEA's two Senior Primary Advisors took a particular interest in the appointment of the new headteacher, Mrs Davison, in 1985. She came with an established reputation for her work on the 'negotiated curriculum' elsewhere in the LEA and subsequently played a key role in both the development and the dissemination of this approach to active learning. Within Greenside, the 'early years' specialist adviser was instrumental in supporting Mrs Davison's introduction of the 'active learning' and a 'negotiated curriculum', and the 'junior years' specialist took a particular interest in curriculum planning and design. In both cases, developments from Greenside Primary were subsequently disseminated to schools across the LEA through booklets and contributions to in-service courses. As the National Curriculum began to be introduced, Mrs Davison was one of those involved in helping the LEA to create a constructive response in terms of curriculum planning and development.

In the absence of national requirements or a strong lead from a Chief Education Officer, the primary school specialist advisers in the LEA were thus able to work with schools to develop a distinctive educational philosophy. However by 1987/8, with a General Election over and the Education Reform Act looming, a new phase of the LEA's development was about to begin.

Building a 'new professionalism'

In 1987 a self-confident and forceful Principal Adviser was appointed to the East-hampton Education Authority. Dr Castle had risen from a primary education background, maintained a considerable interest in teaching and learning issues, and promoted his role as being directly concerned with the improvement of professional practice across the authority. The vehicle which he chose for this improvement was action research. Setting out his philosophy in his first meeting with headteachers, he referred to Stenhouse (1975) and the need to develop professional expertise in the new era of accountability which he foresaw. Over next few years Dr Castle created a significant programme for continuous professional development based on action research and 'reflective practice'.

However, scope for autonomous LEA initiatives was reducing, and by the autumn of 1989, with the National Curriculum beginning to be introduced and local management of schools anticipated, Dr Castle began to apply his 'new professionalism' to the evolving circumstances.

Mediation and incorporation of national policy

As the consequences of the Education Reform Act began to be felt, Dr Castle's responses were clear. First, he sought to assert some control over the new agenda. Thus, with LMS looming he began a major initiative to introduce reflective forms of school management planning based around curriculum, teaching and learning objectives. Headteachers were advised to buy Caldwell and Spinks' book, *The Self-Managing School* (1988) and a new system of 'Institutional Development Plans' was introduced. Additionally, Dr Castle attempted to influence directly the management culture across the LEA. Cascading training from a team of management consultants, all advisers and every headteacher in Easthampton were given experience of new, interpersonally focused management techniques. With the responsibilities of head-teachers beginning to grow, the overall process was received with remarkable enthusiasm. Further, the headteachers who had acted as 'trainers' became strongly bonded and were to remain influential opinion leaders in the years ahead – including Mrs Davison, the headteacher of Greenside Primary School. At the same time, schools were organized into all-phase 'clusters' so that headteachers in particular parts of the city could meet to share perspectives and, in principle, provide support for problems and represent views back to the LEA. Advisers were re-allocated to reflect this new structure.

Dr Castle then sought to incorporate new Government requirements into the professional framework which he had been creating. This was particularly explicit with regard to new assessment regulations which required massive In-Service Education for Teachers (INSET) programmes during 1990–91. Building on the opportunities legitimated by the Task Group on Assessment and Testing (TGAT) report (1988), a programme was constructed based around formative assessment as a means of refining and applying professional judgement in the teaching–learning process. With action research and reflective practice at its heart, this was elaborated both in terms of gathering evidence in classrooms and regarding 'profiling' – the compilation of an annotated portfolio of pupil work. 'Tick-list' assessment systems were frowned upon, but the LEA supported pilot schemes to draw pupils into the assessment process. Incorporation was also attempted as the school development planning movement emerged nationally. Picking up many of the ideas contained in Hargreaves and Hopkins's report (1989) and the School Management Task Force (Styan, 1990), Easthampton's existing scheme was revised to build in a new emphasis on 'priority setting', 'targets' and 'success criteria'.

Accommodation and resistance

During 1992, with the Local Management of Schools well established and Office for Standards in Education (OFSTED) inspections beginning, it was apparent that the powers of the LEA were beginning to wane – a weakening which coincided with Dr Castle's promotion to take on the role of Chief Education Officer.

The LEA provided advice and INSET for teachers as the National Curriculum was introduced, with a strong line that they should attempt to accommodate the new requirements into their existing practices. For his part, Dr Castle resolutely encouraged headteachers to focus on teaching and learning issues and avoid being exclusively drawn into management concerns.

The LEA continued to promote formative assessment while increasingly being required to prepare schools for Standard Assessment Tests (SATs). It also provided covert support for a group of primary school headteachers which formed to oppose the government threat to publish league tables of SAT results. This group, building on their management training experience, their networks across the LEA's school clusters and the principles which had been publicly espoused by Dr Castle, formed one of the largest oppositional headteacher groups in England. They engaged in extensive lobbying of government ministers and opposition spokesmen, stiffened headteacher resolve regarding the SAT boycott of 1993 and, when league tables were eventually published, took advertisements in the local press to explain what they saw as the inadequacies of the information provided and the weaknesses in the educational principles on which the league tables were based.

Overall, however, such acts of resistance were rare. Dr Castle wrestled with the implications of a finely balanced political control on Easthampton's City Council and began to network both within the government and opposition parties. However, the reality was that the LEA's powers had been considerably reduced. The initiative on curriculum, assessment, pedagogy, inspection, accountability and school finance now all rested with central government or its agencies. Operational power lay with schools. The LEA, seen as an interruption in the free market which would raise education standards, was searching for a new role.

The early LEA support for active pupil learning, and the later efforts of Dr Castle to encourage teacher professionalism and school autonomy, were important in providing the context for Greenside Primary School and its staff. In these ways the LEA was a key mediating force (Broadfoot and Pollard, 1996), both promoting a particular learner-centred conception of teacher professionalism, and actively seeking to defend it against new national requirements.

Tables 3.1 and 3.2 below provide an overview and summary of developments in

Academic year, teacher & pupil age	NATIONAL EDUCATION DEVELOPMENTS	LEA DEVELOPMENTS
1984–85 Age 1/2	Keith Joseph, Secretary of State *Better Schools* White Paper *The Enquiring Classroom* (Rowland)	Dr Jones, CEO, takes benevolent pride in schools' achievements within the LEA – but then retires.
1985–86 Age 2/3	Education Act established new rights of governing bodies. *The Curriculum 5–16* (HMI)	Mr Sutcliffe, a CEO 'systems man', manages bullishly and with political effectiveness, but remains distanced from schools. Junior Schools adviser promotes the 'negotiated curriculum'.
1986–87 Pre-school Age 3/4	*Achievement in Primary Schools* (House of Commons) Teachers' industrial action over pay and conditions. *The National Curriculum 5–16: A Consultation Document* (DFE)	Early Years adviser promotes High/Scope for pre-school and infant schools. LEA developments through adviser-backed projects. Strong adviser influence on senior promotions.
1987–88 Reception Mrs Powell Age 4/5	General Election Kenneth Baker, Secretary of State TGAT report published. Education Reform Act passed: National Curriculum Council and School Examination and Assessment Council.	Dr Castle appointed Principal Adviser. Recommends Stenhouse to headteachers and emphasizes developing professional expertise for classroom practice and new accountabilities. Concept of subject curriculum co-ordinators is promoted.
1988–89 Year 1 Miss Scott Age 5/6	LMS circular issued. John MacGregor Secretary of State, July	Dr Castle introduces comprehensive LEA INSET, all based on action research. Early Years Adviser retires.
1989–90 Year 2 Miss George Miss Sage Age 6/7	NC KS1 English, Maths and Science introduced.	Dr Castle advises heads to buy Caldwell and Spinks and to consider curriculum-led school planning. LMS budgeting introduced.

Table 3.1 *National education policy and LEA developments to the end of pupils' Key Stage 1*

English education policy during the period of the study, with particular reference to primary education, and of the responses and actions of Easthampton LEA and its officers.

3.4   GREENSIDE AND ITS PRIMARY SCHOOL

As described in *The Social World of Children's Learning*, Greenside was a highly regarded suburb of Easthampton. With its attractive gardens and mix of between-wars detached housing and relatively spacious semi-detached dwellings, it was recognized as a pleasant place for the prosperous, white middle classes to settle.

Academic year, teacher & pupil age	NATIONAL EDUCATION DEVELOPMENTS	LEA DEVELOPMENTS
1990–91 Year 3 Mr Brown Age 7/8	NC KS1 Technology introduced. NC KS2 English, Maths, Science and Technology introduced. Parents' Charter circulated to schools, September. Kenneth Clarke, Secretary of State, September. John Major replaces Mrs Thatcher as Prime Minister, November. NCC/SEAC powers and significance grow. Pilot national assessment KS1 English, Maths and Science, May.	Management skills training for all headteachers. Institutional Development Plans are promoted, requiring evidence of performance. 'Assessment for Learning' and 'Profiling' training for all schools. All phase school 'clusters' set up across the LEA, with associated link advisers. Junior Schools Adviser retires.
1991–92 Year 4 Miss King Age 8/9	NC KS1 History and Geography introduced. NC KS2 History and Geography introduced. Revised teacher appraisal scheme. Hargreaves and Hopkins publish *The Empowered School*. Alexander's Leeds report – media furore. Alexander, Rose and Woodhead publish 'Three Wise Men' report on pedagogic 'orthodoxies', January. Education (Schools) Act sets up inspection system and OFSTED. John Patten, Secretary of State, April. White Paper *Choice and Diversity* published. KS1 SAT reports published.	Dr Castle appointed CEO, commits to reflective practice and school development planning. New School Development Planning scheme introduced based on 'priority setting', 'targets' and 'success criteria'.
1992–93 Year 5 Miss French Mr Brown Age 9/10	NC KS1 Art, Music and PE introduced. NC KS2 Art, Music and PE introduced. Secondary school 'league tables' published. Dearing review of NC announced. Grant Maintained Schools introduced. NCC and SEAC abolished, School Curriculum and Assessment Authority set up. Teacher boycott of pilot national testing, May.	OFSTED inspections begin nationally. Easthampton advisers reject 'inspection' role. Headteacher campaigning group against assessment league tables flourishes, with tacit LEA support.
1993–94 Year 6 Mrs Chard Age 10/11	SEN Code of Practice introduced. Dearing reports National Curriculum overloaded. National assessment at KS2, English, Maths and Science, May. Gillian Shepard, Secretary of State, July.	Governors', parents' and quango powers grow as LEA powers continue to weaken.

Table 3.2 *National education policy and LEA developments during pupils' Key Stage 2*

Most of the families of our case-study children fit this pattern, as do the four children who feature in this book – three of whom went on to independent secondary school education. Details about family circumstances are provided at the start of each case-study account.

Over the period in question, we can identify three phases in the development of Greenside Primary:

- The 'old school'
- The battle for 'good practice'
- Assimilation and mediation of national policy

This very condensed account creates an impression of rapid change, which is, indeed, how it often felt to the headteacher and her colleagues. However, while deeply affected by the transitions which are recorded, the day-to-day classroom life of each child was experienced more gradually and continuously.

The 'old school'

In the early 1980s Greenside Primary School had a very strong reputation in the community for the quality of its education. With its long history, an affluent middle-class catchment area, and excellent grounds and facilities, it was established as an 'old-fashioned' and 'traditional' school. Children's learning was heavily directed and followed up by regular testing. They were expected to participate fully in competitive games and 'house teams'. Mrs Davison's appointment as headteacher in 1985 represented an attempt by the governors to modernize.

The battle for 'good practice'

When Mrs Davison started her period of headship she faced considerable resistance to her ideas. She was committed to the concepts of 'active learning' and a 'negotiated curriculum' and indeed, had been appointed following an explicit expression of her professional philosophy.

As described more fully in *The Social World of Children's Learning*, Mrs Davison changed some things immediately. For instance, the role of the 'house' system was confined to sport; pupils were no longer explicitly prepared for the entrance exams of independent schools; teachers were required to submit curriculum plans setting out their intentions for the term; Mrs Davison visited classrooms, which was seen as trespassing on teacher autonomy; and she began to discuss with teachers ways of developing new forms of classroom organization and practices which would enable pupils to become more active in learning. This last change led to staff-meeting discussion of developing a 'negotiated curriculum' and strong encouragement of teachers in Key Stage 1 to introduce the 'High/Scope'-influenced procedure of 'plan-do-review' as a form of classroom organization.

Such developments were of concern to many teachers and parents, who felt that the previously stable settlement was being undermined. Teachers felt professionally threatened, and some resisted what they saw as Mrs Davison's 'intrusion'. Resonating with media panics of the period, some articulate parents felt that the traditions of the school and 'educational standards' were likely to be eroded by this new 'progressivism'. However, Mrs Davison had strong support from the governors who had appointed her, including an influential industrialist and the vicar, and she was strongly endorsed by the two Senior Primary LEA Advisers and their exposition of 'good practice'. Both the governors and advisers backed Mrs Davison against the criticisms of some teachers and in a stormy Annual General Meeting with parents. Gradually, as older teachers began to retire Mrs Davison was able to make appointments of younger staff whose views were more in keeping with the new direction being taken. Additionally, some parents began to send their children to other schools, and for a while numbers started to fall. However, they soon rose again as families from a local estate of council housing, Damibrook, began to take advantage of the new opportunity to 'get their children into a better school'.

By the end of 1989–90, the enormous implications of the Education Reform Act 1988 were becoming obvious and new statutory requirements for the National Curriculum in English, Maths and Science were in place for Key Stage 1. The need for strong school management and coherent curriculum planning was now indisputable, and both staff and parents began to take confidence from the leadership which Mrs Davison provided in the new circumstances. Additionally, Mrs Davison, now strengthened by the LEA's management training provision and associated head-teacher reference groups, had became more strategic in her presentation of what the school stood for and more relaxed about how her core beliefs might be interpreted. As she explained:

> I'm trying to get rid of the labels and just say, 'this is the way we work'. In practice though, my philosophy hasn't changed that much, although I know that there are outside pressures and we have to accommodate to them. All my new staff applied for jobs which stated 'the negotiated curriculum' or 'active learning', so they know my expectations. Some of them want advice, as if they want to do things 'the right way'; but I just tell them to, 'get bedded down, teach however you feel comfortable and we'll talk about it later'. So I'm quite happy for teachers to develop their own style around the core philosophy that children should be active, should have access to materials in the curriculum and use this plan-do-review cycle. That's to me a true learning cycle, and it's used throughout life in a way.
> (Mrs Davison, interviewed by Andrew Pollard, July 1990)

As 1989–90 drew to a close, with the new demands of Local Management of Schools (LMS) and the National Curriculum starting to be faced, Greenside Primary School was relatively confident, with the external challenges beginning to draw people together.

Assimilation and mediation of national policy

Mrs Davison's first approach to the National Curriculum was to assimilate its requirements into the curriculum planning systems which had by then been established in the school. Attainment Targets were thus apportioned to various parts of the termly Topic Web produced by each teacher in negotiation with her class – an approach which was offered as a model to schools across the LEA. The school was also one of the first primary school in the LEA to become locally managed, thus increasing Mrs Davison's responsibility for financial affairs but also giving her more control to deploy funds in support of the school's overall philosophy. These developments, then, were assimilated relatively easily.

However, other pressures began to mount. First, there was a gradual increase in government requirements, accompanied by considerable administrative confusion and an unfavourable 'discourse of derision' in much of the media. Meanwhile, Dr Castle's LEA initiatives, intended to mediate some of these requirements, in fact added considerably to the workload. Thus the encouragement of professional development through action research and training in new forms of formative assessment were received with some ambivalence, particularly when the government's Department for Education seemed to outflank such efforts by requiring a standardized assessment test (SAT) pilot for Year 2 pupils. Such external pressures were compounded by continuation of internally generated commitments, with the result that the school struggled. Mrs Davison explained:

> Last year, morale in this school hit rock bottom. And I think it was due to several things, but I think one of the key features was assessment and action research going on, and all the curriculum changes which have been brought in – and somehow we couldn't see a way to cope. At the same time we had some new members of staff who had just come in, and several on short-term contracts covering maternity leave; and we undertook a massive production of *Joseph and the Amazing Technicolor Dream Coat*. Now that put pressure on everybody, and so much was geared up to the production that tempers were becoming fraught and frayed ... So it wasn't just DES changes, though the assessment thing made everybody tense even though it was just Year 2. It was really very disturbing, because everyone knew it was happening and the confidence of everybody went down and it was really a devastating time for everyone. I think it came to a head when they realized that they really could not do any more.
> (Mrs Davison, interviewed by Andrew Pollard, November 1991)

Mrs Davison's strategy in these circumstances was to attempt to mediate external requirements and to prioritize internally generated developments, so that the level of overall pressure could be managed – almost a paradigm case of management of change in a turbulent environment (Wallace, 1994). A matrix approach to curriculum planning was introduced with the express purpose that it would 'stand the test of time'. Some potential pressures were contained with a little sleight-of-hand, such as the Parents' Charter being 'made available' rather than actively distributed to parents. In fact, parental support had grown, and the value of the experience being offered at the school was now becoming recognized:

> We have several parents now who've said that the children are much more confident and much more articulate and better able to plan and keep themselves occupied, even during the holidays, and self organized – than their older brothers and sisters who went through a different kind of system.
> (Mrs Davison, interviewed by Andrew Pollard, November 1991)

The relationship with parents continued to need active management, however. In the summer of 1993, during the period of national opposition to assessment league tables, this was reflected in the decision to issue SAT results to parents, while boycotting the submission of data to the LEA and DFE.

Nevertheless, by the end of the period of study, Mrs Davison had become more confident. Not only could she 'not remember the last time a parent came into my

Calendar year	School year	Pupil age	Class teacher	Class teacher
1987/8	Reception	4/5	Mrs Powell	
1988/9	Year 1	5/6	Miss Scott	
1989/90	Year 2	6/7	Miss George	Miss Sage
1990/91	Year 3	7/8	Mr Brown	
1991/2	Year 4	8/9	Miss King	
1992/3	Year 5	9/10	Miss French	Mr Brown
1993/4	Year 6	10/11	Mrs Chard	

Table 3.3   *The teachers, as experienced by the pupil cohort*

room complaining', but she had also found a way of mediating National Curriculum requirements to reflect the new ethos of the school and her own philosophy.

> We have had to cope with the National Curriculum, but that doesn't mean it has to be humdrum and boring. We've got a curriculum grid now, and all sections of the grid are expressed as questions. That gives a little bit of problem-solving back to the teachers and the children, so that you can have an open-ended outcome in a way, a differentiated outcome. Of course, there is some sort of order of progression as you go down the grid, but across it you can pick out anything from English, Maths, Science etc., which the teacher thinks will blend into a topic. . . . It's a way of getting a little bit more creativity back into the curriculum, back into the classroom, with the teachers, with the children. Because it just seems that we have so much curriculum to cover that a lot of didactic teaching has just taken over, and I think problem-solving does take longer.
> (Mrs Davison, interviewed by Andrew Pollard, September 1993)

In summary, the change of headteacher in 1985 produced a radical change in the character of Greenside Primary School, and there followed several years of difficult adjustment. However, a combination of staff turnover, governor and LEA support, drawing on new catchment area and Mrs Davison's principled resilience and competence eventually yielded a new settlement. When the pressures of the National Curriculum, LMS and inspection came along, there was an initial hiatus and attempts were made to assimilate new requirements. These were followed by strategies of active mediation as Mrs Davison and her staff sought to satisfy external requirements while preserving their internally generated commitment to active learning and a relevant, pupil-orientated and holistic curriculum.

3.5   THE CLASSROOM TEACHERS

The following accounts of the practices of the classroom teachers provide a reference point for later chapters which track the different ways in which the four children experienced them. Those chapters will reveal how the classroom contexts and strategies of each teacher had particular effects on, and implications for, the academic and social experience of each of the children.

Nine teachers feature in the following profiles despite the primary school years being only seven years in duration (see Table 3.3 above). This happened because Greenside's pupil intake was fixed at one and a half forms of entry – a requirement which regularly caused age-cohorts to be divided, even though allocation to classes was based solely on age. Indeed, during their pupil careers at Greenside the case-study cohort was split across classes on two occasions. Thus in Year 2, while most of the cohort were with Miss George, William and Robert were in Miss Sage's Year 2 class. Similarly, in Year 5, when most children were placed with Miss French, William and Robert were again taught by Mr Brown.

As described above, for much of the period of the study Mrs Davison encouraged her staff to work towards forms of 'negotiated curriculum' which would involve children actively in their learning. However, there were important differences among the teachers with regard to the ways in which these expectations were interpreted and fulfilled. Differences were clearly apparent with regard to pupil involvement in decisions regarding the content of tasks, and concerning how, when and with whom they might be undertaken. Teachers' reflections on their work, of which we give a flavour below, showed the additional influence of personal biographies, educational philosophies, previous teaching experiences and a range of institutional, situational and temporal opportunities and constraints (see also Pollard, 1985; Filer, 1993b). A summary analysis of some of the important differences in curriculum organization across the classroom contexts is then provided in Tables 3.4 and 3.5.

Of course, while each child *shared* many aspects of the classroom contexts which we describe, the case studies of pupil careers in Part 2 of the book will reveal the extent to which they were in fact interpreted and experienced *differently*.

Mrs Powell and her Reception class in 1987–8

Mrs Powell was an infant school teacher of many years standing at Greenside School and was well respected within the community of parents for her traditional and well understood approach. At the particular stage in her career at which we meet her in this study, she was finding it especially difficult to incorporate pupil planning and reviews of their learning into her traditional routines of 'work' in the morning and 'play' and 'creative' activities in the afternoon.

> What I found difficult with the integrated day, because I've tried it several times in the past, is really being able to concentrate on something really mucky, and you get covered with paint and glue, and then suddenly someone wants you to write a sentence or something and you're in no fit state to do it. So I always went back to my former way of doing it after trying the new. It was much less stressful and I always knew exactly what the children were doing.
> (Mrs Powell, teacher interview, September 1987, Reception)

However, after a year of considerable mistrust and struggle with the views of the new headteacher, Mrs Powell had begun to establish some compromise between approaches to a negotiated curriculum and well established practice.

> This year I have not been so upset by the negotiated curriculum influence because I had some way of going with it which allowed me still to do quite a lot of what I really wanted to do.
> (Mrs Powell, teacher interview, September 1987, Reception)

Mrs Powell's organization for a negotiated curriculum was based on the identification of five groups of children, each group receiving special attention on one day of the week. Each child had a colour-coded card identifying their group, and the classroom was organized into areas of activity with a limited number of 'pockets' into which children working in the area placed their card. This enabled some choice of activity for children and prevented overcrowding. The traditional activities of infant classrooms of sand, construction, writing, home corner, painting etc. constituted the negotiable part of the curriculum and children would 'plan, do and review' their choices, each of the five groups having first choice of activities, and being called upon to review them, on successive days of the week.

Other groupings were called upon to work with Mrs Powell throughout the day, during which time she continued to set the routine maths and English tasks which she felt important for learning the 'basics'. The system enabled her to maintain a relatively straightforward system of teaching groups as well as satisfying the require-ment to allow children to plan and reflect upon some aspects of their learning. However, neither the substantive content nor the learning processes relating to the 'basics' of reading, writing or number were planned, negotiated or reviewed by the children.

Nevertheless, as a calm, warm and experienced teacher, Mrs Powell managed to adapt to a system which she had mistrusted, and she continued to provide a stable and supportive learning environment for the children entering Greenside School. She retired from the school and from teaching at the end of the Reception year of the children in this study.

Miss Scott and her Year 1 class in 1988–9

Miss Scott spent the early part of her teaching career in the Midlands before moving to a school in Easthampton where falling pupil rolls made redeployment to Greenside School necessary. This move, forced through by the LEA against the wishes of Greenside governors and Miss Scott, was a bitter blow to her:

> I was redeployed much to my disgust and horror, and it totally deflated me. It really knocked me sideways. I was the scapegoat that was just pushed out. I am a conscientious teacher, or I was, up to that point. Well I still am, it's just that . . . I feel a bit embittered by it.
> (Miss Scott, teacher interview, July 1988, Year 1)

However, Miss Scott was allowed by the headteacher at the time to 'just work my own way'. Though regarded as a little progressive for the traditional school and community of Greenside, she nevertheless gradually settled in and eventually took a leading role in developing the English curriculum in line with contemporary educa-tional thinking. The arrival of Mrs Davison and her ideas for whole school develop-ment based on a negotiated curriculum was experienced as a further personal challenge to Miss Scott. She resented the changes, not so much in themselves, as they were not that different from her own philosophies, but as new blows to her professional pride. In particular she felt a loss of autonomy and saw Mrs Davison's managerial style as being 'autocratic'. As the tensions and personal conflicts came to a head during 1988–9 she acknowledged that her classroom practice had suffered:

It is sometimes a bit of a shambles. Because I am an experienced teacher I don't necessarily seem to get myself totally organized. But I've had better organization in the class in other schools. Now, because it's expected of me, I probably don't do it deliberately.

My one fault, I would say, is that I get on the defensive and that brings out the worst in me – not with the children particularly, though sometimes.
(Miss Scott, teacher interview, July 1988, Year 1)

In the year under study, Miss Scott's evolving adaptation to a negotiated curriculum led to each day being divided into three phases. One phase involved every child in a choice of practical or 'pencil and paper' maths, the next a choice of either reading or writing skills, and the third phase involved a choice of creative or construction-oriented activities. Four groups, based broadly on reading attainment and age, were allowed to plan for a maths task, an English task and a creative or construction activity. Thus though the logistics of the two classroom systems were different, Miss Scott, like Mrs Powell, allowed for children planning the timing of some activities, but left intact the routine, teacher-devised tasks for the 'basics' of language and maths. However, in the case of Miss Scott's class that year, her organizational problems and indecisiveness frequently left the children unsure and unfocused, giving rise to motivational problems and difficulties with carrying out her intentions. The underlying stress experienced by Miss Scott at this time further exacerbated such situations so that she would reassert her authority loudly and strongly. Thus, in the year in question, the personal and professional crisis which Miss Scott was undergoing also had an adverse affect upon her relationships with many of the children. They perceived her as 'often getting very cross', and many children talked about being quite frightened of her at such times.

Miss George and her Year 2 class in 1989–90

Miss George was a newly qualified teacher with her first teaching appointment that year at Greenside School. Though initially she was not very confident regarding her skills for delivering the sort of curriculum being developed there, she was enthusiastic and committed to the principle of active learning. In that year Greenside School was also adapting its whole-school planning to take account of the attainment targets and skills associated with the newly introduced National Curriculum. In common with many teachers, Miss George was concerned that the demands associated with its requirements were detrimental to the learning of young children. 'It just seems to take up so much time. And you think, "Well, where do the children come in all this?"' (Teacher interview, November 1989). Despite such additional pressures, however, she maintained her early enthusiasm and commitment. With the active support of the school and LEA, she developed some clear priorities for her early months of teaching:

My main thing has been to get the classroom working, to establish a relationship and get the organization right and I've started getting records ready so that I can check whether I've been there.
(Miss George, teacher interview, November 1989, Year 2)

In accordance with such aims, Miss George constructed a clear and well organized system within which children could understand her expectations for planning and carrying out activities. She organized the children into five groups, roughly based on reading attainment. She used these groups for teaching purposes, and planning time was also carried out within these groups though on a relatively individual basis. Curriculum balance was monitored through Miss George's supervision of planning on the basis of one group each day through the week. In addition, rules existed to ensure, for instance, that a certain number and kinds of maths and writing activities were planned for in each week. As a new teacher, it took Miss George a while to develop the skills required to monitor the tasks and outputs of each child amid the complex activities of the classroom. However clear the expectations, she became aware early in the year that some children were evading less appealing tasks. She experimented with various forms of planning sheet, focusing children's choices more specifically and reviewing her own monitoring systems.

> On the first planning sheet where they had a column and they ticked, they put a mark in if they were going for it and ticked it off when they'd done it. And the idea was that they can't go back to it until they'd done everything, so they are getting a balanced curriculum. But I found that the ones who'd learnt how to work the system were going tick, tick, tick, with no thought, to make sure that they get to whatever they want to do first.

> So that's why with the most able group I started them on the daily planning sheet where they actually have to say what area they are going to go into, what they are going to use and what they are going to do. So they actually have to sit down and think.
> (Miss George, teacher interview, November 1989, Year 2)

Miss George persisted with the development of her planning and group systems and became more proficient at structuring events so that she maintained control and also achieved her educational objectives. Her further priority of establishing good relationships was achieved by means of her calm, firm and constructive approach and she went on to develop a warm rapport with her pupils as the year progressed.

Miss Sage and her Year 2 class in 1989–90

Miss Sage was a young teacher who had graduated in 1987. She spent time travelling and then acted as a supply teacher at Greenside School before her employment there. As one of the teacher appointments which reflected the new ethos being developed by Mrs Davison, Miss Sage expressed a commitment to 'active learning', and wanting 'children to control their own learning as much as possible' (teacher interview, September 1989). However, she was realistic about this commitment and realized that high levels of pupil autonomy and forms of active learning could only succeed within a tight structure of classroom rules and behaviour. In accordance with the developing school policy, she used a strong topic as a source of cross-curricular integration and also as a focus for negotiation with the children.

Thus, within Miss Sage's interpretation of a negotiated curriculum, pupil planning and negotiation were about more than timetabling the movements and choices of individuals and groups across teacher-devised tasks, as it had been in their Reception and Year 1 classroom experience. Miss Sage began the year using a simple system where the children recorded the activities in which they had engaged. From this base she developed a system in which children planned a programme of work for a fortnight. They used a matrix in which curriculum activities were set out in columns and the ten working days set out in rows; the activity requirements were weighted to ensure adequate coverage of maths, reading and writing. Planning took place among groups of children, with a child 'chairing' each group, Miss Sage monitoring to ensure appropriate curriculum balance and children ticking off each planned activity when it was completed. The children were then able to self-direct their work for much of the time, with Miss Sage calling on groups for particular teaching purposes, which might concern maths, science or some aspect of topic work. The classroom organization was thus quite complex, but one in which children were given considerable scope for self-directed learning.

Miss Sage's classroom organization was thus relatively complex and allowed the children a good deal of autonomy. It so happened that the class also contained many of the older Year 2 children in the school, including those who had once been known as 'Mrs Miles' naughty boys'. Miss Sage was aware that, as she put it, she had 'some lively children who could be quite a handful to handle' and her strategy was thus to maintain a tight framework of classroom rules within which the children were given scope for self-directed learning. The rules were discussed with the children on introduction and, if difficulties arose, Miss Sage would seek the children's views on a solution. Having led the children so far into consultation, she would then interpret and enforce the rules very firmly. However, the children seemed to accept the legitimacy of this. As Miss Sage explained:

> They get on fairly well. Well, they know that I'll be on to them if they don't.
> (Miss Sage, teacher interview, November 1989, Year 2)

Mr Brown and his Year 3 class in 1990–91

Mr Brown joined Greenside School as a newly qualified teacher at the same time as Miss George and Miss Sage, though when the children in the study passed through his class he was in his second year of teaching. Like other teachers, he was appointed in part because of his enthusiasm for the idea of children being active in and reflecting upon their learning. Like Miss George, he had needed to learn quickly and make some rapid adjustments in his organization in order to realize his teaching aims:

> I'm a great believer in the basic philosophy behind it. When I came round the school, I thought that's great. And I think what I did wrong in the beginning last year was I threw it too far the other way so at times I wasn't sure quite what was going on in the classroom, and in the end I began to drag it back towards me, to achieve the right balance – it is negotiated, therefore I've got my input as well. But at first I kind of opened the doors and said 'Here you are!' 'Go and explore!' It was a learning process for me.
> (Mr Brown, teacher interview, September 1990, Year 3)

In the year of the study, therefore, Mr Brown was redressing the situation with a fairly highly structured organization framework, though it was, in some respects, not necessarily his ideal model. Following his early experiences of the previous year, he closely monitored the planning process, at the same time attempting to engage children in the process of reflecting on and structuring their learning:

There's a lot to say to them on Monday morning. They all get used to it but it does set the whole week up and it makes every other day easier and quicker to get on with. I now have a weekly review on a Friday where we look back on the week to see what we've got done and look ahead to the next week and see where we're going and what they think ought to be done next.
(Mr Brown, teacher interview, September 1990, Year 3)

Asked about the balance between children doing individual activities that they planned and teacher-devised activities, Mr Brown reflected on the fact that, as yet, he was allowing for little negotiation with regard to the content and the process of tasks:

Well at the moment it's fairly structured. I don't want to start that yet in a way. The activities that they are doing have all come from me, although some may have come from their original brainstorming. Really at the moment they are doing little more than planning when they do things but I'm trying to get them to take charge of going through their books and seeing what needs finishing. Some individuals have come up with fantastic ideas and I say 'Right, OK, fine, go and do it', but I've not gone into that too much yet.
(Mr Brown, teacher interview, September 1990, Year 3)

Thus although his classroom organization in that year was not explicitly encouraging of some forms of pupil autonomy, Mr Brown was warm in his praise of children who challenged his system positively with their own ideas. Over the year he established a special rapport with those children.

Miss King and her Year 4 class in 1991–2

Like the other new teachers at Greenside School described above, Miss King was a young graduate in her probationary year of teaching in 1991–2. She also held similar philosophies although she had a history of being less committed to a career in teaching than the others described here. While now especially enjoying working with children, she expected, in a year or two, to spend time travelling, eventually perhaps teaching 'in a different context, in a different place', perhaps abroad.

Miss King's early classroom organization was based around five large groupings derived from children's friendship choices, with opportunities for children to choose to work at small separate tables with other children, or individually according to the task. Children were moved to other main groupings by Miss King if friendships or working relationships were not progressing satisfactorily. The learning content of tasks was discussed on a whole class basis with children's ideas being incorporated into initial topic planning. On a weekly basis, children produced their own timetables and had a wide range of activities to choose from and develop with their own ideas. Miss King worked with groups for maths activities only. Not surprisingly, and like other teachers new to Greenside School, Miss King found difficulty monitoring pupil activities. However, perhaps because the children were older and more used now to a negotiated curriculum, the problem was not one of pupil evasion but more one of knowing where their enthusiasms were taking them:

I mean, the Head said to us that we can do as much negotiation as we like, that at the moment some of us might not even be confident to do any and how you do it is up to you.. But I think I just went straight in there and had total negotiation and now I think it's coming back at me, because it's not working for me. I just can't keep track of what anyone's doing at all. I mean, I've got records. They are doing what's in the National Curriculum, but just keeping tracks on them to get them to do that because, typically they always want to go off into other things, but you've got to keep track of where they are.

(Miss King, teacher interview, October 1991, Year 4)

As the year progressed, Miss King introduced more teacher-led group work, extending this to science activities as well as maths. More teacher timetabling of tasks in this way, together with fewer activities available at any time, helped her monitor and record children's work.

Additionally, there was some helpful whole-school emphasis on behaviour throughout the year, with a trial of 'assertive discipline' being introduced. Miss King's insistence upon a very quiet, cooperative and orderly classroom working environment helped her to successfully manage pupil negotiation with regard to both curriculum content and the classroom structures which supported it. She held in particular regard those children who exhibited a sense of humour in the classroom, worked collaboratively with peers and in cooperation with her organizational aims, though she also developed particular empathies with other individual children. During her one year of teaching at Greenside before she left for travel abroad, for many children in the class she earned herself a place among the most popular teachers of their primary school years.

Miss French and her Year 5 class in 1992–3

Miss French was a young, recently qualified teacher who joined Greenside School at the same time as Miss King. Also like Miss King, Miss French had a preference for quiet working conditions, though with regard to classroom organization for a negotiated curriculum, they were very different.

Throughout Greenside School, the pupil intake numbers were such that classes were often made up of more than one year-group. In 1992 the numbers of children, together with considerations for curricular organization, resulted in Year 5 being split three ways, two Year 5 classes were mixed with Year 6 and one with Year 4. This latter was Miss French's class and the five girls of the cohort being studied were in that class. The Year 5 half of Miss French's class, along with the rest of Year 5 children in other classes, spent most of Mondays with Mr Brown and each week they were answerable to him, on a weekly basis, for the completion of topic-related tasks. The resulting structuring of tasks by means of worksheets, teacher timetabling, children grouped by year and then by 'ability', was largely a pragmatic solution to differentiated curriculum needs in the class rather than an ideal solution for Miss French. Although the classroom system allowed pupils to extend the given programme where they wished and were able to do so, teacher expectations were nevertheless fairly explicit and activities were heavily directed. Miss French explained her organization:

The organization is based around my planning for the term. I'll take out what exactly I want them to do for the week, of which there will be a core of work which they have to finish by the end of that week, and when I go through work at the beginning of the week

I'll explain what exactly has to be finished. They all have a timetable which is actually quite rigid and there's some class lessons, some group lessons (and) sometimes they'll be doing individual work. Within each area there's also a lot of other work which will carry on to the following week, so there's plenty to keep them going. When it comes to things like maths work, either I'll give their group a sheet – they're actually arranged ability-wise – or they'll be working on the board, so there'll be a progression of things and I'll tell them where they actually start within that. So they're starting at their own level.
(Miss French, teacher interview, September 1992, Year 5)

As topics progressed and as the core needs were covered, then children, again as a *year-group*, negotiated how the content might be extended. For individuals though, any ongoing decisions in relation to content could only be made if they took responsibility for extending their own studies, having completed all other teacher requirements. Perhaps the area of greatest autonomy that the organization allowed for that year was in relation to decisions about presentation of work:

And they've got a lot to say on how they actually go about it, so how they choose to write it, how they choose to present it. For some things there aren't, but for some things there's that sort of flexibility.
(Miss French, teacher interview, September 1992, Year 5)

Though the curriculum was formally organized that year, Miss French was not correspondingly formal in her interactions with pupils. She developed supportive and empathic relations with them as learners, promoting positive and relaxed classroom relations and confidence in classroom discussions. Thus Miss French had much in common with other young female teachers joining the staff of Greenside School over the period of the study. Each was adjusting to their new roles as teachers, needing to be innovative in developing complex forms of classroom organization to meet school curriculum expectations, at the same time as integrating these into requirements associated with planning for, monitoring and assessing the National Curriculum. Each achieved this, in their different ways, while maintaining calm and relaxed environments for learning and warm, supportive relationships with their pupils. These young women teachers were also consistently cited as 'favourites' among the nine children. This was especially so among the girls, with whom they developed particularly confidence-boosting and empathic relationships.

Mr Brown and his Year 5 class in 1992–3

We need not discuss Mr Brown's background here as we have already met him as the Year 3 teacher of the cohort (see above). We have also described the organization of the curriculum in his class in relation to the need to coordinate his Year 5 teaching activities with Miss French. He similarly needed to co-ordinate his Year 6 teaching activities with Mrs Chard that year.

As described in relation to Mrs French's practice, some degree of pupil negotiation was possible, though it was a matter of pupils' individual motivation where this occurred:

We try and give them activities that you can interpret, maybe, in different ways, more problem-solving or (through which) they can express themselves. So with the history, we

give them pointers, questions, things to get them going, but the way they present their information is up to them. In a way, the amount that they do will depend on their ability and also how well they can organize their time.
(Mr Brown, teacher interview, September 1992, Year 5)

As Mr Brown suggests here, the extent to which pupils engaged in alternative ways of structuring and presenting tasks also depended on their efficient organization of their time:

We discuss it on Monday, so it's a sort of weekly cycle. The way we look at it is this. They don't have the option of choosing 'when' but they do have to organize themselves in a better way because they have these pressures of having things done in the week. Last week we found the children said they didn't have enough time to do the history. We said to them, you know the work is set. It can be done in that time. You obviously tried to do too much. So they really have to think 'how long is that and what can I get done?'.
(Mr Brown, teacher interview, September 1992, Year 5)

However, the curriculum had been quite highly structured when the Year 5 cohort were in Mrs Brown's Year 3 class. Rather it was, perhaps, in the field of working and social relationships with Mr Brown that pupils experienced the greatest difference from their earlier experience with him as their teacher. Year 5 pupils were a minority in the class, and their structural and status positions were not what they were before. This was not simply a matter of having lower relative academic positions in the class. The usual year-group status differentiation was greatly exaggerated by the increasing developmental and social maturity, as well as the extra responsibility accorded to Year 6 pupils about to leave for secondary school. Mr Brown was appreciative of the greater social and academic maturity of these older pupils:

I think the problem is that they've been dominated by – not always in a bad way – by having these Year 6 children, and I've got some *very* bright girls (among the Year 6 pupils). When Hannah (Year 5) shines, like when she was a Year 3, I'd have probably given you a different story altogether. I think she's kind of, had to give in to these (Year 6) children, because she's just knocked for six by what they are capable of really. And so am I! Because they do take an *enormous* leap, you know, to Year 6.
  And again, Year 6 children have that maturity. A lot of the girls can certainly come in and have quite a mature conversation and that shows a big difference really that you find you can't have with many of them, I've noticed. Left behind quite dramatically.
(Mr Brown, teacher interview, July 1993, Year 5)

As the case studies will show, this meant that the Year 5 boys in the study experienced less rapport with their teacher than they were perhaps anticipating on the strength of the Year 3 experience. They were also severely challenged by girls, a situation which some boys were beginning to find difficult to cope with.

Mrs Chard and her Year 6 class in 1993–4

Mrs Chard had been the deputy head at Greenside School since 1992, though she had developed her philosophy of active learning and associated classroom practices over many years and in a variety of classroom contexts. Some schools in which she had taught were in areas of considerable economic deprivation which presented a greater challenge to her teaching skills than Greenside children:

Those children came from very poor circumstances, although they were fantastic children, they were so loving and caring. That for me was a brilliant experience but very hard on the teaching front. I had to be terribly organized and it was all about meeting children's individual needs. No way could you group children together and lump them together, their needs were so great that you really had to start very much from basics. I learnt a lot about classroom organization then; about meaningful tasks, because otherwise the children just weren't interested at all.
(Mrs Chard, teacher interview, June 1994, Year 6)

A good number of teaching experiences both before she had a family and while her children were growing up strengthened her beliefs:

I came to Greenside having then been convinced that what I really believed in was children being set a task, a certain amount of negotiation and planning, but in a very highly structured set-up. It's certainly by no means a free-for-all. And [curriculum] planning has to be extremely tight, so you know exactly what you want, but you set it in such a way that the children will have a freedom to choose how they will carry out the task very often, and that's where you're really learning about children's strategies and so on. If you're in there working with a small group of children you really see, 'Yes, this child's needs are such and such, this child's strength is such and such'.
(Mrs Chard, teacher interview, June 1994, Year 6)

For Mrs Chard then, the emphasis was on presenting learners with a challenge, setting high expectations within tight planning schedules and following up with close assessment. These highly negotiated activities were usually achieved within groups, and required initial class discussion with Mrs Chard on the learning aims of the challenge. It then involved children in planning within their groups, in decisions about tasks and roles, research, recording and presentation of aspects of their learning before public presentation and explaining to the rest of the class. We have described above how other teachers organized for tasks so that pupil planning and pupil negotiation of tasks were usually carried out in advance of the activity itself, before they were actually confronted with and engaged on the task. However, in Mrs Chard's class, children were not involved in any very advanced curricular or timetable planning; rather negotiation took place in the context of each imminent and ongoing task. So it was also that systems for children to 'plan, do and review' were incorporated into the structure, meaning and learning aims of each task, rather than, as was generally the case with other teachers' systems, in relation to the weekly or daily organization of curricular experience.

Alongside this active and interactive learning there was also the expectation upon these 11-year-olds for substantial periods of silent, individual work. At such times, outcomes were sometimes less negotiable, being framed by Mrs Chard according to the necessity for a specific content or form of presentation.

Tables 3.4 and 3.5 below provide an overview and summary of developments in Greenside Primary School during the period of the study and of the forms of classroom practice which the case-study pupils experienced.

3.6 CONCLUSION

This chapter offers a contextualizing account of some of the major factors which affected the formal education of our case-study children during their primary

Academic year, teacher & pupil age	SCHOOL DEVELOPMENTS	TEACHER AND CLASSROOM PRACTICES
1984–85 Age 1/2	Church of England primary school, proud of traditions and high reputation among middle-class parents. Traditional pedagogy. House competitions. Coaching for entrance to private schools. Mr Evans, Head since 1965, retires.	N/A
1985–86 Age 2/3	Mrs Davison begins Headship. House competition restricted to Sports Day. Coaching for entrance to private schools stopped. Active learning and classroom innovation promoted.	N/A
1986–87 Pre-school Age 3/4	Negotiated curriculum (with High/Scope influences) introduced. Parental concern develops. Governors support Mrs Davison. Established staff leave.	N/A
1987–88 Reception Mrs Powell Age 4/5	Showcase status: many visitors to school. Curriculum co-ordinators introduced. Parental concern grows among traditionalist families. Number on roll falls. Three established staff retire. Davison appointee now gets a Headship elsewhere.	Mrs Powell: A very experienced, caring but traditional reception class teacher adjusting to Mrs Davison's expectations, which she mistrusted. Many fixed and teacher organized groups for routine and supervised tasks. Some negotiated choice of non-core curriculum activities and of play.
1988–89 Year 1 Miss Scott Age 5/6	Number on roll falls, but Damibrook children start to enter. Parental concern grows: governors meet parents. Rain Forest School Project.	Miss Scott: An experienced and overtly child-centred teacher, but personally and professionally frustrated. Prone to mood swings, including anger. Problems with classroom organization and resentful of Mrs Davison's 'intrusions'. Fixed or teacher organized groups for routine and supervised tasks. Choice of other activities.
1989–90 Year 2 Miss George Miss Sage Age 6/7	National Curriculum English and Maths assimilated into established curriculum planning procedures. First Institutional Development Plan completed. Number on roll stabilizes, with Damibrook intake. Parental concern calms. Staff turnover stabilizes. LMS budgeting introduced. PTA raises £2000 at Summer Fete. A confident end to the year.	Miss George: Newly qualified with great commitment to good teacher–pupil relationships and active learning. Working on classroom organization and skills. Negotiable curriculum for individuals and whole class, combined with teacher-led groups for core curriculum. Miss Sage: Young teacher committed to active learning and negotiation within a tightly organized and firmly controlled classroom. Explicit negotiation of topic work, with more explicit tasks and groupwork for core curriculum areas.

Table 3.4 *School developments and classroom practices up to the end of pupils' Key Stage 1*

Academic year, teacher & pupil age	SCHOOL DEVELOPMENTS	TEACHER AND CLASSROOM PRACTICES
1990–91 Year 3 Mr Brown Age 7/8	National Curriculum Science introduced at KS1, and other core subjects at KS2. Mrs Davison leads attempt to integrate new requirements into topic planning. Parents' Charter 'made available' to parents. LMS seen as an opportunity for independence. Overload of action research INSET. Production of *Joseph and the Amazing Technicolor Dream Coat*. Standardized assessment carried out by Y2 teachers. Staff morale 'hits rock bottom' through work pressure. Two Davison appointees get Headships, three other staff take maternity leave.	Mr Brown: Young teacher, enthusiast for active learning but, following previous experiences, now trying to develop appropriate organizational structures. Limited negotiation of activities by class or for groups only. A mixture of teacher timetabling of group work on core curriculum and group planning of topic work. National Curriculum considerations.
1991–92 Year 4 Miss King Age 8/9	Miss King, Miss French and staff on temporary contracts start. Induction into 'active learning' provided and Mrs Davison is proud of her 'bright new team'. Explicit signs of parental appreciation of 'active learning'. School saves £45,000 from staffing budget	Miss King: Newly qualified teacher, interested in negotiated curriculum idea but expecting to travel. Started boldly with weekly planning for whole class and individuals, but found problems in monitoring pupil work, particularly in relation to National Curriculum. Introduced more teacher-led group work and reduced number of simultaneous activities. Achieved quiet, order and cooperation.
1992–93 Year 5 Miss French Mr Brown Age 9/10	Mrs Davison's connections with the LEA weaken, but school autonomy and financial confidence grow. Mrs Davison engages in conscious mediation and prioritization to manage external and internal pressures. Boycott of submission of SAT results to construct league tables, but results given in annual report to parents.	Miss French: Young teacher teaching a Y4/Y5 class. Committed to developing empathic relationships with pupils and some negotiation. Mix of class, group and individual tasks, with fixed weekly timetable and 'ability' grouping. Felt constrained by National Curriculum requirements and links for topic work with Y5 pupils in Mr Brown's class. Mr Brown: Teaching a Y6/Y5 class in which Y5 pupils were a minority. Felt more constrained by National Curriculum requirements, Y6 expectations and organizational links to other classes. 'Ability' grouping and careful weekly timetabling of class, group and individual tasks. Mr Brown responsible for topic work of all Y5 pupils, drawn from three classes.
1993–94 Year 6 Mrs Chard Age 10/11	New method of curriculum planning developed, based on a subject/year grid with content posed by questions. Designed to allow for teacher and pupil autonomy and to prevent the National Curriculum producing 'humdrum and boring' learning. SATs carried out and reported to parents for the school as a whole and with details on their child.	Mrs Chard: experienced, deputy headteacher. Highly committed and with high expectations for attainment. Tight curriculum planning. Structured timing and groupings, with emphasis on collaborative negotiation within tasks or individual problem-solving. Expected sustained, silent work and 'sensible' behaviour from pupils.

Table 3.5   *School developments and classroom practices during pupils' Key Stage 2*

education. With the progressive implementation of the National Curriculum preceding them, the children were educated through a period of unprecedented change. This has been characterized as an era of ideological struggle between the teaching profession and successive conservative governments (Pollard *et al.*, 1994), and our account provides an illustration of the scale and nature of professional mediation at LEA, school and classroom levels in response to central prescription (Broadfoot and Pollard, 1996). However, it also highlights the strange combination of social trends, political forces, personal biographies and serendipity which influence processes of transition in government, LEA, school and classroom leadership. For pupils however, their classroom relationships with successive teachers are experienced with direct immediacy and, as we have seen, there were both disjunctions and continuities in the forms of practice offered to the cohort at Greenside.

The interface of history and biography is always unique – as it was for the individuals who have featured in this chapter. In the next section of the book, we explore this uniqueness by focusing on four case-study children. We will meet their families, and track the processes of strategic adaption in which they engaged as they learnt and developed their identities through their pupil careers.

Part Two

Case Studies of Pupil Career

Introduction to the Case Studies

Through the following case-study chapters we track the careers of Sarah, William, Robert and Harriet from their entry into Greenside School at age four, through to the time they left at age eleven. We examine the predominant strategies which these pupils used in their learning and as they shaped their individual identities and statuses as pupils. We track those changing patterns of learning and interaction and compare them across the contexts of home and the local community, as well as across classroom, playground and wider school contexts.

As well as tracking the careers of Sarah, William, Robert and Harriet, their case-study chapters also pick up on the stories of Hazel, Daniel, Mary and Sally from *The Social World of Children's Learning*. The experiences of the key children in this book are bound up with them and with the wider year-group cohort as classmates, friends and rivals and against whom they measured themselves and were measured. Thus through the stories, which cross seven years of schooling, readers will become familiar with many individuals and groups, responding differently, interacting dynamically as they carve out identities and careers as pupils. Through the stories we hear the voices of children defining themselves against the wider group of peers, articulating a sense of self as a girl or a boy, as clever or slower, as leader, follower or marginal to the activities of their peers.

As well as through children's own voices and writing, we also tell their stories through the voices and writing of their families, their particular friends and their teachers. They are also told through our own observations, conversations and perceptions as researchers. In this we continue to draw on a complex knowledge of people, classrooms and playground, homes and community of Greenside, built up week by week across the seven years of the children's primary school life.

Readers will observe that the data relating to these case-study chapters was collected by Andrew Pollard for the first four years and by Ann Filer for the latter three years. An account of the methodological implications of the 'hand over' of data-gathering responsibilities and of our collaboration through the *Identity and Learning Programme* generally can be found in Filer with Pollard (1998).

We present below a chart of the case-study children and their successive class teachers through Greenside Primary School.

	Reception	Year 1	Year 2	Year 3	Year 4	Year 5	Year 6
Sarah	Mrs Powell	Miss Scott	Miss George	Mr Brown	Miss King	Miss French	Mrs Chard
William	Mrs Powell	Miss Scott	Miss Sage	Mr Brown	Miss King	Mr Brown	Mrs Chard
Robert	Mrs Powell	Miss Scott	Miss George	Mr Brown	Miss King	Mr Brown	Mrs Chard
Harriet	Mrs Powell	Miss Scott	Miss George	Mr Brown	Miss King	Miss French	Mrs Chard
Mary	*Mrs Powell*	*Miss Scott*	*Miss George*	Mr Brown	Miss King	Miss French	Mrs Chard
Hazel	*Mrs Powell*	*Miss Scott*	*Miss George*	Mr Brown	Miss King	Miss French	Mrs Chard
Daniel	*Mrs Powell*	*Miss Scott*	*Miss Sage*	Mr Brown	Hillside Juniors	Hillside Juniors	Hillside Juniors
Sally	*Mrs Powell*	*Miss Scott*	*Miss George*	Mr Brown	Miss King	Miss French	Mrs Chard
James	*Mrs Powell*	*Miss Scott*	*Miss George*	Easthampton College	Easthampton College	Easthampton College	Easthampton College

Note: Italicized pupil-years are described and analysed in detail in *The Social World of Children's Learning*.

Table 4.1 *The class teachers of pupils during their careers at Greenside Primary School*

Chapter 4

Sarah's Story

4.1 PRE-SCHOOL, RECEPTION AND YEAR 1

Sarah, an introduction

Sarah shaped her pupil identity and career predominantly through that pattern of strategic action which we have termed *conformity*. As we describe in Chapter 2, *conformity* suggests a reification of those four broad categories of structures which we suggest constitute the main areas for career progression in Greenside and in primary schools generally. Those structures relate to curricular expectations and extra-curricular opportunities, to those official social relations which are the concern of teachers and to the unofficial social relations of the peer group and playground. We can expect, therefore, to see Sarah operating within and competently adapting to the mainstream patterns of achievement and cultural norms which are available to all pupils and within which they carve out identities as pupils and ultimately shape their careers.

As we enter Greenside School with the four-year-old Sarah, from what we know of her pre-school years and family life we are not surprised to see her quickly learning to cope with the demands of school and being accepted as a competent member of the class and peer group. Over the first few years at Greenside School, we see her learn a range of strategies which, if often minimalistic and evading in response to tasks, also reduce some of the risks in learning and in the relationships within which learning took place. If it was beginning to be felt that Sarah was not fulfilling her potential, she was for most of the time making good progress and succeeding in being regarded as a 'good girl'. She was also a competent member of a friendship group offering support as well as rivalry in the maintenance of similar classroom identities. If Sarah was not as competitive and striving for academic success in school as some of her friends and an older brother, she was certainly throwing herself wholeheartedly into a sibling rivalry for parental esteem as she strived to match Tom across a range of out-of-school activities.

We have to follow Sarah into her middle years at Greenside School, however, before we begin to get a sense of where her interests and aspirations might lie as opposed to those of her family, peers and teachers. There we begin to see that retreat from conflict and from competition with her peers and the maintenance of a low profile were strategies which were not paying off for Sarah as she began to notice the spiralling careers of friends who took a riskier approach to school life and who were reaping the rewards she sought. Through her later years at Greenside we trace the outcomes of the tensions that emerge between, on the one hand, her competence and strong sense of self and independence and, on the other, her strategy of operating within the structures and patterns of success made available to her by the important people in her life. We trace her patterns of friendship, her relationships with teachers, parents and brother as she strove to reconcile her aspirations for recognition and status with her dislike of conflict and challenge from the people she loved, whose approval she sought or whose support she needed.

Sarah's family

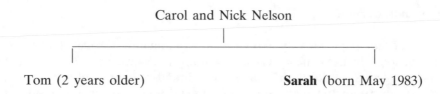

Carol and Nick Nelson

Tom (2 years older)   Sarah (born May 1983)

Sarah was the youngest of a family of four who lived in a three-bedroomed semi-detached house in Greenside. Sarah's father, Nick, was a solicitor and, during Sarah's pre-school and Reception school year, her mother, Carol, worked full-time looking after the family. She also helped at school on a voluntary basis before returning to part-time work outside the home during Sarah's Year 1 at school. Carol's career in office administration gradually developed thereafter.

Mostly through their mother's influence, Sarah and her older brother Tom were growing up with close connections to the church. Mrs Nelson was a Roman Catholic, 'though not strictly so', she explained, and the children were encouraged to accompany her to church from an early age. At the time when the study began, Sarah, at age five, and her brother, were also regular attenders at Crusaders Club. This church-based organization was a popular weekly after-school activity for many children at Greenside Primary and in the neighbourhood generally.

Early learning in the family

From the time when the children were babies, Carol Nelson took an active interest in their learning. However, the experience of learning with her mother was, for the young Sarah, rather different from Tom's before her. Mrs Nelson explained to Andrew Pollard:

When Tom was a baby and growing up, you know, the early days, I was always doing things with him. I am sure that is probably why he is the way he is now because I was always there reading or trying to teach certain things all the time and I always had time to do it. With Sarah I didn't push so much. I don't know whether it was because, you know, in the back of my mind I had thought 'Oh isn't it so nice to have a little girl. I don't have to be so pushy and rough-and-tumble, let's take things a bit more calmly, you know let's do it gently this time, we won't rush things.'
(Mrs Nelson, parent interview, March 1988, Reception)

However, where rather more physical pursuits were concerned, even in relation to an older, stronger brother, no quarter seems to have been given Sarah, and none expected.

She doesn't particularly like rough-and-tumble things. She has had a lot of that at home growing up with Tom being a typical boy and he is quite strong. From the time she was this size until now we have never cosseted her. So she has had to grow up pushing and sort of fighting for herself in that respect. I must admit when she gets together with Tom and his friends she is quite capable of playing the way they want to play. She won't be left out. She likes to prove herself.
(Mrs Nelson, parent interview, March 1988, Reception)

I have never really made either of them as a mummy's or a daddy's boy or girl. We have shared things quite equally and we have never been what I call namby-pamby towards them. If they fall down and hurt their knee we are not one of these who runs up to them straight away and say 'Oh you poor thing, isn't it absolutely terrible'. We just say 'Oh dear that was a bit silly'. You know, get up, rub it better and carry on. I think in most aspects that is the way we have treated it. So I suppose they are quite independent. They are quite happy to go off on their own and do things.
(Mrs Nelson, parent interview, March 1988, Reception)

So, physical and emotional independence and general competence were encouraged in Sarah from an early age, an aspect of family values and parental expectations which seemed to hold irrespective of the sex of the children.

Early learning in nursery school

As was alluded to above, Tom was regarded by his parents as a more active learner than Sarah and this was one of the reasons for their considering that an early introduction to formal education would suit him.

Yes. He was a lot keener on learning things at a very early age. Everything with him started very early and he was always grasping at things straight away and Fairoak [nursery school] was exactly what he needed – little rooms about this size with a few children in actually getting into the routine of what it would be like in school. Some children find it absolutely horrifying but he absolutely loved it. Whereas Sarah wasn't that way inclined as much as Tom. If you offered her information, anything to do with learning she would be quite happy to listen to it but she didn't want to go out and find it herself. I thought that might be a nice environment for her to get into as well. She had a friend who was going. Tom went with a friend who is at Greenside now and Sarah happened to be the same age as his sister, so they went.
(Mrs Nelson, parent interview, March 1988, Reception)

So it was that the nursery experience which the Nelsons thought suitable for Tom was considered also likely to be a good experience for Sarah, though her learning style, it was suggested, was different. Clearly then, aside from any stance that the children had towards learning, the Nelsons had fairly well established views concerning education and the sort of learning environment that they would like for their children. In fact, these views were formed, and certain expectations held in mind, before either of the children was born.

> We had heard before we had children that [Greenside] was an excellent school. They followed the traditional way of teaching. We moved to the area for the school before we had children.
> (Mrs Nelson, parent interview, March 1988, Reception)

However, as we have described in Chapter 3, great changes began to take place in Greenside School between Tom's entry in 1985 and Sarah's in 1987.

> Then when we sent Tom it was the year Mr Evans left and then Mrs Davison came with completely different attitudes and ideas and it really started the parents worrying and thinking what was going to happen. And I know for a fact there will be a lot of children missing next September.
> (Mrs Nelson, parent interview, March 1988, Reception)

A summary of Sarah's pre-school experience

So we see that Sarah was growing up in the context of a set of family values which had been, in part, shaped and informed by the traditional structures of church and education. Clear patterns and expectations were available to Sarah through these structures and organizations and through her older brother who provided a successful role model as he moved through them before her. Their parents had promoted a culture of independence and a certain competitive rough-and-tumble in the children which Sarah threw herself into wholeheartedly. In short then, Sarah had had the sort of middle-class family experience and upbringing that would be likely to prepare her well for her primary school career. If there was a small cloud on the horizon as she entered Mrs Powell's reception class in September 1987, it was that her parents were unhappy that the school was not now offering the sort of education they wanted for their children.

Sarah, Reception, early days in Mrs Powell's class

Mrs Powell was an infant school teacher of many years standing at Greenside School and she was well respected within the community of parents for her traditional and well understood approach. As we have described in Chapter 3 Mrs Powell, at this stage in her career, was finding it especially difficult to incorporate pupil planning and reviews of their learning into her established routines. However, such was Mrs Powell's skill that, although she mistrusted these new approaches and found the adaptations difficult, she continued to provide a stable and supportive learning environment for the children entering Greenside school.

The Nelson family knew Mrs Powell well through Tom's time in her class two years before. So, hand in hand with Alice, her best friend through nursery school,

Sarah embarked upon classroom life supported by a network of familiar and cohesive social relations.

Here is Mrs Powell talking about Sarah, a few weeks after she began school.

Mrs Powell:	Sarah is very independent. That's the one who was working with the shapes. Quite strong-willed.
AP:	Yes, she was being quite creative with those.
Mrs Powell:	Being quite mathematical as well, fitting them together, she put all the circles out just touching each other all the way round.
AP:	She's fitted in all right, has she?
Mrs Powell:	She has a best friend, Alice, and they're a bit naughty together actually, but happy – so that's the main thing.

(Teacher interview, September 1987, Reception)

More formal assessments of Sarah were recorded by Mrs Powell as the autumn term progressed. According to those records, Sarah read well, knew all her initial sounds, was able to spell a few words by herself and had good handwriting. She always had ideas for writing and she was able to write by herself using invented spellings. Sarah was also competent at addition up to 10 and could measure and balance using non-standard units.

Of course it is important to contextualize these not inconsiderable achievements, because of great importance to children's academic and social status within a class is their achievement level relative to that of their peers. Such achievement levels will, moreover, generally bear a relationship to that other social status indicator among children, their age. However, both with respect to academic achievement and with respect to age, Sarah had a reasonably secure structural position in the class. She was the eleventh oldest of 28 children and within the top third of the class in both mathematical and language achievements.

So it was that Sarah quickly adapted to the academic and social expectations of school. Apparently she also felt confident enough to exhibit a streak of independence and a little naughtiness.

Friendships and peer relationships in Reception

We have suggested that one of the reasons for Sarah's successful integration into school life lay in the security that a long-standing close friend gave her. By the time that Sarah had been in school for six months however, her mother, though not over-concerned, reflected in interview upon the fact that Sarah had not widened her friendship base to any great extent. Though Sarah may not have been forming close ties with her peers, she certainly enjoyed social play with many of them. Here is Sarah at a series of 'review times', talking to Mrs Powell and the class about her chosen activities.

Home corner. I was the mummy of Sally and Mary. I made some supper for them and I gave them some medicine. They had a tummy ache and bad throat. They tidied their room and Sally said – oh she didn't want to tidy her room – but she did.
(Sarah, Mrs Powell's records, March 1988, Reception)

Sand. I made a pudding for me and it was your birthday and it was Alice's birthday and Sally's birthday. Then I put some worms in it for Sally. Then we played mummies and dads.
(Sarah, Mrs Powell's records, April 1988, Reception)

I played in the sand and then I wanted to do a marble rolling and then I played in the home corner. Mary and Amanda came after. Then Damien and Nimra came. I made some food for all of the children because I was the mummy. Then I washed my hands after I did the marble rolling. When I was in the home corner I dressed the baby.
(Sarah, Mrs Powell's records, June 1988, Reception)

Records like these kept by Mrs Powell show a strong preference on Sarah's part for social play based around observed patterns of domesticity and family life. Cooking, Mummies and Daddies and weddings were firm favourites of Sarah and of many others in the class. They also show that, if Sarah was not forming particularly close relationships, she was nevertheless accepted as a competent and fully participating member of a peer group of both boys and girls.

Learning strategies in Reception

At the beginning of Spring Term, Mrs Powell said in interview that she considered Sarah to be a quiet girl who was eager to do her best and who took herself rather more seriously than did many others. One factor that seemed to contribute to Sarah's social and academic competence in the classroom was her ability to know what was acceptable to peers and adults and to respond accordingly. Here is Sarah in interview being shown photos recently taken of activities in her classroom. She was asked to order her preferences and did so with easy equanimity and acceptance of her teacher's expectation.

AP: Well now, look, supposing you could do that, or you could do that writing or you could play with Mobilo, or you could do some maths or you could do some painting. Which would be your favourite? Which one would you choose first?

Sarah: Um, writing.

AP: Writing first. And which one would you choose next?

Sarah: (Points at the picture)

AP: Painting, right. And which one would you choose after that?

Sarah: (Taps the picture)

AP: Play in the home corner. And which one would you choose next? Mobilo. And which one next? The maths. That's fine. Now tell me, what's the difference between them?

Sarah: I've forgotten.

AP: You've forgotten. If somebody said, 'Time for your maths now Sarah', what would you think?

Sarah: Got to do it.

AP: And if they said 'Time for your writing now, Sarah', what would you think then?

Sarah: I'll have to do all of the things that are in the classroom.
(Pupil interview, February 1988, Reception)

As is the case with much early learning in school, Sarah was helped along by being happy to remember instruction and fulfil teacher expectations without always fully understanding the reasons for them. In this extract from fieldnotes Andrew Pollard was helping Sarah with her writing.

> I do some writing for Sarah: 'Susan fell off the bench and broke her arm'. Sarah instructs me.
>
> | Sarah: | Then you put a dot. |
> |---|---|
> | AP: | Why? What's the dot for? |
> | Sarah: | It's for Mrs Powell. |
> | Robert: | It's a full stop – like a traffic light. |
>
> (Fieldnotes, Andrew Pollard, May 1988, Reception)

At the end of Spring Term Sarah received her first school report. As suggested by Mrs Powell's records for Autumn Term, as well as everything else here it recorded Sarah's very satisfactory progress and enthusiastic participation across the range of academic, social and creative activities. Sarah's parents, despite some of their early misgivings about changes in the school, were pleased with Sarah's promising start.

Home and family relationships in Reception

Sarah continued at home to be encouraged to enjoy a range of learning experiences. She was beginning to enjoy drawing and painting, and she was an enthusiastic and avid reader. As far as school was concerned, Tom continued to provide a pattern for high achievement through competition with his peers. Mrs Nelson explained to Andrew Pollard:

> The maths group he is in at the moment, there is himself and two other boys who are at the top. It was last year, he was ill quite a bit with throat and ears and he absolutely hated being home because he knew that one of these other two boys were going to be ahead of him by the time he got back to school. That is the way he has always been all the way through school. I am hoping that Sarah will be more and more that way inclined as she gets on.
> (Mrs Nelson, parent interview, March 1988, Reception)

However, it was not the case that Sarah herself was uncompetitive. Rather her competitive energy was directed against Tom, and within the family.

> They go swimming nearly every week – Daddy always takes them on a Sunday. She is always trying to compete and keep up with Tom so she throws herself into the water literally and has a go. She won't be beaten. She won't let him do something that she can't do herself. When we go to the park she is never afraid of going up to the top of the climbing frame and showing she can do as well as any of the other boys and girls there. I don't think there are any problems in that respect.
> We say: 'Go on. Have a go.' As I say we have always treated them like that so she has never had that sort of recourse you know.
> (Mrs Nelson, parent interview, March 1988, Reception)

Later that summer:

> We came away for the weekend and spent the main part of the day on my boss's yacht at Symington Bay.
> Sarah spent an hour or so competing vigorously with Tom crabbing from the pontoons. They were both successful but Sarah's catch turned out to be bigger, much to

her delight. They had a wonderful time and after lunch were treated to a sail along the coast. However, while everyone else was occupied on deck, Sarah spent most of the time below deck, drawing. Mostly pictures of the day's activities and quite detailed.
(Mrs Nelson, parent diary, June 1988, Reception)

So at home, Sarah was able to compete successfully with Tom in a way that maybe she felt she never could academically, especially being two years younger. She held her own and occasionally outshone him in activities requiring physical skills or courage and she was also deemed to be 'better at drawing' than him.

At about this time some changes in Tom's behaviour simultaneously sparked off changes in Sarah's. She had apparently discovered another way in which she could outshine Tom in her parents' eyes.

I have noticed that whenever Tom and I have been having a battle because he is so sort of strong-willed, Sarah has often said to me 'That is not a very nice thing for Tom to say is it. I don't say things like that do I'. I think probably she thinks, well Tom seems to battle on occasions, I'll show mummy I can be a good girl and not do it. I am not saying that we don't have our battles but she will admit defeat if she knows she is wrong.
(Mrs Nelson, parent interview, March 1988, Reception)

Sarah had learnt then, that she could certainly outshine her brother in goodness.

Summary of Sarah's Reception year

During her Reception year, Sarah developed an identity in school of being academically and socially competent while maintaining a degree of detachment and independence. She achieved this within the well structured and emotionally secure environment created by Mrs Powell and a network of school and home relationships. The pattern of independence and competence within clear structures matched that which had been encouraged and experienced at home during Sarah's pre-school years. If the competitiveness for personal achievement that Sarah's parents looked for did not materialize in her schoolwork, it certainly did at home. There, if there was a chance to outshine her brother, she was anything but a passive learner.

At this point Sarah was about to leave behind the comfortable security of Mrs Powell's Reception class and enter a new and altogether different classroom environment in which her independence and competence were to be more severely tested.

Sarah, Year 1, early days in Miss Scott's class

At Greenside School, as we described in Chapter 3, the yearly intake was such that children did not progress from year to year with a fixed year-group cohort. It was for this reason that Sarah found herself in a lower structural position with her move to Miss Scott's class. Instead of being within the oldest half of the class, she now was 27th out of 32 children. From being in the top third in mathematics and language achievements, she now found herself in the middle third. Along with this lowering of academic and social status, Sarah also experienced other changes that gradually affected her sense of security.

As also described in Chapter 3, Sarah's new teacher, Miss Scott, was at the time experiencing some personal and emotional difficulties and a deteriorating relationship with the headteacher. As a result, many of the pupils who passed through her class at this time had, to varying degrees, to adapt to an environment which was more emotionally volatile and, in terms of classroom organization and teacher expectations, more unpredictable than that of their Reception classes.

Sarah almost certainly would have handled these changes more confidently had she not lost the security of her close friend, Alice, who had been removed from the school by her parents. Alice was one of a steady trickle of children who with the passing of the established traditions of Greenside school were being enrolled at a preparatory independent school in the neighbourhood. So it was that Miss Scott's records show Sarah apparently coping with the new situation, but clearly in a less relaxed and happy way than was recorded a year before on entry to school.

> Entered new class with a few tears (her greatest friend has gone to Sheldrake School) but soon settled in fairly happily.
>   Working well and mixing well socially. A little moody on the odd occasion but responding to encouragement and taking interest in all activities.
> (Miss Scott's class records, autumn 1988, Year 1)

> I think she is a very thoughtful, sensitive child and you don't always know what is going on behind those eyes. But, seems fairly well adjusted and doesn't bat an eyelid when I shout.
> (Miss Scott, teacher interview with Andrew Pollard, autumn 1988, Year 1)

It was at about this time that Sarah's parents began to express some of their concerns about some of the new approaches to learning that the school was using.

> Father was quite worried at parents evening that Sarah's writing is, what the term is now called, invented spelling, in that they write what they like. I said this would change, so don't worry. She writes beautifully and what she does do she does well.
> (Miss Scott, teacher interview, autumn 1988, Year 1)

In Document 4.1 we can see a sample of Sarah's writing at the end of her first term in Year 1. It illustrates the use of invented spelling whereby children were encouraged early on to become independent writers, to 'have a go' rather than interrupt the production of ideas by waiting for teacher help.

Sarah's parents, like many others, had a good deal of confidence in Miss Scott's judgement partly because she, like Mrs Powell, was associated with the former, more traditional approaches in the school. However, they failed to be convinced by her reassurances and the school's policy with regard to spelling remained a cause of dissatisfaction.

Document 4.1   *Sarah, Year 1 'Father Christmas' picture and writing (December 1988)*

Friendships and peer relationships in Year 1

With the loss of Alice, Sarah became more frequently associated with a pair of friends, Sally and Mary. These girls, whose stories featured in *The Social World of Children's Learning*, had an ongoing, close relationship, a feature of which was their competitive rivalry both within school and in out-of-school activities. In Year 1, some of this rivalry was becoming particularly acute with Mary having lost some ground in her reading progression and striving to keep ahead of Sally in maths. Sarah, on joining this group, became swept up in the tensions which currently pervaded it and these increasingly became apparent in her relationship with Mary. In an atmosphere where some children were inclined to be wary about 'getting things wrong' (see case studies in *The Social World of Children's Learning*), the three undoubtedly acted as supportive collaborators for each other, minimalizing error and the risk of being told off. At the same time, however, they became rivals in 'goodness', using 'rules' and adult approval to assert control or to score points off each other. The following were taken from a series of exchanges between the two girls on a day in Autumn Term. The episodes concern model making with the two girls working with another, Hannah. The process is being highly directed by Mrs Smart, a parent helper, as other children work in parallel on other models.

Mrs Smart:	That bit's a bit big don't you think? I'm just trying to think how to do this.

Mary plays at eating glue.

Mrs Smart:	'Now hold on. I've got it. If we fold that in there and stick down. So if you put glue in there. And that can go up there, look. And we'll have a little bit of glue just there girls. That's it. Well done. Now we can do the other end. You have a go while I go and help Sally.

Mrs Smart moves to Sally. Sarah and Mary start to argue about how it has to be done. Mary has the glue and insists on 'gluing it in there!' Sarah raises her voice. Hannah looks round *at once* in alarm to see if Miss Scott will react.

Miss Scott:	Who's that?

They resume. Sarah holds the house below the table thus preventing Mary from gluing. Mary appeals to Mrs Smart.

Sarah:	I just want to do one side myself and let her do the other.

Mrs Smart moves to adjudicate. Mary does her side first. Sarah looks bored and cross. Mrs Smart does most of it, Mary applying the glue, Mrs Smart folding the paper etc.

Later in the same session

Sarah argues with Mary about which way the door (of the model) should open.

Miss Scott:	OK, now where's all this silly noise coming from?
Mary:	It's Sarah.
Miss Scott:	OK, well settle down, there's good girls.

Sarah and Mary are waiting to put more bits on. Sarah accepts it (as it is). Mary wants to add.

Mrs Smart:	No. Hold on girls. I don't think you need anything else because the next thing you've got to do this afternoon is paint it. Now, you tidy up the bits of paper and then you can wash your hands.

Mary tidies up with the approval of Mrs Smart.

Mrs Smart:	(to Sarah) What's happened to my cleaning lady?

Mary:	She's not doing anything!
Mrs Smart:	Well she won't get paid then.

Sarah joins in. They tidy up and Sarah goes to wash. Mary remains trying to please Mrs Smart and rivalling Sally in goodness.

After lunch on the same day

Mary and Sarah go off to paint the lighthouse keeper's house. There is *enormous* tension now about who shall do what.

Mary:	I hate Sarah.

I force them to take it in turns. They finish with some difficulty, and go off to wash. As they go Sarah bars the door to Mary. Then they get to the pegs to hang aprons up. Mary drops hers and runs to wash *first*. They race down the corridor. As they return to the classroom Mary comes to me to tell me that Sarah is putting on nail polish using crayons.

(Fieldnotes, Andrew Pollard, October 1988, Year 1)

The sorts of conflicts observed here continued intermittently to the end of the year. During the summer term, a supply teacher remarked to Andrew Pollard:

> There's a lot of tension among the children, particularly the girls. Sarah, Mary, Lois, Charlotte. Is it competition? I've never found it quite like this before.
> (Mrs Smith, fieldnotes, Andrew Pollard, May 1989, Year 1)

Some of this tension surfaced at home during the year with Sarah intermittently upset and complaining of not having friends who wanted to play with her.

Learning strategies in Year 1

During the autumn term in Year 1, Sarah's academic and social competence meant that she coped adequately in this less secure and less predictable context. However, her 'naughty, but happy' identity of the Reception year was replaced with a care to be good, an attention to rules and a dislike of any 'naughty' children, and especially a group of boys which Miss Scott defined as troublesome and who routinely provoked an angry response from her.

The tensions which Sarah was experiencing in the autumn term did not resolve themselves and Miss Scott noted the following in her records in January.

> Towards Christmas [Sarah] became tired and more sulky, parting from mum difficult on odd occasion. Response and general interest has waned. Going through an emotional period when she appears unsure of herself – I cannot think of the reason except that it is attention-seeking. A self-indulgent phase?
> (Miss Scott, class records, spring 1989, Year 1)

With the start of the spring term the situation had deteriorated and Sarah's mother reported in the diary:

> Since the Christmas break Sarah has not wanted to go into school. I cannot get her past the school gates and so have to walk her into the cloakroom and take her into the classroom where Sarah is near to hysterics. She is crying and holding on to my arm with a tremendous force. It usually takes me a good five minutes to leave and even then I have to leave Miss Scott trying to comfort her.
> Miss Scott says Sarah has not appeared to be her normal self in the classroom, since the beginning of term, but nevertheless copes with her work and leads a fairly settled day.
> (Parent diary, spring 1989, Year 1)

Sarah's mother managed to resolve the school avoidance problem with extra reassurance and Sarah continued on the whole to maintain her hardworking and 'good' identity in the classroom. However, there were occasions when Sarah's efforts fell short of her teacher's expectations.

> Sarah's friends were happy to see her back although she didn't appear to get on very well with her schoolwork, maths in particular, and subsequently Miss Scott was, apparently, shouting at her a lot. We tried to find out, from Sarah, exactly what the problem was, but she couldn't explain specifically what was wrong. We didn't pursue the matter but rather played it down and can only hope it was as a result of being away for such a long time.
> (Parent diary, summer 1989, Year 1)

In interview with Andrew Pollard, Mrs Nelson explained the playing down of this incident and some of Sarah's other worries that year. She explained this in terms of her knowledge and support of Miss Scott's practice and her own awareness of her daughter's sensitivities.

> [Miss Scott] doesn't stand for any nonsense, which is quite right. Little sensitive girls like Sarah pick this up and automatically think it's directed at her when it's not, because she's very quick to come home and say so-and-so and so-and-so were being naughty in the class today and Miss Scott didn't like it, she shouted. She picks things up and I think it's probably just her being a bit too over-sensitive.
> (Mrs Nelson, parent interview, July 1989, Year 1)

During the summer term Miss Scott's class records stated that Sarah was 'usually cheerful and helpful' in her behaviour. She was 'a little hesitant', preferring to watch before undertaking an activity. However, Sarah was also 'independent in many ways' and 'not reliant on adult attention'.

Her end of year report recorded Sarah's good progress in all areas of language and her flair for well structured writing with lots of ideas. Similarly she was reported as having a sound grasp of maths concepts. In project work and in creative activities, the picture was of a fully participating and thoughtful approach.

Home and family relationships in Year 1

During a year when Sarah found 'naughty boys' and the tensions and conflicts of the classroom a bit disturbing, she had shown similar responses to ordinary, day-to-day conflict within the home. Her mother, reflecting in interview with Andrew Pollard upon the changes during the year, considered that lately Sarah had seemed to have an increased need for stability and security. This need, at home as in school, can be seen to include worries about the conflicts of others as well as her own.

Mrs Nelson:	She gets terribly upset if Tom is being told off about something.
AP:	Does she?
Mrs Nelson:	Because sometimes he just flips over just silly little things and gets quite naughty at home. And so he's either given a hard smack or just told to go upstairs before anything else happens, to get out of the way. And he stomps off and it upsets

> Sarah. She will burst into tears and come running to either Mummy or Daddy for a bit of comfort. But then of course, that goes down the wrong way with Tom. He thinks that she's getting all the extra attention then . . .
>
> (Parent interview, summer 1989, Year 1)

During the year, Sarah maintained her enthusiasm for a number of out-of-school activities and Tom was feeling increasingly threatened by her abilities in some of these.

> Most of the time, they get on very well and he's a very protective and loving brother [but] there is always this sort of competition, especially with the piano at the moment going on, because they are at reasonably the same level. Tom is just sort of one or two jumps ahead. But whenever Sarah goes in to practise on the piano, Tom is there like a shot saying it's his turn. So we get this fighting over who's going to be playing the piano. There was an occasion a couple of days ago, I could hear Tom saying, 'Are you stupid?' or 'thick' or something. So I said, 'Well, that's not the way to speak to your sister. What's the problem?' And it was just because she was trying to do something that he thought he ought to be doing – 'How come she can do this?'. He was just adopting this attitude that she was just silly. She didn't know anything about it. That upsets her.
>
> (Mrs Nelson, parent interview, summer 1989, Year 1)

Sarah continued to be encouraged by her parents not to be put down by Tom and so, despite her dislike of conflict, she was undeterred by his outbursts.

> She won't let him put her down. She's very strong in that respect. I've always told her that she's had to be and that she must just carry on and not take any notice.
>
> (Mrs Nelson, parent interview, July 1989, Year 1)

During the year Sarah added judo to her out-of-school activities.

> Tom started judo when he was five. So as soon as she came to the age of five, she wanted to start, and Tom wanted her to start also. She's enjoying it tremendously. She has a wobbly tooth at the moment and when we took her last night she was frightened to death that it was going to be knocked out because 'so and so is quite rough at times and I'll just have to make sure that I get hold of him or her first and throw them.'
>
> (Mrs Nelson, parent interview, July 1989, Year 1)

In judo, as in the descriptions of swimming and climbing above, where robust physical activity was called for, Sarah was prepared, literally, to throw herself into the competition. However, in contrast to that vigorously competitive identity that was developing at home, Sarah also gained the identity of 'proper little mother' through helping with babies of friends of the family. In a similar way, during family holidays for example, she often sought out and befriended younger children.

By the end of Year 1, Sarah's mother felt that she had regained some of her confidence in school but was not looking forward to moving on to the next class. Sarah disliked change in her life. She had now got the measure of Miss Scott and Mrs Nelson felt that she would prefer the security of that known situation to having to get used to a new one.

Summary of Sarah's Year 1

In the context of a more volatile classroom atmosphere and with the loss of her close friend, Sarah showed a considerable loss of confidence in Year 1. Although she maintained her academic success and composure in the classroom, a fair amount of stress was apparent on the periphery of classroom life which surfaced in tense relationships with friends and periods of school phobia. Her parents had ongoing concerns in this year both with regard to disruptions and upsets in her relationships with friends and with regard to the school's approach to spelling.

Sarah's identity and career in the early years at Greenside School

Through her first two years at Greenside School Sarah experienced the same classroom contexts as her peers and also as her brother before her. It became clear that her intentions in those contexts, her responses to them and her emerging identity as a learner and as pupil were reflections of her own particular biography. At school she was prepared to accept and fulfil parental and teacher expectations but, at least where academic pursuits were concerned, she did not share the competitive fervour of her brother and some of her friends. Sarah's academic and social competence meant that she coped with the change from a secure to a more volatile classroom context. In so doing she retained something of her 'independent' identity, yet the easy equanimity and the 'naughty but happy' identity of her Reception year gave way to a hesitancy in classroom tasks, an attention to rules and a concern with 'goodness'.

So where is Sarah herself in this account? She seemed to have had the capacity for strong, independent and determined action. She also had considerable capabilities and talents. Yet, so far in her career, her struggles and successes can be contextualized largely within the patterns, expectations and structures that were made available to her by others. Of course, at this point in the story, Sarah was only a little over six years old. We need to move a little further into her story before we begin to get a sense of where Sarah's interests and intentions lay, as distinct from those of the important people in her life.

4.2 YEAR 2 AND YEAR 3

Introduction

In this section we follow Sarah through two classroom contexts which were very different from either that she had previously experienced. Her Year 2 and Year 3 teachers were part of a new influx of staff to Greenside School who were rapidly replacing the teachers of Mr Evans' era. They and others like them positively supported the headteacher and the new ethos of the school rather than, as former staff had done, reluctantly and rapidly having to integrate new ways into existing practices. The new teachers espoused educational philosophies which could be summed up in the belief that the most effective learning took place where pupils

Matrix 4.1 *Sarah, Reception and Year 1, a summary matrix*

Family relationships	Peer-group relationships	Teacher relationships	Identity	Career
Reception: Mrs Powell				
Family move to area expecting 'traditional' schooling.	Sarah begins school with her best friend from nursery, Alice.	Structural position: age, 11/28. Maths and English, in the top third.	By parents, considered to be a passive learner.	Sarah is quick to adapt to academic and social expectations within the sort of well structured and emotionally secure environment she prefers.
Sarah has a brother, Tom, two years older. Compared with Tom she was not 'pushed' as a baby and is seen as a passive learner. Both attend a fairly formal nursery school.	Mrs Powell says they can be a bit naughty together, but are happy. Sarah's parents feel the friendship is over close and would like Sarah to widen her circle of friends.	Sarah is described by Mrs Powell as 'independent', 'strong-willed', 'happy and sociable' and a quieter, more serious girl than many of the others.	Competitive, socially and physically independent at home. Sarah is seen by her teacher as independent, strong-willed, sociable, fairly quiet and serious.	She is accepted as a member of the girls' peer group but prefers the security of a known friend. A pattern of independence and competence with clear structures, together with a strong will matches that which is encouraged at home.
Mrs Nelson is a Roman Catholic, children follow her religion, also attend Young Crusaders. Parents encourage physical and social independence and competing with Tom.	Sarah is accepted as a competent member of the girls' peer culture. She has many party invitations.	Sarah contributes to class discussions, likes the home corner, 'has ideas'.		
Year 1: Miss Scott				
Upsets at home because of Sarah's dislike of her teacher, though parents basically approve of Miss Scott's methods. Some school avoidance.	Alice leaves the school. Sarah expresses unhappiness at home regarding friendships.	Structural position: age, 27/32. Maths and English in middle third. Poor teacher–pupil relationship. Miss Scott says Sarah can be 'moody'. Tears leaving her mother seen as	Sarah sees herself as 'good'. Her teacher sees her as quiet, thoughtful and reserved.	A less confident phase. Sarah shows a need for security and a dislike of conflict, which includes a worry about other people's conflicts.
Sarah dislikes conflict and change, likes to be 'right', likes 'good' children, younger children and babies. She manages conflict with Tom, won't be 'put down' by him.	She plays with Sally and Mary. In the less predictable classroom context this year, the three offer support for each other to 'get things right'. Some conflict as they rival for adult approval, use 'rules' to score off each other.	'attention seeking' and she 'likes situations to go her own way'. An improvement by the summer as Sarah gains confidence. 'Expresses ideas well'. 'Sound' maths understanding.	She also describes her as 'moody' and 'attention seeking', 'not relaxed and friendly'. As Sarah gains confidence in this context her teacher sees her as more cooperative, relating to others.	Classroom structures and relationships are volatile this year. Sarah's social and academic competence means she eventually learns to cope in this less predictable context.

were collaborators in the process. Because of this belief that underpinned their practices, they tended to have rather different expectations of pupils from those of more traditional teachers. As one would suppose, they expected that pupils take more responsibility upon themselves for their learning than previously. They expected them to be active, and interactive, learners in the classroom.

As we have seen, Sarah was able to understand teacher expectations with little trouble and, within these, to exercise a fair degree of competence and independence in the classroom. All of this suggests that she might have come to be considered something of an 'ideal pupil' by these new teachers. On the other hand, in these new contexts would her 'good girl' identity, cultivated with her friends, be useful or not? How would the new philosophy of the school suit someone who had hitherto coped with school through conforming to routine and explicit expectations? Would it provide sufficient structure and clarity for this strategy to work?

In sections 4.2 and 4.3 of Sarah's story we shall discover how she, together with her friends Mary and Sally, responded to the expectations of her new teachers.

Sarah, Year 2, early days in Miss George's class

In September 1989 Sarah entered Miss George's class at Greenside School. Sarah was the third oldest of 32 children in the class and in the top third for maths and language achievement. Her friends Mary and Sally, whose birthdays were close to hers, were still with her.

Miss George was a young teacher in her first post after leaving college. She had been appointed by Mrs Davison, the headteacher, and was therefore supportive of the moves to encourage pupils to participate in curricular and planning decisions.

An example of this practice in action in Miss George's class can be seen in the following observations recorded in fieldnotes. Here, Sarah has selected an activity with knowledge content relevant to a class topic, has decided when she will do it and also which requirement it fulfils in terms of subject area on her planning sheet for the week.

> Sarah has done an excellent sketch picture which names parts of the body, ribs etc. She does a coloured border and says it's part of her plan: ''Cos it's art and craft. 'Cos you can do pictures. . . . I'll put it in my 'All About Me' book.'
> (Fieldnotes, Andrew Pollard, December 1989, Year 2)

In a context where children were only intermittently undertaking similar tasks at set times, a high degree of teacher skill was, of course, required. The teachers needed to monitor each child's planning as well as work completed to ensure coverage of the knowledge and skills on the curriculum.

Miss George gradually developed a clear and well organized system for the planning and carrying out of activities and the children understood her expectations. Understandably though, as a new teacher, it took Miss George a while to develop the skills needed to monitor the activities and output of each child amid the complex of activities going on in the classroom. Sarah, although well attuned to teacher expectations, now found some of the work a little challenging, particularly concerning mathematics. In the new classroom circumstances, she thus began to explore what she could 'get away with'. Here is Miss George talking in interview with Andrew Pollard during the autumn term.

Miss George:	Sarah. There's a strange child. I think she's very bright, she's got it there (*indicates her head*), but she's an absolute genius at avoiding work. I stand back in amazement. She's one of these that really manage to melt into the woodwork and do her own thing. One day I caught her in the home corner for about the fourth day on the trot and I felt quite guilty. She was very pregnant, she was on the telephone, drinking a cup of tea and I had to go in and say 'You've been in this home corner for three whole days. Isn't it about time you came out?'
AP:	Does she plan to do that on her planning sheet or does she do the planning and then ignore it?
Miss George:	'I've lost my planning sheet!' And then at parents' evening when I made them really turn out their drawers, she's sort of keeping about three or four planning sheets on the go so if I do ask her for a planning sheet, she'll bring the one that's going to tell me the story. She's really, really crafty. I can't believe it. Perhaps I'm just attributing her with craftiness!

(Teacher interview, November 1989, Year 2)

Friendships and peer relationships in Year 2

Sarah's friendships continued to be fluid in Year 2. Sally and Mary were still among the closest of her companions and, like them, she continued to wish to project an identity of 'goodness' in the classroom.

AP:	Who don't you play with?
Sarah:	Not Gareth 'cos he's a bully. No way with Gary and Greg 'cos they're naughty. They get told off in service. I'm good.

Later in the interview:

AP:	What sort of things do you like to play in the playground?
Sarah:	Handstands, cartwheels, back flips, roly-polies, chasing. Just girls. Not kiss chase. I don't like it.

(Friendship group interview, April 1990, Year 2)

The reference to 'kiss chase' here gives an indication of one of the ways in which Sarah was beginning to differentiate herself from Sally and Mary. Both of these friends were at the centre of a group of girls and boys who liked to play kiss chase and, increasingly, other flirtatious games in the playground. Such games constituted a strand of playground and classroom culture by which a particular friendship group would gradually emerge. Indeed, children's identification with a range of playground cultures as well as classroom strategies increasingly were to become the means by which the different friendship groups became established and maintained. Such identification, moreover, began to signal distinct and divergent career patterns for Sarah and her two friends.

Learning strategies in Year 2

During the autumn and spring terms, problems of work evasion continued to recur periodically. In the case of some problems, however, it seems not simply to have been a case of Sarah being 'crafty'. During the autumn term she began to have problems with some maths task.

Mrs Nelson:	I wonder whether Miss George has been giving her one or two cards that are a little bit difficult for her and expecting her to get on with them by herself because there was one incident when she came home and said that she just couldn't do them, Miss George was cross, that she wasn't looking forward to going in because she knew that she had to carry on and finish these cards the next day, and she just couldn't do it. So I said, had she actually gone up to Miss George about it, because I said 'that's what she's there for and she'd rather that you asked her than try to carry on and get into a tizzy about it.' And she said 'Yes but she was busy and she said I could do it.' So I'm not quite sure about that.
AP:	But the difficulty is, if Sarah doesn't go and sort of say 'Look I'm getting a bit stuck on it', then she's a bit open to be misinterpreted, isn't she, as not having tried.
Mrs Nelson:	This is what I wonder.

(Parent interview, December 1989, Year 2)

Rather than placing her maths book in the 'unfinished work' tray and risk revealing that she hadn't done the work, Sarah at this point began to avoid getting her work checked by putting it back in her drawer. So it was that Sarah became caught in a vicious circle whereby the more she exploited weaknesses in Miss George's system as a way out of her difficulties with maths, the more Miss George seemed to see her problem as one of 'crafty' work avoidance rather than a mathematical one.

During the spring term Sarah began to avoid maths by 'feeling sick'. Miss George, rather than perceiving the sickness to be a symptom, real or strategic, of Sarah being confronted with difficulties, took it at face value. In March, however, things came to a head. As the following fieldnotes and interview with Miss George reveal, it was finally the actions of the deputy head, Lorraine Madders, that enabled Sarah and her teacher to break out of these recurring cycles of interaction.

> Sarah is crying over doing her maths. Miss George told me that: 'All she's done this week is to hold her chick and do one sum. She did the same last week and she'd do the same next week if I let her! She says she was sick and I sent her down to Marion [the school secretary] who brought her back. Then she did it again so I put her over there with a bucket. Then Lorraine came and read the riot act. Sarah got on and finished half her maths in about two minutes. Then she took the next day to finish it off! I can see I've got a battle on here.'
> (Fieldnotes, Andrew Pollard, March 1990, Year 2)

Despite Miss George's perception that she had 'a battle on here', the cycle was broken and Sarah was pulled back on track by that forceful assertion of school expectation.

> ... and then one day Lorraine really hit into her. I wouldn't have had the cour-
> age in case she was ill, sort of thing and not only did she really tell her off and tell
> her she was a terribly naughty girl, she went and saw her mother and it's miraculous
> the effect it's had. Why didn't I do it in September? (...) So I have questioned –
> did I waste time by pussyfooting around? Was Lorraine lucky or did she see straight
> through her? I still feel, though, that she's making an effort to fulfil her obligation
> and that's it.
> (Miss George, teacher interview, May 1990, Year 2)

Although now working harder at fulfilling teacher expectations, as alluded to in the above interview, the flair and ideas for writing that Sarah had in Reception and Year 1 were replaced by a more minimalistic approach.

> The stories sometimes lack content because I feel she's often only writing them out
> of a sense of obligation. You know, 'Well I've got to do two so that will do'. She'll
> put silly things at the end like, 'So that's all for now. Bye Byeeee'. Talk about treat-
> ing it flippantly.
> (Miss George, teacher interview, May 1990, Year 2)

Although Miss George's lack of experience may have contributed to Sarah's work evasion, it would be wrong to assume that this was a universal effect of her practice. For example, it can be seen in Harriet's story, and in *The Social World of Children's Learning* that, in contrast to the rush-to-finish-the-task response adopted by Sarah and some of her friends, others responded to Miss George with new-found motivation, gaining intrinsic satisfaction from the task of writing.

The feeling continued that Sarah was not fulfilling her potential. Here Miss George, in interview with Andrew Pollard, is reflecting upon the problem and speculating about its origins.

> I've put that she's very slow at completing tasks, which I don't feel is inability or
> lack of competence, but laziness. But on the other hand, after I'd written that, I put
> that on the other hand she does have a clever and likeable older brother who ridi-
> cules her at home, so her mum says. So perhaps she isn't as confident as I think.
> But she is very quick minded, good at mental arithmetic, good reader and speller,
> articulate, dextrous, well coordinated – what can I say? What else can I say?
> (Miss George, teacher interview, May 1990, Year 2)

By the end of the summer term Sarah was showing increased confidence in the classroom. Her end of year report showed that the problems with writing content persisted but that she now had 'a more sensible attitude to her planning' and 'a more mature attitude to her maths work'. As a result of this, Sarah had made 'dramatic strides' in her number work. In contrast to those areas of the curriculum where Sarah's commitment had wavered, her report told of her consistent interest and contribution to project work and her continued enthusiasm for creative, artistic tasks.

Home and family relationships in Year 2

Sarah, at age six, was identifying quite closely with her mother and enjoying a close relationship with her. However, her sensitivity to emotional upsets around this time meant that any arguments between mother and daughter caused Sarah some distress.

We had a nice evening reading, playing the piano and generally just chatting about everything. I really enjoy these sessions and I know she does. We are quite close really and this is made quite obvious when we argue about something – she becomes quite upset and can't do enough to 'make up'.
(Parent diary, November 1989, Year 2)

Sensitivities within the relationship with her mother at this time may have contributed to upset feelings that occasionally emerged over the conflicting expectations of home and school. During the year the fact that Sarah's mother did not approve of the school's approach to spelling meant that Sarah seemed at times torn between the priorities of home and school for writing tasks. She explained to Andrew Pollard:

She does seem to be getting better, slowly. She will be writing things at home here and bring it through and say, 'Is this all right?' and out of a page there will only be two or three silly spellings where she's tried . . .
   She does seem to get into a bit of a tizzy about things if I do look at some of her work and say, 'Well, you have made one or two mistakes.' 'I *know that*, Mummy' – as though it doesn't really [matter] but it *does* matter. 'I know what I want to say and you can read it so what's the big problem?'
(Mrs Nelson, parent interview, December 1989, Year 2)

Document 4.2 is an example of Sarah's writing at school at this time.
Sarah also continued to dislike any conflict between her mother and Tom. However, as was the case a year ago, she was not averse to taking advantage of day-to-day family disputes to assert and contrast her own 'good' identity.

If ever I am having any sort of argument with Tom, she will retreat to her room or somewhere where she hasn't got to be involved at all. And she will see me afterwards saying 'I don't know why Tom was like that, or why he was doing that, because it was naughty, wasn't it'.
(Mrs Nelson, parent interview, December 1989, Year 2)

As was the case a year ago, however, Sarah did not flinch in the face of her own conflicts with Tom. The difference in that relationship was that now Sarah was retaliating verbally.

Mrs Nelson:	She will fight him to the bitter end. Verbally, not physically. Sometimes she comes off the worse for wear but at least she is doing it. She's sticking up for herself. Yes. It's been coming out more lately. She didn't seem to, but just lately she will shout her opinions quite loudly . . .
AP:	But that's mainly with regard to Tom?
Mrs Nelson:	Yes.

(Parent interview, December 1989, Year 2)

Perhaps, during this generally less confident phase of her life, Sarah felt more than ever that she could not afford to be put down or left behind by Tom. Despite her dislike of conflict, where Tom was concerned, it was probably both necessary and, because sanctioned by her mother, safe.
By the end of the school year, however, both Sarah's parents and her teacher were noticing an increased confidence in Sarah. At the same time as her difficulties in school were being resolved, so also her mother reported that Sarah was generally more assertive in their relationship at home.

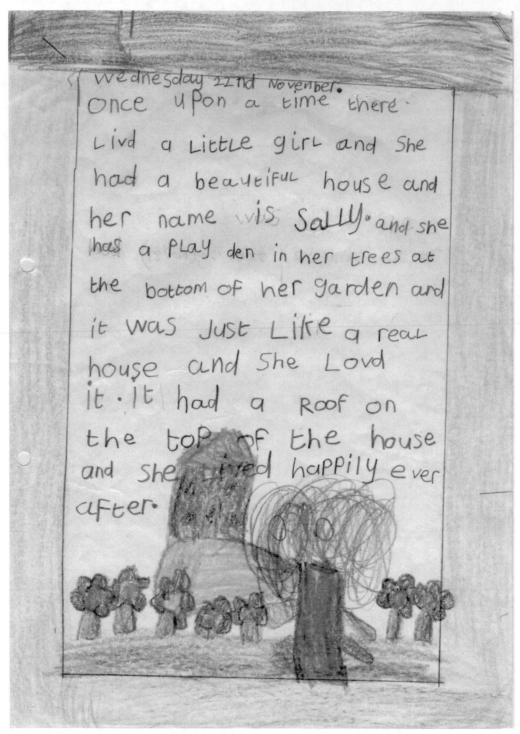

Wednesday 22nd November.
Once upon a time there
Livd a Little girl and She
had a beautiful house and
her name wis Sally. and she
has a play den in her trees at
the bottom of her garden and
it was Just Like a real
house and She Lovd
it. It had a Roof on
the top of the house
and She Lived happily ever
after.

Document 4.2   *Sarah, Year 2, 'Story' (November 1989)*

I've seen quite a big change in her attitude and her growing up. Whereas before if I didn't agree with something that she was doing at home I'd say, 'Look, don't do it', and she would say, 'All right', and that's it rather than get into a confrontation. Now she will turn round and say, 'Why not? Why can't I do this? I'm doing it because ...' And I would have to sit back and think well, I suppose she's right really, she can go ahead and do it. She's got an answer for most things now, whereas before she perhaps didn't, or would answer back and then be upset about it.
(Mrs Nelson, parent interview, July 1990, Year 2)

Mrs Nelson considered that, in part, Sarah's generally increased confidence might be attributable to the advice she had always given Sarah in the face of Tom's attempts to dominate her.

I really just think it's getting older, having a lot more confidence in herself and perhaps me taking her to one side, as I do quite often and say, 'Look, Tom's your older brother but you are you. You have to stick up for yourself. If you don't stick up for yourself, he'll walk over you and so will the other children at school. They'll realize that you're perhaps not as strong as they are. Do something about it.'
(Mrs Nelson, parent interview, summer 1990, Year 2)

Summary of Sarah's Year 2

It is possible that, in highlighting Sarah's changed strategies in the context of the Year 2 class, a more negative impression of her progress in learning has been given than was generally the case. Certainly, the feeling was that Sarah was not fulfilling her potential at school. However, that Miss George should feel this to be so can be accounted for by the fact that Sarah clearly displayed not inconsiderable talents in the classroom.

Sarah's continued sensitivity to emotional upsets and a close identification with her mother created tensions around conflicting expectations of home and school. Where rivalry with her brother was concerned, however, and supported by her mother, Sarah was prepared to face conflict and assert her opinions vociferously.

At this point in her career of course, Sarah and her friends were not only completing another school year but they were also progressing from being infants to being juniors. Although within Greenside School the markers of junior status were few, the transition nevertheless carried its traditional significance. Here Sarah, alone in interview, reflects upon her infant career and anticipates the changes to come.

AP:	How do you think your friends think about how you have got on in school in the Infants?
Sarah:	Sometime they think I'm nice and sometimes they don't. They think that I know lots of words and things 'cos sometimes I help people with words.
AP:	How do you think your teacher thinks that you have got on in school then?
Sarah:	All right. Done well at writing and art. Not so well at maths. Sometimes I can't get the sums right and I have to do them all over again and then I go on to the next thing. Sometimes I'm not sure what to do.
AP:	What do you think it will be like in the Juniors compared with being in the Infants?

Sarah: Nice. I like being in the hut 'cos it's not so noisy and we'll have bigger chairs. Have different planning sheets. Work will be okay 'cos I'll be older, like seven-and-a-quarter and seven-and-three-quarters. I'll get a Brownie uniform.

(Pupil interview, July 1990, Year 2)

Sarah, Year 3, early days in Mr Brown's class

Mr Brown, like Miss George, was a relatively new teacher at Greenside and a keen advocate of the school's learning ethos. As we described in Chapter 3, Mr Brown set out clear expectations for his pupils and systematically monitored their involvement and progress in tasks. Some tasks were timetabled and organized for fixed teaching groups and some through pupil planning of their time and the negotiation of working relationships for them. It was one of Mr Brown's particular concerns that pupils should be both active and interactive learners. In this extract from an interview with Andrew Pollard in the autumn term, he revealed something of these expectations as he talked about the way in which Sarah had settled into the class.

Mr Brown: She's very quiet on the whole. She works hard. She has some good ideas. She perseveres well. She wanted to do a science experiment and I had to get Adrian [the school caretaker] in to collect some turf and she kept badgering me to get things done, which is nice. She is actually a nice child to have in the class.

AP: How is she getting on with her maths at the moment?

Mr Brown: Getting on fine actually. I had Tom last year, who is a whizz-kid at maths, miles ahead of everyone else and she's just a steady worker but she seems to have a good general understanding.

AP: It may be that working in the groups, like you've been doing, suits her from that point of view.

Mr Brown: Yeah. I kept telling all of them that last year my children got more done in their groups than on their own because: a) I can say things once to five or six children, and b) they don't have to wait for me all the time, they can help each other and they can motivate each other. They've all responded well to that on the whole.

(Teacher interview, September 1990, Year 3)

During that autumn term, Mrs Nelson recorded in the diary:

She is extremely happy in this environment at the moment, but I always have the feeling that she shows great potential in a lot of her work activities, if only she would realise that she *can* do it, if she tries.

(Mrs Nelson, parent diary, November 1990, Year 3)

Friendships and peer relationships in Year 3

As Mr Brown's description of Sarah seemed to suggest, she was beginning to look a little more settled in school than she had been since Reception year. This calmer phase was reflected in her peer relations also, with some realignments among Sarah's friendship group. During the year Sarah and Mary worked together in a more supportive and cooperative way than before. Mr Brown told Ann Filer:

> I always think of those two together. They've worked together quite a lot and they seem to get on reasonably well. When I've checked their understanding it's not one leading the other most of the time. I think, if anything, Mary's is slightly advanced in mathematics, slightly more advanced in her understanding. Sarah perhaps more in language, I think they sort of complement each other.
> (Mr Brown, teacher interview, July 1991, Year 3)

Sarah and Mary often worked and played in the playground with Charlotte and Kirsty and Sarah's mother felt that after some of the turbulence of the last two years, Sarah's friendships had stabilized. Undoubtedly some of the reason for this new tranquillity lay in the fact that some of the old rivalries no longer were so apparent. Sally had increasingly begun to separate herself from the other two in the classroom and developed a closer relationship with Hannah. In Mr Brown's opinion, Sally 'knew she was now in the top flight' and had left some of her old friends behind.

In Mrs Nelson's account of friendship shifts also, there is a feeling that separation is coming about, not least because a high-profile, high-stakes strategy was not one that Sarah felt comfortable with in school.

> I'm forever having Mary ring up and saying can Sarah come and play because I'm bored and Sarah does the same thing. Hannah is another girl that comes up [in conversation] quite a lot. Um, Sally used to come up quite a lot but she doesn't seem to be in so much demand now. She's a very extrovert little girl, Sally, you know. She seems to be into everything and wanting to do as well as the older children in the class, I've noticed, and Sarah would rather leave that to someone else to do . . .
> (Mrs Nelson, parent interview, July 1991, Year 3)

As we suggested earlier was to be the case, friendships were also beginning to form around peer-group cultures of the playground. Sarah and many other girls maintained a preference for games within the mainstream of girls' culture involving skipping, clapping, chanting of rhymes. Sally and Hannah, while playing these games, also enjoyed 'kiss chase' and now sometimes played football with the boys as well. Mary maintained a greater playground association with these two girls than did Sarah. She enjoyed these games with boys as well as the language of 'boyfriends' and 'girlfriends', 'going out with' and 'dumping'. Sarah continued to enjoy friendships and classroom associations with boys; however, these flirtatious activities were another aspect of the high-profile culture of Sally's group with which Sarah did not feel entirely comfortable.

Learning strategies in Year 3

Despite the reference early in the year to Sarah's strategies in science, she did not manage to continue to fulfil Mr Brown's image of the 'ideal pupil', the active and interactive learner. At the end of the summer term, Mr Brown told Ann Filer:

> Sometimes people say it's a good idea to make a list of the children in your class. Then the ones you miss out and can't remember are the ones you should target. I think Ellen and Sarah and perhaps a couple of others are probably the ones I'd miss first time round. Because, you know, if I'm firing questions at the whole class her hand rarely goes up and I have to actually pick on her to get her to say something. It's not that she doesn't know the answer or anything, it's just sort of part shyness and lack of confidence really. Their personalities don't come across in the classroom, at least Mary's does a bit more in that she can be a bit silly sometimes whereas Sarah isn't, she's really quite serious about things on the whole.
>   She's sort of plodded along steadily, and very rarely produced anything remark-able. Sort of middle-of-the-road, I would say. No great problems with the work we've done but at the same time I always think she could do better, I'm sure she could do better, you know.
> (Mr Brown, teacher interview, July 1991, Year 3)

With Sarah more settled this year in her relationships in school, the main cause for concern for Sarah's parents was the matter of her not fulfilling her potential.

> She'd rather just get on with the work and do it and remain on the average line of learning. [Mr Brown] feels that she could put a little bit more 'oomph' into it and do something and do better.
> (Mrs Nelson, parent interview, July 1991, Year 3)

Sarah's progress in maths particularly troubled Mrs Nelson.

> Sarah's maths progress, as far as we can see, has been rather slow. She absolutely hates mental arithmetic – whether it is the same at school as it is at home we don't know, but our little episodes at home have not proved very successful – she hates doing it. We feel quite a lot at fault over this. Tom was and is very confident and quick with maths – we should have been giving her more help in order to build up this particular lack of confidence. We are endeavouring to do more about it, and hope it isn't too late.
> (Parent diary, June 1991, Year 3)

At the end of the year Sarah received another very satisfactory report. As in the previous year it recorded that she could put more effort into writing and also into maths but also as before, her general competence and understanding were not in question.

In July, Sarah herself was again asked to reflect upon the year she had just experienced. In the interview she gave Ann Filer a balanced and fairly brief account when talking about classwork. However, consider how she expanded and warmed to the subject when it turns on some other aspects of school life.

AF:	How do you feel that you have got on in the first year of the Juniors?
Sarah:	Some of it's good, some of it's not very good but I've got on quite well. I've had good experiences doing things.
AF:	Can you tell me about some of those good experiences?
Sarah:	Like I said, in drama and choir.
AF:	How do your friends think you have got on then?
Sarah:	In doing my tables they said 'You got on really well' but once I only got 3 out of 10 ... My friends in English some-

	times they said 'Oh that's good'. Other people who aren't my friends sometimes say 'I don't like that'.
AF:	What about your teacher? What does he think?
Sarah:	Pretty good, but I have to catch up with some work.
AF:	Can you tell me how you came to get involved in things like drama and choir?
Sarah:	Well it's like art. First I wanted to do art and stuff and I looked at my pictures and thought they were characters, like in drama. And my brother was in drama and I thought that was a good idea to get involved in it. Also I was a good reader in Class 4 and I had to go on to the library and you saw characters in books as well as characters in art. Characters in books were better and I started acting plays with my brother. When I grow up I want to be either an artist or a nurse or an actor. And I'm quite a good singer. In service I use my normal voice but in choir it's better. It's like a lady's voice then. My mummy says it's like a lady's voice as well.
AF:	Do you think its important to do things like drama and choir in school?
Sarah:	Choir is good 'cos your voice gets exercised and you get better and better. You've got to give up your lunchtime to practise and give up your work somctimes for rehearsals. Then you have to catch up in the lunch hour in the library.
ΛF:	Are there any things that you haven't done that you would like to have done in school this year?
Sarah:	Some people went birdwatching and some people in our class went to that and when I heard I wished I had gone. I had heard about it before they went but I forgot about it.

(Sarah, pupil interview, July 1991, Year 3)

In Sarah's account of her extra-curricular activities at school, as with out-of-school activities there is the tendency to relate her activities to those of her brother. Nevertheless, we can see that her personal commitment and motivation were high and that she clearly saw herself as putting a lot of effort into these activities. Mr Brown, however, seemed unawarc of these interests which were, as we shall learn, an important aspect of the pupil identity she aspired to.

Home and family relationships in Year 3

At about this time in her development Sarah was becoming more aware of her appearance as an expression of her identity.

> Slight problems during the middle of the week in getting ready for school. Sarah is becoming very conscious of the way she wears her hair, the sort of socks she wears, etc., etc.! If she is having a bad day it can cause all sorts of problems first thing in the morning. She takes ages anyway getting ready for school and some mornings can become quite frustrating, for both of us!
> (Parent diary, November 1990, Year 3)

When Sarah became a Brownie that year the 'Artist' badge was the first one she chose to work for and a short time later the 'Rambler' badge was added to her sleeve.

Mrs Nelson: We go away on a walking holiday once a year anyway, whether it's to Wales or to the Lake District. I'm more of a rambler and a trekker, but Tom and Nick are sort of hill walkers and like getting up to the very top of the highest thing they can see so that they can look around. So Tom having climbed the Old Man [of Coniston], what was it – two years ago now I think – she thought that eight was the right age for her to have a go. And she did it! She darn well pushed herself to do it and it was a great achievement that she had actually done it at the same age as Tom. I mean, Tom's coming back into it more and more.

AP: So she's quite sort of determined to hold her own there . . .

Mrs Nelson: Absolutely! And, um, she'd picked this particular badge she sort of wanted to work for at Brownies as well, the walker or the rambler or something and this was one extra thing that she could throw in, that she'd actually done this. Again comparing herself to what Tom had been able to do.

AP: Do you think that's sort of her main yardstick with her kind of, identity? A sense of who she is?

Mrs Nelson: I do. Nick doesn't think as much. I mean he didn't agree with me at the time that I was saying that as soon as Tom leaves the school that I thought that she would get on really well. He didn't agree with me at first. But I think he's coming round to thinking like that and in fact he came home last night and looked around the dining room and said 'Do you realize that we have more pictures of Tom in various events that he's done than we do Sarah and don't you think that we ought to scale them down and have equal numbers of what was going on?'

(Parent interview, July 1991, Year 3)

So, throughout the year, Sarah continued to be competitive and to strive for achievement at home. At the same time she continued to elaborate her 'good' identity, now modelling herself on her mother as she did so.

Mrs Nelson: She does a lot of things for me around the house, without me asking her. On a Saturday morning for instance, she's taken over cleaning the bathroom totally on her own, and [she'll] suddenly appear and say 'I've done the bathroom'. She wants to hang washing out for me. Things like that.

We went through a stage recently where the children were getting pocket money but realizing that they weren't actually doing anything for it. So it's keeping the bedrooms tidy and doing these little jobs, that I think it's her way of thinking, well, I'm actually working for it, you know, even if Tom isn't.

AP: Is this something where she can sort of demonstrate her kind of 'adult responsibility' *vis-à-vis* him?

Mrs Nelson: Yes, yes, and if I'm cross with Tom in the morning because he hasn't got things together or walks out of the door without two or three things that he's supposed to take, she'll start shouting at him as well. 'You haven't done this. Mummy says you haven't done this. Take this to school. I'm always having to bring things to school for you. Why can't you think about it yourself?' I think, do I sound like that? In fact Tom went

out of the door this morning and he said it must be really
nice to be deaf at times!

(Parent interview, July 1991, Year 3)

Summary of Sarah's Year 3

Sarah enjoyed a more settled period in Mr Brown's class than she had experienced over the previous two years at Greenside School. Some realignments in friendship groups meant that she experienced more supportive and cooperative classroom relationships. Her 'plodding' 'middle-of-the-road' approach meant that she coped with the academic requirements with few problems. Her low-profile, quiet classroom demeanour, however, meant that she did not fulfil Mr Brown's expectations for active learning and concerns continued to be expressed, from home as well as from school, that Sarah was not fulfilling her potential.

At home she continued to compete with Tom's achievements and, modelling herself on her mother, elaborated her 'good', 'helpful' identity that contrasted favourably with Tom's.

Sarah's identity and career in the middle years at Greenside School

At this point in her story Sarah was more than halfway through her primary school career. Some patterns in Sarah's learning and in the expectation of her from home and school were becoming clear.

It is notable that the 'independent' identity attributed to Sarah by teachers in her early years is not to be found in any descriptions coming from Miss George or Mr Brown. We might consider whether this is as a result of a change in Sarah herself or as a result of different expectations on the part of teachers. In Mrs Powell's Reception class, Sarah's 'independent' identity seemed to describe an attitude of mind, a sort of strong-willed detachment on Sarah's part. In Miss Scott's class it seemed rather more to do with being able to work without being too reliant on adult attention. Perhaps Miss George's classroom was too open and evolving to suit Sarah. Finally in the context of Mr Brown's expectations of pupils, it is questionable whether either detachment or the ability to work without too much adult attention were what was needed to acquire an 'independent' identity.

Sarah's 'serious' identity remained intact. However, in the context of Mr Brown's classroom, it took on a slightly negative connotation. Insofar as it was considered to contribute to her quietness and low profile it meant that, for Mr Brown, not only did she not fulfil his image of an ideal pupil, but he also felt that her personality did not 'come across' in the classroom. He was thus unaware of interests and aspirations relevant to the pupil identity to which she aspired.

We might also consider at this point why Sarah did not, or could not, adopt the slightly risky, interactive 'into everything' approach of those of her friends that Mr Brown considered to be 'in the top flight'. Would it be right, or sufficient, to say that Sarah's quietness and low profile were simply a reflection of

Matrix 4.2 *Sarah, Years 2 and 3, a summary matrix*

Family relationships	Peer-group relationships	Teacher relationships	Identity	Career
Year 2: Miss George				
Sarah retreats from family conflicts, especially with her mother whom she increasingly identifies with. She is reluctant to offer opinions but will vociferously confront Tom. Sarah experiences conflict between home and school expectations for writing and spelling.	Friendships are fluid, those with Sally and Mary characterized by friction. Sarah enjoys girls' games, finds boys rough. Unlike some of her friends she avoids 'kiss chase' in the playground.	Structural position: Age, 3/32; maths and English, in top third. Sarah has problems with maths, worries about seeking help. Evades maths tasks, 'feels sick'. Later in the year regains confidence and makes strides in maths, though minimalistic in writing tasks.	Once she regains confidence, Sarah's teacher describes her as helpful, mature and responsible. Also says she is quick-minded, good at mental arithmetic and spelling, well coordinated and articulate. 'A genius at avoiding work', however.	Opportunities for evasion of tasks are exploited by Sarah, and problems build up. A reassertion of school expectations brings Sarah swiftly back on track, though a minimalistic approach continues. This phase coincides with a lack of parental confidence in the school.
Year 3: Mr Brown				
Parents feel Sarah is happy at school but lacks confidence and 'prefers to be average'. Her mother thinks she can sometimes be 'a slow learner'. Sarah continues to put much effort into competing with Tom in out-of-school activities such as swimming, piano, hill climbing.	Some realignments among Sarah's group of friends. Friendships stable now, mainly Mary and Kirsty. Sarah continues to be unwilling to participate in flirtatious playground behaviour, leaves 'into everything', high-profile competitiveness to others.	Structual position: age 28/32; maths, science, English, halfway down. Mr Brown thinks Sarah is serious, works hard and perseveres but is not motivated to achieve her potential. Mr Brown does not know her well, says her personality may not come across in the classroom.	Parents consider that Tom's achievements may be a yardstick to Sarah for her identity. Sarah likes to be thought reliable. Sarah has extra-curricular artistic, dramatic and musical interests and aspirations.	Sarah's not extensive efforts in the classroom contrast with her well motivated learning in extra-curricular and out-of-school activities. The year is characterized by friendship realignments, more tranquil classroom relationships and a low-profile pupil identity.

her individual approach to learning and to accept this as perhaps an innate aspect of her identity? A teacher seeing Sarah only in the classroom might believe so. However, we have knowledge of a different Sarah, learning different things in the context of the home and wider community. What also can we make of the independent, active and interactive, extra-curricular learning that she became involved in as she quietly elaborated her own sense of her artistic, dramatic and musical identity over the years?

In the light of these considerations of Sarah's identity, let us turn to her needs. Assuming that Sarah really did have unfulfilled potential, and bearing in mind that many children did very well in Miss George's and Mr Brown's classes, could those teachers have done anything to enhance Sarah's confidence, to change her classroom strategies, to motivate her? Assuming it is the business of schools to identify and maximize potential, in what sort of classroom and with what sort of teacher might Sarah have fared differently?

Perhaps we need to follow Sarah a little further in her career, meet a few more teachers and see how some other pupils fare before we can begin to answer these questions.

4.3   YEAR 4, YEAR 5 AND YEAR 6

Introduction

We began Sarah's career story by tracking her adaptation to school through her Reception and Year 1 classrooms. In those early years a pattern was set of Sarah's social independence and competence in adapting to established structures and expectations which broadly matched that which was encouraged at home. The middle years of her primary career, however, were key years for Sarah in terms of teacher requirements for more active learning and were characterized by concerns that Sarah's approach to some subjects was minimalistic and uncommitted. Questions arose concerning, on the one hand, Sarah's motivation and, from her parents' point of view, the teaching methods at Greenside School.

In this final part of Sarah's primary school career story, we follow her progression through her last three years at Greenside and see her in the context of three more teachers, Miss King, Miss French and Mrs Chard. Like Miss George and Mr Brown, these teachers were recently appointed to the school and were committed to the new ethos being shaped there. As readers will have begun to perceive from Sarah's experience, and as we described in Chapter 3, though these new teachers shared a common basic philosophy, each new classroom context presented pupils with a slightly different set of expectations, organizational practices. Each new context also presented each pupil with different teacher perceptions and interpretations of his or her learning stance, strategies and identity.

Thus Sarah was to continue to meet teachers for whom the notion of an active and interactive learner embodied slightly different implications. In Miss King's class for example, Sarah's strategies and identity were to be assessed in a context where pupil participation and cooperation with peers, and with the life of the class as a whole, were especially valued. In Miss French's class, the expectation was that pupils take some responsibility for their learning beyond given tasks that were, for reasons of year group organization, necessarily highly structured that year. For Mrs Chard, it was important that pupils rise to a clear challenge presented to them by her, and in groupwork, to challenge each other's understanding. As described in Chapter 3, there were many differences between the expectations and perceptions of teachers arising from their individual personal, biographical and professional situations.

Sarah approached these contexts of later years with a fairly well established low-profile, low-risk approach to classroom life and learning. However, at this point in her career it also gradually became apparent to us that Sarah had certain interests and aspirations that she would have liked to incorporate into her identity as a pupil. The extent to which Sarah met the expectations of Miss King, Miss French and Mrs Chard, and the extent to which they fulfilled her expectations of them in supporting this identity, will be just one aspect of Sarah's career story that unfolds through this final part of her story.

Sarah, Year 4, early days in Miss King's class

In September 1991, Sarah entered Miss King's Year 4 class at Greenside Primary School. Sarah was the thirteenth oldest in a class of 30 children and held a position a quarter the way down from the top of the class in maths, within the top quarter in language and a third of the way down in science. Her group of immediate friends, as well as those from whom there had been some distancing, remained with her.

As we have described in Chapter 2, Miss King was in her probationary year of teaching. She held a similar philosophy to other new teachers to Greenside, tending to put a special emphasis on participation and cooperation with peers and in relation to the life of the class generally, and on fluid working relationships. As was the case in Year 3, Sarah's fairly quiet and unobtrusive presence in the classroom meant that, in the early days at least, she was not known well by Miss King. As Miss King explained to Ann Filer:

> Sarah. She's a mystery to me, Sarah is. She's been away for a few weeks and then I realize that this is one girl I haven't really spoken to that much. She doesn't give away much actually. If we're doing a group activity and I'm asking questions and that, she won't participate very much. And you've really got to push her to get something out of her, she'll just look at you a bit lost. I don't feel I really know Sarah, 'cos she's not one that talks to you very much, quite a serious face. But there's something about her personality that I can't quite, you know, grasp on. I actually want to find out more about Sarah because a bit of a mystery to me she is. I don't know really what she's like.
> (Miss King, teacher interview, October 1991, Year 4)

As in Mr Brown's class, children timetabled their groupwork with Miss King as well as whole class lessons and activities and then planned their remaining time so that certain tasks were completed by the end of each week. During this pupil-planned time while she was working with other groups, Miss King had very high expectations for quiet and sustained involvement in tasks. Sarah, for her part, still a little wary of the noisier and 'rougher' elements of the class, liked the class-room context created by Miss King and she also appreciated the new system of 'assertive discipline' techniques adopted by the school, an element of which was that pupils' names were written on the board when they transgress a 'negotiated' rule. She explained to Ann Filer:

> I think it's good because you get to know what children not to mix with, if they are going to hurt you or something.
> (Sarah, pupil interview, June 1992, Year 4)

Sarah settled very quickly and happily into her new class and, for her, as for many other children, Miss King was to become a firm favourite among their primary school teachers.

Friendships and peer relationships in Year 4

Sarah's playground friendships remained much as they had in the previous year. Mary and Sarah no longer worked together much in the classroom but on the odd occasion when they did the old competitive rivalries seemed to surface. At the beginning of Year 4 her mother felt that Sarah was finding such disputes difficult to cope with.

> Sarah still seems to have the same group of girl friends in this class, but doesn't associate much with the boys – they're awful, she says! However, there are still one or two girlfriends she falls in and out of friends with quite easily, one of whom I wish she would just learn to ignore completely mainly due to the upsetting effect it seems to have on Sarah when they aren't friends.
> (Parent diary, November 1991, Year 4)

However, as Year 4 progressed, Sarah's mother noticed that she was able to handle breakdowns in friendship with greater equanimity and they appeared not to affect her so much.

Sarah's social competence meant that she never had any difficulty negotiating her working relationships in the more fluid arrangement in the Year 4 class. The following comments made by Miss King indicate the acceptance that had always been features of Sarah's relationships with her peers.

> She seems to be one of those children that are quite popular. You don't see her with any one particular child. She seems to know everyone and everyone seems to quite like her really. She's quite popular, in a quiet sort of way.
> (Miss King, teacher interview, July 1992, Year 4)

During her first term in the class, although she moved around quite a lot, Sarah worked within a basic group which included Amanda and Charlotte. This initial working relationship did not last long, as her mother recorded in the diary.

> She went through a sticky patch with the 'group' she was in at the beginning of the year. They wouldn't stop talking when she wanted to get on with her work, and already feeling that she was being left behind we asked if we could speak to Miss King about it, which we did, and it was agreed that she could change 'group'. It made a quite noticeable difference in her attitude and the quality of work she was producing. She is still in this group and has not asked to change since.
> (Parent diary, June 1992, Year 4)

After the move away from Charlotte and Amanda, Sarah chose to work predominantly in a group that included Kirsty and Nimra. This quiet and compatible working relationship among the three girls remained in place for the rest of the year. Interestingly, it was to form again two years later when, as we shall see, its same social dynamics were considered by Sarah's Year 6 teacher to be detrimental to her learning.

Learning strategies in Year 4

Both at home and at school, Sarah continued to lack confidence in her own responses. Something of the effect of her reluctance to commit herself to an opinion or an answer at that time can be seen in the following extract from Ann Filer's observation of a maths activity.

> Sarah is working beside Charlotte, with Gavin and Oliver opposite them. Sarah is making a graph of colours of clothes children are wearing. She finishes.
>
> Sarah: Right, what have I planned? I planned my Peak Maths.
>   (*reads from her maths book*) Using a square of paper, three right angles clockwise from North is?
>
> She works out (correctly) that the answer is 'West'. Gavin says that it should be North and they have an argument about it. Sarah changes her answer to 'North'.
>
> More arguments on the next question. Gavin takes Sarah's textbook to demonstrate.
>
> Sarah: Gavin! (*Gavin gives it back*) Can I do my own work please?
>
> Gavin continues to dispute about what Sarah is doing. He tells her:
>
> Gavin: Question seven. Four right angles clockwise from West is West.
>
> Gavin is right this time but Sarah says:
>
> Sarah: It can't be West twice. Gavin, you're going to get them all wrong.
>
> Sarah nevertheless writes down Gavin's answer.
>
> Gavin continues to tell Sarah what to do. Again she tells him:
>
> Sarah: Just leave me alone to get on with my own work.
>
> Then again she puts the answer that he has told her.
>
> On the next question she looks to Gavin for support. He says he's not going to tell her this one. The question concerns how many triangles, squares, rectangles etc. there are in a collection of shapes. Sarah negotiates to get answers out of Gavin.
>
> Sarah checks Charlotte's graph against her own.
>
> Another dispute with Gavin, over graphs this time, how much he'd done and naming of shapes on a bar chart, whether it should be 'rectangle' or 'square'.
>
> Sarah puts a rubber on Charlotte's head and they laugh as Charlotte tries to find it and it falls on the floor. Discussion among the three about who is older than whom. Sarah takes a multi-colour pen out of Charlotte's pencil case.
>
> Sarah: (*to Gavin*) She's got a bigger one than you.
> Gavin: So what!
>
> Sarah asks David about his colour chart. How many blacks he had, how many blues.
>
> Sarah embarks on a social discussion with Charlotte about William's behaviour. Gavin moves Sarah's graph and pushes it up the table.
>
> Girls: Oi, Gavin!
>
> Next task is counting right angles. Again differences of opinion. Sarah counts *all* angles, but Gavin's answer is much too high also. This question is abandoned and social talk with Charlotte continues. After a little while:

| Sarah: | Oh, I want to know how many right angles then I can go on to Book 4. |

Discussion with Charlotte about the problem and Charlotte puts Sarah right on what is a right angle. They pencil in the right angles together.
(Fieldnotes, Ann Filer, February 1992, Year 4)

Miss King also considered that Sarah' reticence to commit herself to an opinion was having a detrimental effect upon her attainment in science, as this extract from her annual report describes:

> She must try to increase her confidence in trying to predict what will happen. Often she has something to say, but she is too shy to come out with it.
> (Miss King, annual report to parents, 1992, Year 4)

In contrast to her former, fairly consistent wish to fulfil teacher expectations, during Year 4 Sarah seemed to become less biddable. Miss King found this puzzling, and, given her preferences for cooperation and participation, did not altogether approve. She told Ann Filer:

> She's a nice little girl, but she's very stubborn. She will never admit when she's wrong. Like today I said right, she's in four things for the sports and I didn't realize I'd put her into four and I said 'Oh you won't mind will you, Sarah, if I take one of yours and give one to Gavin.' (But she said) 'I want to do *all* of it.' And I said 'You know you've got four, that's far too many, you're the only one with four.' She said 'Well, I want to do the relay, and I want to do that, and I want to do that!' and I said 'Well which one don't you want to do then you've got to give one'. And it was 'I don't want to give that one because that's what I like to do!'.
> (Miss King, teacher interview, July 1992, Year 4)

Though never liking to be out of favour with her teachers, Sarah had sometimes been less keen to please at all costs than some of her friends. Nevertheless this did seem to be a significant development in relation to a teacher whom she generally liked. We can begin to look for explanations in Sarah's extra-curricular interests (see for example her 'autobiography' work for a supply teacher, Document 4.3). Readers will recall that Sarah's enthusiasms were somewhat unnoticed and unknown by Mr Brown. This was, moreover, a pattern which was being repeated by Miss King. We might also consider the 'into everything' identities of friends Sally and Hannah, and a series of starring performances and high-profile activities which over the years Sally in particular became identified with (see *The Social World of Children's Learning*, and also William's story in Chapter 5 here) and the picture becomes clearer. In interview with Ann Filer, Sarah's mother, without identifying particular friends, gave something of Sarah's perspective on these matters.

AF:	Does she talk much about other groups of children in the class and how she sees them?
Mrs Nelson:	She has one or two thoughts of a couple of the children, again girls. It's always having things coming their way. You know, 'Why should she get this and I do the same sort of thing but I'm not recognized?'
AF:	What sort of area would that be in?
Mrs Nelson:	Well there has been a lot of mucking about of after-school timetables for various things lately and names have been sort of picked out of a hat. Sarah has always got the short straw

I am writing an Autobiography. Thursday 12th march.

My name is Sarah mary Nelson. I am age 8¾. my hoBBys are Swimming, Netball, bike riding and Art. I was born on 26th of May 1983. I Like school, my savoriote Piece of work is maths because I like learning my Tables. When i grow up L want to be an Artest or a nurse. I want to be a nurse because you can help People Live not die. I want to be an artest because you can draw or Paint Lot's of things. Like sandy beachs or Roads. Trees with Lots of Leaves. My savoriote book that i will Tresure is called the book of brownies. Is about 3 naughty brownies who Play Tricks on People Like Painting a Pig green. Now I will tell you about my best Friend and my second best Friend. My best sriends name is Emily. she is very kind she helps me when I fall over. my second best friend is called Charlotte She is brilliant at netball. and she is kind help full and Pretty.

Document 4.3 *Sarah, Year 4, 'Autobiography' (March 1992)*

so to speak and you know it always tends to be one or two girls who don't miss out and their names crop up quite a lot, you know. But she does seem to feel that things go against her personally a lot.

AF: Is this something at the moment?

Mrs Nelson: No, it's generally always been there.

AF: How do you respond to that, when she comes up with that sort of . . .?

Mrs Nelson: I just try and say that it may seem like it because those names are always there, but it's just how these things happen. It's very difficult to try and get it over. I think I have managed but it's always 'So and so is doing this again', and 'Why should she always do it, when I think I'm just as good as her. Why don't I get a golden opportunity to do these things?' But I think probably that might also relate towards what Tom is doing at school and how he is always getting on and doing things. You know, why can't her name be up at the forefront for a change? It's always that she appears to be pushed into the background. She is not. We never make her feel like that, certainly not here. But it is the impression that perhaps she might be getting.

(Parent interview, November 1991, Year 4)

It seems quite reasonable to suppose that Sarah's increased determination to assert her interests in the classroom were connected to her feelings of being overlooked and undervalued by teachers. As we shall see in other children's stories, she was not the only child beginning to express some long-standing resentments over what they saw as teacher's 'favouritism' of some pupils. Sarah, whose own classroom strategies were so very different from those of her high-profile and competitive friends and brother, seemed to have been especially susceptible to such feelings.

Home and family relationships in Year 4

In contrast to Miss King's perception of Sarah as unwilling to admit being wrong, the opposite continued to prevail at home in relation to her mother.

AF: A bit of a recurring thing is Sarah's dislike of emotional upsets, if she has an argument with you and something goes wrong at home . . .

Mrs Nelson: It is still quite definite. She will go away and think about it and the next minute I get a little letter pushed under the door saying, I'm sorry Mummy, I've thought about it and I shouldn't have done this or that. It's quite upsetting in a way but yes, she always does seem to have had that in her.

(Parent interview, November 1991, Year 4)

The most serious concerns of Sarah's parents however, continued to relate to the general suitability of the school for her. These were now being felt more strongly as clear patterns in Sarah's learning were becoming established, and Mrs Nelson elaborated at length upon their worries.

AF: What are your feelings about the school now? I know you have from time to time expressed reservations.

Mrs Nelson: Yes, um, I'm still not terribly happy the way it's going. They are not pushed on, you know, if they want to learn. I find it very difficult to try and think how Sarah is going to fare over the next few years because with Tom we have really not had any worries. He has been able to cope with it. The teacher doesn't seem to be making time to stop and answer questions. And it's this planning, timetable business. I can't bear it. There must be some sort of teacher looking at what they are doing to make sure that they are not missing out on things but I would still like it to be a set timetable. And for them to be given more of an opportunity to ask where they are going wrong or what they can do extra. I don't think she asks as much as she could. If she's stuck instead of asking a teacher she'll ask a friend and I believe the teacher encourages that. I don't think it's right for someone who needs a lot of encouragement. I know she's not dim by any means, you know, she's always had excellent reports and she's always been of above average ability, but not sort of, she'll be there but Tom's here sort of thing. But I still think she needs the encouragement.

(Parent interview, November 1991, Year 4)

Sarah's parents also continued to be concerned about her spelling and the fact that the school didn't seem to share their concern.

Mrs Nelson: ... But although her spelling has improved tremendously recently there are still areas that need improving. I mean the teachers must have seen this two or three years ago. Why wasn't the encouragement and the help put into it then? We were just fobbed off with 'it's quite good for her age, she's average for her age, these things will improve.' And although we give her help at home here we can't really see any input being made at school. It's just little things like that are niggling me, you know.

She needs help with maths as well. She's getting there and she comes back with some things that I didn't realize that she knew so things like that surprise me. You know, there have been times when we have thought, if Tom wasn't coming up to changing school and finances were better we would move her and just put her into an independent school somewhere, see if that would help. I always think, did I perhaps not do as much work with Sarah as I did with Tom in the early stages? Was I more laid back because it was a girl and I had more time for her and I didn't want to push her on as much as I did push on Tom, because he was a boy and he was the first.

(Parent interview, November 1991, Year 4)

During that year, like many other Greenside parents, Mr and Mrs Nelson employed a home tutor to give Sarah some extra coaching in maths and English. In other respects as well, Year 4 was a full year for Sarah where extra-curricular and out-of-school activities were concerned. She continued to go to drama club after school, though choir had to be dropped because it clashed with the opportunity to go to pottery classes. Sarah picked up on the account of her evenings and weekends:

AF: Is there anything you would have liked to have done that you haven't done?

Sarah: Choir really, 'cos they're doing a concert now so ... (*she looks disappointed*). I go to football every Friday 'cos Sally wanted someone to go with. I used to go to football and now I go again. Including Brownies and tutor, Tuesday is the only evening free. Saturday is piano and an art club down by the canal.

Sarah went on to explain that the art club at Watersway Gallery had been dropped for a few weeks because she was making her first Communion soon and had to go to classes to prepare. On communion classes she explained to Ann Filer:

Sarah: I like it because they tell you stories about how you can help people and make things better and do what you're told. [We were told one about] a boy who did not do what his parents told him to do, but he learnt his lesson when his parents would not do what he wanted *them* to do. So he learnt to do what his parents told him to do.

(Sarah, pupil interview, March 1992, Year 4)

In interview, Sarah's mother discussed the importance that year of Sarah's first Communion, together with something of the role of the church in the life of family members.

AF: Yes, you mentioned that she went to Crusaders. I was going to ask whether Church was very important in your life. It is obviously part of the family ...

Mrs Nelson: It is. Not my husband, but for me and the children. We are Catholic so we go to church every week, but we don't just partake in Catholic things, which is why I let her go round to Crusaders because it's a Christian thing and it does her good. And she is there with her friends. It's not as 'closed shop' being a Catholic these days as it was before, I think. It's more laid back in its attitude and its approach to things. She is becoming more involved in it now especially now that her Communion is coming up next year. Tom did his a couple of years ago now and although she is going through the same work as he did, it's her work and they're her books, you know, and it's going to be her time. It was very difficult at one stage to get her to come to Church and I never forced her to do it because I thought that was the wrong approach. I only wanted her to come if she wanted to come.

(Parent interview, November 1991, Year 4)

As we have already described, Sarah had always been encouraged to be socially independent and this was reflected in the end-of-school year interview with Ann Filer. Her parents told of Sarah looking forward with confidence to a new experience during the approaching summer holidays.

Mrs Nelson: Tom's going off on his scout camp next week and Sarah is going on her own for the whole week to a day camp. From half-past-nine to half-past-four ...

Mr Nelson: ... It's a daily thing, but she's not the slightest bit worried that Tom won't be there. All new people, but she's not a bit worried. Looking forward to it no end!

(Parent interview, July 1992, Year 4)

Mrs and Mrs Nelson also reflected in that interview upon the opportunities that they were able to make available to their children in comparison with their own childhood experiences.

Mr Nelson: It's not just down to money, it's the opportunities ...

Mrs Nelson: There's a much bigger range of things that you can do with children. We can take them to different places and do things with them and give them all the opportunities, I certainly feel anyway, that I never had. And I get incredible enjoyment out of being able to give it to them and seeing them enjoy it. You know, even at times, when you sort of turn round and say 'You know, you're completely ungrateful!'

(Parent interview, July 1992, Year 4)

Summary of Sarah's Year 4

There was increasing concern for Sarah's lack of confidence in her own responses and reluctance to give voice to them during Year 4. Both teacher and parents felt that this contributed to underachievement in school. Her parents also continued to question whether pupils were getting enough access to their teacher in class and whether Sarah was getting enough encouragement. Sarah's strong sense of her own worth, under a quiet exterior, together with feelings of being overlooked and undervalued by teachers, all may have contributed to her attempts at self-assertion. However, her teacher found these difficult and treated them as signs of 'stubbornness'.

Sarah, Year 5, early days in Miss French's class

In September 1992 Sarah entered what was to be one of her most successful years at Greenside School, with regard to both her social and academic status in the classroom. Importantly for her status, she was the third oldest in the class, and within the top quarter for achievement in all core curriculum subjects.

Miss French was a young, recently qualified teacher who had joined the school at the same time as Miss King and, along with Mrs Powell and Miss King, was to become a firm favourite among Sarah's teachers.

Miss French, like Miss King, had a preference for very quiet working conditions. As described in Chapter 3, for reasons concerned with the management of the curriculum with different year-groups within classes, tasks were quite highly structured in Miss French's class. The Year 5 half of the class, along with the rest of the Year 5 in other classes, were answerable to Mr Brown for the completion of topic-related tasks each week. The structuring of expectations by means of worksheets, teacher timetabling and allocation to fixed groups was thus something of a compromise solution, rather than necessarily regarded as the ideal by Miss French.

Although the classroom system allowed for pupils, where they wished and were able, to extend their studies and explore beyond the given programme, teacher expectations were nevertheless generally explicit and activities were fairly heavily directed. Thus, Sarah found herself working within the sort of classroom structures which, as we saw above, her parents felt would be appropriate for her needs.

By the end of the first few weeks in her class, Sarah was beginning to pick up on, and conform to, Miss French's basic expectations for carrying out tasks. However, as we have seen with other teachers, there are often also more subtle and tacit expectations upon pupils. So it was in Miss French's class, as the latter explained to Ann Filer:

> She's settled in, again quite well. Produces some good work. Quite quick to pick up on what she's doing. Where at times I think she needs to push herself a bit more, she produces good work but she doesn't stretch herself within the class. And she doesn't easily take on responsibility for her own learning.
> (Miss French, teacher interview, September 1992, Year 5)

The following extracts from Ann Filer's fieldnotes show the way in which a particular task was both structured and directed so that pupils could work without Mr Brown's presence. It also shows where that 'stretch' and 'responsibility' that Miss French was looking for were missing in Sarah's strategies for completion of the task.

> Harriet and Sarah are together on same table with Edward, Dustin and Ewan. Pupils are in 'ability sets', Miss French has explained.
> After break the Year 5 group are all doing topic writing. They have seen a video on Columbus (with Mr Brown) and had been given questions to make notes on while watching. Now they are constructing a piece of writing from the questions and their notes.
> Sarah is trying to write an answer to a question about where Columbus *thought* he was and where he *actually* was. Harriet is trying to tell her. Sarah is unclear and writing what she is told by Harriet (though in the following exchange Harriet is clearly muddled). Much misunderstanding about India and West Indies. America, North America, South America. Dustin joins in. Harriet is getting cross.
>
> | | |
> |---|---|
> | Sarah: | (*reading*) He thought he landed in India. |
> | Harriet: | No! He thought he landed in the *West* Indies. |
> | Sarah: | No! He *thought* he landed in India. |
> | Dustin: | It was South America. |
> | Harriet: | *North* America. |
> | Sarah: | I'm writing just *America*. |
>
> Before she has written anything Harriet has drawn a very wide border round the page of her topic book where she will eventually make a best copy. She explains:
>
> | | |
> |---|---|
> | Harriet: | (*laughing*) I've made it wide so I don't have to do much writing. |
>
> Sarah works methodically through the questions, ticking as she goes, turning the answers into continuous prose. Harriet oversees her work.
>
> | | |
> |---|---|
> | Harriet: | It's a capital 'N' (for Nina) |
> | Sarah: | (*slightly irritated*) *Okay* Harriet! |
>
> Harriet looks across at me, smiling, sharing the joke of Sarah's irritation. They are trying to answer 'What did Columbus start?' and are having a bit of trouble.
>
> | | |
> |---|---|
> | Harriet: | (*laughing*) I'm going to write it better than Sarah. |

Sarah: (*also laughing*) I'm going to copy Harriet. (*She rubs out what she has written for her last answer and rewrites it.*)

I move to observe Hazel working on the same task with two other girls. They reach a point where they cannot answer a question. Hazel immediately goes to Miss French and asks if she can get a book on the topic from Mr Brown's room. Unlike the situation for children on Sarah's table, of course, it was clear for Hazel that she did not have the option of discovering the answer within her group.

I return to Harriet and Sarah. Sarah has just written an answer to the question 'What did the priests do when they arrived?' she tells me.

Sarah: Phew! I have been waiting ages for the answer to that question.

AF: How did you find out?

Sarah: He [Dustin] told me.

Though she has 'waited' for the answer, Sarah has not gone on to the next question. They are answered in order and ticked as they are completed.

(Fieldnotes, Ann Filer, October 1992, Year 5)

The pattern for working here is very similar to that which was observed in the Year 4 maths tasks. Sarah in both is keen to complete tasks successfully and move on to the next but is held up by her lack of confidence in her own responses and the wish for confirmation and support from her peers. In both she suspended activity, 'waiting' for solutions rather than actively seeking them or carrying on without them. These, of course, are only two examples of Sarah's approach to tasks. However, they clearly illuminate the comments of parents and teachers who cite her lack of confidence in her own responses and a somewhat passive approach to fulfilling teacher expectations as reasons for what they consider to be a very able girl achieving less than she might.

Friendships and peer relationships in Year 5

Although Sarah's playground friendships remained broadly as they had done for some while, with the reorganization of the classes for Year 5, they underwent some changes and realignments. Hannah, Charlotte and Nimra were now in a class with Year 6 children and in interview were clear about the difference that this made to their status and to old friendships.

AF: Are there any children you used to play with that you don't play with now?

Charlotte: We used to play with Sally and Mary, Sarah, Carmel, Harriet and Kirsty and Amanda but we don't play with them much now 'cos we're in separate classes.

Hannah: They made friends with Year 4 and we made friends with Year 6. Like I'm staying with a Year 6 tonight.

Charlotte: We play older games now. They play coloured eggs.

Hannah: We don't talk in babyish voices. I prefer it that we're not all Class 8 [Miss French's] because you get to make new friends. We [Class 9] work with class 10 quite a lot.

(Friendship group interview, January 1993, Year 5)

With the loss of some friends from the class, Sarah, Mary and Sally were back together as close friends. In the classroom, Mary and Sally had been placed in the same 'ability group' and were now regarded by teachers and peers as serious, competitive workers. Though Sarah didn't work with them in the classroom, she was associated with them as part of a group of friends who were pleasing to the teacher and whose efforts were publicly rewarded. Thus one of the boys' friendship groups, in interview with Ann Filer, named the three and Amanda as:

> the group that always gets points on the board and gets picked for the parade of excellence.
> (Friendship group interview, January 1993, Year 5)

As we have already seen, Sarah positioned herself within the mainstream of girls' culture at Greenside. In Year 5, along with the rest of that large group she increasingly joined in talk about 'boyfriends' and boys who were 'sexy', though she continued to differentiate herself from the group in her dislike of the 'bum touch' and 'bum smacks' that had developed out of 'kiss chase' in the playground. In interview with their friends she maintained the opinion that the games were rude, the other girls being accepting of her difference. Girls such as Hazel and Harriet, though they liked some individual members of this group, did not conform to the mainstream culture at all and were generally scornful of it. They were critical of these girls' body, hair and clothes consciousness, for 'showing off' to boys and for being 'teacher's pets' (see Harriet's story).

Learning strategies in Year 5

As we have already suggested, Year 5 was a good year for Sarah in terms of classroom status and in part this was due to her chronological position and to changes in composition of peer groupings. Such changes in fortunes were an inevitable consequence as pupils were regrouped year by year at Greenside Primary School. There were also some academic changes that year, her parents being particularly pleased with her development in maths, in the content of her writing and in her verbal confidence which had improved in the classroom and at home. Also that year, Sarah added flute lessons to her extra-curricular activities and joined the school orchestra. Sports, aerobics and personal fitness were becoming keen interests of Sarah's and an area in which, her mother felt, she was becoming quite competitive. She greatly enjoyed after-school netball games, though she was disappointed not to be picked for the school team. As before, her mother said, Sarah felt disappointed that her efforts were not recognized, and felt overlooked compared with the friends who 'got chosen for everything'. Miss French, however, did recognize Sarah's extensive contribution to the extra-curricular life of the school in her summing-up comments on the report.

> Sarah has worked consistently well this year and produced work of a high standard. She is a popular member of the class and is always polite, helpful and cheerful around the school. She has participated in many clubs this year as well as taking part in school performances and other school events.
> (Miss French, report to parents, June 1993, Year 5)

However pleasing her progress was, the feeling on the part of Sarah's parents and her teacher regarding her underachievement did not substantially change that year. It was felt that motivation was still lacking and her mother reported in the diary:

> Her day-to-day routine at school is becoming, in her words, quite boring. There hasn't been a day over the past four weeks or so when she has come out of school without saying that although she has had a good day, she has been bored.
> Now that she is taking a more active role within the classroom I quite firmly believe that she is wanting to push on with her learning and is unable to do so.
> (Parent diary, December 1992, Year 5)

There was then, as we can perceive from that diary entry, a discrepancy between Miss French's account of Sarah as *unwilling* to take responsibility for her learning and to stretch herself, and her mother's perception that she was *unable* to. Certainly, if it was the more structured and directed routine that caused Sarah to feel bored, she might have lacked the *motivation* to extend her studies and explore beyond the given.

At the end of Year 5, in interview with Ann Filer, Miss French commented that Sarah liked to work with one other child or liked to dominate a group. She suggested that Sarah very much *liked* to lead and was quietly competitive. However, Miss French did not think that Sarah was prepared to risk being different. She liked to conform. She tended to have strong ideas and liked to promote them, but always within a framework (teacher interview, July 1993). This description of Sarah's approach to classroom tasks is interesting and perceptive. Indeed it corresponds well with the tensions which we perceive throughout Sarah's career between, on the one hand her competence and strong sense of self and, on the other, her need to reduce the risk of getting things wrong by operating within available structures and patterns for success.

Home and family relationships in Year 5

Sarah, along with many other boys and girls in her year group at this time, was increasingly developing a more sophisticated and style-conscious identity. Her mother described to Ann Filer some of Sarah's experiments with her appearance.

> She doesn't have to be within [the latest fashion] at all. She's her own person. No, as long as she feels that she looks nice and she feels comfortable in it that doesn't seem to matter. She's paying an awful lot of attention to her hair lately, she actually asked for a crimper for her birthday in May. She picked that out particularly, and in fact she used it yesterday. We were going out to tea at Nick's sister's, a birthday tea, and she wanted to make an impression so she used that – 'Do you think it would be a good idea if I used this?' And she's always looking for different styles. She's asked me lately about using little bits of make-up, which I will let her do occasionally around the place, you know, or somewhere where it doesn't really matter. Can she paint her toenails? – so I let her do that because of course she's wearing socks and shoes all the time, but it makes her feel good when she comes home and changes, and she's got sandals or something like that on. I won't let her do her fingernails. Well, I think she likes to be her own person. She's got her own identity. She doesn't feel as though she has to identify with anyone in particular.
> (Mrs Nelson, parent interview, July 1993, Year 5)

By the end of the year, Sarah's mother thought that Sarah's verbal confidence was improving at home. She was more prepared to contribute to discussions, to offer opinions and to risk being 'wrong' in the context of the family.

Also that year, brother Tom, having passed the necessary entrance exam, was now being privately educated at Rutherford College.

Summary of Sarah's Year 5

Year 5 saw considerable progress for Sarah. Her structural position in class and classroom status were quite high, she gained confidence in expressing opinions at school and at home. Though this was a good year in what were, for Sarah, propitious classroom circumstances, it was still felt that she was underachieving, with some discrepancy between home and school with respect to what exactly was holding her back from full commitment.

Sarah, Year 6, early days in Mrs Chard's class

In contrast to her high structural position in Miss French's class, in Mrs Chard's class Sarah was, chronologically, the twentieth of 26 children. Academically she maintained a position about halfway down the class in the three core subjects.

Mrs Chard was the deputy head of Greenside and had developed a philosophy of active learning over many years of experience and in many different classroom contexts. As we have described more fully in Chapter 3, for Mrs Chard the emphasis in the classroom was on presenting pupils with a challenge, setting high expectations within tight planning schedules, and following up with close assessment. She liked to give pupils the freedom to choose how to carry out tasks and expected them to do so responsibly and to take responsibility for their efforts. In Mrs Chard's class one could observe both high levels of discussion, collaboration and activity among pupils, and occasions when silent, sustained, individual work was expected. Something of Sarah's perceptions of the requirements for success for that year can be discerned in Document 4.4.

Mrs Chard's perception of Sarah – that she was capable of more than she delivered – matched those of other teachers. She explained:

> Well, I feel that Sarah is a reasonably able girl who's not particularly well motivated to turn in the right performance. I think she could be doing far better than she is, and I think for some reason she deliberately chooses to work alongside children who are less able than herself and I feel that she then does appear to be achieving more than they are. But I don't think she is achieving her potential at all. I have reason to think that outside [of school] assessment she does quite well and I think that probably within the school she does the bare minimum really. So she's capable of doing far more.
> (Mrs Chard, teacher interview, December 1993, Year 6)

However, despite those frustrations that were felt by all her teachers, the pattern of Sarah liking nearly all her teachers and having good relationships with them, while also maintaining her individual point of view, also continued:

Monday January 31st.
Successess and achievments.

1. My successess.
2 My targets for change and my strategies for achieving those targets.
3. What i would most like to achieve by the end of the year.

I have had success in lots of things like①, getting my Challenge badges and life Savers badge in swimming and② learning how to to do percentages.

My targets to achieve are,①not to chat so much and② to try and finish my work quicker.③ I will achieve this by not chatting and putting my head down to work.

By the end of the year I would like to①achieve working my hardest and② trying harder in everything I find hard.

Document 4.4 *Sarah, Year 6, 'Successes and Achievements'* (January 1994)

Sarah is always very polite. Can be very stubborn and difficult when she wants to, a little bit of throwing her weight about, but generally a good relationship with teachers. She'll give you a big smile at the end and doesn't hold grudges. You know, at one point she *could* have held a grudge, but she didn't, and we're fine now.
(Mrs Chard, teacher interview, June 1994, Year 6)

Friendships and peer relationships in Year 6

With the move to their Year 6 class, the large group of Sarah's friends were back together again. Sarah for most of the year worked with Kirsty and Nimra, the girls whom Mrs Chard described as 'less able' than Sarah.

Sarah's mother recorded that the pattern of falling in and out friendship, which Sarah for a long time found difficult to cope with, had gone. The reason for this could be clearly seen in the classroom and in the playground for, although her long-standing friendship with Mary and Sally was by no means over, Sarah had withdrawn completely in class and in the playground from the two girls and from the larger group with which they had become closely associated. Mrs Chard commented:

> She doesn't appear to want to fit into that highly motivated group, or doesn't want to join that group.
> They were allowed to choose their own groups and she's chosen. And as far as I can see she has little to do with these others. But I think that they could be seen as quite a threat within the class because they are a very successful group of children.
> (Mrs Chard, teacher interview, December 1993, Year 6)

However, as readers will see in William's story, the 'highly motivated group' of Sally, Mary, Hannah, Charlotte, Vicki and Amanda faced enormous upheavals that year from within, due to rivalries, and from without, due to the resentment from some peers of what was seen as a favoured group. With a knowledge of Sarah's history of dislike of both competitive rivalries at school and emotional upsets, the reader will understand Sarah's lack of involvement with that group perhaps more clearly than was possible for Mrs Chard. It follows that, perhaps contrary to Mrs Chard's perceptions, it is not likely that Sarah would have achieved a higher standard in the emotionally charged atmosphere that sur-rounded the group for much of the year. Indeed, the work of some of the most able and competitive in the group suffered considerably for a while.

Sarah's withdrawal from the group could also have been predicted on the basis of its increased association with boys in Year 6.

AF:	Are there any people that you used to play with that you don't play with now?
Nimra:	Sally, Hannah.
Sarah:	We swap [stickers] with Amanda, not with Charlotte or Mary.
Kirsty:	'Cos they always play football.
Sarah:	They play with the boys.
Kirsty:	Kiss chase.
Sarah:	Not now. That's been banned.
AF:	Why was it banned?
Sarah:	Because the boys were being rough. Hannah and Charlotte got upset.
Kirsty:	Hannah and Charlotte nearly had an asthma attack but they were doing it to stop the boys. Her breathing looked all right to me.

The group explain that their playtime activities include swapping stickers, sitting on the bench talking or sometimes helping teachers, and then talk about the other friendship groups in the class:

Nimra:	Sally, Hannah, Rebecca, Mary, Charlotte. And Amanda sometimes moves on to their table and they think they're the best.
Kirsty:	They've got more boyfriends.
Sarah:	They're always in couples. They dump each other.
Nimra:	It's really stupid.
Kirsty:	They're all right, but when one of her boyfriends comes over to borrow something, Hannah laughs.
Sarah:	That's why we don't play with them much. They're always into boys and we don't like that kind of stuff.

(Friendship group interview, March 1994, Year 6)

Whether the separation was due to differences in the culture of the playground or the classroom, from Sarah's mother's perspective, she was pleased that Sarah had distanced herself from old peer cliques and rivalries that in the past had often been the cause of distress for Sarah and irritation for herself.

Learning strategies in Year 6

Mrs Chard, like Miss French, perceived in Sarah the tension between on the one hand wanting to lead and on the other wishing to feel secure and unchallenged.

> I would say that she wasn't very competitive. I would say that she's cute enough to know what is required, and does that, and doesn't strive for anything greater, will not push herself. She will lead when there is a situation that she feels secure but that means that she will be challenged by another group. Because it's interesting that she has withdrawn from some of the core competitive characters within the class and has established herself within a group where the children don't really challenge her.
> (Mrs Chard, teacher interview, June 1994, Year 6)

Of course, as we have described, a good deal of the learning that went on in Mrs Chard's class took place through cooperation within small groups of pupils in response to a teacher-given challenge. If a small group is rising to a challenge successfully then inevitably, as Mrs Chard suggests, pupils would have faced challenges to their ideas from their peers. Sarah, in ducking out of that challenge which would push her to 'strive for something greater', was failing to fulfil teacher expectations on two fronts. She was failing to gain experience of learning as an active, reflective process and she was also narrowing her field of enquiry and thus limiting the content of her learning.

Again, in highlighting areas of dissatisfaction in Sarah's story, the risk has been that the successes and achievements of the year are overshadowed. Despite the disappointments expressed by parents, teachers and by Sarah, which seemed to have become fixed features of her career, Year 6 was a happy experience for Sarah. Though, on the one hand, in interview with Ann Filer, she reflected:

> In this class I haven't been in the Parade of Excellence once. Some people have been chosen about three or four times.
> (Sarah, pupil interview, June 1994, Year 6)

She nevertheless expressed great satisfaction with the year generally and liked her teacher:

I've got on well with Mrs Chard. She's nice. She answers your problems when you ask questions.
(Pupil interview, June 1994, Year 6)

During the year Sarah took the opportunity, with other Year 6 pupils, to organize and run a stall for the school's annual Charity Day. She continued to attend dance/aerobics after school as well as art club and achieved her ambition of being monitor to an infant class. She greatly enjoyed a week away with Year 6 pupils at the annual school camp and participated enthusiastically in the end of year musical production that was an annual event for Year 6 pupils at Greenside. She also performed on the flute at the 'leavers' concert' and along with several other girls from her class she was selected to dance at St George's Hall in an Easthampton schools concert.

In her final report from Greenside School, which as always was a very pleasing one, Sarah's motivation and enthusiastic participation in the extra-curricular life of the school were acknowledged.

General comments: Sarah has made a lively contribution to Year 6. She has worked well and entered into the spirit of all our big events with great enthusiasm. I know that she will meet great success in the future and I wish her well.
(Mrs Chard, report to parents, June 1994, Year 6)

Discussing Sarah's learning across her school career as a whole, however, her mother expressed slightly ambivalent feelings that she and her husband had always held regarding Sarah's reports.

Mrs Nelson:	Her reports were always that she was coping with the work and she was well above the Key Stage that she should be at the time. So she got something out of that as well because it was always something positive, you never came home with any negative feelings about it. We were very encouraged.
AF:	And the same presumably with parents' evenings.
Mrs Nelson:	Yes, yes. No problems at all. It was almost a sort of courtesy visit, really. But it never seemed to be the time to bring up any real misgivings [...] but I do feel that it hasn't always been because of the school. We sent Sarah to a tutor for a while [...] and the tutor brought Sarah on so well, and made her a lot more confident about some of the things she was doing that she was worried about and not getting the help for. And I think it's been a lot of hard work on Sarah's part, from the extra work she's been doing.

(Parent interview, June 1994, Year 6)

At the end of her primary career Sarah, like most of her friends, declared that they had been very happy at Greenside School and would be sorry to leave. However, she was already keenly looking forward to the next stage of schooling. She told Ann Filer:

I'm going to Rutherford College. I'm excited. I really want to go there 'cos I know some of the teachers and some of Tom's friends and I know a girl that is starting there with me.
(Sarah, pupil interview, June 1994, Year 6)

If Sarah's description here seems familiar to readers, they will recall Sarah's entry to Mrs Powell's Reception class seven years before. The network of familiar relationships described here by Sarah which will support her entry to secondary school matches exactly those which supported her as, together with her friend Louise, she embarked upon her career at Greenside Primary School.

Home and family relationships in Year 6

At the end of Sarah's primary school career, her mother felt that Sarah had become resigned to never quite getting the success in extra-curricular activities that she felt she had worked hard for. She discussed with Ann Filer the way in which, as a parent, she had tried over the years to mediate Sarah's disappointments.

> It has been: 'Guess who's got the two main parts again' – and these two girls' names, ever since Sarah's been at school, they've come up, year after year. But that's been frustrating for Sarah and in some ways for us as parents because how do you explain? But we have to get round it by trying to be positive – she has got a part. It may not be the one that she [wanted] but by being good, or even extra good in that part – so she has gone on thinking, 'I'll show them!', which has been the way round it. Tom's finding it. There are certain boys who are made cricket captain or hockey captain, year after year after year. They always get a bat, always get to bowl, always in the team.
>
>   Now she's nearly finished [at Greenside] she'll just walk in and say 'Yes, so and so got it again' you know, 'but it doesn't really matter because I've got this part and that part.'
> (Mrs Nelson, parent interview, June 1994, Year 6)

Where netball was concerned, feelings that her efforts were not getting rewarded led Sarah to eventually withdraw from the situation.

> Netball: Because she always has been so enthusiastic about it, but has been getting nowhere fast and it just seems a shame. I mean, at the end of the day she said 'Oh, blow it!' She came home one day and said 'I've given up netball. I'm not *doing* it!'
> (Mrs Nelson, parent interview, June 1994, Year 6)

Over the last few years of school at Greenside, for Sarah and her parents, as for all the other children, the question of which school she was to attend for her secondary education assumed increasing importance. As was described in Chapter 3, the socio-economic circumstances of most Greenside families, together with the highly contrasting ones of nearby Damibrook, meant that most Greenside families opted for independent schooling, where the alternative was to send their children to Damibrook Comprehensive School. As the range of perceived options for independent schooling alone covered at least nine schools, speculation among the pupils as to where they would eventually go increased as they progressed through the last few years at Greenside. For much of this time Sarah expressed an interest in the single-sex education offered by Richford High School for Girls. By early summer of 1994, however, after a year in which schools had been visited, options discussed and entrance exams had been sat, the speculation was over for the children. Sarah had won a part scholarship to Rutherford College, where her brother attended, and was to follow him there. With the feeling that Sarah had spent most of her primary school years to some extent 'in Tom's shadow' Sarah's parents, in interview with Ann Filer, did reflect upon whether they had made the right choice of school:

> ... and now with Sarah going to the same school as Tom, one of the things we were worried about was the fact that she might not have her own identity – that she might be known as Tom's sister. But we've accepted, I think, that because there's a lower, a middle and an upper school, that won't happen. Tom assures us that this doesn't happen. I think there'll be occasions where it's 'Oh, you're Tom Nelson's sister', you know, but I think on the whole she'll have her own identity.
> (Mrs Nelson, parent interview, June 1994, Year 6)

Summary of Sarah's Year 6

In her final year at Greenside Primary School Sarah achieved a good degree of academic and extra-curricular success. Though her teacher and parents continued to feel that she had not achieved as much as she could, she had gained confidence, her mother felt, from matching Tom in passing the entrance exam to the independent school he attended. During the year Sarah consciously moved further out of her group of competitive friends and re-established working and playground relationships within a group against which she 'looked good' academically and which more closely reflected her preferred playground culture.

During Year 6, therefore, Sarah fulfilled some important academic expectations, her own and those of others, and had experienced a happy year in the security of the relatively undemanding social and academic context that she had created for herself. On the other hand, although her enthusiastic participation in extra-curricular activities was noted, she still failed to achieve the high-profile involvement to which she aspired in that area of her career.

Sarah's identity and career in the later years at Greenside school

The concluding years of Sarah's career at Greenside School, rather than showing any great change in Sarah's strategies, show the resolution and outcomes of patterns of response adopted early in her career.

Throughout her career, her preference for working relationships in which she was not challenged and for working within teacher-given expectations and frameworks precipitated a continual splitting off from classroom alliances which were themselves semi-competitive. Sarah's dislike of conflict undoubtedly also contributed to this pattern so that, by the end of her primary career, she had certainly created for herself the sort of secure and predictable working relationships she enjoyed. She was also however, continuing to evade some challenge to her ideas and exploration of new areas of curriculum content.

Though she continued to maintain good relationships with teachers and was concerned to maintain a 'good' and 'reliable' classroom identity, she became less striving in her attempts to please teachers than her closest friends from her early

Matrix 4.3 *Sarah, Years 4, 5 and 6, a summary matrix*

Family relationships	Peer-group relationships	Teacher relationships	Identity	Career
Year 4: Miss King				
Mrs Nelson thinks there is a lack of encouragement and access to teachers at school. Sarah prepares for first Communion.	Complete separation from Sally and Mary in the classroom. Sarah works mainly with Kirsty and Nimra, also Charlotte and Amanda. Miss King says that Sarah knows everyone and everyone likes her.	Structural position: age, 13/30; maths and English, in top quarter, science, in top third. Miss King initially found Sarah 'a mystery', 'stubborn'. Good relationships develop. Sarah feels overlooked regarding *her* interests.	A little assertiveness, stubbornness emerging but still sees herself as 'good'. Her teacher thinks she is 'quietly competitive'. Well liked among peers.	Sarah is competent and independent of parents across a range of structured activities of church, clubs, lessons etc. Patterns of success established by Tom. Sarah's strategies have not paid off in school where she feels undervalued compared with her high-profile peers.
Year 5: Miss French				
An all-round improvement in confidence, willing to express opinion, be wrong. Her mother thinks she is being held back in the classroom now.	Changes involve loss of some former friends to another class. Sarah works with Harriet now. Sarah is seen by others as one of the good group of pupils who are pleasing to Miss French.	Structural position: age, 3/29; maths, English, science, in top quarter. Miss French says Sarah produces good work but does not take on responsibility for her learning. Has strong ideas and likes to lead but within a given framework.	'Quietly competitive' popular, helpful and polite classroom identity. Sees herself as good and avoids those who are not. Good at sport, likes netball, aerobics, fitness.	Despite high structural position and classroom status, Sarah maintains a low-risk, low-responsibility approach to learning which her teacher feels is why her potential is still not being realized.
Year 6: Mrs Chard				
Great increase in confidence in challenging parents' views. Sarah passes the entrance exam to go to the same independent school as Tom.	Sarah prefers to work with a non-competitive group of friends who offer her no challenge. Mrs Nelson feels Sarah's enthusiasms in drama, sport etc. have not been rewarded and Sarah continues to feel overshadowed and overlooked in favour of a few high-profile friends.	Structural position: age 20/26; maths, English, science, halfway down. Sarah enjoys a good degree of academic success; however her teacher feels she has not realized her potential: 'She knows what is required and doesn't strive for anything more'.	Teacher thinks she 'likes to lead where she feels secure and won't be challenged by peers'. Also 'polite', 'stubborn', 'doesn't bear a grudge'. Enthusiastic and lively contributor to extra-curricular clubs, events, activities.	Consistently Sarah is considered to have great potential should she be able to risk moving outside given structures. Equally, none of the contexts she met at Greenside fulfilled *her* expectations and aspirations.

years, Mary, Sally, and also Hannah. Indeed, 'strong-willed' and 'stubborn' were also aspects of Sarah's identity variously attributed to her by her teachers over the years. In these later years we hypothesize that this was the response of a child with a strong sense of her own worth who increasingly felt overlooked and undervalued compared with the high-profile extra-curricular identities of some friends. Unfortunately, in the later years we begin to sense that her strategies may not have paid off where her own particular interests and aspirations were concerned. Though she competently fulfilled basic expectations of others, at the same time reducing possibilities of tension in the learning context, the pupil identity to which she aspired was one that she saw being achieved by those with very different strategies in the classroom and around the school.

SARAH'S IDENTITY AND CAREER – CASE-STUDY OVERVIEW

As we have described in the introduction to the case studies, the triadic representation (Figure 4.1) depicts, in the outer triangle, the social context within which Sarah learnt and developed and to which she could contribute. The inner star shows the dynamic relationships between Sarah, her peers, her family and her teachers within which she shaped and maintained her identity. We can thus summarize Sarah's career in terms of the maintenance of low-risk, low-profile strategies and competence in fulfilling academic and social expectations of school and family. In tension with this strategy and success lies a failure to fulfil academic potential as perceived by teachers and parents and disappointment that her some of her own aspirations and expectations were not realized.

We can describe the strategic response of *conformity* in terms of a reification of curricular, behavioural and extra-curricular expectations.

We can perceive this in Sarah's strategies, firstly with regard to her competence in adapting to academic requirements but without any move beyond teacher-given frameworks for success. In the context of her extra-curricular career, it is true, she participated enthusiastically in many sporting, musical and dramatic clubs and a range of events throughout her career. However, as readers will perceive more clearly in the context of other children's careers, participation and enthusiasm were not in themselves sufficient qualities for achieving at the cutting edge of extra-curricular expectations at Greenside Primary School. Something which took the form of a highly interactive, social astuteness, that 'into everything' response, as Sarah's mother described it, was also needed.

With regard to the social relationships within which Sarah learnt, her classroom and social competence, as well as her strong sense of independence, meant that she liked to lead her peers in the classroom. However, she wished to do so within the security of given frameworks. However, such frameworks were also available to all her peers and leadership requires the necessity often to go beyond the given. The contradictions between these two opposing tendencies of Sarah's, the wish to lead and the wish for secure structures, seem to have been resolved in the contexts of her responsibility towards and befriending of younger children, in and out of school, and her leadership of lower achieving peers who offered little challenge.

Thus the implications of Sarah's strategies for her learning and for career outcomes

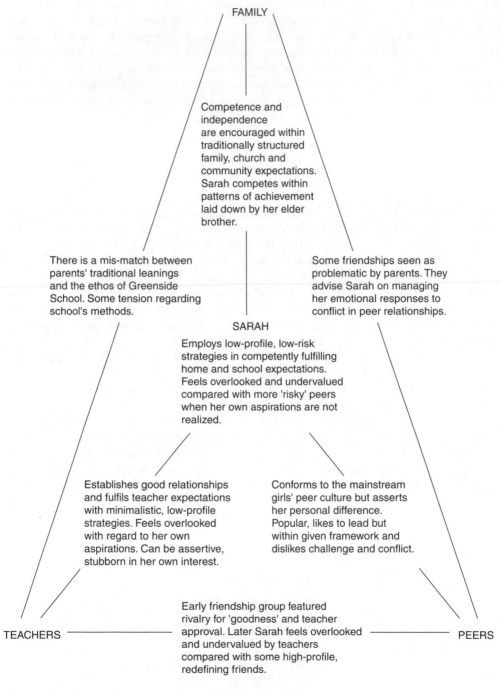

FAMILY

Competence and
independence
are encouraged within
traditionally structured
family, church and
community expectations.
Sarah competes within
patterns of achievement
laid down by her elder
brother.

There is a mis-match between
parents' traditional leanings
and the ethos of Greenside
School. Some tension regarding
school's methods.

Some friendships seen as
problematic by parents. They
advise Sarah on managing
her emotional responses to
conflict in peer relationships.

SARAH

Employs low-profile, low-risk
strategies in competently fulfilling
home and school expectations.
Feels overlooked and undervalued
compared with more 'risky' peers
when her own aspirations are not
realized.

Establishes good relationships
and fulfils teacher expectations
with minimalistic, low-profile
strategies. Feels overlooked
with regard to her own
aspirations. Can be assertive,
stubborn in her own interest.

Conforms to the mainstream
girls' peer culture but asserts
her personal difference.
Popular, likes to lead but
within given framework and
dislikes challenge and conflict.

TEACHERS

Early friendship group featured
rivalry for 'goodness' and teacher
approval. Later Sarah feels overlooked
and undervalued by teachers
compared with some high-profile,
redefining friends.

PEERS

Figure 4.1. *Sarah's case-study overview – a triadic representation*

were clear. Sarah progressed and achieved no small measure of success in her academic career through *conformity* to available patterns for success. However, she suffered some degree of frustration and disappointment as her strategies did not pay off in terms of some of the rewards of which she knew she was capable and which she coveted. Teachers and parents also experienced some frustration that she did not achieve all that they, in their turn, felt she could. Thus, at the heart of Sarah's career biography was a tension between her strategic response of *conformity* with the reification of existing patterns for success and her own sense of self-worth and independence and the desire for a pupil identity which she never quite achieved.

In the following chapter we shall follow the story of William, and will begin to identify a career strategy that involves pupils going beyond the structures and expectations available to them from home, classroom and the peer group. Such strategies involve moving outside *conformity* to given career expectations and involve *redefining* those structures. Through telling William's story, and picking up some more on Sally's story, we shall examine their pattern of strategic action, which produced the sort of outcomes and identities which eluded Sarah.

Chapter 5

William's Story

5.1 PRE-SCHOOL, RECEPTION AND YEAR 1

William, an introduction

Through the preceding case-study chapter we have told the story of Sarah, whose predominant patterns of strategic action at Greenside School have been described in terms of *conformity*. Her story was one of relative consistency of strategy for shaping and managing her pupil identity as she moved through a series of different classroom contexts and teacher expectations.

In telling William's story, we now move along a continuum of pupil's strategic negotiation, whereby the relative consistency of Sarah's approach gives way to change and evolution. Throughout William's story we shall see him actively shaping and *redefining* his identity in strategic response to new sets of classroom expectations as he moves through the school.

It will also become clear that, whereas *redefining*, like *conformity*, is very much *associated* with mainstream patterns of achievement and cultural norms, it implies that pupils are not so much operating *within* those dominant patterns and norms as at the cutting edge of them. Thus through William's story we will see him pushing at the boundaries of expectations, negotiating, challenging and often leading his peers as we will track the emergence and development of his bid for academic and social status.

William's family

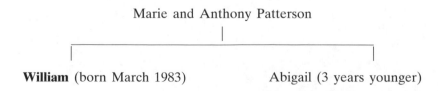

Marie and Anthony Patterson

William (born March 1983)   Abigail (3 years younger)

William was the older of the two children of Marie and Tony Patterson. His father, Tony, was an accountant and Marie Patterson had given up a career in physiotherapy to work full-time at home while the children were young. The family moved to a three-bedroomed, semi-detached house in Greenside in 1987, not far from Sarah's house, and became active members of the parish church of St John. William's parents described themselves as having strong Christian convictions and described their approach to bringing up their children as one in which Christian principles, together with discipline, provided a framework and atmosphere in which the children had the freedom to develop in their own particular ways. William and his sister Abigail were to become regular churchgoers and also, as did Sarah and many of their friends, attended Young Crusaders Club from an early age.

Early learning in the family

By the time he went to school, William had a headstart on many of his peers where reading was concerned. His mother explained to Andrew Pollard how this came about:

> Books feature top of the list of anything they ever do. We read to them endlessly. To really go back to the beginning he was actually a year and 10 months and we had letters on the fridge and I just totally randomly wrote things like 'bus' 'William' whatever, I did about six words on the fridge and within one week he knew them. I jumbled up the colours, I wrote them on paper, I changed the order round and he still knew them. He was less than 2 and he could read about 6 or 10 words. From then on he used to say 'what does that say'. He would point out signs and he wanted to know what it said. I never held him back but I thought he was a bit too young to really get him very far, but he learnt so many so quickly that I thought I might as well take him a bit further if he wants to so we bought the Ladybird Scheme and did the first few books with him. He did really well initially, he was keen, it was only ever when he wanted to do it. Then he started to find them a little bit more tedious because they are so uninteresting – you have pages and pages of boring, no story line at all. We tended to do it sort of during the winter months. Come the summer they are outside and they don't sit down so much. Particularly the summer before he started school, we didn't really do any reading whatsoever. He actually had forgotten a lot of the words. He had a flying start I presume on a lot of the others but he somehow took the whole of the first term to actually begin to enjoy reading at school.
> (Mrs Patterson, parent interview, March 1988)

This description of William's early learning in the home suggests that it was a relaxed and unpressurized experience and his first introduction to institutional learning in the form of playgroup also followed the relaxed approach to early learning favoured by his mother.

Early learning in playgroup

In contrast to the traditionalist nursery school education described in Sarah's story, William's first experience of institutional learning took place in the rather more informal environment of the playgroup. His parents described his response to the new experience.

Mrs Patterson:	We only moved to this house in June, so it was where we lived previously, because we moved here specifically gearing him up for school in September. He had a playgroup he went to three times a week and he positively loved it. Never one single session ever he didn't want to go, or he didn't enjoy it. It was a fairly free sort of playgroup – there wasn't any reading or serious writing or anything like that but he just loved it. From the very first day and it happened to coincide with Abigail being born, which was slightly awkward, but he didn't seem to mind that either – to him it was almost his special grown up let-out of mums and babies and all that. It wouldn't be unfair or whatever to say, he was very popular at playgroup, both to the helpers and to the other children, he was very well liked. He was very outgoing, a lot of them at three were quite shy....
Mr Patterson:	He has always appeared to be reasonably confident when meeting other children, and to a certain extent other adults.

(Parent interview, March 1988)

A summary of William's pre-school experience

On entry to Greenside School in 1987 then, William, as the elder child in a family which was new to the neighbourhood, did not have the sort of knowledge of the school and network of supportive relationships with which Sarah began her school career. However, his confidence at playgroup, his popularity and the evidence of his early learning in the home meant that, like Sarah, he too seemed well prepared for his primary school career at Greenside. Moreover, his parents did not carry the negative expectations and worries engendered by the changes taking place there which was the experience of Sarah's parents and of many others at that time.

William, Reception, early days in Mrs Powell's class

In September 1987, William entered the relatively stable and supportive learning environment of Mrs Powell's Reception class, which we have already described in Sarah's story. He embarked upon his school career with an amazing degree of confidence, as his mother recounted to Andrew Pollard:

> His very first day at Greenside, he was positively excited about it before he started and he ran in and his exact words to me were 'Bye Mum, I don't need you any more'.
> (Mrs Patterson, parent interview, March 1988, Reception)

However, despite his early promise and the advantage of being the third oldest in the class of 28, William only managed to attain a position of about halfway down the class in English and maths during that first school year. His father explained:

It took a lot of time for him to appreciate that he wasn't there to just play all the time. This was a bit of a struggle, a bit of a crisis for him, I think, that he was there eventually to get down and do some work.
(Mrs Patterson, parent interview, March 1988, Reception)

Later at the beginning of William's second term at school, Mrs Powell was able to elaborate to Andrew Pollard upon her developing relationship with him.

He is a very strong-willed boy. He wants to do what he wants to do and there is no doubt about that. He is getting a bit better lately. One example is, after they had been in school I decided to expect them to say: 'Please Mrs Powell' after they had told me whether they wanted school dinners or not. He was determined not to do this. It was really awkward, but you see now he has come round and he does it. I think it is because he doesn't see why anyone should tell him what to do.
(Mrs Powell, teacher interview, February 1988, Reception)

Despite these early struggles over encouraging William to accept the routines and expectations of school life, Mrs Powell was clearly satisfied with William's academic and social skills generally, and in many respects regarded him as a stimulating and responsive pupil. She told Andrew Pollard:

He is a bright boy. He has got a marvellous command of English language. He knows some very difficult words. He is the first 4-year-old I have come across who knew 'deciduous' and what it meant. He hates writing. He can't wait to get away so he can go and play on the mat. Just lately he has become a bit more interested in creative activities. I have not had a lot of trouble with his maths concepts. PE he is all right as he throws himself about. He will say funny things to be laughed at and he likes to make people laugh.
(Mrs Powell, teacher interview, February 1988, Reception)

Despite his appearance of confidence and his growing popularity with his peers, it became clear that William's early adjustments to school were not altogether smoothly accomplished. Soon after starting school, William began to suffer from nightmares, though it seemed that relationships in the playground, rather than those within the security of Mrs Powell's classroom, were likely to be at the root of the problem.

Friendships and peer relationships in Reception

William and his best friend, Richard, had what Mrs Powell described as 'a love–hate relationship' which was characterized by close and constant association between the two boys but also by fights and quarrels. During William's first term of school, the relationship rapidly seemed to get out of hand and became a source of perplexity for his parents, who were unsure how to handle a situation which was clearly causing William some distress.

| Mrs Patterson: | He came home one day with bruises on his back. He said that he had been pushed over – then this was Richard. We kept getting Richard, Richard. In fact he was getting quite frightened when he spoke about things. I left it for a long time. I didn't go in and mention anything about it because I thought, I don't want to start you know whatever . . . |
| AP: | Yes, you wanted to see how it went? |

Mrs Patterson: In the second half of last term, it came to a head one night. He was crying, he was really upset and for the first time ever, and the one and only time ever, he said to me 'I don't want to go to school tomorrow'. He said it was an incident in the playground involving Richard. He was frightened and clinging on to me. I calmed him down because I didn't want to make a great big thing out of it. What I did was the following day I went to see Mrs Powell. Her reaction to us was, they are both very strong personalities, they don't give in to each other which is why they clash, which I mean I fully understand, because he is a strong personality. I don't know Richard, so I don't know how he relates. But I would say certainly up until starting school, William was not ever a violent child. Whether he has become so by copying others I wouldn't like to say. I am sure he learns a bit of elbow room now and again. It is hard to know what is healthy and normal, what is just boys of four and five playing, and what is bordering on the bullish or bullying.

(Parent interview, March 1988, Reception)

During that spring term in Mrs Powell's class, William's mother discussed other new influences upon William that tended to conflict with the norms and expectations of their home. For example, his mother told Andrew Pollard:

He has got quite sexist, I have noticed since he has been at school. Oh yes, it is 'that's girlish' and 'this is boyish' and that is something I have never done at home. He comes home with very definite ideas about girls and boys now, which school has obviously taught him very early. Although he let on to me today he is sewing something for me for Mothers' Day, so I thought, good – getting him to do some sewing.
(Mrs Patterson, parent interview, March 1988, Reception)

Mr and Mrs Patterson were very conscious of the power of peer expectations and Mrs Patterson expressed concern that William should learn to evaluate and resist such pressures.

I worry slightly that peer pressure will get the better of him. It is hard to know how at what age they will begin to have any backbone to stand up and say 'No I won't' or whatever. Peer groups, you know, they are very strong. I can remember at school: do you conform or do you keep up with what is the current 'in' thing to do?
(Mrs Patterson, parent interview, March 1988, Reception)

Learning strategies in Reception

As described above, it was with difficulty that Mrs Powell managed to persuade William to turn his attention to some of the more formal school tasks. Writing in particular continued to be disliked by William and he and several others had discovered an effective strategy for avoiding spending too much time at the task. At this stage in the development of their skills, before they became independent writers, Mrs Powell would adopt the practice of writing to the pupils' dictation for them to write over, and, at a further stage of development, to copy underneath. These pupils, mostly boys Mrs Powell noted, soon realized that the less they said, the less there was to write. She told Andrew Pollard:

Mrs Powell:	Robert and William [do that]. The girls aren't as bad really, they are more verbal anyway.
AP:	But those two have worked that out?
Mrs Powell:	Yes. I think I probably notice those more because it annoys me more with them than it does with the others because I know of the capability there. Others do it as well but, those are the two, because I think they are so able.

(Teacher interview, February 1988, Reception)

By the end of the spring term, however, William was beginning to increase his involvement across the range of activities and tasks. Though he still disliked writing, his report to parents records that his handwriting had improved and that he was keen to read and enjoyed working in the maths area. He had no problem with maths concepts, contributed well to class discussion and was very attentive. He enjoyed stories and was good at PE and games.

However, though William enjoyed working with construction materials and executed his drawings with care, he took the same minimalistic approach to creative tasks that were directed by Mrs Powell as he did to writing. Such activities, involving painting or cutting out for example, tended to be rushed with little enthusiasm or effort put into them. Though William tended to naughtiness from time to time, especially in association with Richard, he was keen to avoid trouble and Mrs Powell tended to see him as:

He's one of those boys who is only naughty when he thinks he won't get caught.
(Mrs Powell, teacher records, autumn 1987, Reception)

On the whole, by the end of the spring term of William' first year at school, although Mrs Powell still found William strong-willed and difficult to discipline, he was clearly beginning to acknowledge teacher authority and accommodate teacher expectations alongside his own enjoyment of school life. His mother recorded in the diary during the spring term that William was always keen to return to school after the holidays and see his friends again. He continued, each morning, to 'rush into school without a backward glance' (parent diary, February 1988).

At the end of his first year of schooling William received a very positive report from Mrs Powell. Among other things, she recorded that he was now trying to write independently, could spell some words correctly and that he knew most initial sounds. He was reading with understanding and was making good progress with his maths. He took an intelligent interest in class topics and had a good vocabulary and general knowledge and contributed to class discussion.

How, though, did William see himself at this stage in his career? He was certainly consciously beginning to shape and articulate an identity and status as a pupil, as his mother recorded in the diary:

William has become very aware over recent months as to how he looks and will only wear certain clothes. He gets very upset if the right clothes are not washed and ready when he wants to wear them.
(Parent diary, February 1988, Reception)

Broadly speaking William does not often compare himself with his classmates. One exception to that is that he has always told us he is one of the fastest runners in his class . . .

William also claims to be one of the best readers in the class and he says that only Robert and Sally are ahead of him. He does seem to take quite a lot of pride from the fact he is ahead of most of the class in reading.

The week before our holiday William made a comment about who he sat with for school dinner. He said that a lot of the other children liked to sit next to him and next to Richard. He quite definitely puts himself and Richard in a position of being popular with their classmates.

(Parent diary, July 1988, Reception)

We can conclude, then, that despite some early setbacks and upsets, that, at this early point in his career William was developing a positive self-image both as a pupil and within the peer culture.

Home and family relationships in Reception

Further evidence relating to William's strategies for learning at that time was accumulated through interviews with his parents. For example, they were asked by Andrew Pollard about the way in which William approached new learning or social situations.

Mr Patterson:	It is difficult to say. In some respects he tends to be a little wary.
Mrs Patterson:	Yes, I would say so too.... Do you remember when he saw that magician. There it was something totally new. He was totally wrapped up in it. He was calling out and wanted to be the one to assist and so on. Yet occasionally he will completely retire and not want to stand up and be seen or heard or anything.
Mr Patterson:	As a rule, normally he meets challenges fairly well. Almost unpredictably, I don't know why, just very occasionally he will back off and go into himself.
Mrs Patterson:	Like with a new toy, for example, Polydron, which now he loves and is brilliant at. But Christmas Day when he got it there were a few tears and a few upsets ...
Mr Patterson:	... because he couldn't put it together.
Mrs Patterson:	Just that initial grasping of it. Once he had done it he never looked back, but he does get frustrated, doesn't he?
Mr Patterson:	If he can't do something immediately, it is not worth bothering with.
Mrs Patterson:	He will physically throw it down and burst into tears and get angry. He is not really 'a trier' whereas Abby is ...

(Parent interview, March 1988, Reception)

As we have suggested above in the introduction to the family, William's parents felt it was important to provide a framework and set of principles for their children's development in order that they developed their own identity. For William's father, however, this was no simple matter, as he explained to Andrew Pollard:

Mr Patterson:	I am very conscious that it is easy sometimes to try and mould your children into someone or something that you think they ought to be, and I personally don't find it easy to ensure that your children have the right environment to

develop their own character and their own desires rather than what you think necessarily. I mean, one minor thing, I have always been very keen on sport and nothing would please me more than to find that William is a star cricketer or a star footballer and I tend to spend time with him if he wants to play football and he is quite good at it. But I have to try and stop myself. I have to fight against myself not to put pressures on him already. I have to be careful because I was brought up in an atmosphere like that in a sense. Pressures were brought on to do well at school. I know kids would crack up under that. Fortunately I don't think I did. But I am very conscious that I don't want to put Abigail or William in that situation.

William's mother, on the other hand, found it easier to resist putting pressure on William to achieve. She explained:

Mrs Patterson: I was brought up the opposite. There was never any pressure, never any pressure whatsoever, academically to achieve.
(Parent interview, March 1988, Reception)

While William was enjoying his first year at school, Abigail, his young sister, was rapidly leaving babyhood behind and was now capable of being both a playmate and a rival. William's parents elaborated on the relationship between the two. They told Andrew Pollard:

Mr Patterson: He sometimes feels a little threatened. Strange, some days they play together superbly, quite happily for hours on end and entertain each other. And William appreciates that I think now she is a little bit older she can be a playmate. But other days, particularly if he is tired I think, he . . .
Mrs Patterson: . . . they spark terribly.
Mr Patterson: Yes, they spark each other off.
Mrs Patterson: She is actually extremely verbal already, I mean she is nearly fluent in speech just as he was at that age, so they argue something terrible verbally, because she has got the command of language.
Mrs Patterson: He regards Tony [Mr Patterson] as 'his' after work. And the fact that you helped Abby with that jigsaw – that definitely triggered off that temper tantrum. Do you remember? He was a bit distraught that night generally but that really threw him off balance. If I play with Abby, that is fine, but after work when Daddy comes home, Daddy is his.
Mr Patterson: I think in a sense that generally speaking Abby tends to be a mummy's girl rather than daddy's.
(Parent interview, March 1988, Reception)

Summary of William's Reception year

In trying to summarize William's career at this point we are faced with a picture that is quite complex. In some respects William demonstrated independence and a degree of social confidence quite unusual in a four- or five-year-old, though he also exhibited the sort of unexpected and often inexplicable fears and inhibitions that are normally associated with that age group. His considerable abilities and enthusiasms contrasted with areas of minimal effort or frustrated withdrawal. His popularity, independence and growing classroom status sat uneasily with a friendship choice that sometimes seemed to have an upsetting influence upon him. Overall, we can conclude that, despite some early setbacks and upsets, William was developing a positive self-image both as a pupil and within the peer culture. The latter, though, seemed to be having a particular influence on his sense of himself as a boy and on gender issues generally.

William, Year 1, early days in Miss Scott's class

The move up to a new class in September 1988 meant that William's chronological position changed from being one of the oldest to being 17th in a class of 32. However, in this new mix of pupils, his academic position remained about halfway down the class in English and in maths. As we have seen in Chapter 3 and in Sarah's story, some of the volatile atmosphere in the classroom that year, and some of the shouting that many children were wary of, could be attributed to the fact that Miss Scott felt the need to assert her control of a group of what she saw as 'naughty boys' coming from Mrs Miles' class. Although Miss Scott had a problem with several aspects of William's behaviour in the classroom, she nevertheless did not identify him as among the naughtier element in the class. As she indicated in interview with Andrew Pollard, she clearly also had a good deal of affection for him:

Miss Scott:	One look of his wide eyes and his pixyish face would make any adult dissolve into granting him his wish. I think he was a naughty boy last year, I picked that up talking to Mrs Powell. He has certainly been a bit boisterous. He is a leader as well. He gets everyone going . . .
AP:	But he is pretty confident with friends and . . .?
Miss Scott:	Yes, he is very assured, very noisy, will think up the ideas and get everyone else doing them, but William is not a fast worker and he will quite happily, like Richard and Daniel to that extent, take quite a long time doing work.
AP:	A going-slow tactic is it?
Miss Scott:	With William, yes. Possibly not with the others. William I think is quite devious. I think he is . . . very attuned.
AP:	Does he sort of play for laughs at all?
Miss Scott:	He probably thought he was quite a laugh, a character. He has actually matured quite a lot but perhaps I am hard on him. My expectation of middle infants is that they have got to grow up and unfortunately they have to grow up quite quickly these days. He can work well but he doesn't really put his mind to it. He has definitely got a better brain than he shows.

(Teacher interview, November 1988, Year 1)

In his classroom relationship with Miss Scott and with his peers, William certainly appeared very assured. Miss Scott commented in her records that first term:

William is often at the centre of some distracting activity. Usually with his friend Richard who gravitates towards him. Confident and outward going, friendly with

relationships well established, he can be quite a strong-willed child insisting on his own innocence even when obviously at the centre of some argument. A leader of his own group of younger boys. Apt to do his own thing.
(Miss Scott, teacher records, November 1988, Year 1)

William continued, then, to display a strong-willed, confident manner, even in the more challenging environment of Miss Scott's class. However, as an interview with William and his friends showed, in his relationship with her he often operated on a knife edge of fear and bravado.

AP:	What happens when you get told off?
Maurice:	It hurts you inside like you're going to cry . . .
William:	I just say 'Naa na-na naa naa, you're not going to tell me off.' You sort of look at your friends and laugh.
Liam:	It feels like your heart is melting when Miss Scott is horrible. She tells me off even when I haven't done it.
William:	I feel like I'm going to run away but I daren't and I'm still looking at Miss Scott and if I laugh she says: 'How dare you!'

(Pupil interview, April 1989, Year 1)

Friendships and peer relationships in Year 1

During Year 1, Stephen joined William's group of friends and along with Richard soon acquired the status of 'best friend'. In his relations with girls, however, William was experiencing more ambivalent feelings, frequently complaining at home that they were 'bossy'. As Mrs Patterson explained to Andrew Pollard:

We'd had some comments about girls and he'd just written them off, 'I don't play with girls any more'. And yet in his first [Reception] year he had quite a few girls that he would call his friends as well. On that Monday morning Miss Scott wasn't in the classroom and I just walked in with him and he was immediately greeted by about four of the other boys, 'William, you're back', and all this sort of thing. But immediately about four girls rushed towards him as well, which really quite surprised me, and they were all sort of 'oh, hello, hello' and all that.
(Mrs Patterson, parent interview, July 1989, Year 1)

Though denying that he played with girls, William continued to play 'kiss chase' and, in interview with his friends, claimed Hannah as his girlfriend.

Despite the numerous brushes with his teachers, it was becoming apparent that William was really quite keen to protect his interests and steer clear of trouble if he possibly could. It was therefore unfortunate that his friends were not quite as astute as William at reading social situations and extricating themselves from trouble:

Mrs Patterson:	There was an incident, I only have the story directly from William so I can't quote it as fact, but from William it was that there was this heavy stone that was used for weighing apparently. Anthony picked it up, passed it to Richard, Richard passed it to him. He claims he told Richard, 'No, I don't want it, Miss Scott will be cross', but an accident happened and Edmund was hit on the head with it. Fortunately, it

	didn't cut, he was OK. But Miss Scott was obviously quite cross about it.
AP:	But William was left holding the rock, was he?
Mr Patterson:	He was left holding it, and he genuinely claims to me that he didn't want any part of it and he knew that they shouldn't be touching it. Now whether that's just because he actually had his antennae going and he knew Miss Scott was going to be coming in there. He couldn't have foreseen the accident happening but he knew if he landed up with it he was going to get into trouble.
AP:	Yes, I'm sure I've seen that before in different incidents where he's seen trouble brewing and tried to get out of it and not been able to do it because some of his friends, who are not quite so canny, were rumbling him into it.

(Parent interview, July 1989, Year 1)

Learning strategies in Year 1

William continued to vary his responses and enthusiasms for school tasks. In interview with his friends, he was asked by Andrew Pollard what he thought about schoolwork:

> Writing is boring and sometimes I start and think and get daydreaming and it's dinner time and then its boring again because you have to keep it neat and because you have to keep on thinking of words and no-one tells you and it goes on and on. I hate construction because you don't get any work done and when your Mum and Dad come there's nothing to see.
> (William, pupil interview, May 1989, Year 1)

In contrast to this last statement, the reports to his parents state clearly enough that William '. . . enjoys all activities, especially construction' (Report, spring 1989) and 'takes a great interest in creative activities, especially construction' (Report, summer 1989). Perhaps William's response here indicates that he was beginning to perceive that there were extrinsic rewards to be gained from classwork as well as the reward of intrinsic interest. For example, as well as the parental esteem which might be gained from filling books, there was also, in maths and reading, the status of classroom gradings to motivate William.

> Maths is brilliant and reading. Some [maths tasks] are fun and some aren't and you try to get on to the different stages. I'm on stage 8.
> (William, pupil interview, May 1989, Year 1)

So, by the middle of Year 1, William seemed to be settling into and more readily accepting the work patterns expected by the school and his parents. By the end of the spring term, Miss Scott considered that he was growing in maturity. Although he was still likely to be at the centre of some distracting activity, he was more ready to accept responsibility for his behaviour and lack of concentration than previously. However, it was clear to his parents that though William enjoyed school, there had been, especially in the first term of Year 1, indications that perhaps all was not quite as well as it might be for William.

As in Reception, however, these small perturbations rumbled on for a considerable time with no definite indications of what might be the trouble. Mr and Mrs Patterson picked up the story, as illustrated in the following section.

Home and family relationships in Year 1

In the first interview of the autumn term of Year 1, William's parents discussed with Andrew Pollard some changes in their son's response to school that year:

> I would say for the first two weeks he said very little about the transitions into a new class. He certainly never ever hesitated about going to school and then gradually it began to creep in, comments like 'It's harder work', 'It's boring', 'It's all work, there is no play, we don't have planning and we don't do this'. Nothing in fact too serious. I probed a little bit to see who he was mixing with, what he was doing and so on.
> (Mrs Patterson, parent interview, November 1988, Year 1)

William's parents were also slightly concerned about his academic progress in his new class and the autumn term parents' evening gave them a chance to consult Miss Scott about their worries.

> We were a bit worried about, basically, how he had settled back in and we were a bit worried about how his reading was going and his writing was going and from what Miss Scott told us, in fact, both of those are going quite well, particularly the reading. But the writing isn't perhaps as bad as we thought it was at all.
> (Mrs Patterson, parent interview, November 1988, Year 1)

However, they were not reassured simply by being informed by Miss Scott that William's academic progress was satisfactory. Their perceptions of Miss Scott, their ability to relate to her, discussions with other parents and with William and their own observations of William all worked together over that term to convince them that there was little to worry about:

> Mr Patterson: She was very reassuring and I quite took to Miss Scott, possibly because she was so positive, I don't know. I found her quite an open sort of person to talk to.
>
> Mrs Patterson: I think she got William sussed out quite quickly. She said he'd sort of settled down and definitely wasn't mixing with the naughty core of kids. From his side, he went through a bit of a phase of 'Miss Scott shouts a lot and he was getting a little bit upset. The noise levels were a bit high in the classroom I think. I sort of said 'Is it at you?', and he said 'No, no it is . . .', and he named some of the naughtier lads in the class. The very few times I have observed him with her, he has no hesitation about going up to her and approaching her. You can see that he is very direct. There is no reticence on his side to approach her. He must have a rapport well enough with her to be able to do that. My own sort of summary in as much as I've spoken with other parents, who have perhaps found her more difficult, is that if he can survive her class fairly intact, then I've got no worries about any other teachers he's ever going to have, I think he'll cope with them extremely well . . .
>
> (Parent interview, November 1988, Year 1)

Having satisfied herself that there was no serious cause for concern, William's mother helped him to adjust to and accept Miss Scott's volatility by interpreting it in everyday, unthreatening terms. She told Andrew Pollard:

> Mrs Patterson:　　I just say to him, well, look, imagine I was teacher, I'd get in a bad mood with you sometimes. I just try and bring her on to a human level to him, and say all of us have rotten days, rotten tempers, rotten moods. Some teachers are more motherly than others. I think he's weathered her really well, as well as probably any of them have.

(Parent interview, November 1988, Year 1)

William's mother's confidence in his ability to manage his relationships with teachers was also founded on her growing perception of him as confident and knowledgeable about people and events around the school generally. He would, for example, give his mother graphic descriptions of other classrooms and Mrs Patterson was surprised to observe his lack of inhibition in approaching other teachers in the school.

During the school year, it was apparent that William continued to be style-conscious, now wanting his hair spiked and gelled, which his parents did not allow, and insisting on having brightly patterned shorts for the summer. Another change in William was in his 'stickability', his mother thought. In contrast to his approach to many creative tasks in school, he now showed greatly increased persistence and increasingly imaginative and creative skills at home, in model-making especially. Also, while he continued to dislike writing in school, he was finding it less of a chore at home. There he would spontaneously write the occasional story, and got much excitement from making a little book as a surprise for his father.

Summary of William's Year 1

In the classroom and playground, William clearly survived and acquired status and the esteem of peers and adults, not least through the use of his considerable social skills. William's parents felt that he had had a good year and were happy about the progress he was making. If there were areas where it was felt more effort was needed, his mother was quite relaxed about that, feeling that he still had plenty of time to grow up. In relation to those areas, however, the evidence suggests that William was beginning to make up for his early minimalistic approach by becoming motivated by extrinsic rewards. There was thus some orientation towards tasks as 'products' with enjoyment gained from them in terms of achieving new 'stages' and parental approval.

William's identity and career in the early years at Greenside School

Some of the contradictions and complexity evident at the end of the Reception year appeared to be resolved at this point in William's story and his identity as a young pupil can begin to be sketched out and perhaps also a career trajectory suggested by the evidence gathered. To assist the interpretation, it is perhaps useful for the reader here to recall and contrast this stage in the career of Sarah.

Sarah was very close in age to William and occupied a similar academic position in the class. The similarities end there though, for it will be recalled, at this point in her career, Sarah's struggles and successes were contextualized largely within the patterns of expectations and structures made available to her by others, whether her family, school or peers. The picture that we have built up of William's identity and career to date is rather different. We get a strong sense in which, at the age of six, he was creating his own patterns of success. He was certainly mindful of the expectations of adults in his life and his growing social awareness meant, it seems, that he was beginning to perceive the opportunities for classroom status and parental esteem through academic success. Sarah's desire to earn status and esteem, it will be recalled, was being played out on the home front at this time rather than in the classroom. However, William's emerging bid for status in the classroom was frequently in conflict with other aims, and the culture of the peer group, his status within it and pursuance of his own interests were strong counter-attractions. At this point in his career, the extent to which the patterns William was creating would be successful seemed to hinge on his continuing ability to reconcile those competing interests. Could he contrive to develop and manage a positive status with his teachers, parents and peers, and satisfy his own interests?

5.2   YEAR 2, YEAR 3 AND YEAR 4

Introduction

At the beginning of his third year of schooling William, along with the rest of his year group, was to encounter a new teacher appointed by Mrs Davison and espousing her commitment to active learning and a negotiated curriculum. As we shall see, it precipitated a phase in his career as a pupil at Greenside in which his regular teachers would now more closely reflect the new ethos of the school.

We have seen in the previous chapter that William's emerging bid for academic status had previously been played out against the strong counter-attractions of his own interests and social aims. Readers who have understood something of the classroom expectations of Mr Brown and Miss King, for example, might like to speculate on William's strategies within the new ethos. For example, how would his sense of autonomy in the classroom and his variable responses and enthusiasms sit alongside the need for pupils to take more responsibility upon themselves for learning? How would William, 'often at the centre of some distracting activity', respond to *expectations* that pupils interact with other pupils?

It will be recalled that the cohort of children being studied were split into two classes in Year 2. Thus, when Sarah went into Miss George's class, William moved into Miss Sage's class, where we now continue his story.

Matrix 5.1 *William, Reception and Year 1, a summary matrix*

Family relationships	Peer-group relationships	Teacher relationships	Identity	Career
Reception: Mrs Powell				
William has a sister Abigail who is three years younger.	William's parents worry that he may be vulnerable to peer pressure.	Structural position: among the oldest few. Maths and English, halfway down the class.	Confidence high, though not predictably so.	Considerable ability and enthusiasms contrasted with frequently minimalistic approach to tasks and withdrawal.
His parents have strong Christian convictions.	He is popular and willing to lead or follow others.	Entered school full of confidence.	Popular with adults and children.	
Parents try to avoid putting pressure to succeed on children.	Some clashes with best friend Richard. Both are 'strong personalities', their teacher says.	'Played' for the first term with no concentration on work.	Teacher sees him as 'Nice' 'Silly' 'A bit tough' 'Strong-willed'.	Strives for autonomy in teacher–pupil relationship.
Mother taught William to read before school.	Picks up definite ideas about appropriate gender behaviour at school.	Minimalist approach to writing and rushes through artistic-creative tasks.	Difficult to discipline.	Concerned to avoid trouble with his teacher.
He sometimes withdraws from situations he does not grasp immediately.	Likes to get the class laughing.	'Doesn't see why anyone should tell him what to do'.	Likes to create laughter in the classroom.	Attains status in the peer group.
			Consciously beginning to shape and articulate a positive self-image as a pupil.	
Year 1: Miss Scott				
Parents concerned over William's progress. Reassured by Miss Scott.	Richard and Stephen are his best friends.	Structural position: age, halfway down class. Maths and English, about halfway down.	Seen as confident and outward-going by his teacher.	Began to show a tendency to be motivated by extrinsic rewards and develop a 'product' orientation to school tasks.
Some complaints from William about school and his teacher shouting.	Complaints at home about girls at school being 'bossy', but he relates well to them.	William says writing is 'boring' but maths is 'brilliant' because of trying to get on to different stages.	Seen by his teacher as 'a bit devious'.	
Mother explains teachers' 'moods' and is satisfied he can handle the relationship.	William's friends are not so astute at disengaging from trouble as he is.	Often distracted in class.	Dominant with peers.	Willingness to strive for status with peers and within the family becoming apparent.
Showing increased 'stickability' at home.		Claims to hate construction equipment 'because there is nothing for Mum and Dad to see when they come into school!'.	Socially astute.	
Occasional 'flare-ups' between William and Abigail.			His social identity is seen as a hindrance to learning.	Able to read social situations to protect his own interests.
			Confident in his approach to teachers.	Despite problems, William continues to enjoy school.

William, Year 2, early days in Miss Sage's class

Miss Sage, like all of the teachers from the children's Year 2 onwards, was part of the new influx of teachers described in Chapter 3. These teachers had been appointed since the new headteacher, Mrs Davison, had come to the school and were generally supportive of the changes taking place. Though their approaches and expectations differed slightly, all aimed to create classrooms in which active and interactive learning could take place.

In Year 2, William was chronologically about two-thirds down the class. In contrast to this lower structural position which his age gave him, by the end of the year his attainment in maths and English relative to this new mix of peers was higher, at a third down the class.

William had not been long in Miss Sage's class before his parents were aware of a change in him. Mrs Patterson told Andrew Pollard:

> It's not even quite a whole term yet, but I think I could say already he is a lot more relaxed and happy again about school compared to last year. Although actually during last year I wouldn't have said it was desperately negative, now you've got a contrast, I would say he is happier again, definitely, and I'm sure it does have a lot to do with the teacher. I think he coped all right last year, but I don't think he particularly enjoyed it. He positively, I think, enjoys school again.
> (Mrs Patterson, parent interview, December 1989, Year 2)

During the year, William developed a close rapport with Miss Sage. With her encouragement, he began to give more time and attention to his writing. This extract from Andrew Pollard's fieldnotes and the writing referred to in it (Documents 5.1 and 5.2) confirm the rapid development during the early weeks in her class:

> His book shows rapid development during the term. A few lines on September 5th to more complete and longer stories now. When questioned about this change William responded '. . . after a bit Miss Sage told me to do a bit more. So I decided I would and I decided I'd do it a bit neater too. So I did. And Stephen and I did a really good story about Mr Belly Button which was great.'
> (Fieldnotes, Andrew Pollard, October 1989, Year 2)

William's approach to artistic pursuits in the classroom remained minimalistic, however. Though he was regarded by Miss Sage as capable of detailed and accurate representation, he seldom devoted sufficient care or time to them.

Friendships and peer relationships in Year 2

William continued to be scathing about girls, both at home and in the school context and, his mother reported, he tended to dismiss their achievements as if they did not count. He continued to deny any association with them:

AP:	Who don't you play with?
William:	Girls, because they're bossy. They make us clean up mess. Trying to be the best and being pretty and doing their hair up and playing with My Little Pony and that, and dolls.

This is Harry. He
can get Dabby [Daddys] Slipuss [slippers].
and it can Get dinu [dinner] Redy [ready].
and he can Reed [read] a Book.

✓

Tuesday 5th
September.

Document 5.1 *William, Year 2, 'Harry' (September 1989)*

> They're not very good. I'd much rather play with some technical Lego.
>
> (Friendship group interview, April 1990, Year 2)

Given William's status consciousness in the classroom, the dismissing of their achievements and the accusation here of 'trying to be the best' suggests that he may have felt a little threatened by the success of girls at school – as he was by his sister's achievements at home. 'Kiss chase' was still played with the girls, however, and William continued to be an active participant in that game.

Though for most of the year William's friendships remained stable, by the end of Year 2 they were about to undergo a major upheaval. Richard, who had been his best friend for three years, left the school and the attachment to his other close friend, Stephen, was loosening. It is also at this point in the story that we begin to pick up on events in the life of Daniel, whose early years featured in *The Social World of Children's Learning*. At this point in Daniel's story, he was worried that all *his* friends were leaving and that he would have no-one to play with in the following year. Mrs Patterson described to Andrew Pollard her understanding of William's new friendship alliance.

> It seems to be quite a recent thing, he suddenly seems to have latched on to Daniel again. I like Daniel, he's a nice little boy. He said, 'I think he's going to be my best friend next term.' He said, 'I still like Stephen. Stephen really likes Ian now, Stephen gets on better with Ian.' 'We still play together', he said, but he seems to have paired Stephen and Ian off slightly. I think with the idea of Richard having left now, he realizes that's what's going to happen.
>
> (Mrs Patterson, parent interview, July 1990, Year 2)

Tuesday 10th october

Magic Belly Button

The malik belly butun [Magic]

In 1980 I went too a iints [giants]

house for tea. and wen I got [when]

thre I saw a nalik belly butun. [there] [that the giant had] [Magic] [button]

and I got a ladur and I poot the [ladder] [put]

ladur up agenst his legos and I [ladder] [against] [legs]

Srtid to Klim up the ladur and I [started] [climb] [ladder]

prest his belly butun and gese [pressed] [button] [guess]

wot hapend. out his belly butun [what] [happened] [of] [button]

came my tea. I cood nt [couldn't]

boollev my Ieys then ι [believe] [eyes]

ett it up [ate]

then ι climd down the [climbed]

ladur and ran home and I tolld [ladder]

my mummy all abat it. at [about]

bed time ι went to bed olly [early]

and nest day ι went to [the] [next]

the prek. [part]

✓

Document 5.2 *William, Year 2, 'The Magic Belly Button' (October 1989)*

Learning strategies in Year 2

It was suggested in Part One that despite some early concerns regarding his relationships with teachers and with peers, William was developing a positive image of himself as a pupil. Part of this positive image resided in his high status among his peers, and also, by the third year of his schooling, William was elaborating this identity with a description of himself as 'clever' and a 'good worker'. Andrew Pollard asked William and his friend Stephen what they thought about school:

William:	I love school.
Stephen:	I think the opposite. I hate it. I only like reading and maths 'cos I'm one of the highest.
William:	We are good, 'cos we are on the library – any book in the school. We read things quite serious. Famous Five is great. *Smugglers Top* is the best story of the Famous Five – it's really good. In *Five on Treasure Island* the girls think the dungeons are haunted.
AP:	Do you like learning new things?
William:	I'm really clever so I like to. I've got real clever as I've got older because I do more work as I get older and in Class 1 there's not much work, 3 more, 4 and you work harder and when we go into class 6 [Year 3] we'll be doing work all day every day and no play at all. We love working anyway. I don't like being *told* to write about things. I like writing when I can choose what to write.

(Friendship group interview, May 1990, Year 2)

In this last comment we can see that the sense of autonomy that Miss Powell and Miss Scott had found troublesome was still active in William's approach to classroom tasks but it was now rewarded.

In the light of this fairly persistent characteristic of William's ('he wants to do what *he* wants to do'), his response to the new events of the summer of 1990 may seem strange. During that summer term, Miss Sage had a prolonged period of sick leave and for three months Miss Jones, a supply teacher, took over the running of her class. Miss Jones taught in a way that was in all respects the opposite of that which was expected of Greenside teachers. Thus children had few decisions to make with respect to the content of tasks, or with respect to how or when they might do them. The goals, rather, were very specific, non-negotiable and decided by Miss Jones. The ideals of active enquiry and cooperation in learning were therefore absent from the classroom for much of that term. William was asked what his teachers thought about how well he had done in Year 2:

> They'd say I've worked well. Maybe not as well as some other people, but I've worked well. Miss Sage doesn't mind us having a bit of fun. It doesn't stop me doing my work. I liked the work Miss Jones gave me and I tried my best – and we got kept in just 'cos we hadn't finished it. She does it the old-fashioned way. I learned quite a lot [but] I like Miss Sage.
> (William, pupil interview, July 1990, Year 2)

Mrs Patterson also recounted William's response to the new regime in the classroom.

Mrs Jones came I think and, as I said, he had a real grumble for the first day or two, 'All work'! 'We're not allowed to play, we're not allowed to do this'. Yet very quickly he turned that completely on its head and said, 'Cor, I did this and this today', 'Miss Sage's going to be really surprised when she comes back and sees how much work I've done in my books'. And he actually turned it all really positively, didn't he, and he even brought a few things home to do sometimes to finish, and in fact, I felt, he rather thrived under being disciplined and being taught traditionally although I think he would perhaps like it tempered a little bit occasionally, with a bit more lightheartedness and a bit of easing up occasionally. I think towards the end of having her, I think he was getting a little bit tired of it, possibly because she wasn't really exactly an extrovert, I don't think you could have a joke with her.
(Mrs Patterson, parent interview, July 1990, Year 2)

In William's enthusiastic response to the opportunity to 'fill lots of books', we have echoes of his perceptions in Year 1, that this would be pleasing for his parents. However, there was also a problem for William in this approach because, within the more formal structuring of tasks and of relationships which it required, he was unable to develop the sort of jokey, relaxed rapport that he had had with his regular teacher. It is interesting, as this account shows, that at least some of the motivation for filling books comes from his anticipation of the return of Miss Sage and his perception of what *she* will think of it.

By the end of the summer term Miss Sage had returned and William immediately picked up on the rapport that had been established before her absence. It was also beginning to become clear that his preferred way of relating to teachers was increasingly through a relaxed, informal approach. Though this was clearly more realizable with the new influx of teachers than it had been in the past, as Mrs Patterson described, William was still learning that there were boundaries to the acceptability of this approach:

It was the very day she was back, the first day back, and William had a sort of light-hearted conversation with her in the corridor which ran something like, she was pretending not to be Miss Sage, he was pretending that he'd gone to the classroom and she wasn't there, and so on and he related quite a lengthy conversation. The problem was he didn't know when to cut off and then went to Mrs Madders (the deputy head at the time) as if to continue the joke, and Mrs Madders was not amused, and so she, not literally, slapped him on the wrist and said, 'Enough. Go back to your classroom'.

He's approached Mr Brown already a few times, his next teacher. I said to him, 'Have you chatted with Mr Brown again', and he said, 'Oh, yes, I chatted with him yesterday'. 'What were you saying to him this time?' and he said 'Oh, I just thought I'd ask him what we'd be doing next year and what sort of things we'd be learning.' And he did a sort of imitation facial grimace. Apparently Mr Brown said 'We'll just have to wait and see' and walked off. But it was the way he'd actually imitated the facial expression as well as the way he's said it.
(Mrs Patterson, parent interview, July 1990, Year 2)

Home and family relationships in Year 2

During William's early years of schooling, his mother was continuing to help his learning with the relaxed approach established before he began school. She described to Andrew Pollard how learning spellings was often made into a family game:

> His spelling is coming on quite well. I'll say to him, 'Spell so and so', and he loves it if I trick him. Like today I said, 'Spell pneumatic' and immediately he said 'N' and I said, 'Neh, caught you out' because he was catching Abigail out, you see, and I immediately caught him out, and I mean, that's just a game and he enjoys that. I think they remember more through trial and error than they do through just learning it absolute sort of verbatim.
> (Mrs Patterson, parent interview, December 1989, Year 2)

As he had done in Year 1, William continued to entertain his parents with descriptions of places he'd seen. His father explained to Andrew Pollard:

> And he will talk non-stop. The last couple of times he went with a birthday party do, they went to Casey's at South Bay. It's *the* place to go apparently if you are six or seven, and he can talk about that and give you a vivid description of every corner of the place for about ten minutes solid. He can come back and he'll describe something in minute detail, and actually it normally is a pretty good description.
> (Mr Patterson, parent interview, July 1989, Year 2)

William's parents considered that there was an element of 'holding the stage' in William's descriptive accounts to them, that he was, as well as sharing his experiences, also using them as an audience. This was also apparent in some of the games he devised at home:

Mrs Patterson:	He's very creative at the moment, in lots of ways. He's doing a lot of just model-making, cardboard and bits of rubbish, that sort of side of thing. He's into putting on puppet shows for us. He's into – what was it the other day? You had a magic session with him, didn't you. He was the magician sort of thing, and woe betide you if you let on that you know what he's up to.
Mr Patterson:	He had some lumps of cardboard a week ago and he and Abby turned them into a little castle with sort of castellations, and everything.

(Parent interview, December 1989, Year 2)

William's mother expressed pleasure at the continuing improvement in his creativity at home that year, though it remained that William put comparatively little emphasis upon such tasks at school.

At the point of William's entry into school, it will be remembered, his parents had little knowledge of the new educational system being introduced at Greenside and no preconceived expectation about its suitability for William. At the end of his first term in Year 2, his mother reported that she was very impressed by the school. She worked in the school as a 'mother helper' one morning a week and found its atmosphere very friendly. She observed that the whole of the infant corridor had the doors open very often and the children were not noisy and they appeared to be getting on. She also expressed appreciation of the warmth of the relationship between Miss Sage and William (Parent interview, December 1989, Year 2).

At the end of his career as an infant at Greenside, William's mother concluded:

William has definitely matured and progressed in his work in school and his whole personality. He remains very happy in school and looks keenly forward to September and life as a junior.
(Parent diary, June 1990, Year 2)

Summary of William's Year 2

By the end of his Year 2 at school it is clear that William had experienced two distinct routes to esteem and classroom status. He had learnt to please and to achieve firstly through a product-orientated concern with completing his work and notching up grades and levels. This motivational system, drawing largely on *extrinsic* rewards and satisfactions, was a highly competitive one. However, he had also learnt to gain esteem and status through rapport and negotiation with teachers and achievement through *intrinsic* satisfaction of tasks, notably writing. William responded to and could successfully operate within either of these motivational systems, and he saw himself as 'clever' and a good worker under both. The former system, that of extrinsic rewards, was effective in that William was both academically able and keen to achieve the rewards of esteem and status that it offered. When intensively applied under the authority and social distancing maintained by Miss Jones, however, though enjoyed for a while, it was beginning to pall for William before she left. On the other hand, the latter system, with its greater space for autonomous development and intrinsic satisfaction, matched the experience which his parents aimed to provide at home. It also drew on and fostered the 'communicator' identity that was emerging in his relationships both at home and at school. The latter rested on positive, affective relationships between teacher and taught, and it appeared to be the means by which William was actively negotiating and elaborating a distinctive pupil identity.

William, Year 3, early days in Mr Brown's class

In Year 3, the cohort of children being studied came together again in Mr Brown's class where William was the 19th oldest of 23 in the class and within the top third for maths, science and English. Readers will have some familiarity with Mr Brown's classroom practice and expectations from Sarah's story and from the description in Chapter 3. In contrast with the way he related to Sarah whom, he confessed, he never got to know well, Mr Brown was to find William almost the ideal pupil for him. We have seen above that William had decided that in Year 3 Daniel was to be his best friend, and indeed they were to work and play closely together for that whole year. Here is Mr Brown giving his impression to Andrew Pollard of the working relationship at the beginning of the new school year:

> Daniel, yeah. He's very pally with William Patterson. They are both very noisy when they first come in, William particularly. But Daniel has amazed me with some of his work, there's a lot more there than it seems, he's just silly sometimes, that's all. I think being with William does him a lot of good because William is very bright and full of ideas.
> (Mr Brown, teacher interview, September 1990, Year 3)

Indeed, over the year, Mr Brown was to become so impressed with the success of the working relationship that, later that year in interview with Ann Filer, he admitted that he had been surprised to discover that it was a new one:

> I'll probably talk about them together, because they go everywhere together – apparently last year that wasn't the case. The way they've been this year I imagine that they've been friends for so long because they work together in such a similar way, they like to talk about what they're doing all the time.
> (Mr Brown, teacher interview, July 1991, Year 3)

Friendships and peer relationships in Year 3

Alongside this new friendship with Daniel, the old one with Stephen was still alive, and though William and Stephen had much less association than previously, it seems that William was still forging a peer identity in the context of that friendship. Here is William talking in interview with Ann Filer and his friends Daniel, Stephen and Ian:

> William: When we're together [Stephen and I] we go mad.
> At this point in the interview, William and Stephen become full of reminiscences of when they used to play together last year – 'Do you remember when . . .' playground stories. The boys refer to themselves as 'the terrible two' and at one point William refers to himself as 'a jester'.
> AF: Where did you get this idea of being a jester?
> William: That's what everybody calls me. Stephen and Daniel are jesters as well. Stephen most. Stephen and me are brilliant jesters. Stephen and me are the most famous jesters in the school. Daniel gets a bit upset at that, when we say that.
> William goes on to explain about teaching each other to be jesters, saying things backwards, silly voices, gestures, mimes.

This friendship group interview seemed to have had the effect of bringing the two boys closer together again. When asked to compare their infant experience with that as a junior, Stephen remarked:

> Stephen: I preferred the infants 'cos I had William and I've lost him now.
> William: Not from this moment you haven't!
> Some discussion follows about who William likes best, Daniel or Stephen. This is quite good-natured between Daniel and Stephen.
> (Friendship group interview, July 1991, Year 3)

As readers of *The Social World of Children's Learning* may recall, at the end of Year 3 Daniel was removed from Greenside School by his parents, who were unhappy about the lack of traditional teaching there. This left the way open for William and Stephen to re-establish their old friendship which was to be maintained throughout the remainder of their time at the school.

During Year 3, as well as having a new friendship with Daniel, William also entered a new phase in his relationships with girls. For the first time since his early days at school he was now ready to acknowledge them as friends. He was prepared to go to girls' birthday parties and was even happy to go to Sarah's as the only boy present, for, despite the shifting group allegiances and their very different classroom strategies, William and Sarah were consistently good friends throughout their primary school careers. Always able to select his companions for work and play, William and his friends began to be associated with a group of high-status girls in the class led by Sally and Hannah (see Sarah's story). Indeed William was now beginning to acquire a reputation among his peers and former friends for being rather exclusive in his friendship choices, as Maurice, for example, described to Ann Filer:

> William and Daniel think they are Mr Smart Guys and they go around 'Blah, blah, blah' and they say 'Go away' (with a push on the shoulder).
> (Maurice, friendship group interview, July 1991, Year 3)

Learning strategies in Year 3

The communicator, negotiator identity that we saw coming to the fore in William's relationships in Year 2 was actively encouraged in the classroom in Year 3. From what readers already know of Mr Brown's pedagogy, and from his remarks below, it is clear that he saw interaction, both with peers and with himself, as integral to the learning process.

> William is very loud, that's the biggest thing, it's trying to quieten him down but he's a bit like Robert, he's an 'ideas man' and thinks hard about things. He's buzzing with ideas, they come shooting out at all times. Wrong times! But very much an original thinker I'd say. He's always saying, 'Why can't we do this? Why don't we do that?', which is nice. If I throw things back at the class and say 'How are we going to solve this problem?', those are the two who I would expect to come up with the answer first.
> (Teacher interview, October 1990, Year 3)

Clearly then, through being able to give expression to his *social identity* in the carrying out of classroom tasks in Mr Brown's class, William was further able to establish his *academic identity* and reputation as 'a good worker'. He even began to devote more time and care to artistic, creative pursuits in the classroom, so that Mr Brown was able to report that in those areas of the curriculum he had produced 'interesting, quality work' that year (Report to parents, July 1991). Ann Filer asked William about his perceptions of the year:

AF:	How do you feel that you've got on in the first year of the Juniors, William?
William:	It seems different from the infants. When I was in the infants I thought Class 6 [his present class] grown up. Being in the juniors means working harder. On the first day I got quite a shock because I couldn't do construction and I had to wait for science and even then [when waiting] we couldn't play. Then I found that the work was quite interesting. Mr Brown told me I was the best working boy in the class.

(Pupil interview, July 1991, Year 3)

Home and family relationships in Year 3

William had become increasingly style-conscious with respect to clothes and hair as his school years progressed. This consciousness was perhaps now beginning to be incorporated into a more general image consciousness. Clues to the sort of image William might have been aspiring to came in the 'terrible two', 'jester', 'challenger' identity that was emerging strongly that year, and it is perhaps epitomized in the following observation by his mother in interview with Andrew Pollard:

> He sees himself as a 'cool dude'. He likes going shopping. He loves buying new clothes. He saw a top in Marks & Spencers about four months ago, he was determined he was going to have it. It just *appealed*, you know what I mean? And I noticed, we were all watching André Agassi on the telly and I noticed he had the same style [shirt]. He said 'That's like mine', you know he immediately just weighs it up. Oh, now I mean, he watched quite a bit of the tennis with me because I'm a tennis fan, and I could see in him, he really responded to somebody like Agassi. You could see that he'd sussed out immediately you know, the long hair, and that sort of thing. He could tell he wasn't just a regular sort of straight player and Agassi appealed in that to him.
> (Mrs Patterson, parent interview, July 1991, Year 3)

The element of challenge to authority that was becoming apparent in the classroom, was also manifesting itself at home during the middle years of William's primary career. Always quite difficult to manage, William had become unpredictable in his moods, 'bolshie' and inclined to be verbally aggressive to his mother and his sister (Parent interview, July 1991, Year 3). Though William rarely explicitly apologized for his behaviour or showed remorse, his parents were sure that he knew the limits of acceptable behaviour:

> He'll suddenly creep down and say, 'Um, would you like me to lay the table for you', or ... I mean, it's his way of saying sorry sometimes, but he doesn't like to actually admit it and say it.
> (Mrs Patterson, parent interview, July 1991, Year 3)

In his relations with Abigail, William continued to be proud of her achievements, particularly her reading skills, and interested in them, but also a little threatened by them. Abigail had begun school at Greenside that year, moreover, and William was keen to maintain their differential status:

> There was a lot of first term 'You're in the *infants* and I'm in the *juniors*' type of thing – that seems to have passed. But it's other comments. He was annoyed once they were on the school field for playtimes and she could now, if you like, get at him, as opposed to being in separate playgrounds. I think she annoyed him a bit by trying to sort of want to play with him at playtimes, and that obviously didn't go down well with him.
> (Mrs Patterson, parent interview, July 1991, Year 3)

Summary of William's Year 3

During his time in Mr Brown's class, we can see William's developing pupil identity as a coherent part of his identity as a person. During the middle years of his career he was actively elaborating his social identity around the school, in the playground and at home. In Mr Brown's class, as with Miss Sage, William's social identity increasingly enhanced and promoted his academic status rather than, as in Miss Powell's and Miss Scott's classes, being regarded as a detraction and obstacle to his learning.

William, Year 4, early days in Miss King's class

In Year 4 of his schooling, as on entry to his Reception class, William once more enjoyed the high structural position of being fifth oldest in a class of 30. Now however, as well as a high chronological position, he also had a high academic position relative to his peers, being among the top few in science, English and maths attainment.

On joining Miss King's class, William was surprised to learn that Daniel was not to return to Greenside School. However, as he had predicted, William and Stephen came together as close friends again. This Miss King described to Ann Filer:

> Yes, very clingy, just the two of them. They can work on their own quite well but they like to plan things together, like they did the poster together, thought about what they're doing together. Everything seems to be together really.
> (Miss King, teacher interview, October 1991, Year 4)

William continued to relate well to staff and his new teacher liked him:

> But William is a funny little character. I mean, I like him because he's sarcastic whereas at this age, you know, if you say something sarcastic everyone else just looks at you like you're mad whereas like, William gets the joke.
> He doesn't like being told off though, because a lot of the time he does everything right and he's OK. But if you get on to him about something he gets very, a bit stroppy about it. I mean like today, he was clearing his tray out and I said 'You haven't planned to clear your tray, I've not told you you can have time to clear your tray'. 'Yes, but it was a *mess* and I thought I had five minutes!' He gets very much like that, you know. Quite strong-minded, but nice.
> He's very good at his work. Great at everything, I think – *very* confident. Basically he's nice. I like him. Very intelligent.
> (Miss King, teacher interview, October 1991, Year 4)

Miss King then, appreciated William's personality and enjoyed his presence in the classroom. However, she clearly did not see his social attributes as contributing to learning in quite the same way as Mr Brown had. Indeed, that was probably to some extent because the working relationship with Stephen was not of the same calibre as it had been with Daniel, and while he was allowed to convert his risky, jokey identity into enthusiasm for tasks, this was sometimes carried to excess. As the following fieldnotes suggest, it sometimes interfered with progress:

> William brings me a 'letter to the editor' about improving the environment that he has written:
>
> Dear Mr Editor
> When you sit on the loo I think you should youse an ozone friendly smell tonic. I agree that your old one would help your smell more though.

Yours Baked Beansley
William Patterson

William and Stephen sit on a table for two tucked away in a corner, partly shielded by the piano. William tells me he always works there with Stephen because they 'have a laugh', says they can't have a laugh on some other tables. I ask what Miss King will think of his letter. He says she will like it because she liked another piece of his writing, which he showed me – a story called '*Peter in discrase*' which contains similar lavatorial humour. Later, when children had gone out to play, Nisha (Miss King) saw William's letter. She laughed and said 'William's funny'.
(Fieldnotes, Ann Filer, October 1991, Year 4)

With the adoption of techniques of 'assertive discipline' in the school that year, William was one of the children whose name was often observed to be on 'the bad side' of the board as a warning for transgressing some classroom rule, usually for talking at the wrong time. However, this did not seem to unduly bother him, or his teacher.

Friendships and peer relationships in Year 4

In Year 4, William's social status within the peer group appeared to rise even more with the somewhat exclusive nature of his relationships in the playground extending to working relationships in the classroom. In Interview with Ann Filer, Miss King described William's social status in the classroom:

Miss King:	Yes, they do everything together, William and Stephen. It's basically those two, William and Stephen and then there's Hannah and Sally that come in when they do group activities. No one else. They just don't let anyone else into that twosome. Like this group, he doesn't really talk to this group very much. They're all boys mostly, real big boys' table! Doesn't ever come across here.
AF:	Clearly they haven't got the status of William and....
Miss King:	Very much like on a pedestal, William. Stephen just under. Everyone likes William and Stephen, Sally and Hannah – and there's very much that little group that *everyone* looks up to in the place really.

(Teacher interview, October 1991, Year 4)

The high-status set which broadly centred round William, Stephen, Hannah and Sally was at the same time forging a new identity as a group in the playground as well as in the classroom. It will be recalled that these children had always been among the core players in games of 'kiss chase' in the playground. Increasingly since the children had been in the junior school, these relationships between the sexes were being elaborated by some of the children and William's group were at the cutting edge of these developments. Hazel, Harriet and Ellen, who, as we shall see in Harriet's story, stood firmly apart from this aspect of peer culture, gave Ann Filer their perceptions of the foursome:

AF:	What is William's group like?
Hazel:	[The boys are] naughty and loud.
Harriet:	Snogging and kissing.

Hazel:	Yeah, and girlfriends and inviting each other out to restaurants.
Ellen:	I wouldn't dare say the word actually.
Hazel:	Sexy.
AF:	Why are they sexy?
Harriet:	Because they go like this to each other (*she raises her middle finger, imitating the gesture they use*) and because Stephen and Hannah are in love.

(Friendship group interview, May 1992, Year 4)

The language within this group, and of the children who associated with it in the playground, was of 'love', of 'going out with' and 'dumping', though to be 'going out' with somebody simply appeared to mean that they were currently acknowledged as 'boyfriend' and 'girlfriend' by each other and by the group.

By the end of the spring term however, the group no longer worked together in class so much. Sally, Hannah, and eventually Stephen also, began to drift away from William to work sometimes with other children, sometimes alone, wishing for fewer interruptions. William meanwhile began a new working relationship with Francis. Miss King told Ann Filer:

> When Stephen and William were together, Stephen never did much work, but now he does more. But William seems to quite like being with Francis, although it gets on *my* nerves sometimes, because they're too much the same really I think, and like to chat and that sort of thing.
>
> (Miss King, teacher interview, July 1992, Year 4)

This break in working relationships coincided with the increasing ambivalence on the part of William, Stephen and some others towards William's longstanding friend, Sally. Sally, whose early years story featured in *The Social World of Children's Learning*, had a reputation for being highly competent and, along with her friend Hannah, for a high-profile, 'into everything' approach to school life. Readers may recall (in Sarah's story in this volume) *her* feelings of being overlooked and in the shadow of these friends' careers. William and Stephen expressed some similar resentment towards the girls, and towards Sally in particular, because of their academic rather than their extra-curricular success. This, they felt, had more recognition from Miss King than did their own. They told Ann Filer:

Stephen:	No one in this class is a swot except Sally.
William:	You would say Hannah was a swot as well if she wasn't your girlfriend. She's a swot too.
Gerry:	I work as well as Sally does but I'm not Miss King's pet.
Stephen:	She doesn't check her spellings and she gets away with it.
William:	I was editing Sally's work and she had 'excellent', 'very neat', and it was rubbish.
Stephen:	When she's sick everyone crowds round her. They think: 'Oh Sally is so cute!'
William:	She always gets to do the good stuff as well, like taking display down and not having to finish her work.

(Friendship group interview, May 1992, Year 4)

Now William, for his part, was well liked by Miss King, as we have seen, and he achieved highly in her class. However, he certainly no longer enjoyed the identity of 'best working boy' that he felt that he had held in Mr Brown's class.

William was, as we have seen, conscious of his classroom status both in the eyes of his peers and his teachers, and this, perhaps with the difficulty still of acknowledging the achievements of girls, may well have contributed to this resentment of Sally's success. As readers will see in the final part of William's story, classroom rivalries among these status-conscious children were to surface again in Year 6, but with rather more explosive and enduring effects in the classroom than these relatively harmless background grumblings produced.

Learning strategies in Year 4

Despite the fact that Miss King was, of all William's teachers, especially keen on having a quiet working environment in the classroom, all of the above show that he was able to work in the sociable way he preferred without too much censure from his teacher but also deliver work of a high standard of acceptability. During the year he continued to devote time to careful art work, began violin lessons at school and, because he had a special aptitude for playing, was allowed to join the school orchestra a year early. William, however, was soon feeling somewhat disenchanted with his violin teacher, as Ann Filer recorded during classroom observations:

> William has just come back from violin practice. I ask him how he is getting on and he says 'OK', but complains that his violin teacher wouldn't let him play the tunes he had learnt at home. 'I practised some at home and I wanted to really impress her', William reported. She wouldn't let him play *The First Noel* that he had learnt.
> (Fieldnotes, Ann Filer, January 1992, Year 4)

The problem was that William's rapid progress meant that his teacher, with a group to teach, could not give him the extra attention he needed. She suggested that he would benefit from private lessons, which William began in March that year. In interview with Ann Filer, Mrs Patterson recalled:

> He did go through a terrible show-off stage, sort of 'I'm better than the others and they are holding me back'. He got on the others' nerves because he was getting too big for his boots about it. But he *is* progressing well and he has got some ability. Oh, I mean he had his usual delusions of grandeur straight away – Nigel Kennedy or whatever. He immediately sees himself as Young Musician of the Year or something, but then that's typical William. But then again, why not? If you don't aspire to greatness then, I mean, you're not going to get anywhere.
> (Mrs Patterson, parent interview, July 1992, Year 4)

However, despite his talent for the violin and his initial enthusiasm, his parents were not altogether sure that William would maintain the commitment that would be needed to justify the expense of private lessons.

Over these middle years at Greenside, William had developed from being a reluctant writer with a minimalist approach to a more creative and original one in which, his father perceived, he gave expression to his identity. He told Ann Filer:

> I was intrigued actually, I had a chance to go through some of his work yesterday evening. I noticed in some of his English essays he was creative in almost an over the top way. There were one or two pieces of work which were quite obscure, but very imaginative, I mean some of the spellings were appalling but it's not his strong

point, but certainly in terms of thinking up a story line and something slightly different. His favourite books are like that too. You know, the Narnia books. He's sort of
almost impatient to read Tolkein and things like that. He knows he's not ready for
it, yet he knows it's the sort of book he's going to like, if you know what I mean.
(Mr Patterson, parent interview, July 1992, Year 4)

During the summer term, William was also chosen from his class for the
school's weekly 'Parade of Excellence' in recognition of his writing about a school
trip.

At this time William was beginning to have a strong sense of his own future
and, of all the children in the study, was the one who talked of the future in
terms of targets and goals. He was asked by Ann Filer how he saw the next two
years at the top of the school:

William:	I like being a big one 'cos no one can boss you around. My target is, ever since I started, in class 5 or 6 (Year 2 and 3) to get into Easthampton Grammar School. I'm trying really hard. If I get into a good school we won't move. We want to move but won't if I've put all that hard work in.
AF:	How did you get interested in Easthampton Grammar School?
William:	I heard about the sports centre there and I thought: 'Now's my chance to get really good at sports.' And I saw some leaflets of it. So I've got to work really hard. And I want to get a good job and not be one of those people on the streets. And I want to do really well with my violin. If I carry on I will get no pocket money for all the autumn and nothing for Christmas 'cos it (the next violin) will cost so much.

William chats on about Nigel Kennedy, Kennedy's bowing technique, the possibility
of doing a music degree.
(Pupil interview, July 1992, Year 4)

In his end of year report, in addition to comments on the curriculum areas
already discussed, Miss King also stated that his number work was of a high standard, that he enjoyed and was a good player of team sports and that he was
aware of fairness in team games. She considered that he was a very caring person, helpful and polite in the classroom with a good sense of humour (Report to
parents, July 1992).

Home and family relationships in Year 4

William continued to be creative and resourceful in his play at home and, as the
Pattersons explained to Ann Filer, as Abigail got older, she was increasingly able
to join in:

Mr Patterson:	He's still quite the showman. He'll still put little plays on. He hasn't grown out of that.
Mrs Patterson:	He's still incredibly creative and resourceful, I mean amazingly so to me. He and Abby, 90 per cent of the time get on really well and he's always the 'ideas man' for the latest game. They have this sort of pattern. They start up a game that sort of evolves over a week and then they sort of scrap that one and then they'll start a new one. This week the

house was converted to a travel agency! You never saw anything like it! I mean maps, and his world, and tickets and the lot, money. It's just incredible. It's not just a sort of a trivial surface game, it's immersion. And I mean poor Abby, I mean, she's quite a bright six-year-old but you can imagine can't you? Sometimes you know he gets a bit impatient with her if she hasn't quite caught on with something she's supposed to be doing.

(Parent interview, July 1992, Year 4)

Summary of William's Year 4

Year 4 was another very successful year for William and one in which he was again able to convert his communicator, negotiator identity into enthusiasm for tasks. He was clearly projecting into the future with confidence and had an image of himself as capable of high achievement. As has been evident in the accounts of William's learning over the middle years of his primary school, he had clearly progressed from his early years when his response to classroom activities was variable. William was now clearly working confidently and consistently and was looking forward to Year 5 in which he was again to have Mr Brown for his teacher. There were therefore at this point no indications that William's career would not continue on its now well established path of success.

William's identity and career in the middle years at Greenside School

At the end of William's 'early years' story we posed the question of whether, for William, the culture of the peer group, his status within it and his pursuit of social autonomy could be reconciled with achieving academic status. In the middle years of his primary career William did indeed accomplish that reconciliation, perhaps not least because of the different expectations of the new influx of teachers at Greenside Primary School. During those middle years, William was able to give expression to his social identity in the classroom through his relationships with teachers who appreciated his negotiating, joker style. In addition, his sense of autonomy which so challenged his early teachers was seemingly channelled into more acceptable forms and interpreted differently in contexts in which pupil negotiation of activities and of lesson content was encouraged. For instance, readers might like to consider the contrast between the 'He wants to do what he want to do' autonomous challenge of William as experienced and interpreted by Miss Powell and Miss Scott and the, 'Why can't we do this? Why don't we do that?' challenge as experienced and interpreted positively by Mr Brown. William's relationships with his later teachers and their appreciation of his learning stance afforded William the space in which his enthusiasm and interpersonal involvement were allowed to support his learning, even though these frequently exceeded acceptable noise levels. In this, the matter of allowing children to choose their working companions and negotiate their working relationships with each other was of vital importance to his learning stance. During these years, William was

Matrix 5.2 *William, Years 2, 3 and 4, a summary matrix*

Family relationships	Peer-group relationships	Teacher relationships	Identity	Career
Year 2: Miss Sage				
William is creative and entertaining at home. Mother says she knows nothing of the school's methods but likes the atmosphere there. Difficult to handle, verbally aggressive to mother sometimes. Gets on well with sister but sometimes belittles her still.	At home and in interview William is scathing about girls – their achievements do not count. Continues to be an active participant in 'kiss chase'. Best friend Richard leaves the school at the end of Year 2. William says he will be best friends with Daniel next year.	Structural position: age, two-thirds from top. English and maths, one-third from top. Miss Sage says he has lots of ideas and shares them. Develops a rapport with Miss Sage who encourages him to give more time to his writing. Also enjoys 'filling books' and formal expectations of a supply teacher.	Seen by his teacher as friendly and sensitive. Seen by himself as clever and hard-working. Does not like to be told what to do. 'Showman' at home.	Develops a rapport with his teacher. Writing now rapidly develops. Had experienced two broadly different motivational systems and could operate either successfully. William develops a relaxed, informal approach to teachers around the school.
Year 3: Mr Brown				
At home, can be critical of school organization and teacher strategies. Some concern and loss of sleep over tests. Parents coach to reduce anxiety. Likes to relate to older boys as a matter of status. Style-conscious. Abigail starts school.	Willliam openly acknowledges girls as friends again. William and friends describe selves as 'The Terrible Two' and 'Jesters'. Has a reputation for being exclusive in his friendships. Peers say '… they think they are the Smart Guys'.	Structural position: age, halfway down class. Maths, science, English, in top third of class. Mr Brown enjoys his company and sees him as lively and enthusiastic. Works with Daniel nosily, likes to articulate problems. Challenges teacher with ideas – 'Why don't we …'.	William is seen as 'ideas man' by teacher. *Social* identity enhances his academic identity. Says his teacher regards him as 'best working boy'. 'Jesters'. William's group '… they think they are the Smart Guys'.	William's communicator, negotiator identity seen by his teacher as integral to the learning process. Thus, as in Year 2, social skills were harnessed for the benefit of learning. Ready to challenge authority. Has a strong sense of his future.
Year 4: Miss King				
William is resourceful in imaginative play with sister Abigail. Begins private violin lessons. Parents report 'delusions of grandeur'. High aspirations generally.	William and friends mix with high-status girls, though boys resent girls as 'swots' and 'teacher's pets'. Daniel has left. He works with Stephen to 'have a laugh'. Later Stephen moves seat to get more work done.	Structural position: age, the oldest. Maths, science, English, among the top few. Has a very good relationship with his teacher. Devotes time to careful work, though seen as noisy and gets his name on the board.	Teacher sees him as funny and sarcastic. 'Gets a joke'. 'Stroppy' when told off. 'On a pedestal' with peers. His group described as 'the sexy ones'. Has an image of himself as successful.	William's jokey identity appreciated and he is allowed to convert it into enthusiasm for tasks. Joins school orchestra a year early. Associated with high-status girls.

stimulated and motivated to move beyond the primarily extrinsic satisfactions of filling books and obtaining grades towards a fuller development of his potential, particularly his creative potential, and towards taking an active responsibility for his own learning. In addition those same classroom structures, expectations and relationships with teachers that enabled his academic status to flourish, also provided a context in which he could carve out the peer group status that was so important to him.

Throughout the account of William's early and middle years at Greenside, readers have been able to see him shaping and elaborating his identity in a bid for academic success and classroom status across a range of classroom contexts. Something of the evolution of William's identity becomes apparent in reflecting upon the move, for example, from the early 'difficult to discipline' and 'work avoiding', through 'clever' and 'good worker', to 'communicator', 'negotiator' and 'Jester'. This transition and elaboration of an identity as a pupil can further be contrasted with the more stable, consistent strategies and identity with which Sarah shaped her career.

If change and evolution of identity and strategy marked the career of William in contrast to the continuity which characterized Sarah's, then we might expect that the next and final phase of his career could still hold some surprises. We will next meet William as he begins his Year 5 with Mr Brown as his teacher again.

5.3   YEAR 5 AND YEAR 6

Introduction

In the third part of William's story we see him among the older pupils of Greenside School and in the last phase in his primary career. However, after having been riding on the crest of a wave over the previous three years, William was now faced with a whole new set of challenges.

In Years 5 and 6, William continued to have teachers with similar philosophies with regard to learning processes as those he had had over the middle years and with whom he had worked successfully. Indeed Mr Brown taught him for a second time and, in Year 6, the deputy head Mrs Chard would be his teacher. Of all the teachers at Greenside School, Mrs Chard was the most experienced and perhaps the most able to realize the ideals of the headteacher.

There were, however, some subtle changes in the expectations of these teachers from those that had held in William's middle years. Teacher regard now had to be shared with pupils who had skills and a maturity William did not yet posses and he faced a threat to his accustomed standing in the classroom from older pupils, from girls, and even from some boys within his own friendship group.

As we have seen, William had previously shown a flexible response to teacher expectations. His strategies and, in turn, his social and academic identity had evolved and he had consistently maintained the esteem of both teachers and peers. There was no reason to doubt that he would continue these adept accomplishments through his later years at Greenside.

In the second half of this section we also again make connections with the career of Sally and of Mary whose early years featured in *The Social World of Children's Learning*. Sally's story contains parallels with William's which help elucidate the strategic position and identity associated with *redefining*.

William, Year 5, early days in Mr Brown's class

In the autumn of 1992, William was confidently looking forward to being taught by Mr Brown, having already established a good personal and working relationship with him. A few weeks into the new term Mr Brown, in interview with Ann Filer, expressed pleasure with the way in which William had settled into his class:

> Well, I must admit I find myself comparing them with when I had them before . . . and I found that William has matured quite a lot more. I think he's settled in very well. He used to be extremely noisy and noticeable but he's not any more. He seems to have a really good attitude and he's very keen to please me, which is very nice. I can't say he didn't work before, but he used to make a lot of noise when doing it, but he's really calmed down and I'm very pleased with him.
> (Mr Brown, teacher interview, September, 1992, Year 5)

Readers with a longer perspective on William's classroom strategies than Mr Brown had access to will perhaps see these changes in William in a slightly different light. Indeed it might be judged that this very sudden switch from William's highly interactive, noisy, jokey norm to a quiet teacher-pleasing industriousness looked more like a strategic response to a new context than a developmental change in William himself.

The longer perspective gained by tracking William's career year by year also helps us to notice a sudden change in William's Year 5 strategy for relating to his teacher. Thus, the following description of William's interpersonal style with Mr Brown in Year 5 stands in contrast with the confident communication and rapport which had formerly characterized his relationships with teachers. Mr Brown told Ann Filer:

> He still has a certain amount of . . . he's *fairly* familiar with teachers, but at the same time he's afraid to go too far. I mean, again, if you mention Stephen, he's much more friendly and easy to talk to, whereas William will only do that when everyone else is, when we're having a joke, and he'll *dive* in then. He would rather only chat to his friends. You know, say first thing in the morning, I can have a very sort of adult conversation with Stephen, but someone like Ian isn't forthcoming to me and William is only sometimes. He's not used to talking to teachers like that I think. And again, it's Year 6 have that maturity. A lot of the girls can certainly come in and have quite a mature conversation, and that shows a big difference really that you find you can't have with many of them.
> (Mr Brown, teacher interview, July 1993, Year 5)

In attempting to account for these changes in William's classroom strategies, the first clue can be perceived in Mr Brown's reference here to Year 6 pupils in the class and to girls in the class. As children moved up the school at Greenside, as we have seen, their chronological position varied from class to class. In Year 5, the cohort under study were again split into two classes as they were in Year 2. The result of this was that William now found himself in a class of 32 children, only five of whom were younger than himself and in which, moreover, two-thirds

were Year 6 children. Now clearly this class composition was likely to have presented William with a challenge, given the high classroom status that he had
always striven to maintain. William's history, in which from time to time there
appears to have been some resentment of the success of girls, may also have
made that class additionally problematic for William, for more than two-thirds of
the class were girls and many of the Year 6 girls in particular were very high
achievers. Many were also held in especially high regard by Mr Brown, as he
indicated above, for their maturity in relation to him, a maturity which many of
the younger children were not capable of. As well as a lowering of academic and
age-related status relative to his peers, William may well have also experienced a
dent to his self-image given the special esteem which he had been used to receiving from his teachers.

In interview with his friends, the high-achieving girls of Year 6, like those in
Year 5 the year before, were dismissed as 'swots'. However, in interview alone
William demonstrated a generous appreciation of the qualities of one particular
girl classmate from Year 6.

AF:	Can you tell me about someone who is especially successful in your class? How is it done?
William:	I don't know her well but Bronwen is clever, gets good marks at tests, gets parts in plays and is good at sports. She's in the netball and rounders and she gets lots of friends. I don't know her but from what Mr Brown said, and you see her in plays and you can tell from the way they are in class that they must work hard to do these things.

(Pupil interview, June 1993, Year 5)

The association with Year 6 children was not however the full extent of the
blow to his structural position and status that William had to cope with that year.
Both Stephen and Ian were selected for school sports teams and the resulting
boost to *their* esteem and standing in the class and around the school seems to
have been felt by William as a corresponding knock to his.

Friendships and peer relationships in Year 5

For pupils in Mr Brown's Year 5 class, there was another route to teacher recognition as well as the usual interpersonal and academic ones. This was especially
so for boy pupils as Mr Brown was a sports specialist with responsibility for the
football and cricket teams at Greenside School. Players for these teams were
drawn from Years 5 and 6 and almost exclusively from among the boys. William
however did not quite make the teams that year, though he was expected to do
so in Year 6. This in itself might not have been too bad a blow for William
because, although he enjoyed PE and many team games, they had never in the
past been a high priority for extra-curricular activity. Though he liked to win,
neither his family nor any of his teachers had considered him to be desperately
competitive on the sports field. Now, although team games may not have been of
outstanding importance to William, they were vital to his friends Stephen and Ian.

The fact of their being selected for teams seemed to have an adverse affect upon William's relationship with them, as Mrs Patterson explained to Ann Filer:

Whether he'll make the cricket team for Year 6 I don't know. But I think that'll be important to him. I mean he *wants* to, because Stephen made the football team and I think he found that a little bit galling.
(Mrs Patterson, parent interview, July 1993, Year 5)

In interview with Ann Filer, Mr Brown also addressed this relationship:

Yes, it's been quite interesting with William, he seems to have gone through stages, at different times where, you know, he's been in with Ian and Stephen, and then other times when they seem to have cast him out. They've left him all alone, you know, and then a week later they'll all be buddies again. I've noticed that happen, I don't know whether it's because of the sport. Stephen's obviously, he's played in the cricket eleven, and he was in the football team. Ian's nearly in and was in the Year 5 football team, or the under tens, whatever, and William wasn't. William nearly got in the cricket team, he was kind of next on my list, but he never did. I don't know if it's *that*. He's been quite upset by it at times.
  He really is desperate to be in the team, to be accepted in that group. I think that in this year's Year 6 there's a very competitive group of boys, and that kind of sets them off, you know, 'cos seeing Stephen sort of coming in here in the school kit, when there's a match, and there's like a spur on to him.
(Mr Brown, teacher interview, July 1993, Year 5)

The new set of circumstances which William had to come to terms with in Year 5 meant that perhaps for the first time in his career he was experiencing the distress of being marginalized by his friends and with little standing in the peer-group hierarchy of the classroom. This change should not perhaps be over-exaggerated in its effect, for he continued to enjoy school and the company of friends. Nevertheless it did seem that, for a while, his way of coping with this blow to his pride was through denigrating others. Mr Brown told Ann Filer:

And the other thing I noticed is a nastier side that I didn't really know. Teasing other children – very subtle – it took me a while to spot. He doesn't make a big thing of it really, but he'll say things to other children aloud, or snigger at them, say at circle time if someone who's a bit different stands up to speak. He'll sort of nudge Stephen and sniggers 'Oh it's *her*', you know, which I don't remember seeing before, and I mentioned it to the parents and they'd kind of noticed some things as well. It's not very *major* but . . .
  He giggles at those who also are rejected usually, people who are *different*, you know, overweight, or whatever, you know, a very cruel side. I've spoken to him about it. He was mortified I'd noticed.
(Mr Brown, teacher interview, July 1993, Year 5)

Of course, with the benefit of this longitudinal study we have an overview of William's career that was not available to his teachers. We would suggest that these actions were William's response to the erosion of his position as leader among his friends and at the cutting edge of peer culture. Mr Brown could not altogether appreciate the issues that were at stake here and, as with many of the strategies that William adopted that year, his response was to see them in terms of qualities in William, rather than as inadequate responses to and struggles with a new situation. If William was not managing to impress Mr Brown with his interpersonal relationships that year, moreover, neither was he being particularly successful in the way he approached classroom tasks. Despite the early pleasure that Mr Brown expressed that William seemed to be buckling down to tasks to please him, in the long term this looked more like a strategy of risk reduction rather than a new 'maturity' of approach that Mr Brown had thought it to be.

Learning strategies in Year 5

Through the story of William's early and middle years we have seen his ability to operate successfully within different systems of teacher expectations. He was able to adapt his strategies, to manage his relationships and to find motivation within a formally structured, teacher-directed approach, as well as through the negotiation of working relationships and curriculum content. In the context of this Year 5 class however, William lost the negotiating, challenging edge that Mr Brown had so appreciated in Year 3 as being supportive of the learning process. Rather, William seemed to be retreating into a search for structure, looking for certainties and checking as a way of pleasing his teacher. Document 5.3 shows one of William's 'Weekly Review' sheets for February 1993.

Of course, this was a strategy that was never likely to win the approval of Mr Brown. In interview with Ann Filer, he was asked about William's approach to tasks and whether William was prepared to risk being different or being wrong:

> Approach to tasks, um, he's not always, he's not as competent as some to go off and do things. Overall, he has all the skills there to take things on and get on with it, but he often needs a bit more support from me in terms of 'Is this all right?'. It's not with everything, but he often says 'Is this what I'm meant to be doing?' and likes to check sometimes. Isn't quite as confident to go for it.
>
> As I've said before he tends to conform. He's a bit more frightened that I'll come along and say 'what are you doing?' but more often than not he'll think of how he's going to approach something, then check with me before he takes the plunge. So you'll find his topic book is fairly, sort of standard, if you know what I mean, in the way he presents his findings or whatever. It's fairly sort of run of the mill. He doesn't kind of think of a really exciting way of doing it very often.
>
> (Mr Brown, teacher interview, July 1993, Year 5)

Substantial though the setbacks and challenges were that year for William, it is necessary to place them within an overall context of hard work and progress on his part. Though his approach may have sometimes disappointed Mr Brown and he clearly lost some of his independence and confidence in himself as a learner, Mr Brown was able to offer a positive report of his progress to his parents that summer. In fact, his *General Comments* on William did not reflect an approach that was substantially different from those of earlier years.

> *General Comments:* William is an enthusiastic, sociable child who has worked hard this year. His progress in all curricular areas has been good but I feel he could achieve even more with greater concentration. He does enjoy discussing his work with others but sometimes this can be at the expense of really getting down to the task. I am pleased with his extra efforts at home which have made a good impression upon his written work.
>
> (Mr Brown, report to parents, July 1993, Year 5)

WEEKLY REVIEW

My best work this week was *my book because I wrote a very neat chapter but I was not so good at spelling in it.* ✓

I need help with *my Volume work because I am finding it very hard.* ✓

I have improved at *my area work because I ∧all my questions right on* ~~Wednesday~~. ✓

How I achieved my aim *This week I achieved both my aims because my handwriting is neater, and I got all my work done for this week.* ✓

My aims for next week
1. *To improve at Volume.* ✓
2. *To improve at my P.E.* ✓

MY WRITTEN REVIEW

My best piece of written work this week was my book, because I have nearly finished it now. ✓ *This week I worked as hard as I could to improve my spelling and handwriting, on Monday I was ill and at home I worked on a different story I am writing.* ✓
I do not work with Mmatthew very well because he chats to me.
I have not been feeling very well this week, but I have put more thought towards my work. ✓ *I enjoyed the geography on Thursday and I came up with some good ideas.* ✓
I have been trying my best to get into the good but but have not done so. Some of my friends have been bralling up from me but I am trying my best to concentrate.

Sp breaking ✓

✓ *An excellent effort that shows what you are capable of. Well done.*

Document 5.3 *William, Year 5, 'Weekly Review Sheet' (February 1993)*

During the month of June, the departure of the Year 6 pupils to their annual camp meant that there was an opportunity to see the effects upon William of a brief restoration of structural position and high teacher esteem. During the absence the older pupils, the Year 5 group from William's class and from a parallel class were taught by Miss Prince, a permanent member of the Greenside staff who worked throughout the school as a support teacher. Mrs Patterson recorded in the diary the following observation:

> During the week when Year 6 were away at camp William seemed to really blossom. He enjoyed having some responsibilities in the school, e.g. the overhead projector in service, and very much appreciated Miss Prince as their teacher. At the end of the week she chose William, among others, for the Parade of Excellence and he told me after school what she had said about him, and he was absolutely thrilled to have been praised so highly for his hard work. He said it was the nicest thing a teacher had ever said about him!
> (Parent diary, July 1993, Year 5)

His parents picked up on the theme in interview with Ann Filer:

> William seemed to positively just *flourish* that week. He was chosen for the Parade of Excellence on the Friday and I've never ever seen him quite so chuffed about *anything*, *ever*. He just couldn't forget it. I think that had a lot to do with it, that Year 5 were king pins for that week, and they all had their little jobs to do, and I think they all felt very important.
> (Mrs Patterson, parent interview, July 1993, Year 5)

In interview at this point in the year, though maybe still flushed with success from these recent events, William appeared to have very positive feelings about the year as a whole. In interview he said he thought it had 'probably been my best year yet', because, he said, he had made new friends and:

William:	I've got down to my work a bit more.
AF:	Why is that?
William:	Being older in the school you've got to. I've liked about every teacher I've had really.
AF:	How well does Mr Brown think you have done?
William:	I reckon [he thinks I've done] well, seeing as my report said that. My reports all said I've improved and that I could do more. Obviously.

(Pupil interview, July 1993, Year 5)

Home and family relationships in Year 5

There were few new developments in William's family relationships that year, changes in the home front taking place mostly in relation to William's interests. These can perhaps most simply be recorded through diary entries and excerpts from interviews.

> William is still learning the violin and last December passed his Grade I with merit. He was a little put out that he did not get a distinction! He seems less keen on the [school] orchestra lately as it interferes with [lunchtime] playing on the field. He is auditioning soon for the Easthampton Children's Orchestra and is annoyed that the

audition clashes with his tennis lesson. He is also not sure about joining the ECO as they practise on a Saturday morning.
(Parent diary, December 1992, Year 5)

Mr Patterson:	He's had two or three Saturday morning tennis sessions so far. He seems to be doing quite well and he's going to do a week's course in the summer ...
Mrs Patterson:	He's made quite an impression, I mean, his first lesson – just knocks up with them across the net and she said normally she would expect them to maybe hit it back twice or three times, before it would get into the net, and William's first rally was 97! And everyone on the other courts were standing clapping. He didn't even mention that. I only found out via her.
Mrs Patterson:	With his friends, these last few months – to me he seems to have less direction with them than he used to ... just milling around the garden really, not actually *doing* anything, and a lot of chat, at one time it would be so much more clear, you know, 'Come on we'll get the Scalextric out', or 'Come on we'll play snooker', or 'We'll play darts', or whatever but now it just seems much more vague what they do together.

(Parent interview, July 1993, Year 5)

In addition to the violin and tennis lessons, William continued to enjoy swimming during out of school hours. In that year his parents also employed a tutor to give William weekly sessions of preparation for independent school entrance exams.

Summary of William's Year 5

During Year 5 it became clear that the change in William's structural position in the classroom had implications for his management of relationships with teachers and peers and for his strategies in approaching tasks. Inevitably William would have entered Mr Brown's class with certain expectations based on their old relationship and the positive memories of his success with him. Readers may recall that William stated his teacher's perception of him in Year 3 as 'the best working boy in the class'. He met instead circumstances in which the highest teacher esteem must have seemed to him to be accorded to pupils of Year 6, especially girls, who had greater maturity and academic ability, and to boys with greater sporting prowess. That William was seen to be somewhat floundering in his relationships and in his approach to learning was not surprising. The identity that he had developed and maintained of being at the cutting edge of teacher expectations and peer-group norms was no longer viable. In effect, he could not sustain the identity of *redefiner* that year. His response, as we have seen, was to retreat into *conformity*, with small forays into deviancy, or *anti-conformity*, which his teacher and parents collaborated to curb. The focus in the analysis here on the loss of structural position and loss of high teacher esteem as being of central concern to William, and at the root of these strategy changes, was supported by the events of the summer when briefly, these forms of status were restored and, once more, in the words of his mother, 'William flourished'.

William, Year 6, early days in Mrs Chard's class

In September 1993 William, along with the familiar cohort of his own year-group, entered Mrs Chard's Year 6 class. Once more he held a relatively comfortable structural position. Chronologically he was almost halfway down the class, but well within the top third for English achievement and about a third of the way down the class for maths and science.

Of all his teachers, William had the least good relationship with Mrs Chard. As we have seen in Chapter 3 and in the comparable part of Sarah's story, in this classroom one could observe both high levels of discussion, collaboration and activity and occasions when sustained, individual concentration was expected. Not surprisingly, it was the latter set of requirements that William found most difficult to carry out. Thus Mrs Chard, as Mr Brown had done the year before, co-opted his parents to support her expectations, and with some initial success, as she explained to Ann Filer:

> William likes to chat and has no concentration and I discussed this with his parents on open night, and they are now working with me on this and this week he has produced the most beautiful piece of English work, really high-quality stuff.
> (Mrs Chard, teacher interview, December 1993, Year 6)

In interview, Mrs Chard described how throughout the year she frequently struggled with her relationship with William:

> William is competitive, yes. He likes to come out as one of the top dogs. He likes his voice to be heard and I don't think he handles not being noticed or chosen too well because that's when the surly side of William comes out and the – 'OK then I'm not going to cooperate'. His feet go up on the chair next to him and the arms get folded and there's this certain 'I'm not going to give you anything today'. William indicates 'The shop is shut, do what you like'. So yes, he is competitive and if it doesn't go his way he can set up quite an opposing force to you – but he's popular, he's well liked and he's good fun and sometimes when we have a task to do and we apply a little pressure, then very often we can get a superb effort out of William.
> (Mrs Chard, teacher interview, July 1994, Year 6)

While some of this description was familiar, in the past William had put a high premium on pleasing his teachers, and the surly, antagonistic response was new. To account for this change of strategy, we need to pick up once more on the stories of Sally and Mary, two girls whose early years stories featured in *The Social World of Children's Learning*. At the same time, we can also pick up on events as they stood when the children had previously been together in Miss King's Year 4 class. At that point in William's story we intimated that there were longstanding rivalries and resentments among the high-achieving pupils that would come to a head in Year 6.

Friendships and peer relationships in Year 6

In attempting to come to grips with the disruptions to teacher and pupil relationships that centred round William's and Sally's groups that year, a useful starting-point is the following extract from a long and very voluble interview with William's friendship group. A question from Ann Filer asking them to outline the different friendship groups in the class opened a floodgate and a catalogue of perceived injustices and critical opinion poured forth:

William:	The middle table of girls, it has to be said, are Mrs Chard's favourite. If Vicki says anything Mrs Chard just cracks up, but if it's us we just get told off. We work really hard at home but we don't get the grades the girls get.
Stephen:	Hannah, Vicki, Mary, Sally. I try really hard . . .
Maurice:	The first five weeks of Parade of Excellence it was all girls.
All:	Girls, girls, girls . . .
Maurice:	As long as we get the work done, why can't we talk? She's one of the best teachers I've ever had, but she's unfair, sexist and biased.
Stephen:	It bugs me. We get work about racism but she is so sexist.
Maurice:	They shouldn't have Parade of Excellence, it's tight on other people.
Alistair:	There's a lot of jealousy. They've got hold of the wrong end of the stick with it. They think they are encouraging but they are de-couraging.
William:	Maybe this is sexist but we should have a boys' Parade of Excellence and a girls' Parade of Excellence.
Stephen:	William is cleverer than Sally but Sally writes a page of 'ands' and 'buts' and gets praised.

The boys go on to make strident complaints about the general running of the school, including the allocation of the school budget, the management of resources and petty rules. They complain about the way in which the school is constantly held up as a model, and that perceptions of it are unbalanced because of its location.

Maurice:	Children in this school come from well-off families who can resource their children. It's a different matter if you compare it with Damibrook where there is a lot of poverty. Comparisons are not fair.

The other boys all clap and agree strongly with Maurice's speech.
(Friendship group interview, March 1994, Year 6)

In this interview can be seen a development of the boys' grumbles about 'swots' and 'teacher's pets' that had rumbled on in the background for a few years without disturbing greatly the boys' relationships either with the 'swots' or with teachers. It was however, significant to the changes that took place in Year 6, that these boys who had three years before dubbed themselves 'the Jesters', now identified themselves as 'the Rebels'. The resentments of the boys had come to a head in the spring term, when it came to light that Sally was becoming seriously upset by verbal attack upon her by one of William's friends. Mrs Chard, in interview with Ann Filer, gave her perspective on the events of that autumn term:

There was tremendous resentment from Stephen towards Sally, that she is everybody's favourite and always chosen for everything and so on. And I said, well this is absolutely not true because I've been making a conscious effort, right since the beginning of September, when I could see the way things were going in the first fortnight. There was this group of girls that were so well motivated towards work and always wanting to do everything, and naturally, if you wanted a job doing you asked them to do it because you knew they'd do it as against this group of boys that never stopped talking and never got anything done. So who got the praise and so on? But they found this really difficult to accept. But there were two separate things

going on at the same time. Both spoiling the class actually, and both sort of festering resentments and bad feelings.
(Mrs Chard, teacher interview, July 1994, Year 6)

The 'two things' alluded to by Mrs Chard included the fact that there were also rivalries *within* the girls' group. Sally, for her part, she thought, was having to confront the fact of her peers catching up with her. Some of the early advantages that she had had over her peers arising from her close association with the school due to her parents' employment there (see *The Social World of Children's Learning*) were now fading away as other children developed their social and academic skills. Mrs Chard thought that perhaps she was finding it difficult when she was not always the 'first' and 'best'. This was particularly significant in relation to her closest friends, Mary and Hannah, also her dogged rivals, always one step behind in her shadow. Mary's efforts were rated particularly highly by Mrs Chard who thought she had 'definitely been a star this year', 'enjoys a challenge' in maths, 'struggles and works with it' to get to the top of the class in English. Her expectations for more 'substance' had not suited Sally so well, however, whose strategy had always been to go for the quick result, finish first, tick it off and on with the next task.

Stresses brought about by internal rivalries for academic and personal prestige, together with the now open resentments and hostility from outside, seriously upset all the girls in that friendship group. Their work suffered and parents were involved because of sleeping difficulties. Mrs Chard finally warned the girls that if they did not 'sort themselves out' they would not be going to annual camp that summer. This, she thought, seriously shocked the group that had always prided itself on being good, model pupils and provided the motivation to resolve their difficulties. Despite her impatience with the girls' disputes however, Mrs Chard continued to maintain that the resentments of William's group towards the girls was unjustified because the boys chatted, challenged and generally did not give of their best unless they felt like it.

Learning strategies in Year 6

We have already explored William's learning and classroom strategies in Year 6, along with those of some other pupils, in the above sections and in the context of both inter-group and intra-group rivalries. Mrs Chard, as we have seen had a clear strategy for encouraging pupils to take responsibility for their learning. However, the setting of a challenge and the requirement for both peer cooperation and sustained independent working meant that the preferred strategies of both William and Sally that had, especially in Sally's case, always served them well, sometimes let them down in this class. As we have described, Sally's strategy of 'goodness' still served her well. However, the learning stance that had run in parallel of being quick and the first to finish, though sometimes regretted by teachers, had never failed her before as it did in this class. Similarly, William's 'jester' communicator, negotiator approach had frequently been on a knife edge of help or hindrance to his academic success and rapport with teachers. However, it had never been seriously disapproved of, nor seen to be such a hindrance to academic success and his relationship with a teacher as it was in Mrs Chard's class. Clearly, a wider range and greater flexibility of skills and strategies were being demanded by Mrs Chard than either of these, and some other pupils, were accustomed to exercising.

However, at about the time when tensions were at their highest, a variety of positive and exciting events took place that saved the year and brought it to a satisfactory conclusion. Firstly, William was chosen for the Parade of Excellence. He had on several occasions let it be known that to be chosen, on his own and not as part of a group as sometimes happened, was one of his aims for the year (see document 5.4) and Mrs Chard granted him his wish in this.

Indeed, William's success in writing had continued to grow. His minimalist approach to the subject he had found 'boring' in his Reception and Year 1, followed by the first pleasure and effort kindled by Miss Sage in Year 2, had now developed so that Mrs Chard was able to report:

> William has shown on many occasions during the year just how talented he is in the use of language. He has written some superb pieces which are rich in description and I believe that he has the ability to go from strength to strength in this subject.
> (Mrs Chard, report to parents, July 1994, Year 6)

Like Sarah and many of the other children in the year-group, William passed the entrance exam for an independent school. Along with his friend Stephen (and with Robert – see Chapter 6), William was offered a place at Easthampton Grammar School, and another of his goals was fulfilled. During the summer the Year 6 pupils, as was traditional at Greenside, organized stalls and a day of fun and entertainment for the school in aid of charity. The children also had a successful summer camp and took part in a Year 6 musical production in which Sally took a leading role and stole the show with her talented portrayal of a dinosaur. On the last day of term William played the violin when the Year 6 pupils displayed their many talents in an impressive 'leavers' service.

Before leaving school, the tradition of the signing of uniforms by friends and staff was observed. William signed his name on Sally's dress with the message 'I love you Sally'. Arms around each other's neck they posed for photographs together with friends; the 'Rebels' and the 'Teacher's Pets' reaffirming their friendship in affectionate embraces.

Home and family relationships in Year 6

During the final interview of William's last year at Greenside school Mrs Patterson reflected upon William's relationship with his teacher. She thought that, although there were clearly aspects of William's character that Mrs Chard liked, he had felt that he and his friends were 'branded as a group, a whole clump of them, that were always noisy' (Parent interview, July 1994). She contrasted this with the instances where William's social identity had been an asset in his relationship with teachers:

> He got on well with Miss Sage because she liked his sense of humour, and she was one of the few teachers who particularly spotted that in him and allowed for that.

William 46

Monday January 31st

School life

tr.a

My successes

English: I feel I have done quite well in english and have produced some good writing.

Maths: I don't think I have done as well in maths but feel I do quite well in tests.

Topic work: Every week when we get a sheet I first put it down in notes then do the drawings and writing up I think that this is a good way of doing it.

P.E. So far this year I feel I have proved my self to be one of the more able ones in running, basket ball, hockey and so on but I will not be to modest.

After sshool: I go to football club and I suppose I can play a fair game.

My Targets

English: I am not really a very good speller and think I can over come this by tgoing maybe a bit harder and by using the dictionary.

Maths: I am a bit slow at working long division out and hope to sort this out by ~~mental~~ – just sitting there doing nothing, but asking for help to understand it better.

P.E.: I would like to improve my football and hope to do this by practicing harder when ever I can.

After School: I think I should try to do my homework more strictly and will do this by telling my mum exactly what it is I have to do.

   <u>Big aims</u>

1. To get into the cricket team.
2. To get a main part in the Y6 production.
3. To produce a piece of writing that will stand out so. much that only I will get into the 'parade of excellence

Document 5.4 *William, Year 6, 'School Life, Successes, Targets, Big Aims' (January 1994)*

She would allow him to go far enough with a joke, which he really appreciates in an adult, being allowed to use his sense of humour.
(Mrs Patterson, parent interview, July 1994, Year 6)

Mrs Patterson was also asked by Ann Filer to reflect upon ways in which as parents she and her husband had interpreted and mediated the school experience with William, particularly his relationships with his teachers. With the comparatively poor relationship with Mrs Chard particularly in mind, Mrs Patterson described the attitude she had been trying to instil in William:

I've just said to him again and again, you know, at secondary school you're just going to have to get on with that, regardless of whether you like someone or not, you work for them and you work hard. But ultimately you're working for yourself, you're not working for them anyway. So that is my chat line. That's the way I try to put it across. He's got to learn to self-motivate more. And if he doesn't ever really get to grips with that, he's never going to achieve what he could achieve and in a

sense no amount of endorsing the school, trying to encourage homework and all this is going to get us anywhere unless William suddenly wakes up one morning and thinks 'Hey, hang on a minute, this is interesting, I'm going to get into this'. It's got to come from *him*.
(Mrs Patterson, parent interview, July 1994, Year 6)

However, the one real 'bone of contention' between William and his parents that year arose from their frustration that, despite his undoubted talent, William did not seem prepared to commit himself to his violin playing.

It is causing a lot of grief and I think deep down I've accepted the fact that he'll give it up. For various reasons he missed Grade II and Grade III. Anthony [Mr Patterson] says the very least he should achieve is to try and get one more grade to actually achieve Grade IV and think – well OK, I gave it a good shot, and I got somewhere.
(Mrs Patterson, parent interview, July 1994, Year 6)

At home, as at school, William was challenging the rules and pushing hard at the boundaries his parents set. His mother considered that he was very much more friendship than family oriented and as parents they were increasingly having to manage conflict arising from the freedoms and activities of friends. Conflicts involving, for instance, where it was permissible to go without parents, what videos it was permissible to watch, were exacerbated, his mother observed, by the fact that William was not very family oriented and that his social life beyond the confines of the home seemed much more important to him. However, this was not viewed altogether negatively by his mother:

In a sense I think it's almost a compliment to us, in some ways, that he is the way he is. You can look at it in that light because he has got a secure base, it gives him a springboard. I think if he was insecure it would show itself in a very different way. Like the day he started school when he shouted to me, you know, 'It's all right Mum, I don't need you any more'. You know, in a sense that said it all, even then, at four and a half. He'd got the base he wanted for those first few years and he was then ready. Another Mum turned to me and said 'I wish mine was like that'. You know they were clinging round legs and not wanting her to go and there was me – 'Bye'. Not a kiss or a hug or anything. Just off.
(Mrs Patterson, parent interview, July 1994, Year 6)

The final reflection of Mrs Patterson on the years of William's childhood was that in essential ways, his personality had not changed. Certainly life was somewhat contentious at the moment with William's growing independence and new freedoms being sought. However, she reflected finally, from the earliest days of being William's parents, life had always been a continuous process of negotiation.

Summary of William's Year 6

In Year 6, William could not achieve recognition through either of the strategies which previously had served him well in the early and middle years. The expectations of Mrs Chard were such that his communicator, 'Jester' identity and his social skills were not the asset to learning and the route to rapport that they had often been in the past. William's other available strategy, that of fulfilling well structured teacher expectations, had of course failed him in Year 5 and was certainly not available to him in Mrs Chard's class.

In Year 6 a pattern became clear in the reactions of children for whom teacher esteem and academic prowess had been so important. As we could see in William's Year 5 and now could be seen among many more of these children, when their habitual statuses became threatened, conflict ensued and we see them 'hitting out' at their peers. In the case of the boys we see them also vigorously condemning the 'mismanagement' of school structures and systems of reward to which they still looked for the recognition and prestige that they felt was due to them.

William's identity and career in the later years at Greenside School

In the middle years of William's primary school career, we saw that the expectations of new teachers at Greenside allowed William to reconcile his social interests and sense of autonomy with his aims of achieving academic status. Interpersonal involvement and sense of fun were allowed to support his learning and promote an intrinsic satisfaction with tasks and an active responsibility for his own learning. This was particularly seen in the development of his writing from Year 2 onwards but also in his enthusiastic involvement in all tasks, not just those that provided extrinsic satisfaction of filling books and achieving grades. This awareness and sense of quality, what Mrs Chard called 'substance', had clearly been taken on board by William but it was not an intrinsic satisfaction alone that motivated him. His drive for status in the classroom and the esteem of teachers meant that he also strived for external rewards and recognitions, grades and a place in the Parade of Excellence.

However, in the later years of his career at Greenside, different expectations of teachers meant that teacher recognition and status were accorded to older pupils with skills and maturity that William could not yet match and to girls who had developed different strategies from William, those of 'goodness', quiet cooperation and sustained concentration. William's social identity was no longer perceived as an asset to learning and to relationships in the classroom. His communicative, interactive identity increasingly gave way to one in which he was perceived as something of a noisy nuisance. At the same time William's expression of his own identity and that of his group changed. The 'Jesters' of the middle years gave way to the 'Rebels' as, at the same time, easy negotiative relationships with teachers degenerated into critical, resentful opposition in Year 6.

WILLIAM'S IDENTITY AND CAREER – CASE-STUDY OVERVIEW

As described more fully in the introduction to the case studies, this triadic representation (Figure 5.1) depicts, in the outer triangle, the social context within which William learnt and developed and to which he could contribute, and in the inner star, the dynamic relationships between William and his family, peers and teachers within which he shaped and maintained his identity. In simple terms we can describe

Matrix 5.3 *William, Years 5 and 6, a summary matrix*

Family relationships	Peer-group relationships	Teacher relationships	Identity	Career
Year 5: Mr Brown				
William mentions school assessment from time to time. Parents say it matters to him what level he has reached. Auditions for city youth orchestra. Enjoys swimming and tennis. Likes to win but is not desperately competitive at sport. With friends, less focused in play. Continues to be image- and style-conscious.	William is not selected for sports teams. Status of friends Stephen and Ian raised by getting in teams. William is marginalized by them sometimes. Continues to enjoy the company of friends, not isolated. Mr Brown says William has mocked, teased those pupils in class who tend to be 'rejects'. William is mortified that Mr Brown noticed. Friends in Sally's group of high-status girls are not in this class.	Structural position: among the youngest few. Maths, science and English, within the bottom third. William perceives that much teacher esteem accorded to high-achieving, socially mature Year 6 girls and sporting boys. Retreats into a search for structure. Delivers a standard run-of-the-mill presentation of tasks as a result. William flourishes when Year 6 pupils go to camp and his status is restored.	Seen by his teacher as more conforming and less confident in relation to him. Some 'deviant' behaviour in relation to peers. Loss of group identities of 'exclusive' and 'the sexy ones' formerly accorded by peers in earlier classes. Very low structural position means that the identity developed of being at the cutting edge of teacher expectations and peer-group norms no longer viable.	Some loss of teacher esteem experienced. Loss of high social and academic status within this classroom. Somewhat floundering in relationships and approach to learning. Retreat into conformity with some anti-conformity, the latter teacher and parents collaborate to curb. William still enjoys school.
Year 6: Mrs Chard				
Takes part in youth orchestra concert but expected to give up the violin. Challenges fairness of school rules at home. Pushing hard at the boundaries at home. Mother says William is friends-oriented more than family-oriented. Being with his parents has always entailed constant negotiation.	William is back with his familiar year group. Longstanding rivalries and resentments among high-achieving competitive pupils become publicly aired in classroom. William and friends think Mrs Chard favours girls and is sexist. William's group dub themselves 'The Rebels'.	Structural position: age, half-way down class. Maths and science, one-third down the class, English, well within the top third. Has an 'abrasive' relationship with Mrs Chard who thinks he talks too much, lacks concentration and does not like not being noticed. William withdraws cooperation from teacher when feels unjustly treated. 'Gives of his best when he feels like it'.	Seen by his teacher as something of a noisy nuisance, 'likes to come out as one of the top dogs'. Also 'fun', 'popular' and talented in the use of language and in his writing. Social identity no longer enhances his academic identity. William and friends redefine their group as 'The Rebels'.	William could not achieve teacher esteem through either of his customary strategies in this class. Easy, negotiative relationships with teachers gradually degenerate into critical opposition. William and friends condemn 'mismanagement' of school systems of reward, to which they still look for prestige.

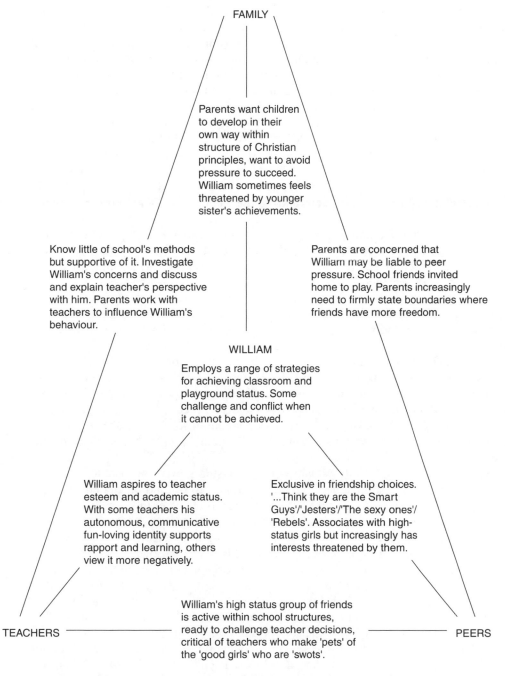

FAMILY

Parents want children
to develop in their
own way within
structure of Christian
principles, want to avoid
pressure to succeed.
William sometimes feels
threatened by younger
sister's achievements.

Know little of school's methods
but supportive of it. Investigate
William's concerns and discuss
and explain teacher's perspective
with him. Parents work with
teachers to influence William's
behaviour.

Parents are concerned that
William may be liable to peer
pressure. School friends invited
home to play. Parents increasingly
need to firmly state boundaries where
friends have more freedom.

WILLIAM

Employs a range of strategies
for achieving classroom and
playground status. Some
challenge and conflict when
it cannot be achieved.

William aspires to teacher
esteem and academic status.
With some teachers his
autonomous, communicative
fun-loving identity supports
rapport and learning, others
view it more negatively.

Exclusive in friendship choices.
'...Think they are the Smart
Guys'/'Jesters'/'The sexy ones'/
'Rebels'. Associates with high-
status girls but increasingly has
interests threatened by them.

TEACHERS

William's high status group of friends
is active within school structures,
ready to challenge teacher decisions,
critical of teachers who make 'pets' of
the 'good girls' who are 'swots'.

PEERS

Figure 5.1 *William's case-study overview – a triadic representation*

William's predominant interest within this web of relationships as that of achieving high social and academic status with a career pattern of strategic responses which we have broadly termed *redefining*.

We can perhaps best conceptualize the notion of *redefining* through a comparison with the notion of *conformity* as described in Sarah's story. *Conformity* was there described as a career strategy in terms of the reification of career structures and the shaping of a career within the patterns of achievement and cultural norms made available by family, the peer culture and the expectations of teachers and the school.

Pupils using *redefining* strategies, we suggest, while being associated with those same mainstream patterns of achievement and cultural norms, are not so much operating within them as at the cutting edge of them. They are pushing at the boundaries of expectations, negotiating, challenging and leading their peers.

As with other career strategies in the typology, we can see this patterned response operating through four broad categories of structures which, we suggest, constitute the main areas for career progression. The structures are those relating to curricular expectations, to the official social relationships of teachers and classrooms and to the unofficial relationships among peers and in the playground, and those relating to extra-curricular opportunities.

We can take both William and Sally as examples of *redefining* pupils and examine parallels in their career strategies. Firstly, with respect to their relationships with teachers and curricular structures, both were cue-conscious and socially adept and both, in their different ways, tested the boundaries of rules and expectations. Thus William in his early years strived for autonomy and operated at the boundary of the permissible while retaining good teacher relationships. In his middle years he developed special, easy, negotiative relationships that won him some indulgences to pursue his own interactive and humorous identity. In his later years, negotiation turned to challenging others' rights to academic status and teacher esteem when it seemed to William that it was withheld from him. His forays into deviancy or *anti-conformity* were brief and neither William nor his friends set up the alternative status systems that would have been indicative of a true 'rebel'. Teacher and parental pressure put William back on track and understandably so, for it was always within the existing academic and social structures that William struggled for recognition and esteem.

It was clear, however, that William's redefiner status was only viable where his structural position was sufficiently high to enable him to operate at the cutting edge of classroom and peer-group culture. This was not a realistic option for him when he was matching himself against the skills and maturity of much older Year 6 children. In that circumstance we saw him retreat into a pattern of *conformity* to teacher expectations with brief acts of *anti-conformity* in his peer relations.

Sally's constant position at the cutting edge of teacher expectations relied on strategies which were, without doubt, more consistently pleasing to teachers than those of any other child in her year group. As described in *The Social World of Children's Learning*, her parents' employment in the school (her father was caretaker) gave her an easy familiarity with the school building and organization, with each of the teachers and their classrooms. As a very small child, before she was even a pupil at Greenside Primary School, she had developed a sense of family ownership of the school and complete identification with it. This, together with an enthusiastic and competitive desire to please her teachers and be 'good' made for easy, highly cooperative relationships with each of her teachers and helped to put her at the forefront of classroom competence.

In relation to other pupils, both William and Sally were leaders within the dominant peer-group cultures of the playground and classroom. William, popular though often the exclusive 'smart guy' in his friendship choices, Sally the competent, sometimes 'bossy' leader of a large group of girls. Both were at the forefront of the sorts of 'sophisticated' social and sexual behaviour associated with the dominant, higher-status friendship groups to which they belonged.

With regard to his extra-curricular and schoolwide identity, William often associated with teachers other than his own and identified with older pupils and the wider school context from an early age. Though William did not make as strong a mark on extra-curricular activities as Sally, he certainly outstripped other pupils in the violin group and together with Sally *redefined* the rules for school orchestra membership by being allowed to join a year earlier than was usually allowed. Sally's sporting and dramatic talents, together with her 'into everything' persistence, meant that, for example, she was chosen often for leading roles and, in her final year selected for the hitherto boys-only cricket team. Her familiarity with after-school clubs and activities meant that, in her infant years especially, she often joined in with the older children, either officially or unofficially, a year or so early.

Thus, with different approaches, both William and Sally carved out careers at the cutting edge of classroom, playground and school life generally. *Redefining*, for the autonomous William was, in many respects, a risky operation, frequently carried out on a knife edge of social approval. For Sally *redefining* was a matter of high confidence and competence and the maintenance of social approval. For both it was a socially astute, highly interactive and competitive bid for status and a vehicle for the development of identity.

Chapter 6

Robert's Story

6.1   PRE-SCHOOL, RECEPTION AND YEAR 1

Robert, an introduction

In the preceding chapters we have told the stories of Sarah and William, whose predominant patterns of strategic action we have described in terms of *conformity* and *redefining* respectively. In William's story we also began to appreciate some ways in which pupils' predominant patterns of response can be disrupted as they become no longer viable when children encounter new classrooms and experiences.

In this chapter we tell the story of Robert, whose predominant strategy was that of *non-conformity*. Patterns of strategic action associated with *non-conformity* suggest a degree of detachment and self-determination in relation to curricular, teacher and peer expectations. As we track Robert's career through Greenside School we will see that he brought to school his own distinct interests and autonomous approach to tasks. Unlike Sarah and William, Robert set many of his own goals in the classroom and he did not identify with many of the dominant forms of interaction within the wider peer culture.

Of course, Robert was not able to shape and maintain his identity as a pupil independently of context and unconcerned for the responses of others. As we shall see, the ways in which teachers perceived Robert, the learning contexts they created and the perceptions of his peers were all crucial to the maintenance of his sense of autonomy in the classroom and the operation of his own interests. They were crucial, that is, to the maintenance of his identity and status as a pupil, and therefore crucial also to his happiness.

Robert's family

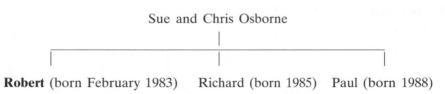

Sue and Chris Osborne

Robert (born February 1983)   Richard (born 1985)   Paul (born 1988)

Robert was the oldest of the three children of Sue and Chris Osborne. The family moved into a semi-detached house in Greenside shortly before Robert was born; two years later his brother Richard was born, and, during Robert's Reception year at Greenside, the family was completed with the addition of Paul.

During Robert's years at Greenside School, Sue Osborne worked full-time in the home bringing up the young family of boys while Chris was a Director/Partner in an agricultural by-products business.

Shortly after they moved to Greenside, it was suggested that they should begin to consider the education of the as yet unborn Robert. As this interview with Andrew Pollard indicates, however, although Robert was by now in his Reception class at Greenside, the whole question of appropriate education for their children continued to be an open one for the Osbornes.

Mrs Osborne:	Educationally it is still very early. We haven't any fixed ideas. We don't know what. Where he is now, he is there because it is the nearest school and the lady next door said her children were there when we moved in. I think I was expecting Robert and she said 'You must get him in to that school. My children started there. It is very good.' We had thought about other education. A friend of mine who is a teacher is into this Steiner. We went up to The Forest Waldorf School and we had a look round there. We were very impressed really but they seemed a bit hippyish, you know, men going round in suits and sandals with no socks. We were really taken with it though. We were quite interested but in the end thought perhaps it wasn't very practical.
Mr Osborne:	I'd say we know more about the Steiner method of education than we do Greenside School's.
Mrs Osborne:	But it was all very free and easy with no pressures put on the children. It sounded wonderful. It sounded as if you could come out of it as a seventeen- or eighteen-year-old who could cope with anything. But then we thought, well, what happens if you have to do an exam. That was what we were worried about.
AP:	Yes, well that is right. There is no pressure on people but, I mean, Greenside is an area where a lot of parents do put pressure on their kids, so that is quite a difference in approach. How do you see that?
Mr Osborne:	Yes, definitely. I don't know. It is so difficult isn't it? When you are first married you have a fair idea what you want out of life and how you are going to get it so you can make long-term plans. But when you have children you just have to take it day by day really. Beyond him and Richard going

> to Greenside, we haven't even considered looking beyond
> that.
> (Parent interview, March 1988, Reception)

In their tendency to be attracted to a non-traditional form of schooling, their tentativeness of opinion, and their willingness to take things 'day by day', readers will appreciate that there was a clear difference between the Osbornes' approach to their children's education and that of the predominant culture among Greenside Parents. In common with most Greenside parents however, they were keen to ensure that their children's pre-school experience of learning was a rich and varied one.

Early learning in the family

Robert's early learning in the family included a wide experience of books, stories, talk and play, as well as social encounters with adults and children beyond the immediate family. Diary entries show the foundations for Robert's later skills of literacy being laid through the employment of inviting resources of both a material and cultural nature. What is suggested in the writing of Robert's parents is that his early learning took place within the context of day-to-day routines and relationships of the family and of the wider community, rather than as a result of any overt intention on their part to formally teach:

> Before school Robert was never happier than when being read to. The book at bed-time was an early institution that has now carried on with Robert now reading his schoolbook. At home books were made available at an early age and have been treated with due reverence since. Taking out a book to read has always been a sure fire way to quieten both boys down should they be over-excited.
>   The magic of forming letters into words and word into meaning has always been of keen interest to Robert. Party invitations were studied and replied to from an early age, with street names, signposts and poster advertisements always good for distraction if necessary. Writing paper, pens, crayons, markers etc. are available at home and are used daily (nearly always) by both boys. Robert is in charge of the best equipment!
> (Parent diary, Summer 1988, Reception)

These diary descriptions of Robert's early learning in the home and community suggest that his parents created a particularly relaxed and stimulating learning environment. It was consistent with this unhurried approach, that Robert experienced a low-key build-up to school attendance. Mrs Osborne told Andrew Pollard:

> I didn't go on too much about the school. I feel, you hear a lot of women saying, or husbands, whatever, at Easter, 'My child's looking forward to going to school'. I think it is months and months away. It's built up too much for them. So Chris and I didn't say an awful lot about school, just kind of mentioned it at odd times so Robert wasn't thrown in out of the blue. I didn't want him to get too keyed up about school.
> (Mrs Osborne, parent interview, March 1988, Reception)

Early learning in playschool

Like William, Robert experienced the informality of playschool from the age of three, rather than the greater formality of Sarah's nursery school experience. Unlike both William and Sarah, Robert experienced no formal teaching of literacy skills before school. From the perspective of Robert's fast developing reading skills in his Reception class, Mrs Osborne, talking to Andrew Pollard, expressed doubts about early formal education either institutionalized or in the home:

> I would say he has got on very well because I think it is very young to be bothered with that. I think it is very young. I mean, I am not a teacher, I know nothing really about education in the formal sense, but you know, you hear about people teaching them at playschool how to read and mothers teaching children to read before they go to school, and what's the rush really?
> (Mrs Osborne, parent interview, March 1988, Reception)

There was then clearly a consistency between Robert's parents' attitude to his early learning and their earlier attraction to some elements of the Steiner school of educational philosophy. This was most notable with respect to the practice in Steiner schools of discouraging early attempts to formally teach skills of literacy and numeracy. Readers of *The Social World of Children's Learning*, and of the accounts in this book, will appreciate that Mrs Osborne was expressing a view that was distinctly unusual among Greenside parents with even the least traditional perspectives on education.

A summary of Robert's pre-school experience

When we put Robert's parents' views about learning and their lack of knowledge of Greenside School into the context of other families and the changes underway in the school, an interesting comparison can be made. As we saw in *The Social World of Children's Learning* and in Sarah's story, very many parents had moved to Greenside and had made an early decision to send their children to Greenside Primary School on the basis of strong belief in an educational ethos that in fact no longer existed by the time their children got there. It was ironic therefore, that the Osbornes, a family with no educational plans or preconceptions, should appear nevertheless to have an approach to learning that would match much more closely the emerging ethos of the school.

As we shall see however, Robert did not have to wait for the new ethos to emerge before the match between his learning at home and at school would be apparent. From the earliest days at Greenside he was ready to engage actively with the opportunities to learn that Miss Powell's classroom offered. However, as Robert's story will reveal, there were some aspects of classroom life in those early years at Greenside to which Robert's learning intentions were less well adapted.

Robert, Reception, early days in Mrs Powell's class

Robert entered Mrs Powell's Reception class in September 1987 with the advantage of being the oldest child in the class. He was one of the highest achievers in maths and in reading and English generally. In those early days in Mrs Powell's class, Robert's favourite classroom activities usually involved the use of construction equipment. However, as his mother suggested in interview with Andrew Pollard, in the carrying out of his ideas, Robert frequently experienced a fair amount of frustration:

> [His favourite is] the marble game as he calls it, this helter-skelter construction kit. Apparently he wanted to build it as they show it on the box and Mrs Powell says it looks as if they put it up, took a photograph and the thing fell down because it isn't stable. Of course, he loses his head every time this happens. Every now and again I say 'What do you like about school Robert?' – 'The marble game.' – and it is always the same answer.
> (Mrs Osborne, parent interview, March 1988, Reception)

Mrs Powell reflected on the same aspect of Robert's classroom behaviour:

> Robert is a highly intelligent and volatile little boy. If he's playing with something and he has an idea in his mind of how he wants it to be and he can't achieve that he blows his top and screams and cries and whatnot and you have to calm him down. If someone comes along to play with him and moves something that he doesn't want to move, oh, ructions!
> (Mrs Powell, teacher interview, September, 1988, Reception)

From this account it becomes clear that in the classroom Robert was also experiencing his peers as a source of frustration.

Friendships and peer relationships in Reception

In Sarah and William's stories we saw their reciprocal play with friends and classmates generally as a source of satisfaction and their increasing competence in this sphere of classroom and playground life as contributing to their identity as socially acceptable members of their peer group. However, in a classroom situation where resources were limited and shared, Robert's plans for achieving the ideas in his head were frequently frustrated. As Mrs Powell suggested above, other children would often take and use the pieces of equipment that Robert had in mind to use and he was therefore more likely to see them as a source of frustration in the classroom than as useful cooperators in play. Sharing and cooperating are seen as important aspects of learning to be a pupil in English primary school classrooms, and so Robert's strategy in which his construction ideas had priority over any need for relating with his peers came in for some negative criticism from Mrs Powell:

> He is not good at sharing the resources but he will play in among them. I wouldn't say he is terribly cooperative because Robert is still the Number One.
> (Mrs Powell, teacher interview, February 1988, Reception)

If reciprocity was lacking in Robert's classroom relationships with his peers at that time, it was, perhaps because Robert did not seem to *need* other pupils to any great extent. In Daniel's and Mary's story in *The Social World of Children's Learning*, for example, and in Sarah's story in this volume, we see that friends provide, among other things, both academic and social support in the classroom. They enable pupils to compare their responses and check their efforts, minimalizing the risk of being 'wrong' or incompetent in the eyes of their teacher or their peers. Robert's high structural position in the class, his autonomous approach to many classroom tasks and his teacher's regard for his intelligence, of which we will see more below, would all have rendered Robert less vulnerable to some of the evaluative aspects of classroom life than were many of his peers. This apparent lack of need for his peers extended to the playground, where, we have seen, the predominant culture of Greenside boys of Robert's age was characterized by a robust participation in running, chasing and fighting games as well as, for some, 'kiss chase' with girls. Such activities held no appeal for Robert, however, as his mother explained to Andrew Pollard:

> He runs like this, with his arms down by his side. He can't run. He really can't. I say 'Loosen up, Robert. Bend your elbows', but he hasn't an idea. He is like an old woman trying to run. It really is funny. He's not an outdoor child, is he really? You have to coax him into the garden really, unless it's something interesting he is not too keen on going out. If you are doing the grass or something like that he will go out. He will go on the climbing frame. They pretend that it's a pirate ship. He will climb and slide a bit [but] he doesn't like to potter or run around or kick a ball so much. He might do if you encourage him.
> (Mrs Osborne, parent interview, July 1988, Reception)

It would be wrong to consider Robert as in any way a social isolate where his peers were concerned. As Mrs Powell suggests, he liked to play in among them and, indeed, he seemed to have had a need and capacity for close friendship. His mother described to Andrew Pollard his relationship with his friend Hazel, whose story featured in *The Social World of Children's Learning*:

> Hazel came to tea the other afternoon. I think he is quite fond of her, pally, or whatever. I don't know what kind of relationship you would call it. Robert had his train track down and Hazel was playing with his garage and they almost ignored each other for the couple of hours that she was here, but she said she had a good time. Robert was delighted she was here. He kept saying 'Will you come and play with me? Come and play with me again.'
> (Mrs Osborne, parent interview, March 1988, Reception)

The friendship between Robert and Hazel was an interesting one in that, as Hazel's story shows, friendship for Hazel was very much on her own terms and related to her own distinct interests rather than those of the mainstream shared culture of the peer group. Here too, with Robert, we begin to see that the dominant ways of interacting and the shared concerns of the predominant group culture were at odds with Robert's agenda. He and Hazel seemed to share mutual needs and understandings which were satisfied through their parallel play.

Learning strategies in Reception

As was alluded to above, Mrs Powell regarded Robert's intelligence as exceptional. This was not simply a matter of his attainment relative to the other children in the class. Rather, it was that she perceived something distinctive in the strategies he brought to learning:

Mrs Powell: Yes, you see people like Robert can learn from any situation whatever. He sort of sees possibilities in apparatus and others will only do what you tell them to do with it.
    Robert has got a good general knowledge and good vocabulary. Very interested in everything. He approaches any activity, I think, with a different slant.

AP: Yes, you were saying that even if he might be bored he looks for something that is interesting in it.

Mrs Powell: Yes. His drawings are good and they look like what they are supposed to be.

(Mrs Powell, teacher interview, February 1988, Reception)

In terms of Robert's academic attainments, during the spring term of 1988, Mrs Powell noted in her records that he 'always has ideas for writing', has 'good handwriting' and 'can spell some words'. However, she also noted that he 'doesn't write as much as he could' (see, for example, Document 6.1). As is described in William's case study Robert, like William, had adopted the strategy for avoiding too much writing by dictating little to be copied:

Mrs Powell: Robert and William [do that]. The girls aren't as bad really, they are more verbal anyway.

AP: But those two have worked that out.

Mrs Powell: Yes, I think I probably notice those more because it annoys me more with them than it does with the others because I know of the capability there. Others do it as well but those are the two because I think they are so able.

(Mrs Powell, teacher interview, February 1988, Reception)

Mrs Powell also recorded that Robert had 'well developed number concepts' and in her report to Robert's parents during his second term at Greenside, Mrs Powell stated that in project work:

Robert takes an intelligent interest in all that is going on. He has a good general knowledge and is able to contribute much to class discussion.
(Mrs Powell, report to parents, Spring Term, Reception)

Also during that Spring Term, Mrs Powell was able to report that, with respect to social aspects of classroom life:

Robert is learning to cope with sharing resources with the rest of the class and the bouts of unacceptable behaviour are fewer nowadays and short-lived.
(Mrs Powell, report to parents, Spring Term, Reception)

Thus Robert's single-minded attachment to his own agenda was something that Mrs Powell hoped was being modified by life in the classroom. It was, though, something that continued to give his parents some cause for concern.

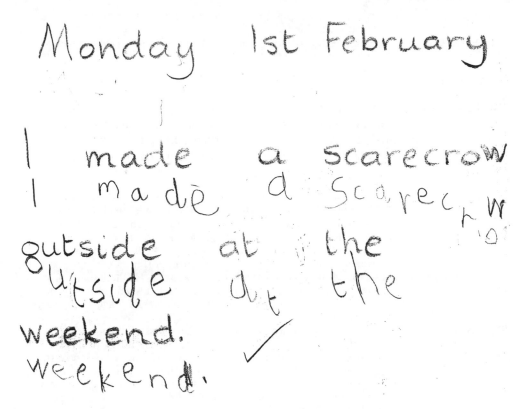

Document 6.1 *Robert, Reception, 'I Made a Scarecrow' (February 1988)*

Home and family relationships in Reception

Just as Robert's desires were inevitably going to clash with the organizational and human demands of a busy classroom, so too were they with those within the home. While Robert's parents wished to respect Robert's needs and minimize his frustration, they also had to consider the needs of the rest of the family. They were, moreover, frequently perplexed as to the best way to handle the situation, as they describe in interview with Andrew Pollard:

Mrs Osborne:	As far as I am concerned I feel as if the relationship sometimes isn't very good because you are just pushing all the time. If he wants to do something you have to say 'Well, we haven't got time now we will have to do it again', you know.
AP:	Robert sort of flourishes best in his own time I think, doesn't he?
Mrs Osborne:	Yes!
Mr Osborne:	. . . and as long as it all goes smoothly he is all right.
Mrs Osborne:	It is when things go wrong we have problems. The slightest thing can set him off and he just loses control.
AP:	Has he always sort of approached things that way?
Mrs Osborne:	Yes, he is very, not touchy, perhaps 'particular' is a better word. I mean if he is building something and he can't get it

	just right, well, he just goes crazy and it's hard to know what to do with him really.
Mr Osborne:	He has toned down since going to school because obviously they are not going to stand for fits of pique every ten minutes or so.

(Parent interview, March 1988, Reception)

Robert's tendency to be 'particular' and to insist on getting things right was a trait that, in the home and school examples here, applied to his own plans for models, to games and practical activities. In interview, his parents were asked to reflect also upon situations in which his efforts were more likely to be evaluated by others.

AP:	You see, I am thinking that there are lots of situations in school that some up where, because the kids feel a bit evaluated, it is a threatening situation and they have to take risks. You have to write something down and it is right or it is wrong or whatever. So the way they actually approach a risk-taking situation, I think is quite an important issue.
Mr Osborne:	I was just trying to think of his writing. He had some problems, letters back to front, and it doesn't seem to worry him that much. He will accept that, 'Oh yes, I have done that backwards'.
Mrs Osborne:	He says, it doesn't matter, he doesn't fuss about it.
	To us [his reading] seems very good, not knowing how other children have progressed. Most of the schoolbooks he brings home now he can read. Obviously there are words he doesn't know but he will make a good shot at it, and even if it is wrong he will get part of it right.
AP:	He is eager to have a go.
Mrs Osborne:	Yes, he is very keen. Very keen.
Mr Osborne:	He is keen to have a go at tackling a strange word and he is not bothered too much whether he gets it right or wrong.
Mrs Osborne:	I usually praise him if he makes a shot at it. I say it is 'a very good try Robert'. Then I say whatever it is, the word. I try to emphasize the positive and avoid the negative.

(Parent interview, July 1988, Reception)

Thus, if Robert was relaxed in his approach to learning to read and write at home, so too were his parents. They did not 'get in a fuss about it'. Rather they reduced the risk for Robert by creating a learning environment in which 'making a shot at it' and 'getting part of it right' were viewed positively and reinforced with praise.

We saw above that, like William, Robert usually tried to minimize any writing task in school. Also like William, and as he had done from his pre-school days, Robert enjoyed writing for his own purposes at home:

He enjoys writing, although Mrs Powell says he doesn't do his writing in school, but he does do a lot of pictures with words here and there at home.
(Mrs Osborne, parent interview, July 1988, Reception)

Stories and imaginative play continued to be among Robert's favourite home pastimes, as this diary entry extracted from a day in the life of Robert and his family shows:

Robert asked for a story to pass the time getting to school and was happy to listen to 'A little boy called Robert' which is a true recollection of a family holiday in Scotland when he was 18 months old. A great favourite, one he hasn't asked for, for a long time until recently. [This evening] Robert said he had a good day at school when asked, but had forgotten what had happened – not uncommon! He read his schoolbook with interest and enjoyed dinner chatting about when he was a baby, what he liked to eat and things he used to say. After dinner had no interest in his 'word tin', a real battle to get him to do a few new ones, wanting only to play. Into pretend – a newsreader tonight. Helped to prepare a desk with phone, news sheets and computer [cardboard boxes]. A very imaginative report, with Mother and brother roped in to assist. Pleasant half-hour prior to bedtime. Robert helping to clear up before bathtime – very rare. Daddy late tonight, arriving at the end of story time – memo to self, must improve timing – and immediately handed a book to read an extra story for a few more minutes. Relaxed, happy evening.
(Parent diary, February 1988, Reception)

The relationship between Robert and his brother had always been good, his parents felt. Indeed Robert did not resent even the amount of time and attention that Richard as a baby had demanded. However, as we see in this diary entry, brother Richard was now becoming old enough to join in Robert's play and, as it was with his peers, play between them was usually conducted on Robert's terms. Mrs Osborne told Andrew Pollard:

Well the other day he was playing something with Richard, and Richard came out in tears because Robert was insisting that Richard do something the way he wanted to do it. He had a bridge, he builds two chairs facing each other and he had a toy box and a couple of chairs trying to make a drawbridge. And Richard instead of say stepping on the drawbridge, Richard was just sneaking in the back door which didn't go down at all well and Robert was losing it, and Richard came out in tears upset because he wasn't just doing what he should have done, in Robert's eyes anyway. Robert was getting upset with Richard. He has definitely improved but he still has a tendency to go a bit wild if you don't comply, or if Richard doesn't comply. But generally they play very well.
(Mrs Osborne, parent interview, July 1988, Reception)

Having reflected on the fact that earlier in the year they felt that they had little knowledge of Greenside School or of education generally, at the end of Robert's first year at school the Osbornes were asked what they now felt about the school.

AP: You have been happy with Greenside have you, so far?
Mrs Osborne: I suppose I am. I don't know an awful lot that goes on. Like Chris says, we certainly know very little about the school. I know it is open if you want to go in and help out, which I think is a good idea because it gives you an idea of what goes on. At the moment it is not very easy.

Mrs Osborne was referring here to the fact of having a toddler and a new baby to look after, though Robert's lack of interest in discussing anything at home connected with school compounded his parents' lack of knowledge:

It has been like this all along. You say 'What did you do at school today?' It is 'I've forgotten.' That is all you get. I say 'Did anyone come in?' or 'Did you do anything new?' He just has no interest in saying anything about school. He loves going. It is not that. He just really doesn't want to talk about it.
(Mrs Osborne, parent interview, March 1988, Reception)

However, though they may have known little about how Robert spent his days in school, the Osbornes felt pleased with Robert's progress and development:

Mr Osborne: I think he enjoys school so much the way the day is structured at the moment. There again I don't know how the day works at school but it seems a very relaxed routine. He seems quite happy with that. Particularly at weekends his mind is like a sponge, you can say things to him, it goes in and it's still readily available a couple of days afterwards and on some subjects he will just want more and more information. I am running out of things that I can truthfully say to him that I know are correct. We were talking about comets and meteorites.

Mrs Osborne: I wasn't part of all this I can assure you!

Mr Osborne: This was when you were in hospital, the whole weekend nothing but questions about this. I was searching frantically in the evenings through the encyclopedia trying to find some more information ... but that is the sort of thing. I mean it obviously works for Robert the way they are doing it at school. What I can remember of school was very regimented and that was less interesting for me. I just don't want it to happen to him.

(Parent interview, July 1988, Reception)

Clearly then, by the end of Robert's first year at school, his parents felt that he had settled well at Greenside and considered that the school's approach was suiting him.

Summary of Robert's Reception year

In Robert's first year at Greenside School we see him setting his own goals and interpreting those of his teacher in creative ways. If emotionally and socially he did not always conform to the expectations of either his teacher or his peers, his independent approach to learning and his originality nevertheless enabled him to begin to achieve status in the classroom in the eyes of his teacher. For Robert, his peers were at worst an interference to his plans, at best almost, it seems, an irrelevance.

At this early stage in his career, Robert's parents are unaware that there was a broad match between the expectations and learning environment they created in the home and the new ethos which was beginning to sweep through the school. Readers of Sarah and William's stories will appreciate that Robert would not experience that change at classroom level until he met the new influx of teachers in Year 2. In the meantime the relaxed and secure atmosphere of Reception was to give way to what was, for many, the greater challenge of Miss Scott's Year 1 class.

Robert, Year 1, early Days in Miss Scott's class

The new mix of children that Robert experienced in Miss Scott's Year 1 class meant that he was no longer the oldest, but that half the class was now older than him.

However, he maintained his high academic position, achieving the highest attainment for reading and literacy generally and the second highest attainment in maths. His independent stance in the classroom also remained unchanged, as Miss Scott's remarks to Andrew Pollard confirm:

> He has this extraordinary general knowledge and amazing interest in everything, anything. Quite independent. We are planning our day – 'I don't think I want to put my plan in that silly thing. We can't get them out. We can't see them. I will put mine in my drawer and then I will know where it is, and you will know where it is. Much better'. His plans are all fantastic drawings and squiggles.
> (Miss Scott, teacher interview, November 1988, Year 1)

> I met his parents. They seem very normal. I said he was a very gifted child. They didn't seem particularly bothered either way. They accepted it.
> (Miss Scott, teacher interview, November 1988, Year 1)

In his Year 1 class, as in Reception, Robert continued to exhibit independence of purpose and frustration when things did not go according to the plans in his head.

> Self-oriented still in many respects and displays an immature behaviour when things do not go his way in his own work or social confrontations.
> (Miss Scott, teacher records, November 1988, Year 1)

Although Robert continued to say little about school at home, it was clear that, unlike any of the other children in the study, he seemed relatively impervious to Miss Scott's volatility. His parents reported to Andrew Pollard that he had settled well into his new class:

> AP: The first weeks went OK then?
> Mrs Osborne: Fine. No problem whatsoever. I waited for about a week to say anything, and I said 'How are you getting on? What is your new teacher, Miss Scott, like?' [He said] 'She is lovely.' And that was all I got really. Very happy. Very pleased. No problem at all. He very seldom says anything about school.
> (Parent interview, November 1988, Year 1)

If Robert's approach to school remained unchanged with his change of class teacher, so too did his responses to his peers. Although he had lost his position as oldest in the class, for Robert, being in a class with older children was helpful.

Friendships and peer relationships in Year 1

Robert in Year 1 continued to reject the involvement of other children in his work and plans. However, the fact that he was prepared to include some of the older children suggests that he had more potential for social and cooperative relationships in the classroom than he had sometimes been given credit for. Miss Scott to Andrew Pollard:

> He is a bit, like, an oddball. He is the odd professor. The children tolerate him. Robert is Robert and he probably doesn't mix terribly well because if things get taken or people ruin things by taking one piece of his junk or model, he gets terribly upset. But there is less of that now. I don't really know who he goes with [in the playground]. He seems to wander because he has so many ideas about models and problem-solving things. Children tend to like to see what he is doing and perhaps copy and perhaps interfere, which does

cause problems. So he perhaps gets older children to look at his work. Like Liam. They get together. Or Marcus, but then he tends to work on his own.
(Miss Scott, teacher interview, November 1988, Year 1)

So, if Robert continued to be 'tolerated' by his peers and his outbursts ignored, this was, in part, because of the respect and interest that his ideas and achievements commanded. It was probably also because he was deemed, despite his temperament, to be 'well meaning' (Teacher records, November 1988), 'a friendly boy' and 'a warm, open child' (Teacher records, January 1989).

As his mother described, Robert was not interested in the sort of running and chasing games that predominated within the mainstream boys' culture in the playground. In addition, of course, there was a lack of reciprocity in his relationships with his peers. Robert, however, did not appear to see his isolation in these terms. For him, it seems, the rejection came from others. At home, when asked by his mother who he played with at school, his response was,

'I don't play with anybody. Nobody wants to play with me.'
(Parent interview, July 1989, Year 1)

There is a suggestion here, and in his appreciation of older children in the classroom, that Robert was not the loner by choice that his teacher seems to have perceived him to be. Although friendship and association with Robert would clearly have to be on his terms, the indications are that companions who shared his interests would have been appreciated.

Learning strategies in Year 1

As suggested above by his achievements relative to his peers, Robert continued to excel in all aspects of schoolwork. His writing was now developing with Miss Scott reporting that he had 'a very individual style and expresses his thoughts well in writing' (Report to parents, spring 1989). Robert told Andrew Pollard about his favourite activities in the classroom:

AP:	What do you think about work at school?
Robert:	I'm good at maths. I like maths cards. Construct's my favourite. I got to play with that all morning one day. No-one noticed. It was very good.
AP:	What about reading?
Robert:	I'm not actually too keen on reading. I'd rather play in the maths all day, non stop. I've shot up now. I'm on Stage 2 of cards. I think I'll be on Book O next. That's a very, very, very, very hard one.
AP:	Does it matter if you don't do things the way your teacher wants them?
Robert:	Most of the time I get it right. It's difficult to tell but I just work it out and think about it. Nearly all the time I get things right. It doesn't surprise me now. But the best at maths is Luke. He's already on Book O, I think.

(Pupil interview, May 1989, Year 1)

Robert's sense of autonomy in his learning meant though, that teacher expectations were not always fulfilled, as Miss Scott's records showed:

Robert is always deeply involved, but again at those activities which interest *him* and these activities may result in his inattention at class oral times and his simply not listening to instructions. And so many of his ideas aren't followed through in the detail one anticipates from his ideas . . .

However, there is no doubt that Miss Scott saw Robert as a positive force and resource in the classroom:

He is a marvellous source of ideas and often stimulates other children into their own discoveries. An exceptional child.
(Miss Scott, teacher records, summer 1989, Year 1)

Such praise for Robert's intellect was, Miss Scott had suggested, received with equanimity by his parents, and readers may well wonder at this calm acceptance. We shall now, therefore, turn to the Osbornes' response to Miss Scott and her perception of Robert's development.

Home and family relationships in Year 1

During Robert's first autumn term in Year 1, Andrew Pollard again visited Mr and Mrs Osborne at home and asked about the recent parents' evening in the school.

AP:	What did you get when you had the parents' evening and you went to Miss Scott? What sort of thing did you get from her?
Mrs Osborne:	He had glowing reports, it was almost embarrassing to be quite honest. I think that he is quite a bright child, but then mothers perhaps think that anyway of their children, you know, everyone thinks their own is wonderful. But, the questions he asks, he is quite clever. You hate saying this really. You hate admitting it in one respect. I didn't know where to look. [. . .] This thing about the lighthouse project, she was amazed at that. Getting the basket back to the house [from the lighthouse]. He had an idea about how he was going to do it although they hadn't done anything about pulleys yet. She said he was talented, gifted. Like I say, it was most embarrassing. I thought, 'Oh gosh'.
	Chris wonders how we are going to keep him enthusiastic about learning and how we are going to feed him with information and facts. Not necessarily to try to teach him things but to keep him interested and try to keep life interesting and learning interesting. But I don't think we have changed our approach really or thought about treating him in a different way.

(Parent interview, November 1988, Year 1)

Though, as we have seen, Robert's parents used praise to encourage his learning, they did think that care was needed with regard to the way in which Robert might perceive himself relative to others.

He did come home one day and he said 'Miss Scott said I was clever', and I thought, um, well, I wouldn't have said that to a child. They might go around and say 'I am very clever' and that is going to get someone's back up straight away isn't it? Who wants to see a five-year-old coming round saying 'I am very clever'. It is dreadful isn't it? Again it was something to do with the lighthouse. She probably said 'That was a clever idea' or something like that. I presume it was something that just tripped off her tongue.
(Mrs Osborne, parent interview, November 1988, Year 1)

The relaxed approach that Robert's parents had taken to the development of the formal skills of literacy in his pre-school years continued into his early years of school. Thus, though they considered Robert's spelling to be 'erratic' they were nevertheless confident that experience would put that right. As we have seen, how to sustain Robert's enquiring nature concerned them more than the acquisition of more formal evidence of learning, and they gave credit to the school for maintaining that through into his second year of school life. They did, however, regret the fact that Robert seemed to have a dogmatic point of view about everything. Moreover, they occasionally viewed Robert's questioning with some ambivalence, as they described to Andrew Pollard:

Mrs Osborne: I think another six months and that will be it. I won't be able to answer any more questions!

Mr Osborne: Sunday he was in here before breakfast and I came down and he was watching BBC2. It was one of those advanced school programmes about Newtons. So since then I've been plagued with – 'I want to know what a Newton is', and I said to him, 'Why don't you ask Miss Scott or someone at school to find you a place in the library where there is a book that can tell you all about Newtons' – 'I'm not allowed to do that. What's a Newton?' – he just runs along one track all the time.

On other occasions the opposite approach could be equally vexing:

But sometimes he will ask you a question and I might be thinking really hard to try and give him the right answer, and I'm in the middle of this long involved explanation. . . . But while you are trying to answer the question, he's thinking of something else and he's going to ask you something else, or he's looking at something else and it's, you know, 'If you want to ask a question, please listen to the answer!'
(Mrs Osborne, parent interview, July 1989, Year 1)

Robert's tendency to 'blow ups' when frustrated were becoming fewer and, although he was still 'difficult' his parents felt it was important to give him the time and space to operate in. Though respect for the child's point of view and agenda was not always easy, Mrs Osborne was particularly clear on this point as, she felt, some of Robert's temperament may have been a reflection of her own.

Very often it is a hassle. No matter what you want Robert to do, you have to ask him over and over again. I try to ask him nicely initially – 'Come on Robert, we will do it again' – and eventually it is 'Right Robert, we do it *now*!' I am not the most patient person and I think quite often Robert gets a lot of his traits from me, where he loses his head quite easily when things don't go right.
    If I find I am cross when I shouldn't be, I always apologize afterwards because I expect them to apologize when they do something naughty so I don't see why we shouldn't apologize to them. They are a proper person. A little person.
(Mrs Osborne, parent interview, November, 1988, Year 1)

So it was that there was something of a match in the way in which Robert's outbursts were understood and responded to at school and at home in his early years. If they were tolerated at school, this was not least because of the respect in which his ideas and work were held by teachers and peers. At home, Robert was given time, space and emotional support out of straightforward respect for a child as being 'a proper person'. In both cases however, it was clear that, irrespective of the more powerful adults in his life, Robert was insistent in his focus upon his own agenda and active in the creation of the opportunities to carry it out.

Summary of Robert's Year 1

So it was that Robert sailed through his second year of schooling at Greenside. His responses to frustration in the classroom remained virtually unchanged, and though labelled 'immature' and 'self-oriented' by Miss Scott, this identity was increasingly being subsumed within a more powerful and positive one arising out of his intellectual response to classroom tasks. It will be recalled that in William's story, the presence of older, more competent pupils represented a threat to his status and the strategies he had evolved in the classroom. Robert's structural position in Year 1 was not diminished, but rather strengthened, with the influx of many children older than him. Not only could he match them academically, but they provided opportunities for the sort of sociable and potentially cooperative classroom relationships which had been lacking with his slightly younger peers. What is more, unlike any of the other children in the study, Robert remained relatively unperturbed by the more volatile environment of Miss Scott's classroom. Indeed, his classroom strategies and learning stance were apparently unaffected.

Robert's identity and career in the early years at Greenside School

If Robert was instrumental in creating his own space, whether through emotional outbursts or quiet refusal, he was in a powerful position to do so. At home he was the oldest of Chris and Sue's children and his parents were prepared to negotiate a compromise between his needs and the needs of the rest of the family. In school, his autonomous stance and social distancing were to some extent indulged by his teachers as an element of his 'oddball', 'odd professor' identity, while the tangible quality of many of his achievements enabled him to maintain respect and status among his peers even while dissociating himself from most of their activities and interests. Though, as a result, Robert was perceived by his teachers as something of a loner from choice, there are indications that this may not have been the case and that Robert did have a need for companions. As Robert's career story unfolded and his identity and status within the peer group evolved, so the nature of those needs becomes clearer.

In the meantime, at this point in his career, Robert's confident position looked fairly secure. As he moved into Year 2 and the new ethos at Greenside School, as might have been predicted, he continued to go from strength to strength. Ahead, in the future, lay some less assured and less altogether happy periods at school for Robert, as well as some more equivocal perceptions of his abilities. For the time being, however, Robert moved happily and confidently into Miss Sage's class.

Matrix 6.1 *Robert, Reception and Year 1, a summary matrix*

Family relationships	Peer-group relationships	Teacher relationships	Identity	Career
Reception: Mrs Powell				
Robert has two younger brothers, Richard and Paul.	Robert is not a physically active child, does not run well and is not very interested in outdoor play.	Structural position: age, the oldest in class. English and maths, near the top.	Robert sets his own goals in the classroom and begins to achieve classroom status through his independent approach to learning and his originality of ideas.	There is a broad match between the expectation of the home and the ethos being developed in the school.
Relaxed approach to learning in the home. No formal pre-school teaching of literacy. Low-key build-up to school.	Robert experiences great frustration in the classroom where peers can be disruptive to his plans, especially where limited resources have to be shared.	Mrs Powell says he has original ideas and makes original use of apparatus. 'He can learn from any situation.'	Regarded as 'highly intelligent', and 'volatile' by his teacher.	Home and school learning environments can be characterized by the emotional and temporal 'space' accorded to Robert by his parents and by teacher.
His parents have no fixed ideas about education but think the school's relaxed atmosphere benefits Robert's learning.	Robert's autonomy, high stuctural position and teacher regard suggest he does not *need* the support of peers in the classroom.	'Well developed number concepts', 'can write independently', 'always has ideas for writing'.	Does not conform to peer-group norms.	Robert is also active in creating his own space and structural position in family and class also mean he is in a powerful position to push through his own agenda.
Robert taxes his parents' knowledge with questions.		Develops strategies for avoiding too much writing but writes at home for his own purpose.	Maintains an attachment to his own agenda at home and school.	
Tends to have tearful rage when his plans are frustrated.				
Year 1: Miss Scott				
Robert never talks about school at home.	Older boys in this class provide opportunity for more sociable classroom relationships. Robert rejects the involvement of others in his ideas. Peers tolerate him.	Structural position: age, 16/32. English top, maths 2nd.	Teacher describes him as 'self-oriented', 'highly intelligent in thinking, immature in actions'.	Early indication of his supportive, inspirational role *vis-à-vis* his peers as Miss Scott uses his ideas to stimulate other children.
Parents feel some embarrassment at Miss Scott's praise of his intelligence. Feel that school has maintained his thirst for enquiry. Robert has 'a dogmatic point of view about everything'.	He is often alone in the playground, complains at home that no-one wants to play with him.	Miss Scott uses Robert to generate ideas. Peers like to see what he is doing but interfere, causing frustration.	'Oddball', 'odd professor'. Seen as a loner by choice at school.	Negative aspects of his classroom behaviour, e.g. low cooperation with peers, frustrated outbursts, subsumed within a more powerful and positive intellectual role and identity.
Imaginative play with brother Richard punctuated by occasional flare-ups.	Has friends home to play, on his terms.	Parents say he loves maths and reading, finds many school books boring. Teacher says his writing has flair and originality.		

6.2   YEAR 2 AND YEAR 3

Introduction

From this point in his career, Robert was to follow the same track as William, so he was now about to move through Miss Sage's class and then Mr Brown's.

In the early years of his career, as we have seen, Robert had impressed his teachers with his originality, independence of approach and ability to set his own learning goals. Robert, perhaps of all the children in the study, therefore, was likely to respond enthusiastically and successfully to the new ethos in Greenside School. However, his working relationships with his peers had proved to be a problem for him in the past. How might Robert fare therefore, with the increased expectations upon pupils to cooperate interactively with their peers?

In the middle years of his career at Greenside, Robert's relations with his peers did indeed continue to be regarded as something of a problem. Yet we will also see some important changes as Robert learnt to reconcile expectations upon him for cooperation and for sharing resources and knowledge with his own interests and agenda for learning. In Part Two of his story we see an adjustment to new contexts, as Robert actively constructed a classroom identity that was acceptable to his peers as well as his teachers.

Robert, Year 2, early days in Miss Sage's class

In the autumn of 1989 Robert moved into Miss Sage's class, along with William and with Daniel, whose story featured in *The Social World of Children's Learning*. Robert settled quickly into his new class, where both his chronological and academic position remained virtually unchanged from the previous year.

Miss Sage's early perceptions of Robert were not dissimilar from those of his previous teachers. She told Andrew Pollard:

> Robert. An oddball. Very intelligent but immature. Bit of a loner. Very interesting. Prone to tantrums? You can see his lower lip curling as he struggles to control himself. Gets very interested in things he has chosen. Loves the computer and would love to spend all day exploring, investigating it.
> (Miss Sage, teacher interview, September 1989, Year 2)

The love of computers alluded to here was a new development in Robert's career and was to become an important aspect of his identity as a pupil and his classroom status in the years to come.

As described in Chapter 3, within a highly organized and monitored framework, pupils in Miss Sage's class were encouraged to be active learners, taking a good measure of responsibility for their own learning. Robert had always strived for, and thrived on, the sort of self-direction which he was now able to achieve in this class. However, along with taking greater control over their own learning, pupils in Miss Sage's class were also expected to achieve higher levels of interaction and cooperation with their peers than formerly. On his previous record of classroom relationships, the latter might have been expected to be more of a problem for Robert. However, other developments that occurred during that year shed some further light on Robert's working relationships with his peers.

Friendships and peer relationships in Year 2

At the beginning of the year, we see Miss Sage describing Robert in much the same terms as his previous teachers had. He was 'a bit of a loner'. To a great extent this continued to be the case in relation to Robert's playground activities, and though he had some regular companions he could also frequently be observed in lone activities. He gave an account of his playtimes to Andrew Pollard:

AP:	What sort of things do you like playing in the playground?
Robert:	On the apparatus and walking on the wooden parts of the thing that holds the bank in and running on the terrace and the field. Kicking a ball with Luke and I play dinosaurs with Naomi. She's not my girlfriend – just one of my friends. And I like to see how the new plants are sprouting. Class 8 planted them.
AP:	Are there any children you don't you play with now, who you did play with before?
Robert:	I don't see Hazel so much 'cos she's in another class now. But I like playing dinosaurs and dragons.

(Robert, pupil interview, May 1990, Year 2)

It may be recalled that Hazel was something of a special friend of Robert's, though this continued to be more apparent in their home settings than in school. As can be seen in Hazel's story in *The Social World of Children's Learning*, and in Harriet's story, games of dinosaurs and dragons were very much the invention of Hazel and closely associated with her playground and classroom identity.

Though his playground activity continued much as before, Robert was becoming more closely associated with the pair of friends, Daniel and Andrew, who readers will also have met in *The Social World of Children's Learning*, and also with Luke. These three boys constituted what Robert's mother jokingly referred to as his 'wimpy clan' – boys who, like Robert, were less active in some of the more rumbustious forms of playground activity, with which William, for instance, associated. Daniel and Andrew were inclined to find Robert 'bossy' . As Andrew put it: 'He always makes us do what *he* wants to do' (Friendship group interview, April 1990, Year 2), and so Robert's association with the group did not become particularly strong.

Though Robert's playground activities did not undergo any great change in Year 2, his working relationships with his peers in the classroom did. In earlier years, Robert had, as we have seen, tended to 'blow up' at the interference of his younger peers in his plans and exclude them from his activities. Now Miss Sage reported that Robert still: '. . . occasionally gets worked up if situations don't conform to his expectations' (Miss Sage, report to parents, spring 1990). However his peers were concerned this was less often the case. Rather, Robert increasingly assumed a more inclusive 'explaining' role in relation to his peers so that Miss Sage was also able to report:

Robert has formed some good relationships with peers and adults. He can work very cooperatively with others and be an inspirational influence on them.
(Miss Sage, report to parents, spring 1990)

Of course, it is difficult at this point in Robert's story to conclude that this development was attributable to the change of classroom context or alternatively to a general maturation and adaptation to the peer group that would have occurred anyway. Certainly, in Miss Sage's classroom the organizational structures, rules and expectations for behaviour supported cooperative and interactive learning in a way that the children had not previously experienced. It is also clear that Robert, despite not sharing many of the concerns of the mainstream peer culture, nevertheless needed their interest and support for the maintenance of his classroom identity and status as an 'inspirational influence'. This in itself may have been sufficient motivation for the cultivation of their respect and support. However, we shall have to allow another couple of years to pass in Robert's career and analyse some classroom contexts which were less supportive of Robert's relationships in order to move forward our understanding on this.

Learning strategies in Year 2

During Robert's second term in her class, Miss Sage wrote that she considered him to be 'talented in all areas of the curriculum' with the exception of sport (report to parents, spring 1990). Her comments on his approach to tasks included the observations that he 'displays flashes of insight and intuition' and 'is gaining the concentration and self-discipline to follow his ideas through'. At the beginning of that term however, Robert, for his part, indicated to Andrew Pollard that he was relatively unsure of his teacher's perceptions of him and less confident of his ability to succeed than might have been supposed:

AP:	How are you getting on at school?
Robert:	Well, I'd rather not say, really.
AP:	Oh, well, is that because you're doing so well?
Robert:	Well, not really.
AP:	Oh.
Robert:	Well, I'm really a bit lazy, really. It's particularly with long things and writing things. I like to do short things where I can do them quickly. And if it's writing it makes my hand ache.
AP:	What do you think your teacher thinks of how you're getting on?
Robert:	I don't know really.
AP:	Good?
Robert:	Well, not really. She thinks she has to keep an eye on me and some things are quite difficult. Sometimes I don't understand them.
AP:	Oh, what sort of things?
Robert:	Well maths cards for instance. I'm on Level 3 and some are quite hard and I don't know what I have to do. Goodness knows what Level 4 will be like.
AP:	What do your friends think about how you're getting on?
Robert:	Good.

AP: What do your parents think?
Robert: (*very emphatically*) Brilliant.
(Pupil interview, January 1990, Year 3)

Documents 6.2 and 6.3 show the sort of writing activity that was 'long' and made Robert's hand ache.

As some of Miss Sage's remarks above indicate, Robert continued to make good use of opportunities to carry through his own plans and ideas. However, readers of William's story will recall that during that year Miss Sage was away from school for three months and a supply teacher, Miss Jones, took over. She brought a very different philosophy and approach to the structuring of tasks. For William, it may be recalled, working his way through a series of highly teacher-directed tasks, filling exercise books and anticipating the approval of his *absent* teacher proved, for a while at least, to be a very motivational process. In the case of Robert, however, there was a mismatch between Miss Jones's non-negotiable approach to tasks with highly specified outcomes and Robert's desire for a measure of autonomy in relation to his learning. During this time, Robert was asked by Andrew Pollard what he thought about school:

Robert: The best thing I like is playing outside. I wish we weren't kept in so often. Just since the supply teacher. I like Miss Sage better.
AP: Does it matter if you don't do things the way your teacher wants them?
Robert: I'm not used to doing things the way the teacher wants. I prefer to do things the way I normally do. I can get into a little bit of a muddle to get it how she wants it.
(Fieldnotes, Andrew Pollard, April 1990, Year 2)

Later in the school year, Robert reflected in interview on his time in the infants:

AP: How do you think you have got on at school in the infants?
Robert: Quite well. My favourite class is Miss Sage. I don't remember Miss Powell very much, but I think that Miss Scott came number three. Mrs Jones was a bit different 'cos I've got much more interesting ideas than her.
(Pupil interview, July 1990, Year 2)

These fairly matter-of-fact replies of Robert were also characteristic of his responses at home where he was reluctant to reveal that, during that stage, he was having a fairly unhappy time at school. However, his parents detected that all was not well with Robert:

Mrs Osborne: It is probably good for him to see that different teachers have ideas of approaching the class in different ways. But he wasn't very happy with that set-up.
AP: Did he come back and talk about it or did he just come back upset?
Mrs Osborne: The first couple of days he came back upset and didn't want to go to school the next day. The first time I had had that (. . .) At first he didn't want to talk about it. Any time he has been upset by anything he has never wanted to say what it was but eventually then he got a bit upset and he said he

Type of Story	Time	Setting
Funny	1990. (Future).	Make Believe.

Character's name	Description of character
Tom	Blue hare, Red eyes. Age 15 a Bignose

Ideas for the plot	The ending
he takes somefig from the musem.	he goes to Prisen

Story title	The RoBarre

Now write your first draft.

Document 6.2 *Robert, Year 2, 'Story Planner' (November 1989)*

kept being shouted at because he wasn't getting on with his work, and couldn't get on with his work because he was being shouted at. So this circle was going on and on and I've since heard that one day he was very upset in the playground and was crying. Certainly he didn't like the fact that he had

Thasday 2nd November

The ROBARE [Robbery]

One day well Thasday [Thursday] it wasin

the Sunday Timse [Times], "Rober [Robber]

TOM Stiks [strikes] agen [again] !!!" this time

he had RoBd [robbed] the city musem [museum].

So the PoLLes [police] and over [other] PePol [people]

hay to find him. Wehn [When] tha had [they]

Conerd [cornered] him, they Loox't [locked] him up

in Prisen [prison]. Sevs [serves] him rit [right] dosantit [doesn't]

Yes it dos [does] !!!!!!!!! !!! .

Document 6.3   *Robert, Year 2, 'The Robbery' (November 1989)*

to sit down and do things, didn't have much time to do his own thing. He didn't say very much other than that really, so I just said, 'I know why you don't like it, it's all work and no play. It's not like with Miss Sage, all play and no work' – just to see what he would say. And he said, 'Yes. No, no. We can *choose* what we do. We can *plan*'. I just wanted to see what he would say, comparing the two.

(Parent interview, July 1990, Year 1)

Of course, the overview of Robert's career, which this longitudinal analysis allows, gives us some further insights into the possible cause of Robert's unhappiness at this time. From this perspective we can see that it was not simply a measure of autonomy and the opportunity to investigate and explore his ideas that Robert had lost during that three-month period. While he was confined to a chair carrying out teacher-directed tasks, he had also lost the highly visible and tangible identity of 'inspirational influence' that flowed from it. It was this identity, moreover, that, in one form or another, had always underpinned his classroom status and his relationships with his peers as well as with teachers.

Home and family relationships in Year 2

At home, Robert's parents reported that his talking and questioning remained as lively as ever, but they suggested, his listening was still not as good. This they felt was because Robert had a very strong conception of what he thought he knew, which tended to overpower his listening and what he might gain from others. The 'explaining' role that was developing in the classroom came into play in all sorts of contexts now, as shown in Sue Osborne's description of a family visit to the Science Museum in London:

Mrs Osborne:	Whereas Richard will stand and just look, Robert will dive in and he will see perhaps a wheel or something going up and down. I remember on two occasions he looked at whatever it was and there was a man standing beside him and he started to go on to this man, explaining this model of a mill. Robert was trying to explain it to this man and he could hardly get away from him.
AP:	In a way, his self-confidence in terms of explaining technical things is way ahead of his actual knowledge.
Mrs Osborne:	Oh, yes. Definitely. Which maybe is quite a good thing really.

(Parent interview, December 1989, Year 2)

It may be that in this sort of case, explaining to another was Robert's way of exploring his own knowledge and explaining to himself. He also loved to explain things to Richard now, though in this case his mother felt it was more a case of airing his superior knowledge before his younger brother:

Mrs Osborne:	Every now and then he will come along and say 'this is how you do this, Richard' and 'Let me explain'. For instance, letters. He will say 'This is how you do the letters, Richard'. Whereas before he was just doing his own thing and not really bothered. Now he thinks that being a top infant he is more grown up and that he can show off his knowledge to Richard.

(Parent interview, December 1989, Year 2)

In contrast to Robert in his Reception class, Richard was not settling easily into Greenside School but Robert was prepared to spend time with him in the playground while he gained confidence:

Mrs Osborne:	He hasn't been very happy, but he's settling a bit. I try to encourage Robert to try at lunchtime to play with him, and he does. I think he takes an interest in him.
AP:	So Robert has been acting as responsible older brother a bit?
Mrs Osborne:	Oh, I would say so, yes. Definitely. Maybe not so much at

> home if they're arguing over something but when they're in
> school, definitely.

(Parent interview, December 1989, Year 2)

Apart from the period with Miss Jones described above, the only other school upset of which Robert's parents were aware was in relation to sports day, as this extract from the diary reports:

> His one weakness lies in the sports field. Carl Lewis can definitely sleep easy in the knowledge that Robert will not present any competition for him! Sports day is not a favourite for Robert, who can, and has, got very upset about the thought of coming last – again!

(Parent diary, July 1990, Year 2)

The annual upset at each sports day suggests that, though Robert may have not been *interested* in the more active pursuits of many of his male peers, he certainly was not *indifferent* to them and to the implications for status that they carried within the mainstream pupil culture at Greenside School.

Summary of Robert's Year 2 at Greenside School

During Year 2, we see Robert developing a showing, explaining role which is given expression in the classroom, at home and with strangers as well. Perhaps encouraged by both his Year 1 and Year 2 teachers, Robert was increasingly coming to regard himself as knowledgeable and of superior intellect. However, although his parents were pleased with his confident and enquiring nature, any arrogance and bossiness continued to be frowned on and discouraged.

If Robert thrived intellectually and was at his happiest in a context in which he had a good measure of control over his learning, it now appeared that that self-direction was also important for Robert in the construction of a classroom identity that carried status.

At this point in career we cannot be *sure* that Robert's unhappiness with Miss Jones could be attributed to the loss of a classroom identity that underpinned his relationships with his peers. By the same token we cannot know *for certain* that it was Miss Sage's classroom organization that enabled Robert to operate in ways that were helpful to his relationships with his peers. What was becoming clearer was that Robert was not indifferent to his image in the eyes of his peers, and in Year 2 we saw him actively elaborating a pupil identity that was increasingly acceptable to his peers. This, moreover, was in a way that was distinct from the more obvious academic, social or physical means to this end, such as those competed for by boys such as William. If we follow the track of Robert's career for a few more years, the relationship between teacher-organized contexts, the ways in which Robert was perceived by teachers, and his role and status with respect to his peers will become clearer.

Meanwhile, with the new interests of computers and science added to his technological stature, Robert moved into his Year 3 class, able now also, one would imagine, immediately to take on the role of interactive learner that we have seen to be Mr Brown's ideal.

Robert, Year 3, early days in Mr Brown's class

In the autumn of 1990, Robert again very quickly settled into a new class, maintaining about the same chronological and academic position as in the previous two years. His reputation had gone before him and so, to some extent, Mr Brown knew what to expect. He gave his early impressions of Robert to Andrew Pollard:

> He's generally very intelligent but he seems to get worked up about silly things, but when he's chatting to me he's always got fantastic ideas about things. He was doing science today and he looked at the grid I'd given them to complete and he said, 'Instead of "what happened" couldn't we put "results"?' and things like that, and I keep thinking 'Oh, pat on the head. Marvellous'.
> (Mr Brown, teacher interview, September 1990, Year 3)

Mr Brown also emphasized some scattier elements of Robert's approach that other teachers had not:

> I think he's a kind of forgetful person. He'll leave a mess behind somewhere, not because he's lazy. He's just forgotten about it. He will go and do something else because he's thinking about the next thing, like a mad professor in a way. It's just always commonsense things as well. He might put something in the wrong place and not see what he's done wrong.
> His work is beautifully presented. He's great.
> (Mr Brown, teacher interview, September 1990, Year 3)

Miss Sage did not use the description of 'professor' in her comments about Robert, but now we see that again, as in Reception and Year 1, Robert is attributed that identity by a teacher. Now, moreover, the tag 'mad' has been added and, as in Reception and Year 1 also, we see in Mr Brown's account, an indulgent attitude towards classroom behaviours associated with a form of the 'professor' identity. Robert's parents, in contrast to Mr Brown's perception, had, in interviews since Year 1, described Robert as 'lazy' due to his habit of getting brothers, friends, and anyone that would, fetching and carrying for him.

We suggested above that Robert, through his experience in Miss Sage's class, was now in a position to be the sort of interactive learner that Mr Brown also valued. Indeed, in the early days in his class Mr Brown did perceive that Robert's relationships with his peers were quite satisfactory:

> AP: How is he getting on with other children?
> Mr Brown: Fine. No problem as far as I can see. He doesn't seem to have one friend, but he's always got someone with him.
> (Teacher interview, September 1990, Year 3)

However, as the year wore on it became clear that Robert was not integrated in his working relationships with his peers in quite the same way as he had been in Miss Sage's class.

Friendships and peer relationships in Year 3

At the end of Year 2, some children had left the school and new friendship groups formed in the playground. Observations and friendship group interviews with Ann Filer showed Robert's relationships and play activities continued much as they always had done, with several boys happy to play with Robert if they were not playing football or some other running, chasing games.

> Marcus, Maurice and Robert play scientific games. Pretending they can turn into bicycles. They're really clever.
> (Stephen, friendship group interview with William and Daniel, July 1991, Year 3)

> I play with Robert when I'm not playing football.
> (Marcus, friendship group interview with Maurice and Robert, July 1991, Year 3)

Robert also remained popular with many of the girls and was not averse to joining in the culture of 'love' and 'girlfriends', although, as this conversation during an interview with Ann Filer shows, he could not always manage the casual banter that went with the scene:

> Maurice: Belinda put a love letter in your drawer today.
> Robert: I don't mind. That's all right. Some people get silly about that sort of thing but I think it's all right.
> Maurice: Oh, listen to him! Don't get so serious about it! He really gets serious about it.
> Robert: People are always making fun of me because I'm in love with Belinda.
> Maurice: She's fat and tubby.
> Robert: It doesn't matter what people look like.
> (Friendship group interview with Marcus, Maurice and Robert, July 1991, Year 3)

Robert was also friendly with William and Daniel and though he played with these and other friends out of school and they went to one another's houses for tea, there was a tendency sometimes to marginalize him, as also became apparent in group interviews:

> I try to play with Daniel but he says 'Push off, we're having a private conversation'.
> (Robert, friendship group interview with Marcus and Maurice, July 1991, Year 3)

> I had to hide my birthday invitations from Robert 'cos we're going to Southwater Lagoon and Robert cries. He's not like us. He doesn't like football and things. He does computers all the time after school.
> (Daniel, friendship group interview with William, July 1991, Year 3)

Indeed, as we shall see, swimming was another activity that Robert was going to have to come to grips with if his pride was to be upheld before his peers. However, family holidays over recent years had shown Robert developing some expertise as a skier, though unfortunately his peers were not privy to his courage on the ski slopes.

We suggested above that Robert, in Mr Brown's class, was not as integrated with his peers in the classroom as he had been in Year 2. Mr Brown's account of Robert's working relationships tell a similar story to that which held in his early years of schooling. He told Ann Filer:

> He has a tendency to get frustrated, especially if he's working with others who don't come up to his level of understanding or ability. He can get into little temper fits at times, especially if it's technology because he knows exactly what he want to do and nobody's going to stand in his way and if they do, if they get to the hammer first, or

he's supposed to be working with them and they don't like his design, then he can get really frustrated and end in tears.
(Mr Brown, teacher interview, July 1991, Year 3)

In other respects Robert's peers were enabling for him in the classroom. A feature of his relationships with peers in Miss Sage's class had been the 'showing' and 'explaining' role that she had encouraged at this time. He had been an 'inspirational influence'. Now, with his growing interest in computers and the increasing gap between his skills and the rest of the class, Robert was able to develop this explaining role to his own ends. Not unnaturally, Robert was the person to whom pupils turned when 'stuck', for not only did he know more than they did, but also more than Mr Brown. Robert's tendency on such occasions was to 'take over' in his demonstrating role, and this not only gave him plenty of access to his beloved computers but also provided a legitimate escape from less appealing tasks. Of course, it was peer acceptance and respect for his knowledge and for the help offered that gave him access to this role, but such time as was spent away from routine tasks also needed at least the tacit support of Mr Brown, and this was forthcoming.

Learning strategies in Year 3

As suggested, Mr Brown did recognize that Robert's troubleshooting role could be a problem, as he described in interview with Ann Filer:

> But, I mean, he's been disappointing sometimes so he's not consistent and he's produced some work which is absolutely outstanding, you know, but it's sporadic. Other times he's too busy sorting out with the computer to concentrate on his own work. So his maths has been steady. In science and things like this occasionally he's produced this fantastic work and his understanding is superb, but, you know, he's had a sort of up and down.
> (Mr Brown, teacher interview, July 1991, Year 3)

Where written work especially was concerned, Mr Brown considered that Robert did not 'put in the necessary effort' (Report to parents, Spring Term 1991). Where computers were concerned, though, Robert simply took complete control of his learning and amazed everyone with his understanding and expertise. Mr Brown told Ann Filer:

> As I say, the computer is his life. His knowledge of the computer is just astounding. He's read the handbook, the sort of adults' handbook, for his computer at home, which is the same as ours. So he comes in and asks me these questions which in *no way* can I even begin to answer and he's found out things that I didn't know, and we don't need to know actually, but he's gone into new fields and messed me around sometimes by changing the background colours and things when he should be doing what he's asked to do on the computer. So when the computer is on, he gravitates towards it.
> (Mr Brown, teacher interview, July 1991, Year 3)

Thus, though Mr Brown might have regretted Robert's sporadic attention to other less appealing tasks, he was clearly very impressed by Robert's knowledge and he both acknowledged and promoted his 'boffin', 'troubleshooter' identity and role in the classroom:

> Robert is our computer 'expert' in the class who solves all problems. His knowledge of the computer is completely comprehensive.
> (Mr Brown, report to parents, Spring Term, 1991, Year 3)

Home and family relationships in Year 3

As we have seen, the Osborne family now had a computer at home, though Robert's early enthusiasms caused a few problems:

> Robert late after school, tonight being his chess club evening. On arriving at home continually asked when Mr James would come. Mr James is a friend who is 'into computers' and has been invaluable in sorting out the problems caused by the recent purchase of a computer. All the problems, needless to say, have been the result of Robert's flying fingers and his inability to freeze mentally when confronted by a computer screen. Mr James has been able to reprogramme the wretched machine on a couple of occasions and seems amused by Robert's excited state when exploring the limits of each programme.
> (Parent diary, June 1991, Year 3)

Another diary entry for that year reflects upon the fact that Robert's lack of sporting prowess was increasingly becoming a problem for him:

> The only thing Robert really hates about school is sports, and particularly sports day. There has been no improvement re his athletic prowess and he will only enter the minimum number of events he is obliged. By the way, the two events are the obstacle race and the three-legged race – we pity his poor partner. Robert hates losing, or at least being seen to lose, and obviously thinks that he has no chance to do well and will not even try.
> (Parent diary, November 1990, Year 3)

Where swimming was concerned, it was the indignity of wearing arm bands that finally persuaded him to accept swimming lessons:

> Mrs Osborne: He never wanted to swim. Never wanted swimming lessons. No, no, no. Now he has actually started to have swimming lessons. He's not very good but he can get across the pool. He can join in now without arm bands . . .
> AP: And that, you reckon, was because Paul started?
> Mr Osborne: I think it was a combination, yes. Robert going and seeing Paul the baby with arm bands on and a lot of children his own size in the pool without arm bands on.
> (Parent interview, July 1991, Year 3)

Robert's parents also reported that he was able to cope much better now with disappointments and with events not going according to his plans, and he continued to be self-assured and self-sufficient, socially. His parents during this year bought some commercially available maths assessment materials to give Robert some extra practice and, though they remained fairly relaxed about Robert's erratic spelling and his difficulty learning tables, they gave help to ensure that these were learnt for weekly tests at school. In other respects Robert's parents still felt that they knew very little about his life at school and it continued to seem to them that home and school were completely separate existences for him.

Summary of Robert's Year 3

Robert may have lacked interest in sport but he certainly could not remain indifferent to it. Football was increasingly becoming an area of competitiveness with the boys now they were in the junior school, and the high status accorded to sporting prowess among his peers could not altogether be dismissed. This was likely to have been more so with Mr Brown being a sports teacher, as we have seen in William's story.

In other respects though, teacher support seems to have helped ensure that Robert enjoyed high esteem in the eyes of his peers. The image of Robert that Mr Brown as their first male teacher promoted and validated in the classroom was still a strongly, if stereotypically, male one. That promoted image of 'computer boffin' may have compensated for Robert's weaker involvement in the mainstream boys' culture, for, despite his unconventionality, Robert was accorded a good measure of acceptability and popularity by boys of high status in the peer group.

Robert's identity and career in the middle years at Greenside School

It is now becoming clear that, in relation to the typologies of strategic action described in Chapter 2, Robert's strategies predominantly followed a pattern of *non-conformity*. This pattern entails a degree of standing outside the academic, social and extra-curricular structures of the school and Robert did so both in his unconventional and independent learning stance in the classroom and in his rejection of the alternative routes to status available, for example in the playground and sports field. However, as we increasingly perceive, he could not dissociate from them as easily as he appeared to do in his early years. In the middle years we see that Robert *did need* his peers, not only for companionship, for he was not the 'loner from choice' that was sometimes assumed, but increasingly we perceive that he was reliant on peer support and respect for the maintenance of his identity and interests-at-hand in the classroom.

In terms of the typology it is also apparent that *non-conformity* produces a certain variability in the pupil's relationships with teachers. So far, teacher support and admiration for Robert had been almost complete and, perhaps for this reason, the extent to which Robert was reliant on such teacher support was only gradually becoming apparent. We can see, for instance, that Robert was reliant on certain organizational practices of teachers for carrying out his interests in the classroom in relation to his autonomy and the working practices he enjoyed. Also, it appears, he was reliant on them to promote and sustain a viable classroom role with respect to his peers. All of this teacher support in turn provided the conditions in which Robert was able to develop and maintain his identity and status, in the eyes of his teachers and his peers, both as a pupil and as a boy. Only

Matrix 6.2 *Robert, Years 2 and 3, a summary matrix*

Family relationships	Peer-group relationship	Teacher relationship	Identity	Career
Year 2: Miss Sage				
Robert's talking and questioning are still good but listening not so good, his parents say.	Working relationships with peers improve. He can work cooperatively with them, his teacher says, and can be 'an inspiration influence' on them.	Structural position: age 15/ 27. English and maths, 2nd in class.	Robert sees himself as knowledgeable and of superior knowledge. This has been encouraged in the early years in school, but is discouraged by parents.	Robert's high structural position together with not feeling the need to conform to peer norms continue to put him in a powerful position with regard to his independent stance in the classroom.
Robert has more control over his temper now.	Robert now has what his mother jokingly refers to as his 'wimpy clan' of friends who are not involved in some of the tougher forms of playground activity.	Robert develops a love of computers and science. Miss Sage says Robert is talented in all areas of the curriculum except sport.	Robert's identity as an 'inspirational influence' and his 'explaining' role develop now.	However, his evolving influence and role in the classroom entail gaining the respect and recognition of his peers.
Likes to explain to Richard and show off his knowledge. Any talk of 'cleverness' is discouraged.		He dislikes the loss of autonomy with a supply teacher and claims his ideas are better than hers.	He could not sustain this identity with the supply teacher.	
Upsets at home about sports day and coming last in his race.				
Year 3: Mr Brown				
The family buys a computer. A curfew has to be set on Robert's use of it.	Frustration with peers because others do not match his ability. He reverts to working alone most of the time.	Structural position: age 17/ 33. Maths, English and science, in top few.	Computer 'boffin'. 'Mad professor'	Though Robert lacks interest in sport, he cannot be indifferent to it. The high status accorded to sporting prowess in the peer group cannot be dismissed.
Robert enters the minimum of events for sports day because, his parents say, he hates to be seen to lose.	'Troubleshooter' role enables good relations and the respect of peers, also access to computer activities.	Robert directs his own learning where computers are concerned. Attention to other tasks 'sporadic'. Results may be 'outstanding' or 'disappointing'.	Characterized as 'skatty', and 'forgetful' by his teacher as elements of his 'professor' identity.	Despite his problems with the mainstream boys' culture, with teacher support, Robert is developing a strong 'male' image that is acceptable to boys.
Parents are relaxed about his indifferent spelling and difficulty learning tables.	Robert can also be socially marginalized by friends because he is 'not like us'.	Mr Brown supports his computer 'troubleshooter' role in relation to his peers.	Robert's parents are less indulgent and describe similar behaviours as 'lazy'. Other boys see Robert as 'not like us'.	

briefly did we see, in the case of Miss Jones, the supply teacher, that things might go less well for Robert should his preferred ways of operating be withdrawn. Further than that, we can only hypothesize that Robert was also unhappy at that time due to the concurrent loss of role, identity and status in the classroom.

In Year 4, the hypotheses can be tested a little further. For the first time, Robert was to experience a year throughout which his class teacher, Miss King, was not altogether in empathy with him. Neither did Miss King during that time recognize or support the identity that Robert had evolved over his first four years of schooling.

6.3 YEAR 4, YEAR 5 AND YEAR 6

Introduction

As we continue to track Robert's progress we will see him facing considerable challenges to the classroom status and identity that he had maintained and developed through his career thus far. In Year 4, Robert, at times, seemed less happy than he had previously been through his career at Greenside, and unaccountably so from the point of view of his parents and Miss King. However, from the longitudinal perspective which Robert's case study offers we can perceive that new classroom and peer-group structures, as well as different teacher expectations and perceptions of Robert, resulted in a loss of power to act independently in the classroom, and a loss of his former classroom identity and role in relation to his peers.

However, Robert's return to Mr Brown in Year 5 did not produce an immediate reversion to his former classroom status. Like William, Robert was to find now that former roles and status in the classroom were occupied by Year 6 pupils. For the first time in his career Robert was considerably outshone academically by his classmates and for a while he, like William, no longer fulfilled the same kind of 'ideal pupil' image in Mr Brown's eyes. Robert also had to overcome the challenge of Mr Brown's doubts and misunderstandings regarding his independent approach to learning in Year 5. We will show how Robert, with teacher support and a new friendship, overcame these less than propitious circumstances to recover his previous identity and role in relation to his peers as well as a measure of autonomy in relation to curricular expectations.

In Year 6 Robert and William were reunited with the other case-study children in Mrs Chard's class and we shall see why Mrs Chard came to hold more equivocal views on Robert's intellect than any of his former teachers. On a more positive note, we again are able to see the power of a teacher to support and nurture a pupil's identity and to note how Robert's former classroom status and happiness were maintained for his final year at Greenside.

As we follow Robert through these years, though he suffers some setbacks, he also developed some new strategies and made some special friends. Together these helped to affirm Robert's identity and to restore his former happiness at school.

Robert, Year 4, early months in Miss King's class

In the autumn of 1991, eight-year-old Robert, along with the rest of the children in the study, moved into Miss King's Year 4 class. This year his structural position changed. He was the third oldest in the class, within the top few for science and maths and within the top quarter for English. This was very similar to his position in his Reception class, though the composition of the class was different now.

For the first time since his entry to school, Robert was slow to settle into his new class, as his mother described to Ann Filer:

> Well, we thought he had settled well but we're not so sure now. A couple of times Miss King has asked me to come in after school because he had burst into tears for no reason and I don't know if he is happy or not after all this. Robert has never given us much feedback from school, you know. Any information is dragged from him, so I won't say I was shocked but I had assumed he was settling down nicely.
> (Mrs Osborne, parent interview, November 1991, Year 4)

Though in the past Robert had sometimes cried at school, the reasons had always been understood and, apart from his time with Miss Jones, the supply teacher, no-one had assumed Robert to be basically unhappy. Now things seemed different and no-one, least of all Robert, could give an explanation for his tears. Miss King explained:

> We were all just experimenting making musical instruments with junk and at the end of the session he was just *crying* and I said 'What are you crying about?' and he said 'Because my elastic band keeps coming off my instrument and it won't stay on.' I said, 'Well what's wrong? I mean, you could just ask someone to help you. I could have helped you'. He said 'Yes but the point is it *keeps* coming off'. It wouldn't stay on there. He got so frustrated that he started to cry about it. Three times that's happened now, he's cried. That's when I saw his mother. And he actually said to me 'Will you tell my Mum for me?' I think he's so intelligent like that. He was getting frustrated about *why* he was crying because when I asked him he said 'I don't know why I'm crying. I really don't know, 'cos I know I shouldn't be crying but I keep crying'. And then when I told his mother she was really confused, but she said she'd keep an eye on him and she saw me about a week ago and said 'I really do think it's because he's got no friends in the class'.
> (Miss King, teacher interview, October 1991, Year 4)

Mrs Osborne continued to monitor the situation, going into school from time to time to talk with Miss King, because, as the term progressed it also became clear to his parents that Robert was not working well:

> But he's not doing what he should be doing, I think. He tends to want to do his own thing and unless someone says 'Do that, that and that, NOW', then he tends to be left on the side. We are not ones to push and make him do things and it's very easy going [here at home], isn't it? We don't do a lot with him out of school but I think generally he needs to be pushed along.
> (Mrs Osborne, parent interview, November 1991, Year 4)

Throughout this time, Robert's parents were sure that he liked his teacher and observed that he was never reluctant to go to school in the morning. Certainly he had lost friends and familiar peers with the move to his new class, though, as his mother pointed out to Ann Filer:

But if I say 'He's lost his friends', I never know how much he needs the friends anyway.
(Mrs Osborne, parent interview, November 1991, Year 4)

Perhaps it is not surprising, then, that everyone was slightly confused about the cause of Robert's troubles at that time.

Friendships and peer relationships in Year 4

As frequently happened during the study, with some children leaving the school and the reorganization for a new class, the children's friendship groupings underwent some disruption and restructuring. For Robert, disruption came about because Daniel had left, Marcus and Maurice were in another class and William renewed an old friendship with Stephen and, as we described in William's story, became more exclusive in his friendship choices. Now although Robert had never had particularly close classroom associations with these friends, what he did have in the past was a role in relation to them and their acceptance and respect. This indeed was important as they were mostly boys with quite a high standing in the peer group and with teachers. Now in Year 4, in contrast, we see Robert being at best ignored and sometimes rejected by high-status boys such as William and Stephen. Miss King recounted her observations:

> Definitely a loner but I feel sorry for him actually because I think he really tries to get on with the other children but they push him out for some reason. Like today. We were playing Chinese whispers on the floor. They were all in a circle and he accidentally just sat on Stephen's foot and he said 'Oh, I'm sorry Stephen' and Stephen, I can't remember what he said but something horrible. And Robert said ' I'm sorry' and he was trying to talk to Stephen and Stephen just shut him out. He's a very intelligent little boy you see and sometimes I think the other children may not want to work with him because a lot of the time he likes to get on with something on his own, but I think, occasionally, when he does really want to talk to some other children or get in with a group they just push him out.
> (Miss King, teacher interview, October 1991, Year 4)

Now the picture becomes clearer and, from the perspective which we have of Robert operating in other classes, we can probably conclude that Robert was not a loner by choice. Certainly, as his former teachers have understood, because his peers often represented a frustration to his goals, he frequently wished to work alone in the classroom. However, he also needed the companionship of his peers and he had, over the years, evolved a viable way of relating to them *and at the same time working with them*. He had maintained these relationships and status among his peers, with teacher support, through his showing, explaining and helping roles and had been respected by his teachers and respected and accepted by his peers for it. Clearly, what was missing for Robert in Year 4 was that special role in the classroom. Now Miss King certainly wished for pupils to work cooperatively and supportively of each other; indeed it was one of her criticisms of Robert that he did not do so. What she clearly did not do was to accord to Robert the public recognition of that particular identity that he had been used to, whether in the form of 'professor', 'inspirational influence' or 'troubleshooter'. It followed that, unlike any of his former class teachers, neither did she take an indulgent attitude towards the 'oddball', 'mad' forms of behaviour and ways of working which they associated with the stereotypical 'professor' identity. Rather, she perceived Robert's individualism and his attempts to take the lead with ideas and to push them through as a problem both for him and for his classmates. In her report to parents she commented:

> Science: He is able to plan an experiment in a group but needs to listen to others more without taking over. His collaborative skills could be improved.
> PE: He seems to find it very hard working in a team. He often does not listen to the rules and when he is 'out' he often will not accept that it is the rule. He needs to develop his teamwork skills a little.
> (Miss King, report to parents, summer 1992, Year 4)

Also, many informal conversations between Ann Filer and Miss King generated a similar perspective, as recorded in these fieldnotes:

> Miss King tells me that Robert still does not get involved with other children or include them. His exclusion of others is sometimes quite hostile and he won't listen to others ideas, she says. I referred to Naomi telling me Robert was 'a professor' and to his former identity as such. Miss King said the 'professor' thing is a hangover from Mr Brown's class and Naomi thinks Robert is wonderful, so that is why she used it. Miss King didn't think any of the others viewed Robert in this light any more. She never sees them getting ideas from him, she told me. She also said Robert never joins in review or class discussion.
> (Fieldnotes, Ann Filer, March 1992, Year 4)

What Miss King could not have perceived was that the former respect and status as a source of ideas for his peers had been facilitated by *teacher support* of a role and *teacher promotion* of an image, and that now that support and promotion were no longer in place. This become particularly relevant where Robert's computer skills were concerned, for, though Miss King recognized his considerable abilities in the area, as the classroom observations below indicate, any gravitation towards the computer or involvement when others were working with it were discouraged.

The picture drawn from Miss King's observations above is a sad one, though perhaps Robert's moment-to-moment classroom experience was not quite as lonely or isolating as it might seem from that picture. Observations of Robert in the classroom would, on the one hand, certainly corroborate his exclusion by, for example, William and Stephen. However, the friendly sociability that all his teachers have described was undiminished, and though he did not have many shared interests through which to relate to many of his peers, he could certainly competently reciprocate at the same level of classroom fun and social exchange. For instance:

> 1.35 pm
> Robert comes into the classroom and is one of the first to settle with a book. After the register has been called, Robert cuts some paper for a drawing task. Whilst putting the guillotine away, he passes William and Stephen who are working on the computer.
>
> Robert: (*to William and Stephen*) Oh, that's excellent, you've got 180 degrees rotation. (*No response. He repeats*) You've got 180 degrees rotation.

The boys still do not respond. Robert returns to his table to draw. He does a quick tour of the classroom looking for a rubber. He asks Naomi and uses hers.

1.45 pm
After drawing quite a lot, intermittently rubbing out, Robert turns the paper over and begins again. He is drawing a red desk-tidy composed of different length cylinders with red pens in it. Naomi comes up to him and asks him why he is drawing his own object (from the selection available). She pokes Robert on the bottom with the point of her pencil in fun and Robert takes it in that spirit. She does the same to Edward. Edward has a quick word with Robert.

Robert: (*to AF*) This is an easy thing to colour 'cos I just have to take the felt tips out.

(. . .)
Sally (the caretaker's daughter) comes up to me (AF) and tells me about the leaking roof and then remarks to Robert about his drawing:

Sally: That's good, Robert.

Another child speaks to Robert as he passes. Robert compliments Alan on his drawing of a skeleton.

Robert: (*to AF*) Look. What all great artists do. (*Robert has signed his picture*)

Robert takes his picture to Miss King who talks about it with him, discussing colour matching. She tells him it is good. Robert cuts it out.

2.05 pm
Robert has finished the drawing task. He goes over to the computer and again talks to William and Stephen about their work on it. He has said very little before Miss King goes over:

Miss King: Robert, what have I told you? [. . . about going over to the computer]

Robert rushes back to Alec and Matthew and tells them that William and Stephen are 'hacking in' to their computer work. He turns to me (AF) and tells me:

Robert: It's OK. They're allowed to.

Robert cuts two 'snowflakes', quickly, out of paper and gives them to me (AF). He goes to Alec and Matthew and makes a suggestion about their colour mixing. He goes over to Gerry and asks him if he likes his (Robert's) picture.

2.15 pm
Robert: (to AF) What I like best [on his signature] is the way the R and the O go into a line, look. Now what shall I do?

He goes to Naomi and talks briefly. He writes his name on a pencil and pokes her on the bottom with it. She responds and a game of this follows. They both go over to the carpet together, look at books and talk together.

2.30 pm
The bell goes for playtime. Miss King tells everyone to sit in their places.

The children are dismissed. Robert and Naomi play together in the playground. They play with two small circles of paper that they took out from the classroom and bits of twig. They are making 'twirlers', intermittently chatting to each other.
(Fieldnotes, Ann Filer, January 1992, Year 4)

Interestingly, several of the children that Robert was relating to in this these fieldnotes were to become of special significance to him within a few months. Though at this time, as we have seen and heard, Naomi was his main classroom and playground companion, he was to discover an affinity with the three friends Edward, Alec and Matthew. They became a closely knit group and Robert for the first time in his school career was regularly each playtime seen to be playing with the same group of boys. For the first time, Robert had found a group of friends that could share his interests and develop play around those interests and from the group interviews with other pupils at that time, it became clear that the group had acquired a distinct identity. One of the girls' groups, for instance, named the four as a group and described them as: 'A bit boring. They play Julius Caesar and Time Machines. Things like that.' (Mary, friendship group interview with Emily, March 1992, Year 4).

William and his friends also identified the four as a group and said:

William:	(*mockingly*) They talk about *really sensible things*, like the line chart [in the classroom] and we don't know what they're talking about.
Gerry:	It's quite boring what they talk about.
William:	Robert's the one with the ideas in that group. He's the computer expert.

(Friendship group interview with William, Stephen, Ian and Gerry, March 1992, Year 4)

Robert's group were asked what they liked doing in the playground.

Robert:	Space ships. And films. We have this cowboy setting and pretend we're on TV. We rob a bank.

The boys tell the story of the action and they all know their lines for the shots which they 'film' in the game. They talk animatedly about their parts in the play.

AF:	What is this year like, with Miss King, compared with last year?
Alec:	I like this year better. We know Robert now which we didn't before.
Edward:	It's better with Robert. He really helps you out when you're stuck.
Robert:	I like playing with our group.

Robert's activities with this these boys and their appreciation of Robert, then, seemed to have the effect of affirming his previous identity and role. Within the confines of this group of friends at least, his ideas and his imagination were again being valued and used.

Learning strategies in Year 4

At the same time as he was becoming integrated into this new group, Robert also became more settled at school and his parents and teacher reported no more tearful breakdowns in class. By the summer, his parents felt that his overall progress had recovered, though his teacher continued to regret the inconsistency of Robert's approach. She felt that he did not always listen well, with resulting work not as she had intended:

... like the activity last week when I said I wanted describing words. He wrote sentences and I didn't want sentences. If he'd come out and asked me about it he would have found out, but he just carries on.
(Miss King, teacher interview, October 1991, Year 4)

He would do so much better if he tried to listen attentively a little more.
(Miss King, report to parents, July 1992, Year 4)

At the end of Year 4, as at the beginning, Miss King felt that Robert still seemed to 'go up and down a lot'. He was still 'switching off' and 'always in a world of his own, daydreaming' (teacher interview, July 1992, Year 4).

Now although in the past Robert had tended to develop strategies for avoiding less enjoyable tasks, he had always substituted these tasks with his own ideas and plans. As we have seen, although his former teachers had regretted Robert's attachment to his own agenda and failure to apply himself to many routine tasks, they had consistently valued the outcome – the different slant that Robert brought to classroom activities, the source of ideas and inspiration and help for others that he provided. With the loss of teacher recognition of that approach, and his loss of power to act independently in the classroom, Robert did not now fill his time applying himself to the full range of tasks. Rather, as we see, he filled it with episodes of inactivity and daydreaming. Whereas, in the past, the view of his teachers had been that Robert had always been working and learning in any classroom situation, now he spent considerable amounts of time doing neither.

Home and family relationships in Year 4

During Year 4, Robert's home and family life continued with little change. As always, there was a tendency for his parents to be to be slightly perplexed by some aspects of his behaviour, as Mr Osborne explained:

> He can be extremely exasperating because he can talk to an adult almost as an equal, but he dissembles very well and can project himself quite well too. So he can appear very mature – but at other times he's unbelievably backwards. A complete contrast. It's quite hard for us to follow really.
> (Mr Osborne, parent interview, July 1992, Year 4)

What his parents described as Robert's 'backwardness' showed itself in many social and practical situations, some of them having parallels in some of the descriptions given by teachers of Robert in the classroom:

> Robert is happy to relate to other people provided it is on his own terms. Unless a person is able to interest Robert he will make no effort to give them his attention. We can see this clearly with his brother Paul, who idolizes and mimics Robert and is destined to be another handful. We pity the teachers in September.
> (Parent diary, June 1992, Year 4)

> We're still waiting on Robert each morning. There's always something. He hasn't got his lunchbox or he hasn't got his folder. Last week it was his spelling book he hadn't brought home – 'I put it in the folder. You or Mum must have moved it!' He does find it hard to accept he's wrong. 'Somebody else' has moved it. He's *never* moved it. He can never find anything unless it's *there*. Scatty.
> (Mrs Osborne, parent interview, July 1992)

Robert's younger brother, Paul, was now, as we see, about to start school and of an age when he was becoming more involved with his older brothers. As with Richard, the relationship had its less tranquil moments, especially as Paul was becoming increasingly interested in the computer:

Play at home is usually very good between the boys (although Paul very often gets in the way). Robert is becoming more helpful with Paul although he is never happy when Paul goes into the study to interrupt computer work. Sometimes Robert will let Paul on the computer but never for long and it nearly always ends with Robert and Paul screaming at one another.
(Parent diary, October 1991, Year 4)

Later in the year, however, Robert became more tolerant with his brothers, as his father reported:

Well, he's *mellowed*, I suppose to a certain extent. He's definitely prepared to go more than halfway on occasions with Richard, to play with him, particularly in the evenings.
(Mr Osborne, parent interview, July 1992)

We might speculate whether Robert's new mellowness with his brothers came about in part as a result of more fulfilling and reciprocated relationships with schoolfriends.

Summary of Robert's Year 4

In this section relating to Robert's time in Miss King's class, we have devoted a lot of space to an examination of his relationships and roles within the peer group and in both classroom and playground. We have argued that the issues surrounding Robert's position and status *vis-à-vis* his peers have always been crucial for the maintenance of his identity and for the fulfilling of his interests in the classroom. Year on year, our analysis of the patterns of Robert's school relationships have suggested that teachers played a crucial role in facilitating and supporting classroom relationships with his peers in the maintenance of those interests and identity. In the next section we see Robert back in Mr Brown's class and readers will be given some further insight into Mr Brown's perspective on Robert's learning stance and his role as teacher in accommodating it. Readers of William's story will be prepared for the fact that, now that the cohort of Year 5 were to be outnumbered by Year 6 pupils, fresh challenges were likely to face Robert and he would not be able to simply pick up on the old relationships and roles experienced in Year 3.

Robert, Year 5, early days in Mr Brown's class

In his Year 5 class, Robert was to experience a much lower structural position than he was used to. In a class of twenty Year 6 pupils and twelve Year 5s, there were only seven pupils younger than him. Additionally, it was a new experience for Robert to have many pupils more advanced in science and maths than he was. Nevertheless, he had been looking forward to returning to Mr Brown's class. His parents were somewhat mystified therefore, when in the early days in Mr Brown's class Robert broke down in tears at home, saying he found it difficult to concentrate in school, he had no friends, and was lonely. In school, moreover, Robert continued to show something of the same tendencies that he had in Miss King's class. In the following extract from an interview with Ann Filer, Mr Brown was asked to reflect upon any changes in Robert since he last taught him:

Robert has stopped wandering, which he used to do. He used to stand by the computer all the time, but he doesn't do that, though he's still there if he's needed. His concentration is *better* but still there is something missing. Today we were watching a video on the Aztecs and his recall of it was quite disappointing for someone of his intelligence. And I find with him that his mind wanders. I don't know what it is, it's hard to pin down, but you know, he does tend to switch off for a period and then he gets really excited about something, then, fine, he's absolutely giving one hundred per cent. But Robert doesn't seem quite the same. He's a lot calmer and more mature but it's just this question of his concentration that I'm a little worried about at the moment, or commitment, or whatever it is. I don't know.
(Mr Brown, teacher interview, September 1992, Year 5)

Mr Brown also reflected on the fact that Robert had had to accept a change from his usual position of being one of the most successful pupils in his class to one in which not only were there Year 6, but also some particularly bright girls who, in terms of their scientific and mathematical understanding, far outshone him in the classroom. He wondered whether Robert was having difficulty finding a place for himself in this new situation.

So, for the first few weeks, there was some puzzlement on the part of both Mr Brown and Robert's parents at his failure to thrive as well as they had expected. In terms of our analysis we can believe that Mr Brown had probably correctly identified part of the problem. However, Robert had never been competitive with his peers and so it was difficult to see the problem purely in terms of his relative academic status. However, although Mr Brown was unable to change Robert's structural position, he was, as we shall see, able to do much to support a change in his classroom status and identity, and this, together with a new friendship, eventually helped to restore his happiness and motivation in school.

Friendships and peer relationships in Year 5

Although Robert continued to play with Matthew, Edward and Alec, his three friends from Year 4, they were now in another class and, as usually seemed to happen when friends were split in this way, the closeness was difficult to sustain without the shared experience of classroom life.

However, after being in the class for a few months, Robert began to develop a relationship with one of the Year 6 boys. Toby was, perhaps, more closely matched to Robert in his interests and classroom strategies than any of Robert's previous friends. Toby liked football though, and on days when that was permitted to be played in the playground, Robert said that he 'just walks around' (Robert, friendship group interview with Robert and Toby, January 1993). Other boys in William's group, however, saw Robert as being more integrated into their playground games now:

AF:	What do other groups like doing in the playground?
Stephen:	Robert and Toby. Robert's playing our games now.
William:	Yeah, Robert's OK.
Ian:	He's not in our group but he plays our games.

(Friendship group interview with William, Stephen, Ian, Lawrence, Philip, January 1993, Year 5)

Robert and Toby also gave an account of their play together. The following transcript indicates both their shared interests and the way in which, as was usual with Robert, interview conversations became diverted on to more fascinating topics:

AF:	What do you like doing in the playground? What's your group like?
Robert:	Argumentative.
Toby:	We have this argument that I don't think there are any black holes in space and we have this discussion about whether there is any proof of black holes.
	(Toby in his argument makes some reference to 'air' in space and Robert corrects him)
Robert:	We talk about what there is in space.
	(Our interview conversation continues with an animated, if not perfectly informed, discussion on the subject of leptons, gluons, neutrons, electrons, what might have caused the big bang and whether there was anything before the big bang.)

(Friendship group interview with Robert and Toby, January 1993, Year 5)

The two boys worked and played closely together for the remainder of the time in Mr Brown's class, though, as a Year 6 pupil, Toby was to leave the school at the end of the year,

Learning strategies in Year 5

It seemed to Mr Brown that once Robert and Toby got together in the classroom, Robert's motivation and enthusiasm began to be restored. As he explained to Ann Filer:

> Its been a tremendous partnership because the last time I had Robert he was really quite a loner and I think he would have been again really, but with Toby he's got someone who's got a similar way of thinking and also somebody who gets very excited about scientific things and technology and computers and this kind of thing. So they kind of spark each other off with word games and quizzes and anything like that. They're always bringing things in and really get sort of carried away with it [...] as a working relationship, they've done really well and it's not been one of them leading the other. Robert wouldn't allow that anyway. He's very sure of his opinions and what he wants to do.
>
> (Mr Brown, teacher interview, July 1993, Year 5)

We cannot assume that Robert's restored enthusiasm and motivation to work were solely as a result of finding a friend. Certainly that had not been the pattern in Year 4. In the following description of Robert, we see that something else occurred this year that did not occur in Year 4. He was now also regaining the recognition and respect of the wider peer group, and again became integrated with them and had a role in relation to their work:

> And as we've said, about being this 'professor', he doesn't seem to mind that at all, this image that he's got, because I think he gets his kudos or whatever from being a whizz-kid, you know, and people go to him for help and therefore he's respected for that. You know, the computer's a big thing obviously and you know, often during maths people ask him things, and in science or whatever.
>
> (Mr Brown, teacher interview, July 1993, Year 5)

This is a very different description from that which Miss King gave of him in relation to his peers and, moreover, in terms of structural position of Robert, the conditions for the maintenance of this status were so much less propitious in Year 5. We need therefore to consider what could have brought about this reversal from last year. Again, we might examine the expectations of the classroom teacher and his perceptions of Robert's learning stance and classroom strategies:

> But in general he rarely waits for me. Sometimes, when I *want* him to, you know, he'll get really down if I tell him that he should have asked me about something. He likes to go off on his own and explore things and I'm very happy about that most of the time, but sometimes he goes at it at the wrong time, you know, when he goes off to the library and he hasn't asked me or something like that. Yes, he will, you know, go off and he'll follow a line of enquiry through, especially say in science where he's produced his own investigation, raised a question and designed an investigation and will follow it through, explore all the avenues and so on. And Toby's very similar.
> (Mr Brown, teacher interview, July 1993, Year 5)

> Often I feel guilty for jumping too soon and saying 'What are you doing, Robert?' But [what] he's actually doing, you know, [is] being independent. And occasionally I think 'Oh, why did I do that?' Why didn't I just say 'That's great. Well done'? He's done it *his* way, you know, and my initial reaction looks like he's doing something completely different. When I think he's not listened he'll have started it and gone off on a tangent and done it his way.
> (Mr Brown, teacher interview, July 1993, Year 5)

We can now further support our analysis of the role of teacher in promoting Robert's classroom identity through a comparison between this and Miss King's understanding of Robert's learning stance and classroom strategies. Miss King experienced Robert's failure to fulfil the requirements of a task in the expected way as irritating and somewhat frustrating, not least because it seemed to stand in contrast to an intelligence and ability which she recognized. She thus interpreted Robert's alternative approach as his failure to listen. Mr Brown, on the other hand, has reached a conclusion that his initial perceptions that Robert has not listened may have been mistaken. As we can see, he increasingly interpreted Robert's independent response as a *sign of his intelligence* rather than as a *contradiction of it*. Though Mr Brown sometimes clearly felt uncertain of his judgement of the situation and therefore, as in Year 3, his support may have sometimes been more tacit than explicit, we can contrast the outcomes with those of Year 4 where Miss King's perceptions lead her to a more negative appraisal of Robert's stance and to reprimand the alternative activity.

Home and family relationships in Year 5

Robert's home relationships remained relatively unchanged during Year 5 at school and a few excerpts from his parents' diary entries will serve to acquaint readers with a few new activities in his life and some of his parents' ongoing thoughts about his education:

> Robert has really enjoyed this year with Mr Brown and it's really hard to remember him talking about his class describing problems. This year we have been giving some thought to secondary schools, having visited several during 'open evenings' but as yet no decision

has been made. Although we feel Robert is very capable in school, we are a little anxious that perhaps he needs some help in preparing for examinations should we choose to go along the independent school route. After talking with some other parents, we decided to send Robert to a local tutor on a weekly basis for a bit.

His interests are very much the same, with the addition of piano lessons. Robert has always shown an interest in playing and has been on a waiting list for two years. We think he will do very well and can pick up a tune very easily. Chess, glockenspiels and swimming are the other after-school organized hobbies. At home his interests remain the computer, the game player (a Nintendo clone) and reading. Now he has discovered science fiction, Chris's collection is re-emerging in Robert's room.

(Parent diary, June 1993, Year 5)

We see here that Robert's parents, in line with the many Greenside parents, were increasingly considering not only secondary education but the implications of independent schooling. As for William and Sarah, extra tuition was considered necessary if the child was to manage the necessary entrance exams. Robert, meanwhile, though keen to have the matter of which school he was to attend settled, expressed no preferences from among the independent and state schools visited with his parents and with the school. He also seemed unperturbed by the prospect of exams. His parents for their part were hoping that the solution would emerge from their visits and consideration, but this did not seem to be the case as his mother observed:

I was hoping lights would flash but it doesn't seem to work like that.
(Mrs Osborne, parent interview, July 1993, Year 5)

Summary of Robert's Year 5

Robert's lower structural position in relation to the many able Year 6 pupils meant that, like William, he could not secure the academic status that he had always previously held. However, measuring his achievements against his peers, or in order to please parents or teachers, had never been a source of motivation for Robert. Rather, classroom status had been secured in relation to his special roles and identity. Thus, although Robert initially lacked motivation and enthusiasm, with Mr Brown's recognition and support for his former 'explaining' role and 'professor' identity and for his independent learning stance, he went on to renew his enthusiasm and commitment.

Of course, Robert also found a special friend in one of the Year 6 boys, and Mr Brown considered that this made a significant difference to Robert's motivation and enthusiasm. It is impossible to analyse the relative importance of the two factors – restoration of his role and identity and a close relationship with a friend – in restoring Robert's full enjoyment of school that year. However, in his previous year in Miss King's class, we observed that finding special friends who shared his interests was not enough to restore Robert's classroom motivation in a context where he could not establish a positive pupil identity and working relationships with his peers. In Year 6 to follow, moreover, the position was to be reversed, for Robert was not to find a replacement for Toby. He was, nevertheless, able to skilfully negotiate teacher support to elaborate his classroom roles, thus gaining more time for following his own interests in the classroom and gaining increased respect and acceptance from his peers. At the end of Robert's Year 6 story, readers will thus be in a position to assess more confidently the relative importance to Robert of close friends in the classroom and the maintenance of his special classroom identity.

Robert, Year 6, early days in Mrs Chard's class

As we described in Chapter 3, Mrs Chard, as a fairly new deputy head to the school, was experienced in organizing for active learning and offered the sort of opportunities for independence of approach that one would assume would suit Robert very well. It also seemed likely that she would perhaps interpret his needs in similar ways to Mr Brown. As she explained to Ann Filer:

> Teacher planning has to be very tight, so you know exactly what you want, but you set it in such a way that the children have a freedom to choose how they will carry out the task very often, and that's where you're really learning about children's strategies and so on. You're in there, working with a small group and you really see – yes this child's needs are such and such; they need *that*, this child's strength is such and such so they need *that*.
> (Mrs Chard, teacher interview, June 1994, Year 6)

However, like other teachers from time to time, she was concerned with the contradiction between what she saw as abilities and the finished product of his work. Her predominant concern was to bring the two into line and to this end she was, in her own words, 'struggling' in her relationship with Robert. Her comments to Ann Filer with regard to Robert's written work are certainly reminiscent of those of Mrs Powell, his Reception teacher, to Andrew Pollard six years previously:

> Robert's probably an outstandingly able person I think, who gives very little on paper and I'm working with Mum and Dad at the moment to exert some pressure on Robert to produce the quality we're expecting from him. Maths he's able in and likes, so you get a good performance. Science, if it's electricity or something you get a good performance. If Robert likes it he'll do well but what *I'm* after is Robert's contribution, one hundred per cent contribution, right across the curriculum. His English work could be outstanding, but it's a scruffy presentation, it's as little as possible. So we're doing a lot of work with Robert, and on Robert, to really get what we want, because there's real quality in there and we want it out.
> (Mrs Chard, teacher interview, December 1993, Year 6)

Mrs Chard, perhaps of all his teachers, most rigorously tested Robert's thinking and, over the year, as we shall see, this led to her holding a more ambivalent view of Robert's intellect than that of any previous teachers. Despite the 'struggles', however, Mrs Chard expressed the view that Robert seemed keen to establish a good relationship with her:

> I think he might see me as a bit of a dragon – but he is anxious to please and he is anxious to share things with me about computer discs and findings and so on. He brought me a piece of beautifully written-up computer work the other day.
> (Mrs Chard, teacher interview, December 1993)

Readers may perceive that Robert perhaps had an interest at stake here over and above that of establishing a good relationship with his teacher and, as we shall see, Robert was also developing a similar one with his peers. From the developments that followed that year, we might conclude that Robert was engaged in negotiating a classroom role and status in a much more active way than he had in previous years.

Friendships and peer relationships in Year 6

The loss of Toby was not felt too badly by Robert, Mrs Chard believed. He was, she said, certainly never isolated in the classroom. Ian, Alex and Anthony were his main classroom friends now and William and Stephen could still be counted among his friends. Robert, along with Alex, Ian and Maurice, formed a band in which Robert played the keyboard and some public performances, notably of 'Rock Around the Clock', were given at school events and concerts.

Unlike in the previous two years, Robert did not have any special friends for sharing his interests, however. Ian, Alex and Anthony liked football and 'kiss chase', and Robert was rarely observed playing with them in the playground:

> Alex: Robert's into computers and he's mastermind in the school with computers.
> Liam: Robert usually stays inside and does computer and reads books.
> (Friendship group interview with Alex, Liam, Anthony and Barry, January 1994, Year 6)

However, Robert's position outside the mainstream of peer culture was perhaps more accepted and respected in Year 6 than at any time:

> Maurice: I used to play with Einstein Robert a lot and I would, but he wants to do his own thing. He's got his own ideas. When he wants to play with us he does. Robert's OK.
> William: Too technical.
> Maurice: We tried to get him to tell some jokes but he's too much in his own head. He sat back and did not want to get involved. Robert's OK. He's getting more interested in what we do. He does get some laughs going and Ian picks it up from him.
> (Friendship group interview with Maurice, William, Stephen, Gareth and Alistair, January 1994, Year 6)

The identity of 'Einstein Robert', as a friend who was 'OK' was not confined to a small group of friends, albeit high status friends. It rather represented a generalized regard for Robert across the class, as the following extracts from Ann Filer's fieldnotes indicate. The children had been given instructions by Mrs Chard to continue working on projects for a Year 6 class assembly. Mrs Chard was going to be absent, however, and a supply teacher was taking her place. When asked by Ann Filer what he would be doing Robert replied that he could not work on his task, reasoning that as his partner was away it would probably be best if he helped other people. The freewheeling nature of Robert's activities that afternoon was therefore not typical of what routinely would have been permitted. However, because the teacher did not know the children, it probably went unnoticed by her. Fieldnotes recorded the events:

> 1.35 pm
> Barry and Liam are making a picture for presentation with the overhead projector. They are tracing a cross-section of *The Victory* in coloured felt-tips. Robert watches, lends

advice, checks results with a piece of paper put between the acetate and the book being traced from. He tells me:

Robert:	It's like when you do a tracing. It looks good until you take the paper off.

A short while later, Robert is by the computer where Maurice, William and Alistair are working. I wander over. Maurice tells me that they are having trouble with the printer and Robert is fixing it:

AF:	Well he looks confident enough.
Maurice:	Robert's always confident around computers.

(. . . . .)

1.58 pm
Robert helps Edward carry a board with some rocks (fossils) on it from the technology area outside the classroom. Miss Reed, the supply teacher, tells me that they are intending to stick rocks on the board to make an abseiling rockface. Robert uses the glue gun to make patches of glue and Edward places the rocks on the patches.

2.01 pm
Edward takes over the glue gun and Robert watches.

(. . . . .)

2.10 pm
Robert is back on the glue gun, now putting glue on the back of the rocks. The board is back in the technology area. I go out there and Alan tells me:

Alan:	Some of the rocks have fallen off, but not the big one.
AF:	That's interesting. Why not the big one?
Alan:	Probably because it's got the flattest bottom.

2.13 pm
I return to the classroom and Robert is on the computer with William. Robert, in control, has got the keyboard and is in front of the screen. He gets up and takes a picture out of the printer. I ask about it but Robert does not know who it belongs to. Maurice comes along and claims it as his. Robert wanders off.

(. . . . .)

After play time
We are in the technology area and Robert's younger brother Richard and a friend come to look for some materials. Maurice does not realize that I know Richard and introduces me:

Maurice:	This is Richard, the second member of the Einstein family.

Robert is back with the rocks. They have all fallen off by now. Robert finds some ModRoc (plaster impregnated sheets of bandage-like material) which he suggests they use instead of rocks. He wets some and screws it in a ball. He then leaves it in the bottom of a bowl full of water and tells the others he needs to siphon off the water. He gets a tube and shows the others how to suck to start the siphon. They are intrigued and call him 'a genius'.

Edward:	I'm glad we've got Robert helping us.
AF:	Robert, why does the water needs siphoning off?
Robert:	So that it slowly drains off so the ModRoc won't dry off too quickly.

I am not sure that the ModRoc should sit in the water at all, but Robert has disappeared to consult Naomi who apparently knows all about the material. He comes back and tells the others it will take seven hours to dry and that they must make as many as possible and paint them tomorrow. I continue to write my notes but Robert tells me to come and look. They have a production line routine and are saying 'Dip, squeeze, soak', putting the material into a second bowl to soak. I express my doubts about this:

AF:	Do you have to soak it? Don't you just have to dip, shape and leave it to dry?
Robert:	(*agrees*) Yes you do.

He then looks doubtful and goes to consult Naomi again. Edward tells me, as he waits for Robert.

Edward:	Robert is brilliant at this.

Robert returns.

Robert:	Don't soak it. Shape it and let it dry.

Naomi joins them and all four together shape rocks and put them on a paper towel.

Robert:	Model them with a flat bottom.

Naomi starts to put them directly on to the board.

Robert:	(*to Naomi*) No. Oh! Will it stick if you put it on? Right, stick them on the board. Do we need any more?

They rush, anxious to do as many as possible before tidying-up time.
(Fieldnotes, Ann Filer, April 1994, Year 4)

Now although some of these incidents are very amusing, as is some of the admiration for Robert, they serve to show very nicely exactly why he coveted and elaborated his troubleshooting, helping, explaining role in relation to his peers. These roles enabled him to relate to his peers through shared interests and experiences as he was not able to through the usual cultural forms within the boys' peer group. Everywhere that Robert went he was admired and complimented. His help was welcomed and he was allowed to take control. He had a very positive identity; he was 'Einstein', 'a genius', 'brilliant' and although this was an extreme example, it makes clear exactly why teacher support, however tacit, was necessary to enable the sort of contact with peers and their tasks that made it possible.

The data also suggests that Robert was, in addition to his usual helping, trouble-shooting role, also putting more effort into his relationships with his peers in Year 6. Some of this effort was observable in the production of a class newspaper. The effort involved in typing, designing the layout of all the contributions and printing them was considerable, so that the event found a place in the diary report which his parents were writing at that time:

December 6th Robert was washed and dressed by 8 am, able to play with Paul before helping with taking a neighbour's two girls to school. Robert was particularly pleased to have done some work to show his teacher [a newspaper report]. His teacher was so pleased with the work that Robert was asked to do more – to print out reports for the whole class!

December 7th Robert awake just before 8 am. Rushed breakfast, washing and dressing to disappear into the study and use the computer to print out some schoolwork. He was called several times but still delayed the migration to school long enough to make everybody late. Sue 'explained' to Robert that he didn't have time in the mornings for the computer – his ears should have recovered by midday. After school, television at home and then a disappearance to the study for more work before Robert's lesson with his tutor [. . .] Back home for more computer work. Robert is very keen to do the work, even keener for us to go over the drafts, checking for mistakes.
(Parent diary, December 1993, Year 3)

Thus it was that, despite Mrs Chard's more ambivalent perceptions of Robert's established intellectual identity, his role in relation to his peers was being supported in the classroom.

Learning strategies in Year 6

Mrs Chard had an interest in the teaching of science, and she was particularly concerned to develop scientific skills within the National Curriculum. She considered the knowledge content to be less important in developing their scientific thinking. In the development of scientific skills she often liked, as in other areas of the curriculum, to pose a challenge to the pupils, then seeing herself as 'mentor' rather than 'teacher', promoting independence and pupils' own input. As his reflections on the difference between Year 6 and Year 5 indicate, Robert, for his part, enjoyed the science in Mrs Chard's class:

> There's more history work to do and less maths, I think. I don't like the maths as much this year. I don't know why. English is the same, still boring with stories. I hate writing stories. The science work is more interesting. You don't have to watch plants grow. We virtually had to do that last year.
> (Robert, pupil interview, May 1994, Year 6)

However, the rigorous approach demanded by Mrs Chard frequently challenged Robert's confidence in his own knowledge and his occasional dissembling. She explained:

> He's one of those children who's got a mind full of jargon which he doesn't really understand. When he's trying to set up an investigation he'll go for something really complex, but he can't really prove it or test it, because it's something he's heard or read or seen, there's no doubt about the ability but it's 'Now hang on a minute Robert. Stop and explain what you're doing'. And there was a tussle over there being a skin on water the other day and he said 'Yes there is', and I said 'Well is there really or is there just an appearance?' 'No, no, there's a skin on water'. He stuck with his idea. Never really accepted that there's not really a skin. He's a little bit stuck with his prejudices. You know, he thinks he'll test me out with various things and I just stick with the simple – 'What do you mean, Robert? Explain yourself', and very often he can't.
> (Mrs Chard, teacher interview, June 1994, Year 6)

Mrs Chard's emphatic and questioning approach meant that she held a more ambivalent perspective towards Robert's scientific intelligence than any of his other teachers. Interestingly this view was to some extent in accord with the view that his parents had always held and that we have seen in some of the early years interviews. As we saw in Year 2, Robert's mother thought that it probably was a good thing that he had the confidence to explain scientific and technical concepts that were beyond his present understanding, However, his parents also felt that what Robert 'thought he knew' and his part factual, part imaginative bluff often got in the way of listening and learning from others.

The struggle to get Robert to produce across the curriculum what she knew he was capable of continued to exercise Mrs Chard throughout the year:

> I've striven and striven with Robert to tap some of the depths . . .

but as she saw it:

> He's been almost playing a game with me of trying to get away with the least possible. It's almost been 'Can I beat the system?' as the way I see Robert's mind working. Now when we did our topic on data handling last half-term there was no child who was more

into it than Robert because it was right up his street and he was setting up a computer program for everybody else and he did a great job.
(Mrs Chard, teacher interview, June 1994, Year 4)

While Mrs Chard was supportive of Robert's efforts to establish his preferred role in relation to his peers, she was also quite prepared for him to pursue his own agenda without them. Ann Filer asked about Robert in relation to his peers and the extent to which he was prepared to lead or follow others. Mrs Chard explained:

> Well, as Robert likes to stand outside, leading or following or group dynamics are not really part of Robert's agenda, I don't think. He's very much about what *he* wants to come to school to do that day and people, including staff, are an irritation in his path, they stop him from achieving his goal. And if we didn't interfere with him he'd be really very happy with that. And I think in many instances it fits within the things we are doing. We have to allow children to be like this because as adults we like our solitude and we don't all like to be part of a group and we don't all get on in groups.
> (Mrs Chard, teacher interview, June 1994, Year 6)

Again we have the perception of Robert as 'loner by choice' that all his teachers have articulated. Yet our longitudinal view shows us just how much and in what ways Robert did need his peers and just how unhappy he was and how his motivation and enthusiasm for learning suffered when these relationships were not supported by teachers' actions and perceptions of him. It would be fair to say that none of his teachers, however supportive in this regard, perceived the connection between their actions and perceptions of Robert and his role, acceptance and status within the peer group.

If Mrs Chard regarded Robert as out to 'beat the system', we can certainly see him negotiating it perfectly to his own ends in Year 6. Just as we saw above that Robert was now more active in negotiating a role for himself in relation to his peers, so he was in negotiating the space in which to follow his own interests in the classroom. In discussion which included all the children in the study, Ann Filer suggested to Mrs Chard that there was a similar conflict between her requirements and those of both Robert and Hazel (see Hazel's story in *The Social World of Children's Learning*). Mrs Chard outlined the difference between the two as she saw it:

Mrs Chard:	Very much a conflict, I think, but again I think that Robert can cope with it by doing what you ask, keeping you quiet and then getting on with what *he* wants to do, whereas Hazel finds it that much more difficult because it takes her that much longer to *give* you what it is that you want. So Robert has that great advantage – 'All right then, if she wants a page I'll dash her off a page and she'll be quiet then and then I can read my book or go on the computer.'
AF:	So he has that freedom, if you like, to negotiate in a way that Hazel perhaps doesn't because she's struggling.
Mrs Chard:	She does [struggle]. It takes her much longer too. She's much more *stubborn*, in a way, than Robert. I think that Robert has accepted – 'Oh well, I think I'll just give in to her and get her off my back, whereas Hazel will quite stubbornly resist the situation for perhaps three-quarters of the lesson and then have to be pressurized into giving you what you want. Two different strategies –

AF:	Due to her lack of understanding?
Mrs Chard:	Yes, and then having to cope with the frustration of everybody else has got a page done by now and she's only got one word.

(Teacher interview, June 1994, Year 6)

If Robert in this was negotiating for a situation that was largely antagonistic to his teacher's expectations, he was, in the area of his preferred interests, negotiating a more positive role and relationship to her.

> He has spent time trying to educate me on the computer and he's been very good about that and he's asked me if he can stay in every day to work with this because we had a new Nimbus halfway through the year and he's asked every single day. He's not interested in going out to play with groups of children. So he does all these weird and wonderful things and then he wants to involve me. He wants to show me and tell me about it.
>
> (Teacher interview, June 1994, Year 6)

Document 6.4 shows something of Robert's attempts to involve and educate Mrs Chard in his computer interests.

As well as helpful roles in relation to pupils and teacher, Robert in Year 6 had extended his troubleshooting role to the rest of the school and was the official 'call out' for other members of staff or pupils experiencing difficulties with computers.

Some of the success experienced by Robert in negotiating his classroom relationships and developing his own fields of interest are perhaps encapsulated in his response in interview:

AF:	Can you tell me about Year 6. What's it been like?
Robert:	I think it's been a very good year. I've had lots of fun. More than usual. And in what you're allowed to do. In Year 4 and 5 you do a lot of work but you don't do very much of the things I like. In Year 6 we've done a bit more science and technology than usual which is what I like.

(Pupil interview, May 1994, Year 6)

Home and family relationships in Year 6

We saw that at this point in William's case study, conflicts with parents were beginning to arise. These conflicts concerned the activities and freedoms permitted to friends and the importance William attached to a social life with friends beyond the confines of home and family. Robert's position in relation to the mainstream peer culture was, as we have seen, very different from that of William, who was frequently at the cutting edge of peer-group expectations. Conflicts between on the one hand the child's imperative to be part of and accepted by the group and on the other parental concerns and restraint were clearly not an issue in the relationship between Robert and his parents, as they explained to Ann Filer:

Mr Osborne:	At the moment he's not a follower of the crowd. He hasn't been up to now. I just wonder if that will change.
Mrs Osborne:	Is that down to friendship again? I mean, Toby and Maurice called here one night and Barry, Ian and Marcus. They were on their bicycles and Ian called for the money [for a purchase for Robert]. But they'd obviously been going up and down on their

Processor	8088	8086	80286	80386	80486	Pentinum (80586)
Average RAM (direct from shop)*	0.512	0.64	1	2	4	8
Maximum RAM**	1	1	4	16	64	256
Lowest clock speed (in mHz)	4.7	8	8	8	12	50
Highest clock speed (in mHz)	4.7	8	16	16	66	110

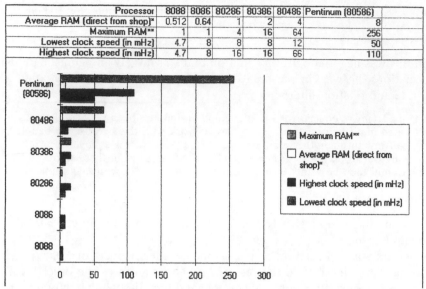

Note: * For the 8088 and 8086 processors, RAM is measured in kilobytes. For the others, it is measured in megabytes.

Note: ** For all the RAM here is measured in megabytes.

This is a performance rating for some types of computer.
It lists the processor and how much RAM each usually has when
bought, the maximum RAM available for that type of computer, and
the lowest and highest clock speed for the computer. RAM
stands for RANDOM ACCESS MEMORY. It is the thinking space of the
computer. It is measured in bytes, kilos, megas + gigas, tera + yte.

The clock speed is the thinking "speed" of the computer. It is measured
in Mega Hertz (how many millions of pulses of electricity pass
through per second. The higher the number, the faster the machine is.

You have lost me with this Robert. Please put the
masking tape on the back of your work.

Document 6.4 *Robert, Year 6, 'Computer Performance Ratings' (June 1994)*

bicycles (. . .) but Robert saw them and didn't fuss about the others and just saw Ian and that was it – 'Goodbye'. And, you know, they were all in their big sloppy tee shirts and, you know, caps and things, but he's not really into any of that, fashion or trainers, which we are quite pleased about obviously. But then, if he's not going out with a crowd he probably wouldn't care about these things. He doesn't seem to bother about what others are doing or where they are going.
(Parent interview, July 1994, Year 6)

At the end of Year 5 we left Robert's parents at the point where they were still undecided about his secondary education. They picked up the story in the diary:

The work provided by the local tutor made us happy to sit Robert for the [entrance] exams last January. In the event, although he didn't receive the offer of a scholarship at Easthampton College he was offered a place at both Rutherford College and Easthampton Grammar School. After an interview at the CTC (City Technology College) Robert also received an offer of a place there. Robert was happy to leave the final choice of his secondary school to us, we believe he could have been happy at any of them, and in the end we plumped for Easthampton Grammar School. That sounds very easy but neither Sue nor I want to go through the agony of indecision for at least another eighteen months!
(Parent diary, June 1994, Year 6)

In contrast to William's enthusiastic appraisal of the 'amazing' social and sporting opportunities ahead of him at Easthampton Grammar, Robert, for his part, was ready to admit to a quite natural ambivalence regarding the changes ahead:

AF:	Are you looking forward to going?
Robert:	Yes. Half of me is and the other half of me doesn't want to go.
AF:	Do you think you would feel that wherever you were going?
Robert:	Yes, it's not knowing what to expect really. Hard to put into words. Just nervous.

(Pupil interview, May 1994, Year 6)

Summary of Robert's Year 6

Although Robert's teacher saw Year 6 in terms of her failure to draw out the best from Robert, he himself felt it to be perhaps 'his best year'. Despite Mrs Chard's ambivalence regarding the way in which he worked the system and his relationship with her for his own ends, she was supportive of his interests in securing plentiful access to the computer. Though she was unaware of it, like many of his other teachers, she supported his need to develop an identity and status in relation to his peers.

Year 6 saw Robert more active in negotiating these relationships and roles in the classroom than he had been in former years. The helping, explaining roles that he had been elaborating over the years now extended beyond responding to difficulties. He was now taking on something of the role of supportive tutor and facilitator, offering tangible benefit in the structuring and production of computer-assisted work. This, together with the deployment of other knowledge and skills in this area, also supported the work of his teacher, as well as of his relationship with her. Though the work for others may have been on Robert's own terms, perhaps Mrs Chard did not realize just how much more Robert was contributing to classroom relationships than he had done in the past, nor how much more he was getting out of them that year, despite the lack of any special friends.

Robert's identity and career in the later years at Greenside School

The later years of Robert's career at Greenside Primary School can be characterized as distinct from his early years in two respects. First, they were different with regard to the nature of the challenges faced by Robert and secondly they were also different with regard to the development of his range of strategies in dealing with those challenges.

From Year 4 onwards, we have seen that the almost unconditional support and admiration on the part of earlier teachers became more qualified. There was also, from Year 4 onwards, a corresponding lack of indulgence towards some of the more non-conforming aspects of Robert's identity as a pupil. Understandably, as the pupils moved up the school and curricular demands increased, the academic and social expectations of his teachers regarding the tasks that needed to be done and the way they were carried out assumed greater importance. Although each of the three teachers saw Robert, his needs, his abilities and his strategies very differently, the pressure was undoubtedly greater for Robert to conform and to realize his full potential through the curriculum.

For instance, in the first few years of school simple fascination on the part of teachers and peers in his activities and ideas, together with the occasional emotional outburst from Robert, was enough to secure a useful identity as 'oddball', 'professor' and associated indulgences. It is possibly a result of leaving behind some the freedoms with regard to practical activities and exploratory play of the early years classrooms that he developed his 'inspirational influence' with regard to peers and an explaining, troubleshooting, boffin identity. As expectations became more structured that new role in relation to his peers, incorporating *their* interests as well as those of his teachers into his own, certainly gave him increased freedom to follow his own interests, especially in relation to computers.

However, these new roles and the associated identities that evolved around Robert in those middle years were fairly easily accomplished by him for, as we have shown, teachers nurtured, facilitated and supported them. In the later years however, Robert's preferences for his own activities and alternative approaches and outcomes increasingly produced a struggle and conflict, most notably in Years 4 and 6. Even with Mr Brown, with whom he had previously established a satisfactory compromise, doubts and indecision about letting Robert 'have his head' were a feature of their relationship.

Thus what in Reception was viewed as a positive and inspiring approach to classroom tasks and learning became a potential source of struggle and conflict between Robert and his teachers. Accordingly we see Robert, across his later primary career, having to more actively negotiate to secure some of the autonomy and working practices he had enjoyed during his early years at Greenside School.

ROBERT'S IDENTITY AND CAREER – CASE-STUDY OVERVIEW

As we have already described in the introduction to the case studies, the triadic representation (Figure 6.1) depicts, in the outer triangle, the social context within which Robert learnt and developed and to which he could contribute, and in the

Matrix 6.3 *Robert, Years 4, 5 and 6, a summary matrix*

	Family relationships	Peer-group relationships	Teacher relationships	Identity	Career
Year 4: Miss King	Parents puzzled that Robert is unsettled at school, monitor the situation. Robert is still outgoing, confidently 'dissembles' with adults, strangers. Some battles with brothers over use of computer, is more 'mellow' by spring.	Miss King expects pupils to cooperate. Robert is seen as failing to participate. Loss of role and status. Sometimes ignored, rejected by high-status boys. Finds a group of like-minded friends and is happier by spring.	Structural position: age 3/30. Maths, in top few. English and science, in top quarter. Robert is tearful and slow to settle in this class. Miss King does not recognize or support his former special identity and role.	Miss King sees Robert as often inattentive, inactive daydreamer. Seen as sometimes 'very mature', often 'unbelievably backward' by parents. Robert and friends seen as 'sensible' by other boys.	With new structures, new teacher expectations, Robert loses his special identity and the role in relation to his peers. He loses status with teacher and peers and power to operate independently in the classroom.
Year 5: Mr Brown	Robert has tuition for independent school entrance exams. He enjoys chess, swimming, piano, science fiction. Paul is following Robert's pattern for 'getting his own way' in the family.	'Whizz-kid' identity and helping role supported by teacher and restored, despite many able Year 6 pupils in the class. Loses his friends to another class, now enjoys friendship with Toby, sharing scientific interests.	Structural position: age 25/53. Many able Year 6 pupils outshine Robert in maths and science. Early lack of effort. Interpretations of his independence as 'not listening'. Later regained teacher support for his independent stance.	Independent learner. 'Whizz-kid' identity and helping role restored in the classroom. Robert is regarded as 'OK' and more inclined to play other boys' games now.	Robert is faced by the challenge of low structural position, Mr Brown's disappointment of his effort, and doubts about his independent stance. He successfully negotiates a return to teacher and peer esteem and an independent stance.
Year 6: Mrs Chard	Home life continues as before with Robert continuing to maintain separation between home and school. Robert leaves decisions about secondary school to his parents. He passes the entrance exam and an independent grammar school is decided on.	Toby leaves. Robert's role now extended to more active support and structuring of peer's computer work. Rarely seen in the playground. Stays in and works on the computer. Robert is admired for his ideas, his help welcomed by all.	Structural position: age, half-way down. English, maths, science, in top third. Mrs Chard 'struggles' to get Robert to produce what he is capable of. Through computer expertise negotiates a relationship with Mrs Chard and extends his support role schoolwide.	Teacher sees Robert as 'playing the system' for time to follow his own interests. 'Probably oustandingly able' but 'a mind full of jargon', 'stuck with his prejudices'. To peers he is 'Einstein', 'a genius', 'brilliant', 'too much in his own head' but accepted as 'OK'.	Year 6 sees Robert increasingly active in negotiating relationships and roles in the classroom. His teacher in supporting access to the computer was also, like many of his teachers, supporting his ability to shape a positive identity and status in the peer group.

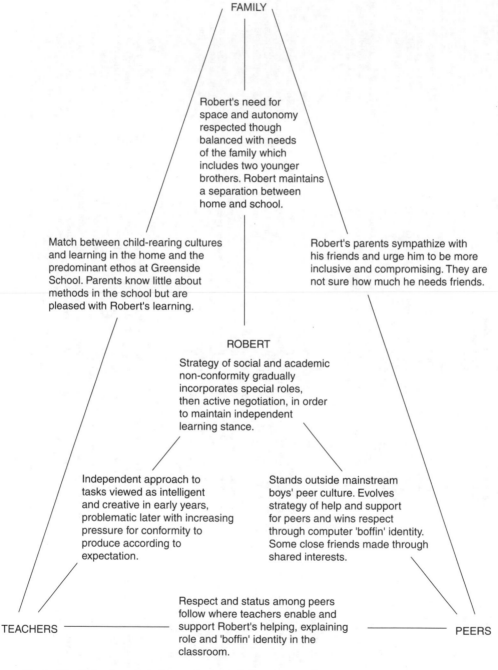

Figure 6.1 *Robert's case-study overview – a triadic representation*

inner star, the dynamic relationship between Robert, his family, peers and teachers within which he shaped and maintained his identity. In simple terms we can thus describe Robert's predominant career interest within this web of relationships as that of maintaining an independent learning stance and his predominant career strategy at Greenside school that of *non-conformity*.

We can now also summarize Robert's identity in terms of the career strategies which constitute and give rise to the description of *non-conformity*. We have described *conformity* in terms of reification of a range of career structures and *redefining* as representing the cutting edge of those structures. The strategic responses associated with *non-conformity*, however, can be conceptualized in terms of a greater detachment from those structures. Thus we see Robert throughout his career taking an independent stance in relation to curricular, teacher and peer expectations rather than adapting to them as we saw Sarah and Mary doing, or testing and extending the boundaries of them as did William and Sally.

As with other career strategies in the typology introduced in Chapter 2, we can see this patterned response operating through the four broad categories which we suggest constitute the main areas of career progression. These career structures are those relating to curricular expectation, to the official social and relational expectation of teachers and classrooms, to the unofficial social relations and expectations of the peer group and to a range of extra-curricular and school-wide opportunities.

Thus in relation to curricular expectation Robert's independent stance is reflected in his autonomous approach whereby, in Mrs Powell's words, 'he approaches any task with a different slant' and for his Year 6 teacher 'he's very much about what he wants to come to school to do that day'. We have seen further that these twin facets of Robert's learning stance, that of pursuing his own agenda and carrying out the school's agenda in his own way, were maintained by Robert throughout his primary career. They did though, become increasingly challenged by pressures to conform and produce according to expectations.

Our analysis further suggests that it was as a result of that increased challenge to his preferred learning stance that Robert adapted his strategic responses with regard to classroom relationships. In his early years his creative yet temperamental approach, which earned him the identity of 'oddball', 'professor', empowered him to push through his own agenda with a certain amount of teacher indulgence, peer admiration and tolerance. The evolution of his ability to maintain his own agenda so powerfully culminated in Year 6 with Robert actively negotiating a good relationship with his teacher and his peers and extending his supportive roles in relation to them, simultaneously creating and extending his preferred sphere of activity in the classroom and school. In response to her 'struggle' and 'striving' to motivate Robert towards official curricular expectations, Robert is 'playing a game with me' of 'can I beat the system?'.

Non conformity also entails a degree of standing outside the norms and expectations of the peer group and Robert's rejection of the mainstream male culture of the playground and sports field put him at risk of isolation and rejection by his peers. However, the pupil identity of 'boffin' and computer expert was also a powerful 'male' identity, crucial to Robert's acceptance and status within the boys' peer group.

Robert's story reveals that the maintenance and elaboration of an identity that was both academically and socially rewarding relied on more than the development of certain strategic responses. As with William's *redefining* identity which was only viable within certain contexts, Robert's too was affected by teacher perceptions, their social and academic expectations of pupils, by features of the learning contexts they create and by his structural position *vis-à-vis* his peers.

In the typology of career strategies introduced in Chapter 2, we suggest that a feature of *non-conformity* is variability in teacher–pupil relationships. These may be characterized by either empathy and rapport or incomprehension and exasperation on the part of teachers. We have seen something of this variability in Robert's story, though predominantly their empathy and rapport were forthcoming, not least in relation to their perception of Robert as intelligent and creative and of high academic ability. In Robert's story we have also met his friend Hazel, whose early years story featured in *The Social World of Children's Learning*. Hazel's predominant strategy was also that of *non-conformity* and teacher perceptions of Hazel and the degree to which they could empathize with her independence were much more variable than in Robert's case. These variable teacher–pupil relationships, as well as Hazel's struggles with some areas of the curriculum, made the maintenance of her individual identity and classroom agenda much more difficult to accomplish.

In the following chapter we meet Harriet, another pupil whose career strategies were predominantly those of non-conformity. Harriet and Hazel were 'special friends' in the way that Robert, also constructing a career outside the mainstream peer culture, needed special, like-minded friends. Readers of *The Social World of Children's Learning* will therefore be able to pick up Hazel's story again through the telling of the story of Harriet's career.

Chapter 7

Harriet's Story

7.1 PRE-SCHOOL, RECEPTION AND YEAR 1

Harriet, an introduction

In our final case study we track the career of Harriet. Like Robert, Harriet tended to adopt strategies of *non-conformity* in relation to the academic and social structures within which the children of Greenside School fixed their goals, shaped their identities and, ultimately, their careers as pupils.

Strategic responses associated with *non-conformity* involve a desire for a good measure of independence and control on the part of the pupil in their learning and in the contextualizing social relations. Though there were parallels with Robert's career in terms of such responses, there were also important differences with implications for the viability of their strategies and for career outcomes.

A common pattern in the lives and careers of the *non-conformers* in our study, Harriet, Robert and Hazel (see *The Social World of Children's Learning*), lay in their having strong interests, and associated identities, which were nurtured and developed largely outside school. It is these interests which when imported into school by the children began to shape their identities as pupils and to override in importance the social and cultural norms and expectations of classroom and playground.

However, a significant difference between Harriet and Robert lay in the nature of their special interests. Robert's computer interest and scientific and technical abilities were directly relevant to the academic life of the classroom and carried considerable status within it. Harriet's knowledge and skills in relation to horses and riding were not so directly, if at all, valued in the classroom, any more than was Hazel's fascination with dinosaurs, dragons and later, also horses.

Throughout Harriet's story we shall track her fortunes as she, and later with her friend Hazel, struggled to incorporate her personal knowledge into her classroom learning and establish her distinct identity in the playground as well as through a series of classroom contexts. Like Robert, Harriet and Hazel found contexts which were supportive of their growth in learning and in which they could shape an identity and a certain classroom status. However, they more often found themselves on the margins of the mainstream current of classroom life, somewhat detached from the goals and interests at hand of teachers and the majority of their peers.

Harriet's family

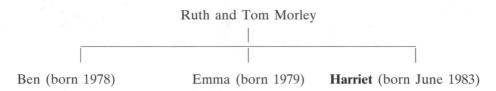

Ruth and Tom Morley

Ben (born 1978)   Emma (born 1979)   **Harriet** (born June 1983)

Harriet was the third child of Ruth and Tom Morley, brother Ben being five years older than Harriet and sister Emma, four years older. The family lived in a spacious detached house on the outskirts of Greenside, a busy main road which ran through the centre of the suburb and a considerable walk separating them from Greenside Primary School and from the majority of families that sent their children there. Tom Morley was an actuary with a busy professional life, with less time to spare for the family than either he, or they, would have wished. Ruth Morley at the time of the study worked at home for the family and in bringing up the children. She also volunteered her time helping in the classrooms at Greenside School as well as at nearby riding stables, among other activities assisting with Riding for the Disabled. Indeed, the whole family shared an active interest in horses, and increasingly as Harriet grew up were immersed in the related cultures of hunting, gymkhanas and riding lessons. These, together with the work associated with the owning and stabling of horses, were an important focus of both family and social life for the Morleys. Mrs Morley, like Sarah's parents, had considerable reservations about the way the school was developing under Mrs Davison, and would have preferred a more structured and traditional approach. There was then a sense in which the family's separation from Greenside School community was more than simply a matter of geography. Rather the geographical was symbolic of a degree of cultural, social and emotional separation which, over the years of the study, increasingly came to characterize the relationships of Harriet and her mother with Greenside School.

Early learning in the family

In spite of being the youngest by some years in a busy and active family, Harriet was both powerful and effective in influencing the rest of the family, including her grandmother, in her own interests. Like Robert and also like Hazel, whose story featured in *The Social World of Children's Learning*, Harriet's approach to learning, from her earliest years, took on the characteristic pattern that we have described as *non-conformity*. Thus, we found that issues of control and of self-determination emerged as important features in Harriet's relationships and approach to learning. Here Harriet's father describes to Andrew Pollard a tussle with four-year-old Harriet over teaching her to ride her bicycle:

> She has in the past been very stubborn about it. She might say that she would like the stabilisers off but as soon as you take them off she decides, no, she wants them back on again. Then we have a couple of battles of wills and I am insisting that she must try. You plonk her on the bike and she just goes limp and will refuse to have anything to do with it.
> (Mr Morley, parent interview, March 1988, Reception)

Andrew Pollard suggested that Harriet seemed to be quite good at negotiating to get her own way in the family, though her parents described her determination in stronger terms:

> Mr Morley: I think it's more demanding than negotiating, isn't it? She will start off a negotiating line when she says 'I want a story'. You say 'No it's too late' and then it is 'Just a few pages' and then you start and when you have read four pages or whatever she will then start demanding the rest.
> AP: You described her at one point as stubborn. In what circumstances does she react in that way?
> Mrs Morley: Well, we have ever such a kind dentist but she has never let her look at her mouth or teeth yet. The idea is to have them from a very early time but she hasn't even got on the dentist's chair.
> (Parent interview, March 1988, Reception)

However, it was not simply a matter of Harriet's determination that enabled her frequently to take a controlling stance in her family relationships and push through her own agenda. Like Robert, she was also in a powerful position to do so in many instances due to the spirit of compromise within the family, particularly in Harriet's case, of her mother and sister:

> Mrs Morley: Harriet is the noisiest and bossiest. Emma has always been a real little mother to Harriet.
> Mr Morley: Emma has always to an extent given way for Harriet, hasn't she? Emma has been playing with something and Harriet has wanted it. Emma has been the one to give up the pen or . . .
> Mrs Morley: Because it makes life easier for me as well. It isn't just that Emma is being weak. I wouldn't really in many circumstances want them to fight it out. I would rather that she did give way.
> Mr Morley: Certainly when Harriet screams.
> Mrs Morley: I hate them all crying and quarrelling over things. I know that families do do that, but she is getting quite clever at trying, maybe let Harriet have it for a short while and then . . . not have a head on confrontation with her.
> (Parent interview, March 1988, Reception)

In further comparison with Robert, we suggested that his independent stance, as well as being accommodated by his parents, was also supported by his structural position as oldest of three children. Paradoxically, the particular age relations of the Morley children, as well as her mother's relaxed response in the face of Harriet's resolution, meant that there was some advantage to Harriet in being the youngest. Her parents described Harriet's play in her bedroom with her dolls:

> Mrs Morley: ... and she talks a lot, whether there is anybody up there or not. She talks just as much to herself as if she is not by herself.
>
> AP: So she has quite a little world going. She is quite self-contained in a way, is she?
>
> Mrs Morley: Yes, she is. If I try and keep the light off – it just sounds as if she is disobedient but I just don't think it is that important – but she will just go and switch it on again as soon as I have gone down. I used to be a lot stricter with the other two because having them close together I couldn't [manage without being].

(Parent interview, March 1988, Reception)

Harriet's parents felt they could possibly attribute their more relaxed response to Harriet to the fact that as a baby she had a heart murmur which 'knocked her out' if she caught a cold or became over-tired. For the first year of her life there had been, therefore, as Mr Morley explained, 'a subconscious feeling that we had to look after her a bit more'. However, Harriet had quickly grown out of it and never tired as a toddler and in fact, from her earliest years had been growing into a strong and energetic girl:

> Mr Morley: I think she enjoys the ballet that she goes to.
>
> Mrs Morley: She is happier with a hockey stick. She is really good with that.
>
> Mr Morley: She has always had very good coordination either for kicking a ball, virtually as soon as she could walk she could kick a ball very well, and she can whack a ball with a hockey stick.
>
> Mrs Morley: She hasn't really got the build for ballet dancing, I don't think. It's just somewhere to go because Emma goes.

(Parent interview, March 1988, Reception)

As in Robert's family there was, before school, little formal attempt to teach Harriet the skills of reading and writing in the home, though some early reading activities did take place at playgroup. However, Harriet had a special relationship with her grandmother who lived nearby and she was very skilful in, for example, instructing Gran on how to write stories for her to copy. With two older siblings at school, and parents as well as Gran to cajole into extra story reading, Harriet was actively taking control of her literacy learning from a very early age.

Early learning in playgroup

Along with many of the children she was to begin school with, Harriet attended playgroup at St John's church hall in Greenside. Her mother and father, in interview with Andrew Pollard, described their satisfaction with the playgroup:

> Mr Morley: She progressed quite well, didn't she? It is structured so they had a separate little group for early reading skills and things like that. She got on well there.

AP:	She started picking up her reading then, did she? Because she is a good reader.
Mrs Morley:	Yes, she likes it. They had the Red Hat series there.
Mr Morley:	Yes, I think St John's made a conscious effort to get early learning, early reading books, which did follow on to Greenside School.

(Parent interview, March 1988, Reception)

However, on the basis of her experience of Greenside School, Mrs Morley clearly felt less than certain that Harriet's future education would be as structured and as satisfactory as her early learning, as she explained to Andrew Pollard:

Mrs Morley:	I like the skills laid first, and they are not there. Not from what I have seen anyway.
AP:	So is that the main source of your unease about it in a sense?
Mrs Morley:	What, the whole system? I would like them sitting in twos, listening to blackboard teaching and playing in the afternoon when the work is done. But that applies further up the school. They have been mostly under five this year which is a bit of a 'playgroup like' introduction to school.
AP:	Sure, they are very young, aren't they.
Mrs Morley:	But they could manage more. Didn't the *Sunday Times* say that this week?

(Parent interview, March 1988, Reception)

At playgroup, Harriet's closest friend was Daniel, whose story features in *The Social World of Children's Learning*. The families had known each other since the two children were babies, their older sisters having attended playgroup together. Daniel and Harriet were to continue their attachment on entry to school, and though Harriet's mother slightly regretted that her daughter had not yet made any real friends among the girls, she felt that this would come in time and that Harriet would be the happier for it. Meanwhile, Harriet was confidently looking forward to going to school, the uniform and the lunchbox being the main attractions, her parents thought.

A summary of Harriet's pre-school experience

As in the other children's stories, we can at this point consider Harriet prospects as a child about to embark upon her primary school career. Now that readers are familiar with Greenside School and the learning contexts that Harriet was to experience, they may wish to make their own conjectures about how Harriet might fare there. Certainly, from the perspective of Harriet's academic competence, as well as her physical and social confidence, she looked well prepared for a successful start to her school career. With regard to her approach to learning, certainly Robert's experience, as a child also with a sense of self-direction and an independent approach, was predominantly a positive one. However, we have seen from Hazel's early years story (see *The Social World of Children's Learning*), and in this book, that a similar approach, without Robert's particular identity and strategic responses, might be much more difficult to sustain and her year-on-year experience a lot less predictable.

We also might consider that while Mrs Morley accepted, and to a degree encouraged Harriet's autonomy and self-direction in her relationships and in her approach to learning in the home, her expectations for institutional learning were somewhat different. It was not the case, as it was for many parents, that Mrs Morley particularly distrusted the new ethos at Greenside School. It was, rather, that she was concerned that a lack of emphasis upon formal learning of basic skills prevailed in primary education generally. Indeed, she had been dissatisfied with her children's schooling before the change of headteacher at the school. Thus while Harriet was enthusiastically and confidently looking forward to her entry into Greenside School, her mother was feeling less than optimistic that the school would develop her potential.

Harriet, Reception, early days in Mrs Powell's class

At the age of four years and three months, Harriet was chronologically 13th of the 28 children who entered Mrs Powell's Reception class in the autumn of 1987. During the year she maintained a position within the top third in the class for attainment in maths and English. The transition to school was smooth and after some initial uncertainty on Harriet's part, Mrs Powell found her to be full of 'bouncy self-confidence'. As she described to Andrew Pollard:

> Mrs Powell:　She is quite bright and quite confident really. She likes to be with Daniel but she is all right without him. Certainly when he has been away she has been fine. She always seems to have boundless energy actually. I think she is basically a jolly sort of person. Nothing too much really gets to her.
> (Teacher interview, February 1988, Reception)

During those early days, Harriet and Daniel, in their teacher's words, 'didn't go far from each other'. However, despite the closeness of the two from a very early age and the mutual security they had gained from each other, the friendship was not to survive for long in the context of the gendered expectations of the wider peer group. Increasingly these began to impinge upon four-year-old Daniel's awareness.

Friendships and peer relationships in Reception

When Mrs Powell was asked by Andrew Pollard to describe Harriet in relation to her peers, the description she gave bore a resemblance to the relationship of Harriet in interaction with her siblings:

> Very vociferous. Wherever she is, she is shouting about it. She enjoys the construction activities more than most of the girls and that is because Daniel likes to go there and so she is there as well. She enjoys it, and the home corner she is very happy in. She is probably a little bit bossy.
> (Mrs Powell, teacher interview, February 1988, Reception)

Though Mrs Powell saw Harriet's involvement in the things boys preferred to do as following Daniel, her mother perceived that this was simply a reflection of Harriet's interests which were less traditionally gendered than most of her peers' were becoming at this age. While Harriet loved her dolls, she also enjoyed activities traditionally more associated with boys:

Mrs Morley:	When I have seen her there she is not loud. She just concentrates on Daniel all the time.
AP:	When you say that, do you see it as a mixed blessing?
Mrs Morley:	No, I like it. She likes doing things that boys like doing, like climbing trees or chasing around in the garden or playing with Mobilo more than . . .
AP:	. . . playing in the home corner or whatever.
Mrs Morley:	She likes the home corner too, but then, boys quite like the home corner.

(Parent interview, March 1988, Reception)

It was the case though, that while Harriet's association with boys and their activities was acceptable to other girls, for Daniel, to be friends with a girl was becoming a problem. As his story in *The Social World of Children's Learning* tells, Daniel's need was greater than Harriet's for the mutual security their friendship offered. However, the need to shape an identity that was accepted within the mainstream boys' culture was of overriding importance and, despite his subsequent insecurity, it was Daniel that forced and maintained the separation.

As the school year drew to an end Mrs Morley thought that Harriet was not quite as happy as when she had started. Harriet had not yet made any special friends among the girls and though Mrs Morley was keen for this to happen, she also had a fairly ambivalent view of the culture of the main girls' groups at Greenside:

Mrs Morley:	School is not something she is dying to get to but I don't have any tears about her going either in the mornings.
AP:	Why do you think she may be less happy than she was before?
Mrs Morley:	I always think it is to do with friends – not work because they don't do enough work to worry about.
AP:	So you think it is how secure she is feeling with other children?
Mrs Morley:	Yes, if she had someone she can tag on to. They can be horrible to each other saying 'You're not playing', 'I don't like what you've got on', 'You are not allowed to do this'. I hate all this business. I wouldn't think she ever said, 'you're not allowed to do this', 'you're not allowed to do that'.
AP:	But you think some of the others might?
Mrs Morley:	Yes, I think if they wear the wrong thing, it they take in a toy, they very quickly say 'You're not allowed to do that'.
AP:	You said something about her being aware of hair slides or something like that. There are one or two who are very good at what they are allowed to do and what the rules say – pedantic.
Mrs Morley:	If anything I rather like to break the rules. I think she should do what she thinks is right.

(Parent interview, July 1988, Reception)

However, as her reports to parents confirmed (Spring Term and Summer Term, 1988), Mrs Powell continued to regard Harriet as a happy and sociable girl who cooperated well with her peers. From her perspective of Harriet, she would seem to have been a child well able to approach with equanimity the pressures and expectations of the peer group.

Learning strategies in Reception

As might be expected from the accounts of her achievements through her early learning in the home and playgroup, as well as from these accounts of her social responses in the classroom, Harriet was able to respond to teacher expectations with ease. Of course, other responses of Harriet could have prevailed but in this context there was no reference to Harriet's 'stubbornness' or to a wish to control others, or to a 'battle of wills'. Where learning in Mrs Powell's class was concerned, Harriet appeared to accept the discipline of school and do what was required:

> Mrs Powell: She has got this relaxed, sort of jolly attitude to everything. She is not serious about it. She is doing it because I have asked her to do it and she has got to do it.
>
> AP: She doesn't bother too much about that. She just gets on with it, does she?
>
> Mrs Powell: Yes, she just has a good old chat and a laugh. Nothing too much really gets to her. If she did something and you weren't very happy about it, it wouldn't worry her, the fact that you weren't very happy about what she had done.
>
> (Teacher interview, February 1988, Reception)

In Robert's story we saw that Mrs Powell was unhappy that some of the children, even very able ones like Robert and William, minimized the writing task by dictating very little to be copied. Girls, Mrs Powell felt, were less likely to deploy this strategy perhaps because they were 'more verbal'. Certainly, Harriet's easygoing acceptance of teacher requests such as Mrs Powell describes here, as well as her ability to fulfil teacher expectations, can be seen in her approach to writing tasks:

> People like Harriet, she will dictate about four pages of five lines each maybe and copy it all, after having concentrated for perhaps half an hour colouring her picture, so she evidently likes it. Although she doesn't choose it, she is quite happy to do it. She doesn't mind writing the extra and copying it.
> (Mrs Powell, teacher interview, July 1988)

Indeed Mrs Powell was pleased with Harriet's accomplishments across the curriculum. She reported to Harriet's parents, among other things, that:

> Harriet is willing to talk about her experiences and always has ideas for writing. Her handwriting is much improved, most letters being formed correctly.
> Harriet is interested in class topics and always listens well.
> Harriet enjoys all creative activities. Her drawings are improving, she is adding more detail and sometimes works on the background.
> (Mrs Powell, extracts from report to parents, Spring Term 1988, Reception)

Harriet reads very well with good expression and understanding, with obvious enjoyment.

Harriet enjoys practical mathematics and number work and has made good progress.

She spends a lot of time on her drawings and enjoys using colour with delightful results.

She enjoys PE and games activities.

(Mrs Powell, extracts from report to parents, Summer Term 1988, Reception)

However, if Mrs Powell was happy with Harriet's progress over her first year of school, Harriet's mother, as she had anticipated, was somewhat less than satisfied.

Home and family relationships in Reception

If we consider some entries in the parents' diary of June 1988, we can see that Mrs Morley had a different perception of Harriet's literacy skills at the end of her first year of schooling than did her teacher:

She enjoys doing her reading to us and always seems to be reading and willing to read her schoolbooks and any books at home. She doesn't mess about or fidget when she reads but I don't know if she always knows what she has read. She loves being read to, but again, I don't know if she concentrates on the story. She will stop me several times to ask where a certain word or phrase is and I have to go back and show it to her.

I think she finds writing quite hard work. She doesn't do much at home, if any. I keep meaning to do more but time just goes. She is nearly up to the standard she was when she left playgroup last year. We get a lot of tracing paper bits brought home. She seems fairly proud of them but really, they could do more at school.

(Parent diary, June 1988, Reception)

Mrs Morley's perceptions and expectations clearly differ from Mrs Powell's on several counts in relation to Harriet's reading and writing. However, perhaps the most startling observation of Mrs Morley's was that she considered Harriet's writing to be 'nearly up to the standard' of the year before. In interview, Andrew Pollard questioned further:

Mrs Morley:	Yes, and I mean it.
AP:	In what way is that? Do you mean in the formation of letters?
Mrs Morley:	It seems to me that she has done so little during the year that it has almost gone back to nothing.

(Parent interview, June 1988, Reception)

Now, this clearly indicates such a gulf between the understandings of Harriet's teacher and her mother that we might suspect either a breakdown in communication to the effect that Mrs Morley did not *know* what Harriet was doing in school and how much she was writing, or a tremendous difference between the expectations of Mrs Powell and those of Mrs Morley. It appears that the latter was probably the case and that Mrs Morley's perceptions of Greenside's best efforts fell short of what she would ideally wish. Andrew Pollard asked about

Harriet's parents' long-term aspirations for her. Among other thoughts, Mrs Morley commented:

> Obviously healthy, happy mostly. Those are the really important things. To have a good, broad outlook on everything. By eleven, educationally, I would like her to be better than what Greenside School wishes to turn out.
> (Mrs Morley, parent interview, March 1988, Reception)

Following this statement in March moreover, there was a further deterioration in Mrs Morley's confidence in the school brought about by a series of incidents that Mrs Morley felt were unprofessionally handled by staff at the school. Just after the summer half-term, Mrs Morley recorded in the diary, Harriet moved up to the next 'reading box':

> The next box was in Miss Scott's room. We went in together the first day and found the box and took a book. Fine. In the morning she took it back and quite honestly Miss Scott 'jumped' on her saying, out of the blue 'So what was so great about Billy's day?' in a horrible stern voice. We were both taken aback having been used to Mrs Powell's friendliness. Harriet thought she was being told off and couldn't answer. Miss Scott said 'There! It's not good you pushing her. She does not know what she's read. It's a waste of time. No good coming in here getting books . . .' – on – on – on. Result: Harriet and I fed up and Harriet is afraid to go and change books and definitely won't do it by herself. No pleasure at all. Miss Scott refuses to acknowledge my presence now. Very moody individual.
> (Parent diary, June 1988, Reception)

The next event to precipitate a rift between Mrs Morley and the staff at Greenside occurred just after Harriet's fifth birthday and was also recorded in the diary:

> I went shopping that morning and knowing Harriet was having a packed lunch I didn't get home until 1pm. I found a note on the door saying 'Harriet is with me – Lois'. I dashed over the road to my neighbour, Lois. She said 'Don't worry. Harriet was here but she's been collected and is back at school'.
> (Parent diary, June 1988, Reception)

Harriet, forgetting she was to stay in school at lunchtime, had left her classroom and the school. Not finding her mother at the school gate she had proceeded to walk the considerable distance home, crossing two busy roads and through some parklands. Mrs Morley was, naturally, upset and angry, and it was also, of course, a very worrying incident for Mrs Davison, the headteacher, and Mrs Powell. Mrs Davison concurred with Mrs Morley's suggestion that the collection of children at the school gate should be supervised. Mrs Powell was, according to Mrs Morley 'very angry', accusing Harriet (to her mother) of being 'deliberately deceitful' in misleading her about whether she intended to go home. Mrs Morley commented:

> This behaviour from Mrs Powell was incredible and totally wrong. The whole episode has been a misunderstanding on Harriet's part and was unprofessionally handled by Mrs Powell.
> (Parent diary, June 1988, Reception)

Some of the bitterness of these clashes with teachers can probably be attributed to the fact that relationships between Mrs Morley and the staff at the school were already strained. As we have seen, Mrs Morley felt that pupils at Greenside 'could do more', and she had taken into school a *Sunday Times* article suggesting, Mrs Morley recalled, that 'children respond to more of a structured approach'. She sought Mrs Powell's opinion on the issue:

Mrs Morley:	That went down terribly. Mrs Powell interpreted it as I was finding fault with Mrs Long. Emma is in Mrs Long's class. I never mentioned Mrs Long but there is so much tittle-tattle in that school, all those women there and not enough men teachers. I was called in by Mrs Long – did I have any complaints about her teaching? It was awful. So unprofessional.
AP:	My goodness, so you have had a few ups and downs.
Mrs Morley:	Yes, I have recently. All these teachers are going. I suppose they are so fed up. I haven't found Mrs Davison (the head-teacher) to be too bad really. It's the others. These people who are leaving.

(Parent interview, July 1988, Reception)

Among the happier events in Harriet's family life recorded in the diaries that year was a very significant one for Harriet – her first riding lesson:

At 2 pm we were at the riding stables. Harriet had been waiting for this moment to arrive all week. We have let the children go for rides on ponies while on holiday but this was the first real lesson and now they were ready to hop on.
Each child was led to a nearby field and they practised all sorts of things. Ben said Harriet answered up very well when the teacher asked questions mostly about names of different parts of the pony and saddle. Enjoyed by all.
(Parent diary, February 1988, Reception)

Throughout that year Harriet continued to be strong-willed and self-determining at home, qualities which, her mother felt, embodied considerable strengths:

She is wilful at home but she is fun and she is interesting to be with. She will always have a go at anything. If you say 'Make me a cup of coffee' or anything like this, even if I know she can't do it, she will say 'Oh, yes, what shall I do?'. Whereas if I say anything like that to Emma, who is older, it is 'I can't do that. I don't know how to do that'.
(Mrs Morley, parent interview, July 1988, Reception)

Harriet's Reception year at Greenside had clearly been a rather unfortunate one from the point of view of home–school relationships. However, Harriet seemed to remain relatively unscathed by it and Mrs Morley felt that her own relationships would improve in the school when the staff from the previous head-teacher's administration had left. That, however, was in the future. In the meantime the news was that Harriet was to go into Mrs Scott's Year 1 class in the following September, and as we can judge from the events above, that was not well received by Mrs Morley.

Summary of Harriet's Reception year

From her parents' perspective Harriet's first year at school was predominantly characterized by abrasive relationships and disappointment at her academic progress. These unhappy clashes seemed to have left Harriet unscathed, however, and perhaps it was the case that, as Mrs Powell suggested, 'nothing much gets to her'.

Indeed, Harriet had settled into the expectations of Mrs Powell's classroom remarkably well. At home she was forceful in taking control of her learning over family members who were in the position of supporting that learning, whether the issue was learning to ride her bicycle or having a bedtime story. In Mrs Powell's class however, she accepted the discipline of school and did what was required, though ultimately indifferent to either pleasing or displeasing Mrs Powell.

Similarly, Harriet seemed relatively indifferent to the pressures and opinions of her peers. Perhaps not unconnected with this indifference, there are early indications here that Harriet might shape an identity outside the expectations and the norms of the mainstream culture of the girls' peer group.

Harriet, Year 1, early days in Miss Scott's class

Harriet's structural position in Miss Scott's class was lower than it had been in Reception. She was now almost the youngest in a large class of 32 children, attaining a position over the year within the top third for English still but almost three-quarters the way down the class in maths.

The abrasive relationship which we have seen existed between Harriet's mother and Miss Scott had stemmed from the time when her sister Emma had been in Miss Scott's class. A lot of data from interviews, from Andrew Pollard's fieldnotes and from Miss Scott's extensive records illustrate both a poor teacher–pupil relationship and a poor relationship with Harriet's mother. It unfortunately appears that Miss Scott, as a result of her relationship with Mrs Morley, and as a result of the stress she was under at the time, felt an almost instant antipathy towards Harriet, as she described to Andrew Pollard:

> Harriet is the youngest girl and I am afraid there is a slight problem in that I know Mrs Morley, we know each other from old. Harriet – I didn't from the instant ... OK, you can't blame the child for the mother, and I have taught Emma and Emma was slightly like it, but Harriet was so rude in her way that she speaks to you in that she would be very abrupt and surly. I can't think of the right word. I suppose I am on the defensive in many respects because of the situation in the school probably, but also partly because her mother does come in and she would take over Harriet's education if she possibly could, or definitely her reading which she thinks is obviously the 'be all and end all'.
> (Miss Scott, teacher interview, November 1988, Year 1)

As she recognized, Miss Scott's personal antipathy towards Mrs Morley and what she saw as her misguided childrearing practices spilled over into her professional dealings with Harriet, as she described:

Miss Scott:	There was an unfortunate incident last week which was rather funny when she cut her hair and that I must write down about because it's like the incident when she went home when she shouldn't have done last term. The mother came to me on Tuesday morning to say Harriet was going to be late as she was going to have her hair cut because the night before she had got some scissors and hacked away

quite merrily. The mother made it quite obvious to me – she
is going to come in at lunchtime and you mustn't say how
awful she looks. You mustn't make her feel uncomfortable.
[However, when Harriet returned to school] Joyce Lane [a
nursery teacher] came in. It took her by surprise. 'How
lovely Harriet, your hair looks beautiful' and I said 'Don't
say that' and then at some point – I know, knowing me – I
made some crack about the scissors 'Well we know what scissors are used for, but they are not used for some things they
are used for cutting paper' or something like that ... which
put her in her place.

AP: What did she do?
Miss Scott: She just looked at me.
AP: Did she say anything about why she had cut her hair?
Miss Scott: No, I didn't talk to her about it. I didn't want her to think
she could cut her hair to get attention and she could cut her
hair anytime because it didn't matter. She doesn't seem to be
at home reprimanded for things she shouldn't do. My ploy is
not to give her the attention she obviously thinks she might
want.

Miss Scott went on to describe how relations were mended with Harriet by the
end of the week:

Miss Scott: Anyway, that was the beginning of the week. On that Friday
we were writing firework poems. She came to me with a
superb poem, and I was pleased. I sort of screamed, saying
'How marvellous' and hugged her and her response was
amazing. She was overjoyed. I had made a breakthrough.

However, she thought Harriet remained socially insecure in the classroom:

Miss Scott: I wouldn't say she mixes. I think she is still quite a surly
child. She does seem to play once again with Daniel Jarrett
these last couple of days. I don't know why, but he's been in
a funny state recently as well.
(Teacher interview, November 1988, Year 1)

Perhaps it was a measure of both Daniel and Harriet's insecurity in these circumstances that they came together again briefly. Certainly Harriet had not yet
made any real friends among the girls at the time when, as we have seen in
Sarah's story and in *The Social World of Children's Learning*, many children particularly felt the need for them because of the volatile atmosphere in Miss Scott's
classroom.

Friendships and peer relationships in Year 1

During the first half of her year in Miss Scott's class, for the first time in her
school life Harriet seemed troubled by a lack of friends and she complained at
home of having no-one to sit by or play with.

As the year progressed and with, as we shall see, improved relationships with
her teacher, Harriet's classroom confidence returned. As her mother put it in the
diary:

According to Miss Scott, Harriet is coming out of her shell. I wasn't aware she was in it.
(Parent diary, June 1989, Year 1)

However, Miss Scott continued to regard Harriet as 'a bit of a loner' (Teacher records, May 1989). Like Robert however, Harriet was not 'a loner' by choice; rather her interests were simply quite distinct from those of most of her peers. This, together with the geographical distance from their homes, contributed to a sense of separation from them. Already however, Mrs Morley was beginning to identify a certain shared perspective between Harriet and Hazel:

Mrs Morley:	I think Harriet daydreams quite a bit, lives in a little world of her own. And I think Hazel does that as well.
AP:	Hazel does that, yes. Harriet's world is the horses and things? What sort of world?
Mrs Morley:	Yes, well, horses and perhaps the family ... But out of school, school doesn't really come into it. This is the trouble. I think you need to live in an area where all your friends are neighbours. She isn't a ballet type – in fact we are giving up ballet actually. But a lot of those girls at school are and I can see that they move and dance really well. Well she isn't that type. Apart from Hazel I can't think of anyone of the girls that are really her type.

(Parent interview, July 1989, Year 1)

Hazel is mentioned as a friend here because, as the year had progressed, Harriet had become more closely identified in the classroom and playground with her and also with Nimra, though she was somewhat marginalized by the two. A close friendship with Hazel was not really to take off until the following year.

Learning strategies in Year 1

As we have seen, Harriet experienced a shaky start to the year with Miss Scott feeling some considerable antipathy towards her and Harriet, for her part, withdrawing the happy compliance that she had shown in Mrs Powell's class. Miss Scott in her records (November 1988) and in interview (November 1988) described Harriet variously as having 'a difficult attitude', 'stubborn', 'not relaxed', 'quiet', 'sullen', 'rude'.

As her structural position with regard to academic attainment might suggest, Miss Scott found a greater discrepancy between Harriet's skills across different areas of the curriculum than did Mrs Powell. Of course, Harriet was one of the younger pupils in the class now and her skills were being measured against a different cohort. Nevertheless, there was a qualitative difference between the two teachers' assessments of her progress. Thus, whereas Mrs Powell was pleased with Harriet's writing both with regard to skills, content and length, Miss Scott recorded:

Harriet finds writing difficult thus the skill is immature and still does not match her reading. Similarly her maths.
(Miss Scott, teacher records, January 1989, Year 1)

With regard to maths especially, Miss Scott regarded Harriet as 'vastly behind' (teacher interview, November 1988).

However, by the beginning of the summer term, Harriet's progress began to improve so that by the end of the year Miss Scott was able to report:

Language development Her language skills have consolidated. Revealing a growing interest in writing with imagination and skill is developing.

Maths Harriet has made recent rapid progress now that her understanding of basic concepts has been attained. She is revealing a deeper awareness and interest in all aspects.
(Miss Scott, report to parents, July 1989, Year 1)

This progress occurred at about the time when Harriet was, as Miss Scott put it, 'coming out of her shell'. While it is impossible to attribute the change in Harriet to any definitive cause it is possible that, like Sarah and many other children, she 'got the measure' of Miss Scott and had learned ways of coping in her classroom. However, there were also other changes, instigated by Mrs Morley, which reduced the tension between home and school which had so influenced Miss Scott's dealings with Harriet.

Home and family relationships in Year 1

As the year progressed Mrs Morley felt less involved in Harriet's schoolwork, especially her reading, and knew little about what Harriet was doing in school. She had begun to withdraw from the school situation as she explained to Andrew Pollard:

AP:	Could you tell me a little bit more about how you see Harriet's self-confidence with maths?
Mrs Morley:	Well really, not being in the classroom, I can't say, and I always find it very difficult to find out exactly what is going on because if you ask too many questions you're labelled anxious. So I can't tell you. At one time I was helping her to choose the books but that went out of my control completely. And I didn't find the books very good that she was bringing home. It makes it sound as if I am very pushy and anxious but in the end I thought, I can't go in. I won't do anything at all. Just let it slip.
AP:	So really, your policy over the year was to 'keep your head down' in a sense.
Mrs Morley:	Yes. I mean, I wish that teachers would appreciate parents who are anxious to find out what their children do. Why don't they? Tell me.

(Parent interview, July 1989, Year 1)

During what was in many ways not a very successful or happy year either socially or academically at school, Harriet was rapidly developing a range of knowledge, skills and confidence – but in an altogether different context.

Mrs Morley:	Well, she started riding just over a year ago now, but she's got plenty of confidence on that and there's never any hesitation about approaching the horses or trying new things. My

daughter Emma is very hesitant about cantering and things like that, but Harriet just seems to do them and she gets on with the people there. We've just been to this place, a farm near Symington Bay, and she gets on ever so well there – Harriet bossing people about, telling fathers who are leading their children that they are doing it the wrong way, and she's right in what she says. But I don't think that confidence comes over particularly in [the school situation].

AP: It's interesting the confidence in the riding situation. Do you remember how it started? Have the other children done anything . . .?

Mrs Morley: No, it's just natural. She doesn't hesitate about going up to animals. It doesn't matter how big the animal is, she'll go straight up.

AP: And she's always done that, has she?

Mrs Morley: Yes. Other children do tend to hold back. She'll probably end up being kicked. She's been bitten a few times by the horses but that doesn't put her off.

AP: So she's developing the idea that she's good with animals and that's obviously given her a lot of positive reinforcement.

Mrs Morley: Yes. That's her thing.

(Parent interview, July 1989, Year 1)

By the end of the summer term, Mrs Morley's unhappy relationships with staff were almost behind her and she was more optimistic about the year ahead than she had been at the beginning of Year 1. While she did not know who Harriet's teacher would be for the following year, her hope was for 'someone quite strict, but fair and fun'.

Summary of Harriet's Year 1

Compared with her Reception year, Harriet's experience with Miss Scott was marked by a poor pupil–teacher relationship, some loss of social confidence and a withdrawal of the easy classroom compliance and cooperation that had marked her relationship with Mrs Powell. Harriet also found greater difficulty with integrating satisfactorily with her peers that year and her progress slowed in both maths and writing. An improvement in Mrs Scott's relationship with Harriet towards the end of the year coincided with a return to a satisfactory level of progress.

Contrasting with her classroom life, Harriet, out of school, demonstrated a tremendous social confidence and a knowledgeable competence in the context of learning to ride. The slight cultural as well as geographical distance that had separated her somewhat from her peers now became more marked. Harriet, at five years old, was beginning to shape an identity and status in horse riding circles, as well as within her family.

Harriet's identity and career in the early years at Greenside School

By the end of her second year of schooling Harriet showed no clear identification with any aspect of her formal schooling. She had developed no clear sense of 'belonging' yet. The positive sense of self as 'good with animals' and knowledgeable regarding horses and riding that was emerging out of school had no parallels in school.

As we have already indicated, Harriet's predominant strategic responses in school can be described, like Robert's, in terms of *non-conformity*. For both children, school and home were separate domains and once at home school was set aside. There was also, for both of them, a corresponding sense of emotional distance from school, and this was characterized by a certain indifference to pressures to conform to the expectations of teachers, as well as those of peers. Both children were seen by teachers as 'loners by choice' in relation to their peers, though a broader perspective on their experience shows that they had a limited choice of peers who were able to share their particular interests and goals.

At this stage in her career it was still difficult to perceive what goals Harriet might have in relation to school. Unlike Robert, she had as yet found no scope in school for the maintenance or development of her special identity, either in the classroom or playground. In this respect her experience matched Hazel, whose early years story features in *The Social World of Children's Learning*. In the following school year, both Harriet and Hazel would be taught by Miss George, the new member of staff in her first year of teaching, whom we last met in Sarah's story. In Miss George's Year 2 class, the two girls came together as friends and began to forge a mutually supportive relationship that would last throughout their primary years. Within this relationship, and with others that joined the group, the two girls struggled, with varied degrees of success, to shape and give expression to their distinctly individual identities and classroom agendas. We will follow those struggles through the next two instalments of Harriet's story.

7.2   YEAR 2 AND YEAR 3

Introduction

Through the middle years of Harriet's career at Greenside, we begin to see more variability both in teacher–pupil relationships and in the support offered for the development of her positive self-image as a pupil. At this point in his career, Robert, whose predominant strategy was also that of *non-conformity*, went from strength to strength in impressing his teachers with his independent stance, negotiating a classroom role and status independently of teacher expectations. Unlike Robert, the identity which Harriet sought to shape in school was unrelated to the formal curricular content. Nevertheless, we see Harriet begin to give expression to her special interests, in the classroom through writing, talking and artwork. However, the expression of her interests in this way depended upon the level of freedom permitted to pupils to negotiate the knowledge content of tasks, and it may have been the absence of such freedom that prompted Harriet to find an alternative route to maintaining her identity and status: one that was not vulnerable to teacher control. Like Robert, Harriet also found that, with friends who shared special interests, she could give expression to and elaborate a distinctive identity within the peer culture.

Matrix 7.1 *Harriet, Reception and Year 1, a summary matrix*

Family relationships	Peer-group relationships	Teacher relationships	Identity	Career
Reception: Mrs Powell				
Harriet comes from a busy and active family with close association with horse-riding community. She has an older sister and brother and is the 'noisiest and bossiest'. Harriet likes to be in control of herself and her learning. Tense relationships exist between Mrs Morley and some Greenside staff.	Distance of home from peers' homes limits Harriet's out-of-school access to them. Mrs Morley concerned that Harriet has no good friends among girls. Harriet enjoys games traditionally associated with boys. Cooperative with peers. Friendship with Daniel wanes as he withdraws from relationship with a girl.	Structural position: age, 13/28. In top third for English and maths. Harriet could read before coming to school. Teacher sees her as happy, relaxed, vociferous and cooperative. Works and plays closely with Daniel, Harriet leading and dominating. Fairly indifferent to teacher approval or disapproval.	At home 'noisy', 'bossy', 'independent', resents control by others. In school, 'happy', 'relaxed', 'vociferous', 'independent'.	Accepts the discipline of school and does what required but indifferent to adult and peer pressures. Harriet does not greatly identify with the mainstream girls' culture in the school. Some tensions in home–school relationships.
Year 1: Miss Scott				
Mrs Morley is more pleased with the school generally though lacks confidence in Harriet's teacher with whom she has a poor relationship historically. Mrs Morley feels less involved in Harriet's learning, is beginning to withdraw from a tense classroom situation and knows little about what Harriet is doing in school. Harriet gets on well in horse-riding circles.	Teacher describes Harriet as 'a bit of a loner'. Harriet expresses unhappiness at home over having no-one to play with and sit by at school. She is on the margins of the friendship group of Hazel and Nimra.	Structural position: age, 29/32. English in top third, maths, three-quarters down class. A shaky start to the year, poor relationship with Harriet's mother affecting Miss Scott's perceptions of Harriet who she sees as 'stubborn', 'sullen', 'rude', 'not relaxed'. Later in year Harriet regains some confidence, is seen as 'alternatively noisy and hesitant'. Also 'strong-willed'. Maths progress picks up and she develops an interest in writing.	At home, good with animals, confident in horse-riding circles. Described by Miss Scott as 'stubborn', 'sullen', 'rude'. Later in year described by Miss Scott as 'noisy', 'hesitant', 'strong-willed'.	Harriet withdraws with some general loss of confidence in the classroom due to the loss of Daniel's friendship and less secure classroom structures and relationship with teacher. No clear identification with any aspect of school. No sense of belonging yet. A pattern of home and school as largely separate spheres of existence for Harriet is beginning here.

Harriet, Year 2, early days in Miss George's class

In September 1989 Harriet entered Miss George's Year 2 class where she was the fifth oldest in a class of 32 children. Her structural position in this class in English, within the top quarter, was also higher than in previous classes, though she remained three-quarters the way down in maths.

Miss George, it will be remembered from Sarah's story, was one of the new members of staff who were rapidly replacing those of the previous administration. More about Miss George and the organization of learning in her classroom can of course be found in Chapter 3 and in Sarah's story. From the point of view of Harriet's story, however, what was important was that the relationships surrounding her learning were likely to be improved now that the antagonism between Mrs Morley and the teachers of the previous administration were in the past. So it was that Miss George reported to Andrew Pollard that Harriet had settled well into her class. Despite her perplexity and amazement at Harriet's independent stance, we can discern a degree of good-natured tolerance in her account of her early impressions of Harriet, an account which contrasts strongly with Miss Scott's antagonistic reactions to her:

Miss George:	I found Harriet a bit strange when I first met her. She is very long-winded, she takes ages doing anything, she takes ages planning. Sometimes it's gone breaktime and you say 'What have you planned?' – 'Oh, I haven't finished my planning yet' – 'Well what have you been doing, it's ages'. And I remember the first week I gave her some work to do and when I went back ages later she hadn't written a single mark on the page. I said 'What have you been doing all this time?' – 'Thinking!' She's quite strident, isn't she? 'Thinking!' – as if I was really stupid. Of course. She'd been thinking, so that was all right. She didn't have to put a mark on the page as long as she'd been thinking. She's a really good reader. Anything she writes is horses. That's all she talks about.
AP:	Would you say she is as obsessive about horses as Hazel is about dinosaurs and things?
Miss George:	Pretty close, yes, because she got all the reading books out of the library. I was going through the pink tickets because I seemed to have rather a lot there and if it was a horsy type book they'd say 'That's Harriet'.
AP:	Are there other children with a similar 'obsession', if you like?
Miss George:	I don't think any of them on that. A few of them talk about ballet like that.

(Teacher interview, May 1990, Year 2)

Here we see Miss George both acknowledging and allowing Harriet to give expression to an area of development in which her competence and self-esteem were high. An example of Harriet's writing conveying her feelings about her horse-riding activities can be seen in Document 7.1

As we described in Chapter 3 and in Sarah's story, the organization of learning and the planning of tasks in Miss George's class now enabled pupils to have a greater control over both the content and the timing of tasks. Harriet certainly used this greater autonomy to begin to carve out an identity and a classroom

Tuesday 24th April

on Thursday I went to Byways
and I rode on James and
Pebble and Alice
took our lesson Pebble
is good on lessons James
is good on Hacs I like
riding James on Hacs
and Pebble on lessons
Pebble Pebble is nice
to ride James is nice
to ride as well I
like Taffy too I have
not liked when I
was a baby I am six
now but I whant to be

status which was distinct from those of most of her peers. It was not, however, so very distinct from Hazel's, and it was through their similar self-determining approaches to the expression of similar interests that Harriet and Hazel began, later in the year, to form their close attachment. Miss George, for her part, was

7 I really do want to be 7 and I am 7 in June Alice said I am a good horse rider I lov. being a good horse rider horse-riding is fun horse-riding is some times funny I like hot riding Emma likes riding Emma rides Taffy two

really want.

Document 7.1 *Harriet, Year 2, 'Horse-riding' (April 1990)*

to come to feel an attachment and empathy with the two girls such that, at the end of the year, she was to acknowledge them as the two in the class she would especially miss when she left the school.

Friendships and peer relationships in Year 2

Of the children in Miss Scott's Year 1 class, only six, including Harriet, transferred to Miss George's class. Among those six were some of the girls with whom Harriet had in the past associated without forming close relationships. These included Sarah, as well as Sally and Mary whose stories feature in *The Social*

Harriet is self-confident and friendly. She has worked particularly well with a special friend this term.
(Miss George, report to parents, summer 1990, Year 2)

Home and family relationships in Year 2

During Year 2, Mrs Morley maintained the stance of rather distancing herself from Harriet's classroom, as she explained in the diary entry for Harriet's first term in Miss George's class:

I just can't write about school. I know nothing about it (points of failure I know!). She always comes out confident and happy. Harriet seems to like Miss George.
(Parent diary, November 1989, Year 2)

However, if she was still not happy with Harriet's education at Greenside, at least she had reduced the tension in her relationship with the school and tried to change the image that she felt they had of her, as she explained to Andrew Pollard in interview:

Mrs Morley: I don't want to appear an anxious mother because I'm not, although I'm typecast as that at the school – so I try not to be. I feel, in a way, the least I know about what's going on [the better], then I won't be annoyed about it. They're not really finding what she can do and what a short time at home it can take her to learn something. I think, what on earth do they do all the time there? But if I don't know that, then I just think she's fairly happy at school and let it jog along like that.

AP: But one way of insulating yourself from it, from making sure you don't get upset about things is to draw back and try not to get involved. So the consequence is that you are drawing back from getting involved with what Harriet is learning at school.

Mrs Morley: Yes. It is bad that. I know the type of work they produce could be much, much better. That sounds awful but it's so difficult to deal with – there's 31 in the class. So I just let her jog along.
(Mrs Morley, parent interview, December 1989, Year 2)

We go up on parents night and think 'isn't it awful' but somehow by Year 6 they all write quite well.
(Mrs Morley, parent interview, July 1990, Year 2)

Mrs Morley went on to say that she sometimes bought the commercially available maths exercise books for Harriet to complete at home which she did quite happily. It was difficult keeping it up in the evenings though, she explained, with three children to transport to swimming, Brownies, piano lessons etc. and a husband who worked long hours and wasn't often around to help.

At this point Mrs Morley was apparently becoming a little more philosophical and relaxed about the primary education of her children. It perhaps helped that the Morleys, living where they did, were able to send their children to a state maintained grammar school.

I'm pleased that Ben has gone to Halberton and I'll feel quite pleased if Emma just follows on, and Harriet, and there isn't really a need for them to achieve lots at eleven just to pass an exam. I'd rather they just float on.
(Mrs Morley, December 1989, Year 2)

Families that lived on the other side of the main Easthampton Road nearer to Greenside School, however, found it almost impossible to get their children into Halberton Grammar and, as we have seen, most of them considered their nearest comprehensive school, Damibrook, an unacceptable choice.

As every year, the diary and the interviews that year also recorded the day-to-day events and relationships in the life of six-year-old Harriet out of school:

The thing that is most different at home this term is that we have a border collie puppy. She is sixteen weeks. Ben seems more interested in television than in her, Emma is afraid, but Harriet takes on a lot of the walking and playing with her. 'Mo' can be very rough and often loud screams and cries come from Harriet.

Harriet went to piano. Mrs Thorpe, her teacher, said she is a very determined young lady and doesn't like to be wrong. I think Mrs Thorpe has a lot of patience with her. As with most things, Harriet doesn't want to practise but when Tom [father] does sit down with her and encourage her, she succeeds.

After piano we all went to Gran's for tea. Harriet likes to take over and we listen to her sing a few songs just for fun. The old ladies love it but everyone has to do exactly what Harriet says.

I'm glad Miss George told the girls to keep their hair tidy because Harriet insists on doing her own and by the end of the day it's terrible. Don't know what goes on – no buttons left on her blouse and shoes all scuffed.
(Extract from parent diary, November 1989, Year 2)

She's not a child that likes trying on clothes. I can't get her to do that. She hasn't got much patience.
(Mrs Morley, parent interview, December 1989, Year 2)

Where her brother and sister were concerned, Mrs Morley described Emma as 'an ace at relationships' who would hang back or say the right thing and manage to be tactful and so she and Harriet had a good relationship, her mother felt. Ben, however was 'totally intolerant' at this time. 'It makes so much trouble unnecessarily', his mother thought. Harriet, for her part, responded to her brother with 'screaming, crying and being very loud'.

Summary of Harriet's Year 2

In her Year 2 class Harriet discovered a route to establishing an identity and status through classroom tasks. In Miss George's class conditions existed for greater pupil autonomy than she had previously experienced. She had greater control over her learning which was something she asserted at home. Harriet was supported by the teacher in giving expression to her out-of-school identity and expertise with horses so that she incorporated it into her learning with a resulting increase in motivation and intrinsic satisfaction in writing tasks. This in turn promoted a partnership with Hazel and the beginning of what was to become a new friendship group.

Harriet, Year 3, early days in Mr Brown's class

As in Year 1, Harriet was again this year one of the youngest in the class, with only three children younger than her in a class of 33. Mr Brown, her teacher, gave his early impressions of Harriet:

> My first impression of Harriet was that she was very noisy but I've got on really well with her since and she wrote on her review sheet, I think last time that 'I like you'. We've got on really well. She's been a lot more sensible and she produced some really nice work and she's a fantastic reader, I think she really does understand [what she's read]. I couldn't believe what she was reading – one of the Narnia books and understanding it. She came in last week at lunchtime. We were planning our service and we wrote a play. She's full of good ideas.
> (Mr Brown, teacher interview, September 1990, Year 3)

Mr Brown, as we have seen in all the children's stories, supported the philosophy of active learning and pupil negotiation of the curriculum in the planning of tasks. However, as we described in Chapter 3, different teachers tended to interpret the concept of 'negotiated curriculum' in different ways and their interpretations, of course, became translated into the way the planning and organization of activities were carried out in the classroom. One of the differences that we identified was in relation to the freedom which pupils had to negotiate the knowledge content of tasks. So, for example, Miss Sage and Miss George's class were characterized by ongoing negotiation of the content of tasks on an individual and a group basis. In Harriet's case, as we saw, this gave her a platform for the expression of her individual identity, as it did for Hazel. In Mr Brown's class, however, as we also described in Chapter 2, negotiation of the specific content of tasks took place on a whole class or sometimes a group basis. This meant that there was little room for pupils' *spontaneous* creativity with respect to introducing new ideas:

> OK, we've got the web [i.e. topic plan] and their ideas but they may have other ideas as they go along. Some individuals have come up with fantastic ideas and I say 'Right, OK, fine. Go and do it'. But I've not gone into that too much yet. I think it will be more them planning their ideas properly, for me to say 'That's OK', so that I know what's going on.
> (Mr Brown, teacher interview, September 1990, Year 3)

Of course, in addition, as we described in Robert's story, as the children left the relative freedom of infant classes behind, the requirements of the National Curriculum and the need for more formally structured expression of knowledge crowded out the opportunities for freedom of expression that were a feature of the early years. It was partly as a result of the progression through the school in this way, we suggested, that Robert had to devise strategies for making opportunities to pursue his own interests and maintain his identity in slightly different ways than he was able to manage in his early years. Certainly, however, it was the case that no distinct expression of Harriet's identity surfaced in Mr Brown's classroom that year. Nor were her out-of-school interests celebrated or supported by Mr Brown in the same way that Robert's more obviously curriculum-related interests were. It may have been a consequence of the stronger framing of knowledge in the classroom that year that Harriet began to elaborate her identity more strongly in the playground in the context of a new friendship group.

Friendships and peer relationships in Year 3

While no distinct expression of Harriet's or indeed Hazel's identity surfaced in the classroom that year, that identity was being highly elaborated by the girls in the playground within their new friendship group. Harriet described their activities to Ann Filer:

> Well, my little gang I was talking about, Hazel, Ellen and Ned, they all like what I like and we all go on hands and feet and I'm not the odd one out and Hazel's not the odd one out and no one is 'cos they all go around on hands and feet.
> (Harriet, pupil interview, July 1991, Year 3)

'Going on hands and feet' had been one of Hazel's games from first coming into school and her speed and agility at it were a source of pride. Now Ned and Ellen, both relatively new pupils in the school, had joined the two girls and the four children spent their time in the playground imaginatively immersed in games of dragons, horses and other animals, mythical and real, as they described to Ann Filer:

> AF: What do you like playing in the playground?
> Hazel: We like to play Dragons and Unicorns.
> Harriet: And back fights. You sit with backs together and push against one another.
> Hazel: Play fights. You jump over each other like a tiger does.
> Harriet: We like cute wasps and bees.
> AF: Are wasps cute?
> Ned: Oh yes, 'cos we really love nature.
> (The children tell of finding and naming snails and children from another class stepping on 'their' snails. They recognized the pattern on the shells they said, so they know it was theirs.)
> (Friendship group interview, July 1991, Year 3)

These distinctive and frequently high-profile activities were looked upon with a mixture of amusement and amazement by their more conventional peers. The general opinion expressed to Ann Filer was that the four were 'mad' and definitely 'weird':

> They play weird games of dragons. They go down with their bums in the air. They're always doing something weird.
> (Jessica, friendship group interview, July 1991, Year 3)

As we see in other children's stories, the children's friendships at about this time in their careers began to form around shared interests and perspectives. We saw for example how Sarah began to somewhat distance herself at this point from friends such as Mary, Sally and Hannah who liked 'kiss chase' and had more competitive classroom profiles and were 'into everything'. Thus as well as shaping a group identity in terms of shared interests that were distinct from their peers, like other individuals and groups they were also differentiating themselves from others on the basis of what they were not. Ann Filer asked the group if there were children in their class that they didn't play with:

Harriet:	We don't play with Stephen.
Ned:	'Cos he's mean.
Ellen:	Not Sally.
Harriet:	'Cos she's a bit bossy.
Ellen:	Hannah we don't play with. She's a bit like Sally.
AF:	What about Diana?
All:	Eugh!! She steals stuff.
Ned:	And she kicks and punches. If you're a boy she pulls your pants down and if you're a girl she lifts your dress up.
Ellen:	At my party she was really rude. She said 'Simon says lift your dress up and pull your knickers down'.
Harriet:	She kept spilling drinks on purpose.
Ellen:	What really spoilt it was that she snatched a party bag from my Mum. Diana sometimes plays with Naomi, but Naomi is nice. When I first came to this school she was kind to me and waited for me to finish my dinner.

(Friendship group interview, July 1991, Year 3)

As well as disapproving of rudeness or vulgarity in their peers at this time, neither did they concern themselves with the talk of 'love' and 'boyfriends' that was increasingly becoming central in the cultures of the mainstream, and especially high-status boys' and girls' groups at the time. Similarly, although Harriet had had a brief association with it, neither did Harriet, Hazel or Ellen concern themselves with the chants, rhymes and clapping games that occupied a lot of playground time for the majority of girls. By the end of the year, therefore, in contrast to their relatively low profile in classroom and extra-curricular activities, the four had created for themselves a high-profile well defined playground identity, which was distinctly different from those of their peers.

Learning strategies in Year 3

During her time in Mr Brown's class, Harriet made reasonably good progress as her report at the end of the year indicated:

English Harriet is an articulate girl who contributes well in group and class situations. At review times she always explains herself clearly logically and fluently. She enjoys writing and has produced some interesting work. She must learn to check her work more carefully however.

Maths Harriet has shown a solid understanding of the work covered. Her output has sometimes been a little disappointing however.

Science Harriet has good scientific skills and is capable of carrying out investigations in a methodical, careful manner. Her understanding of all the attainment targets is good.

General comments Harriet is a lively, sociable girl who has a good group of friends. She has worked steadily all year and has made good progress overall.
(Mr Brown, extracts from report to parents, July 1991)

However, Mr Brown felt that Harriet was not achieving all that she might. Certainly her progression and attainment in maths, as always, lagged behind her understanding. In addition, however, although Harriet's writing was described as 'interesting', the enthusiastic and prolific response which she had brought to writing tasks, especially in Year 2, were missing that year. Indeed it seemed that, within the context of the structuring of tasks in Mr Brown's class, her freedom to give expression to the identity that she had been shaping since her entry into Year 2 was largely curtailed.

Mr Brown attributed Harriet's relative lack of progress to the attention she gave to supporting Hazel in the classroom. However, he conceded that this was not the cause of Harriet's slow progress in maths. The children were then grouped according to achievement and for this subject she did not work with Hazel. However, he was sure that a greater separation was necessary:

> ... but I did say to Harriet that I think sometimes Hazel is holding you back, because Harriet is very bright and she spends all her time with Hazel, checking her work, helping her out, explaining what I've just explained to everybody else. So I did say to Harriet, try and work with other people some of the time and then Ellen came in as a new girl and they accepted her into the group with Ned. And so Harriet's been relieved of the burden to a certain extent. It got to the stage when Harriet was answering for her. I'd go over to the table where they were working and say, whatever – 'And why haven't you been getting on Hazel?' and Harriet would answer and I would say 'No, let *Hazel*'. And she'd come out to me and say 'Hazel's upset because she doesn't know what to do' and I'd say 'Why couldn't Hazel tell me that?' It was getting silly.
> (Mr Brown, teacher interview, July 1991, Year 3)

Readers will need to refer to Hazel's story in *The Social World of Children's Learning* to appreciate the loss of rapport with her teacher and loss of classroom confidence that this account indicates, compared with her previous year in Miss George's class. However, as Mr Brown's accounts showed, he was never wholly successful in persuading Harriet away from Hazel, and moreover, working separately from her did not promote any great difference in the quality or quantity of her work. He further reflected:

> I wonder how she would have developed being with someone like Sally all year. I think that would have dragged her along, pulled her up a lot quicker.
> (Mr Brown, teacher interview, July 1991, Year 3)

However, our understanding and analysis of the very different motivational impulses of Harriet and Sally do not support Mr Brown's hypothesis. As we saw in Sarah's story, Mr Brown regarded Sally as 'in the top flight' now. Sally's classroom strategy of assessing, and speedily fulfilling, the basic requirements of teachers was motivated by a desire to be first to finish and to please her teachers. This strategy was fuelled by a highly competitive, constant comparison with other high-achieving peers (see Sally's story in *The Social World of Children Learning*). Conversely, although Harriet liked to be praised by her teachers, she was largely indifferent to their urging and was clearly not in competition with her peers. Rather, where she had excelled, for instance in writing, it was intrinsic satisfaction with the task that was the prime motivator.

As we have observed in the other case studies, their first year in the junior department was a time when many of the children began to develop extra-curricular interests. For some, this led to high-profile identities in relation to the school beyond their own classroom. Thus drama, choir, musical instruments and sports became increasingly important for many pupils, not only for their intrinsic interest but also for the status which was conferred. Their fortunes in their preferred activities, we have seen, were of vital importance to all the children in the study except, so far, Robert. However, Harriet, and also Hazel, were also relatively unconcerned about such issues as who got in the cricket team or who had the starring role in the Christmas play, though they joined in some of these activities from time to time on a relatively uncommitted basis. In interview, Ann Filer asked Harriet about her involvement in these things:

Harriet:	Well, last year and a tiny bit this year I did glockenspiels but I sort of lost interest. The music went very fast and I only had to do one beat and it was boring.
AF:	Do you think it's important to do things like that at school?
Harriet:	Well, if you're in choir it's important to carry on doing it 'cos you're in concerts and you have to practise. You don't have that with glockenspiels so it doesn't matter. It doesn't matter because if you're in the middle of a game in the playground, like I was in the middle of a game with Hazel and Ned and Ellen, you have to stop when the bell went and it was time for glockenspiels and I was winning.

(Pupil interview, July 1991, Year 3)

Home and family relationships in Year 3

Mrs Morley thought that Mr Brown was a competent teacher but again, with over 30 children in the class she felt that Harriet's progress was unlikely to change. She also felt that Harriet had not adapted very well to the new class that year, as she explained to Andrew Pollard:

Mrs Morley:	She did not adapt very well at all. In fact she hated it. I think being more or less the youngest in the class. I think Mr Brown found she acted a bit immaturely which makes sense because she is young. It wasn't until Ellen came, and then Harriet was a bit happier, and then this foursome, you know, Ned, Hazel, Ellen and Harriet.
AP:	They have really struck up quite a strong relationship.
Mrs Morley:	Yeah, they are four odd bods.

(Parent interview, July 1991, Year 3)

In relation to Harriet's friendship with Hazel, Mrs Morley recorded in the diary:

Hazel came to tea. We took the dog for a walk before coming home. She got on very well with Harriet and was polite to me. A nice girl.
(Parent diary, November 1990)

However, in relation to Harriet's progress Mrs Morley continued to be less than satisfied. She felt that all the children would have benefited from homework and she also worried that in school 'there is a constant noise in the classrooms' and wondered how children managed to learn anything under the circumstances. Nevertheless, the diary ended on a positive note as it had begun:

> Apart from these comments, she is a very happy girl again and I know that's important.
> (Parent diary, November 1990, Year 3)

During the year family relationships and activities continued relatively unchanged from the previous year. Unlike many of her peers who were becoming increasingly style-conscious, Harriet didn't have much interest in fashion. Her mother thought that she would probably have liked to dress like her slim friends but didn't give much consideration to what, as a bigger child, might have suited her. She hated clothes shopping. Though she had been 'desperate to have long hair' the previous year, she 'didn't care what her hair looked like' (parent interview, July 1991). Harriet's mother also described her as interesting, articulate, funny to listen to, kind and sympathetic and enthusiastic. She also reported that she never thought of teasing others and was not 'a point scorer' (parent interview, July 1991, Year 3).

Summary of Harriet's Year 3

Harriet experienced less autonomy with regard to curriculum content in Mr Brown's class and no distinct expression of Harriet's identity surfaced in the classroom that year. Rather, that identity was expressed and highly elaborated by Harriet in the playground within her new friendship group. Though the group was regarded as 'weird' by the other children, Harriet remained popular with others in the mainstream girls' culture.

Harriet's identity and career in the middle years at Greenside School

In the middle years of her schooling, Harriet discovered a way of incorporating an out-of-school identity into her pupil identity, giving expression to it through classroom activities, especially writing. In the following year, where classroom conditions were less propitious, she elaborated a distinctive playground identity through high-profile, imaginative play.

The theme of Harriet's emerging identity as distinct from that of the mainstream girl's and boys' culture at Greenside Primary School is now becoming evident. Her interest in all things to do with horses was strongly family-based and her lack of interest in the developing trend and style-consciousness, flirtatiousness and other 'sophisticated' concerns of many of her peers was endorsed by her mother.

After a period in Miss George's class when Harriet began to merge home and school identities and forge closer contacts with a range of friends, the pattern of separation and disengagement re-emerged in Harriet's career. The increasing distinctiveness of identity being expressed by Harriet in relation to her peers, the relative geographical isolation of the home from the school, and the increasingly

Matrix 7.2 *Harriet, Years 2 and 3, a summary matrix*

Family relationships	Peer-group relationships	Teacher relationships	Identity	Career
Year 2: Miss George				
Mrs Morley would like to see more formal structuring of tasks in school. She continues to hold off from school, feeling she has been stereotyped as an anxious parent. Is prepared to let Harriet 'jog along' as long as she is happy. Harriet is enrolled in piano lessons but rebels over practice.	Initially identified with one of the dominant girls' groups. Later, through shared interests in animals and story writing, a special friendship with Hazel develops. They read their stories to infants at playtime. Friendship with Ned, another horse-rider, also begins.	Structural position: age, 5/ 32. English, in top quarter, maths, three-quarters down the class. Seen by her teacher as self-confident and friendly. Pupils have greater autonomy in this class. Harriet talks, reads, and writes about horses. She is slow at less appealing tasks and indifferent to teacher urging. Enjoys writing and gains intrinsic satisfaction from it.	Home and school identities merge and Harriet is perceived as confident and friendly, skilful and knowledgeable about horses at home and school.	Harriet discovers a route to establishing identity and status through classroom tasks. Harriet has more control over her learning now, something she asserts at home. She is encouraged by her teacher to give expression to her identity and she incorporates it into her learning. This increases motivation and promotes the beginning of a new friendship group.
Year 3: Mr Brown				
Parents continue to feel unhappy about aspects of Harriet's education. Harriet's lack of interest in the trend and style-conscious concerns of many peers is endorsed by her mother. Harriet described as interesting, articulate, funny to listen to, kind and sympathetic, enthusiastic, not a 'point scorer' or one who teases.	A closely knit group of Harriet, Hazel, Ellen and Ned develops. The group spends playtimes in imaginative immersion in game of dragons. They are tagged 'mad', 'silly' and 'weird' by peers. Unlike most peers, Harriet's group do not concern themselves with talk of 'love', 'boyfriends' and 'girlfriends'.	Structural position: age 30/ 33, maths, three-quarters down class, English, half-way down. Harriet was slow to adapt to this class and slow to establish good relationship with teacher. Concerned for Harriet giving too much support to Hazel, Harriet's teacher encouraged her to work with others but with limited success.	Within her family, Harriet is perceived as 'interesting', 'funny to listen to', 'kind', 'sympathetic.' Her teacher describes her as 'lively and sociable'. Her friendship group is tagged 'mad', 'weird', 'odd bods'. Harriet's emerging identity as distinct from the mainstream peer culture beginning to be evident now.	No distinct expression of Harriet's identity surfaced in class. Rather, identity is highly elaborated through play. She maintains popularity with other girls' groups. A pattern of separation, disengagement, assertion of distinctive identity continues to emerge through home, school, peer-group relationships.

separate spheres of home and school, came together and combined in a coherent theme at this point in Harriet's primary school career.

As we track Harriet through the last few years of her career we will trace the development of her sense of self and phases in her engagement with the concerns of her teachers and peers. Through those years, as she struggled to leave behind the more childlike forms of expression through play, we shall see Harriet begin to confidently articulate her perspective on her peers, her teachers and on her own distinctive identity.

7.3   YEAR 4, YEAR 5 AND YEAR 6

Introduction

As we track Harriet through Years 4 and 5 we will examine two classroom contexts in which, as in Year 2, her experience was characterized by rapport with her teachers and support for her classroom identity and status. Harriet's academic and social qualities were appreciated by these two teachers. Harriet responded to them with enthusiasm, showing progression not only in her preferred writing tasks but also across areas of the curriculum where she had formerly shown reluctance. Though remaining close with Hazel, sharing and articulating distinct and separate identities from the mainstream girls' culture, Harriet also widened her relationships with other girls. In so doing she became more conscious of the opinion and the pull exerted by the dominant girls' groups. Through the stories of Harriet's Years 4 and 5, we analyse the effect upon Harriet of these contradictory claims to her developing identity and the role of her social competence in maintaining popularity and status among her peers.

The chapter continues with an examination of why Harriet's increasing clarity of identity within classroom and peer relationships should become eroded and disappear through Year 6. We examine some of the complex reasons for her drift to the margins of classroom life and the concerns of most of her peers through that final year at Greenside.

As observers following each one of Harriet's later years, we are offered insights into the ebb and flow of Harriet's commitment to the life of the classroom as she confides her perspectives on her peers, her teachers and her own distinctive identity.

Harriet, Year 4, early days in Miss King's class

In September 1991, eight-year-old Harriet entered Miss King's Year 4 class where she was, chronologically, 18th of the 30 children in the class. Her structural position with regard to academic attainment in the class was the highest it had been in her career so far. She was now in the top few for maths and science and in the top quarter for English. Like most of her teachers, Miss King was somewhat uncertain what to make of Harriet until she got to know her better, as she told Ann Filer:

> I like Harriet, actually. She's nice. At the beginning I wasn't too sure of her because
> she used to look at me like she didn't really know what was going on sometimes.
> (Miss King, teacher interview, October 1991, Year 4)

> Harriet is very bright, and in the first term I don't think I actually was aware that
> Harriet was as bright as I'm aware now.
> (Miss King, teacher interview, July 1992, Year 4)

We have seen that a pattern is beginning to emerge whereby Harriet is able to maintain a particular out-of-school identity in the classroom only within certain contexts. Thus where pupils had a greater freedom to negotiate the knowledge content of tasks, there was a greater opportunity for Harriet to give expression to her out-of-school identity and maintain a particular status within the classroom. Now, Miss King's interpretation of what aspects of the curriculum were negotiable with pupils, and at what point in the planning procedure, was different from Mr Brown's. As we saw in William's story, pupils were now allowed a greater freedom with respect to the content of their writing than in Year 3. It will be recalled that William gave Miss King much amusement as he expressed his particular sense of humour through this medium in what his father described as a 'quite obscure but very imaginative' creative tendency (parent interview, July 1992). Thus, for Harriet and Hazel, horses were back on the curriculum in Miss King's class. They found their way into stories, into their journal writing and into any 'topic' writing that could be slanted to include them (see for example Document 7.2), all accompanied by careful artwork.

In fact horses seemed to fill their classroom days, as a morning of observation of the two girls records:

> Every spare moment for social exchange between Harriet and Hazel seems to be
> filled with horses – after registration, at playtime, at tidying up time.
> (Fieldnotes, Ann Filer, February 1992, Year 4)

The revival of motivation and enthusiasm in the two girls, as well as the rapport that they were to develop with Miss King, had implications for their achievements across the curriculum. This showed itself particularly when, for the first time in her career, Harriet was in the top attainment group in maths. Hazel's classroom and academic confidence also soared.

Friendships and peer relationships in Year 4

Perhaps because Harriet was now projecting a well-defined identity and status within the classroom, the need to maintain her high-profile activities in the playground was correspondingly receding. The three girls were certainly as close as ever in their playground games and, as indicated above, the themes of horses as well as mythical creatures ran through them. One morning during February, Ann Filer joined Harriet and Hazel in the playground to discover what they were playing.

> Hazel and Harriet spend playtime discussing ponies. Hazel has to guess the breed of
> Harriet's ponies. Having gone through all the breeds she knows, which to me seems
> considerable knowledge, Hazel is reduced to making 'silly' answers based on

THE STORY OF MY LIFE
Name: Harriet Morley   Age: 8

I was born in Easthampton

Maternity Hopislal with my

friend Hazel Farthing I grew

up as a horse adict. I do

have my own pony now. My

hobbies are horse riding, ice stateing,

and galoping on my pony.

My worst accident that has

to be appendicitis My worst

food is b sprots pots

Document 7.2   *Harriet, Year 4, 'The Story of My Life' (Spring Term 1992)*

Harriet's clues – 'bouncy ride pony', 'kicking pony'. Hazel takes periodic 'gallops' around the playground in between coming up with answers. Harriet stays in one place, near me, all playtime. Harriet tells me that in the imaginative games they play she is a chestnut unicorn and Hazel is a red, green and purple dragon.
(Fieldnotes, Ann Filer, February 1992, Year 4)

Although Harriet continued to enjoy her games with Hazel and Ellen, she was also clearly becoming concerned to disengage from some of the 'weird' and 'silly' aspects of her playground identity. Though she predominantly worked and played with these girls, she was also now enjoying a wider association with many other girls in the class and also was coming under some pressure from them to conform to a more commonsense, collective playground identity. Another playground observation, a few months later, captured the following exchange, recorded in fieldnotes:

Hazel and Harriet are having an argument with Naomi in the playground as I approach them:

Naomi:	(*to AF*) Hazel says she is a dragon and that's stupid because dragons don't exist. They are mythical.
AF:	Yes, but people can imagine all sorts of things, they don't have to be real do they?
Naomi:	But Hazel does not *imagine*, she says that she *is*. (*Naomi then turns to Hazel and tells her . . .*) I managed to get it out of Harriet that she is not *really* a unicorn and you are not *really* a dragon.
Hazel:	Harriet only said that because you were being unkind to her. You *are* a unicorn, aren't you, Harriet?'

Harriet, who has not said anything since I joined them, at this point gives a non-committal shrug and walks off.
(Fieldnotes, Ann Filer, May 1992, Year 4)

So it was that Harriet was having to walk a tightrope between the preservation of a valuable friendship and the protection of an acceptable image in the eyes of the wider peer group. If Naomi was a threat to Harriet's balancing act, then other girls were more tactfully understanding of her dilemma:

AF:	What do the other groups do in the playground?
Emily:	Hazel, Harriet and Ellen. They play dragons and unicorns.
Mary:	Hazel makes believe she is a dragon and Harriet pretends to believe in it when Hazel's around so she won't break friends with Hazel.

(Friendship group interview, Mary, Emily and Naomi, May 1992, Year 4)

As well as having a wider association with other girls in the class, Harriet also very briefly became involved in a friendship with Sally. This came about as a result of the children being asked to write something about the person they were sitting next to. Miss King explained:

Sally Gordon had written 'I would really like to get to know Harriet and I'm sure a lot of people would but we always feel that Harriet doesn't want to talk to anyone else'.
(Miss King's account of Sally's writing, teacher interview, July 1992, Year 4)

By means of an end of term parents evening, Sally's statement filtered through to Harriet, the outcome being that Harriet took up the offer of friendship. Miss King picks up the story:

> Yes and today, at review time, Sally was really excited. She had this little letter and it was three pages and it was from Harriet saying would she come and stay at her house and see her ponies and things. And I think that's the new friendship because I looked round and there's Harriet sitting with Sally and I've seen Sally saying 'Come and sit next to me'.
> (Miss King, teacher interview, July 1992, Year 4)

The friendship was very brief, though. It was over by the end of term and never observed by Ann Filer. Nevertheless, the incident is worth recording here as an indication of Harriet's status with the dominant girls' groups in the class and the considerable pull they were exerting on her at this time.

Learning strategies in Year 4

Like Mr Brown, Miss King considered that working with her friendship group was holding Harriet back. Also like Mr Brown, she found it difficult to separate them as she described in a conversation noted by Ann Filer:

> Nisha [Miss King] has reorganized the groups in order to encourage the two halves of the class, those that came from last year's Class 5 and from last year's Class 6, to mix more. Nisha said she wanted to get the close-knit group of Hazel, Ellen and Harriet to separate a bit but it didn't work putting Ellen on another table. She was miserable and so the three are back together again, which defeats the object of the reorganization as far as these three are concerned.
> (Fieldnotes, Ann Filer, March 1992, Year 4)

However, the perceived problem of the girls' close classroom relationship became resolved during the latter part of the year. Not only was Harriet widening her classroom associations as well as working with Hazel, but Hazel now had a greater classroom confidence and needed the support of Harriet less:

> But I feel now that Harriet is ready to break away from it [the close association]. But in a way, I think Hazel's not so bothered any more, because when Harriet's gone off working with Sally it doesn't affect Hazel because she's so into her stories, she's just sitting there doing her own thing and Hazel's talking to a few more people now.
> (Miss King, teacher interview, July 1992, Year 4)

The relationship between Miss King and Hazel was such that for the first time in her career Hazel was gaining confidence in maths and science. She began to enjoy the subjects and be proud of her achievements in them so that she was no longer so reliant on Harriet for support in them.

Harriet certainly reflected some of these positive aspects of the year when interviewed during the spring term by Ann Filer:

> AF: Can you tell me about this year compared with last?
> Harriet: This year is better. I don't know why. It's because I've got more friends – Amanda, Hazel, Ellen, Emily, Nimra, Hannah, Naomi and Charlotte.

AF:	How do your friends think you are doing at school?
Harriet:	Well. Very well.
AF:	What about your parents?
Harriet:	Excellent. I'm working harder. I don't know why I'm working harder but my Mum says I'm working harder in Class 7.

We also picked up on Harriet's extra-curricular involvement that year:

AF:	Apart from schoolwork, have you been involved in anything special that you feel pleased about this year?
Harriet:	Well, my tie-dye turned out right [a table cloth in after-school art club run by Miss King]. Also in choir. I get on good with that 'cos the spring concert is coming up soon.
AF:	How did you come to get involved in that [art club]?
Harriet:	We had slips given out. I signed in pottery and that was all taken so I joined art club. I discussed it with Hazel and we both said we must do art and pottery so we will be together.
AF:	Do you think it's important to do things like that at school?
Harriet:	No. I just wanted to do them. If Hazel left choir I would leave.
AF:	What if you left? Would Hazel leave too?
Harriet:	Yes.

All the indications are therefore, that despite Harriet's disengagement from some of the more fantastic imagery surrounding this friendship, and despite having other sources of classroom and playground company and support, Harriet still needed this particular friendship as much as Hazel did.

Home and family relationships in Year 4

As Harriet suggested, her parents were more pleased with her progress that year and they liked better what they saw in the classroom:

Mrs Morley:	I haven't felt that [negativity] with Miss King at all. It really is the first time [that I haven't] and I think Harriet's done quite well with her. She also liked Miss George and that is the type of teacher I think she likes, young lady, soon out of college who has probably been taught the way they are supposed to teach up there.
AF:	Mmmm. You picked up on the spelling and the tables [in the diary]. Do you get a sense that there's a bit more structure with those this year?
Mrs Morley:	Yes, I really do and I think it's good. And I've been pleased to see myself, just how easily she can learn spelling, otherwise I wouldn't know, because I certainly wouldn't bother doing spellings with her in her spare time [...] I like Miss King. From what I can tell she keeps them quiet and they can concentrate and the system works with her.

(Parent interview, July 1992, Year 4)

Mrs Morley continued to be happy with Harriet's friendship choices. In many ways she found many of the other girls of Harriet's age more mature than Harriet. She thought this showed in their being 'more organized' and seeming 'quicker to put their own case forward'. On the other hand, she found Hazel and

Ellen, as well as Harriet herself, very pleasing for being 'unshow-off-y'. Sister Emma though, conscious of the ways in which Harriet differentiated herself from the majority of her peers, warned her that she will have to 'go with the trends more' if she wants to get on at Halberton Grammar School (Mrs Morley, parent interview, July 1992, Year 4). For the present though, Harriet was about to embark on a new school year, again with the sort of teacher with whom her mother thought she got on well. Miss French, like Miss King and Miss George, was another young woman teacher who had very recently left college.

Summary of Harriet's Year 4

The incorporation of Harriet's interests and identity into her life in the classroom once more coincided with an advance in her attainment across the curriculum. For the first time in Harriet's career her mother had no negative feelings about the school. Also coinciding with the advance of her identity and status in the classroom, there came a reduction of the more extreme manifestations of identity in the playground that had developed last year. Although Harriet did not at any point engage with the more traditional pursuits and culture of the mainstream girls' groups, she developed wider friendships within them in Year 4. She became rather more mindful of her image in the eyes of these girls and was careful to disengage from the more 'mad', 'weird' aspects of her group's identity.

Harriet, Year 5, early days in Miss French's class

The spread of Harriet's year-group across several classes meant that, just as William and Robert found themselves in the minority in a class of Year 6 pupils, so Harriet and the girls in the study found themselves in a class, half of which were Year 4 pupils. It was because of this year-group distinction, as well as because of age and attainment, that she enjoyed a high structural position again this year. Chronologically she was sixth in a class of 28 children, and academically she was in the top quarter for attainment in maths, science and English. Unlike any of Harriet's other teachers, Miss French did not go through an initial period of uncertainty with regard to appreciation of her qualities and abilities. Soon after the beginning of the new school year, in interview with Ann Filer she observed:

> Harriet's settled in and seems to have settled in very well. She's quite bubbly, very enthusiastic, seems to have very few problems with her work. She seems quite confident with what she's doing and seems to approach it with quite a mature attitude.
> (Miss French, teacher interview, September 1992, Year 5)

Harriet for her part was also aware from very early days in the class that her teacher liked her. In fact that was established publicly when she was chosen by Miss French for the Parade of Excellence, a regular feature of Friday morning assembly, when a child or a group was nominated from each class for special recognition. Harriet told Ann Filer about it:

AF: How does Miss French think you are getting on in this class?

WEEKLY REVIEW

My best work this week was   my book review

I need help with

I have improved at my Maths because   I like it now but i
didn't before.

How I achieved my aim   I achieved my aim by doing lots
of english

My aims for next week are topic and my handwriting

MY WRITTEN REVIEW

I have enjoyed this it has been a
happy week no one bossed me about
I am pleased with my self and my
work

Document 7.3   *Harriet, Year 5, 'Weekly Review' (November 1992)*

Harriet:	Very well. She said in the Parade of Excellence when I was picked, that I was picked for 'general kindness'. [This was because] if Miss French hadn't changed the date [on the blackboard] I would change it.
AF:	Is there anything else you do?
Harriet:	Well I tidy up other people's things. When it's tidying up time I clear up other people's things if they have left them. Sarah won't. She just leaves them.

(Pupil interview, September 1992, Year 5)

As well as being kind, Miss French told the school, Harriet was nominated because 'she always comes in smiling in the morning' (Fieldnotes, Ann Filer, September 1992). Further evidence of Harriet's satisfaction with her new class, and her work and relationships in it, could be found in many entries in her 'weekly review' during that first term (see for example Document 7.3).

As we have described in Chapter 3 and in Sarah's story, for reasons concerned with the management of the curriculum across the year 5 classes, tasks were quite highly structured by Miss French that year. With different year-groups within the class and with the Year 5 pupils answerable to Mr Brown for their 'topic' work, the consequence was that timetabling was tight, expectations for content to be covered fairly explicit, and pupils allocated to fixed groups for most tasks. This, we have seen, was something of a compromise situation for Miss French rather than a reflection of her preferences for classroom and curriculum organization. However, the expectation was that, where they wished and were able, pupils should extend their studies independently beyond the basic expectations of the teachers.

In relation to her written work this is what Harriet did do that year, so that both in interview and in her report to parents Miss French expressed the view that, in her writing 'Harriet's creativity shines through'. Given the easy relationship that Harriet had with her teacher, and given that she took the opportunity to extend her writing, we might expect that horses would find a place in the curriculum. Certainly when the opportunity arose Harriet would share her interest and achievement with her teacher and the class. For instance, on one occasion she brought in rosettes won at a gymkhana and on another told the story of her pony taking off and running away with her. Nevertheless, the high-profile classroom and playground obsession with horses and with mythical animals gradually gave way this year to a more profound conception of their identity as Harriet and Hazel began to define and assert their identities in terms of the dominant peer culture which surrounded them.

Friendships and peer relationships in Year 5

As we have indicated, dragons and horses were now dying out and Harriet and Hazel walked and talked more in the playground. They did so, however, in a desultory, bored sort of way which was reflected in their account of playground activities in interview with Ann Filer:

AF:	What's your group like? What do you like doing in the playground now?
Harriet:	Playing with Katie [Hazel's younger sister].
Hazel:	Sometimes she fusses and gets on our nerves.
Harriet:	Just stand around chatting.
Hazel:	That's all there is to do really. There are no climbing frames and no secret places to hide like in the infants. We're a rather funny group.
Harriet:	The rest of the groups are pratts. Snobs.

(Friendship group interview, January 1993, Year 5)

Despite the 'pratts' and 'snobs' labels, however, by the end of the year Harriet was to revive some of the fleeting playground associations she had had with other girls and with their games as a result of a classroom friendship with Sarah.

As the imaginative, high-profile expressions of their identity, which had become socially uncomfortable for Harriet, were dying out in the playground, the girls were beginning to articulate their identities in new ways. The interview continued:

AF:	How are some [children] snobs?

Harriet:	They say 'I'm better than you' [...] Showing off. Their hair, their body. Like this [*Harriet flicks her hair*]. Sally Gordon always tries to make her hair curly and nice for all the boys in school.
AF:	Do others show off their hair?
Hazel:	Mary and Sarah and all that group.

Harriet shows Ann Filer how Sally walks to 'show off' her body.

Hazel:	And they like to make themselves all tidy with shiny shoes and little squeaky voices.
AF:	So your group is different.
Harriet:	Yes. We're normal.
Hazel:	No, we're not normal. Some people say we're crazy. They bring in Barbie books and dolls and trolls.
Harriet:	And silly little pencils with trolls on and Barbie pencil cases.
AF:	So you don't go in for that sort of thing.
Hazel:	No. I just use any pencil that works.

(Friendship group interview, January 1993, Year 5)

The two girls were now for the first time articulating a more fundamental distinction from the mainstream girls' groups than that represented by special interests and playground games. They were now confidently distancing themselves from a gender stereotype of identification with body and style consciousness which the majority of girls were giving expression to. Harriet was, moreover, doing something similar in relation to her classroom identity and in opposition to the competitive 'goodness' that characterized the strategies of the dominant girls' group.

Learning strategies in Year 5

As we described above, the pupils in Miss French's class now, for most activities, worked within assigned groups. Only infrequently, and only when Miss French permitted it, did Harriet and Hazel work together. Harriet worked in her group quite closely with Sarah and something of their easy compatibility can be discerned from Year 5 classroom observations in Sarah's story. In interview with Ann Filer, Miss French talked about Harriet's working relationships in the classroom that year:

> Harriet mixes well with others. She can be a bit of a dreamer but she tends to work well most of the time on task. She is more competitive than Hazel though not *very* competitive. I think she takes a pride in her own work, she's not behind by any means. She's not competing to be first in the class, she just likes to keep pace and she's doing that quite easily. I wouldn't say she's a natural leader, although she makes her fair share of contributions, she doesn't try to dominate. But I wouldn't say she was easily led either.
> (Miss French, teacher interview, July 1993, Year 5)

As we have indicated, as well as expressing a gender identity that was distinct from the mainstream girls' groups, Harriet was also at this point articulating her rejection of the competitive and teacher-pleasing approach of the dominant girls' groups in the class.

AF:	Can you tell me how you think some children get to do well in school?
Harriet:	By being teacher's pet. Someone like Sally Gordon. Gets everything right.
AF:	Do the friends that children have make a difference to how well they do in school?
Harriet:	Well Mary and Sally, they are two people who really suck up to each other but if Mary gets ahead Sally will rush to finish to get with her. Sally might say 'Well it wasn't me that did that picture' if it wasn't good, 'it was Mary', because she doesn't want to get told off.

(Pupil interview, June 1993, Year 5)

Though Hazel, like Harriet, had a good rapport with Miss French and was well supported by the way classroom tasks were structured that year, she was unhappy with being separated from Harriet in class, not least because Ellen was now in another class. By the end of the year and with the further weakening of their playground association, Hazel was feeling somewhat abandoned by Harriet who was now enjoying both an academic and a social status independently of their relationship. She was asked about her Year 5 experience:

AF:	How well does your teacher think you have done this Year?
Hazel:	Miss French is one of the nicest teachers I've had. On my report she said I was good at most things and I was kind and helpful and had a wonderful sense of humour. I like that report. It was nice.
AF:	What has this year been like with friends compared with last year?
Hazel:	Well everyone likes Harriet and they seem to treat her like the best in the class because she's one of the teacher's pets, but not as posh and boasty as Sally Gordon.

(Pupil interview, July 1993, Year 5)

Harriet for her part declared that the year had been 'brilliant' and that Miss French had said that she had been 'a pleasure to teach'.

In Year 5, therefore, we can see that Harriet's classroom confidence and enthusiasm were established in the context of teacher relationship in which she felt valued and in which public recognition was given to her personal qualities as well as any academic qualities she showed. This year, Harriet did not need an identity imported from her out-of-school life with which to support her classroom status in the eyes of teachers or peers.

Home and family relationships in Year 5

Mrs Morley recognized that Harriet was happy and that she liked her teacher that year. She was not confident, however, that Harriet was doing as well in maths as teachers reported. She explained to Ann Filer:

Well, you know, they always write really nice reports but I imagine they probably do for most people and I honestly don't think Harriet's got much of a clue in her maths

and yet they all say she's got a good grasp. But delve below the surface and she knows very little.
(Mrs Morley, parent interview, July 1993, Year 5)

Moreover, her mother believed some of Harriet's maths improvement in Year 5 was due to the extra tutoring they now were paying for, but which Harriet was resisting:

AF:	. . . and presumably she has homework to do [for the tutor] does she?
Mrs Morley:	Yes. Well, she does it fairly reluctantly. Because they're not used to doing this at school she can't see why she's doing it and she's just that type of person that makes such a *fuss* about everything. It's too easy to give up on her rather than fight her all the time. She's so definite about things.
AF:	And you're holding out on this one?
Mrs Morley:	Mmmm. *I* haven't got the right temperament to help her, but Tom, my husband, can and he needs to help her out with the work this woman gives her. It seems that there's quite a lot that we've got to catch up on now. English doesn't seem too bad.

(Parent interview, July 1993, Year 5)

In general, the more positive feelings that her parents had about school in the previous year continued through Year 5. Although concerned about Harriet's maths, Mrs Morley continued also to express a somewhat philosophical perspective on the children's education. She thought that, with a busy family life which did not leave a lot of time for over-close supervision of learning, they were, as parents, probably not 'pushy' enough to see high academic success coming from their children. For the same reason she felt relatively relaxed that Ben and Emma did less homework than they should have done. She understood their perspective if they wanted a less 'chasing around' and demanding life than they saw their father lead.

Summary of Harriet's Year 5

With the move away from the more childish and pervasive expressions of her out-of-school identity and status, Harriet was now differentiating herself in more fundamental ways from the culture and interactional styles that were predominant in the wider girls' peer group. In the classroom, though highly regarded by her teacher for personal as well as academic qualities, she nevertheless distanced herself from the strategies of competitive 'goodness' adopted by the dominant girls' group. Thus in terms of classroom status, in terms of learning and in terms of her growth towards a more self-confident assertion of her identity, this was a very successful year at Greenside School for Harriet.

Harriet, Year 6, early days in Mrs Chard's class

In her final year at Greenside School Harriet once more found herself one of the youngest in the class, with just three pupils younger in a class of 28. While attainment in maths about a third the way down the class would suggest that she maintained progress in that subject, there was a distinct difference in her English position over that year. Looking back over the year, Mrs Chard was to explain:

> Her English is patchy and variable. She can give a really good performance. You can have a bad day with Harriet when she will appear to be in the bottom third, but on a good day she's much higher.
>
> (Mrs Chard, teacher interview, June 1994, Year 6)

Reflected in these evaluations was a sense of disenchantment on Harriet's part which was gradually to take root during that year. Certainly there were no surprises in Mrs Chard's description of Harriet in the early days in her class:

> Harriet I feel, has really come to the fore this year. She's a delightful, bubbling, sparkling personality and is contributing well to the class. She's a very self-sufficient person and has a very fulfilled life out of school and is a very much *loved* girl and has this lovely confidence and this lovely air and can tackle any task in any way. Not outstandingly able, I don't think, but is happy to have a go at anything. I feel that she is maybe more able than she has shown in the past and we are actually working at the moment on Harriet achieving her full potential. I think if she's allowed to she will be sloppy and slapdash and doesn't really care, and I want the *quality* that I think is in Harriet really to come to the fore.
>
> (Mrs Chard, teacher interview, December 1993, Year 6)

Some of Harriet's own reflections on her work can be found in her evaluation of her history topic work for the spring term (Document 7.4). As we have indicated though, Harriet's Year 6 experience was not to develop quite as Mrs Chard had hoped. Indeed, Harriet, over the course of the year, felt less happy with regard to her classroom relationships than these early perceptions of Mrs Chard indicated and as the year progressed she was to express dissatisfaction with her teacher and was to find difficulty maintaining satisfying relationships within the peer group.

Friendships and peer relationships in Year 6

Since Year 2, Harriet had predominantly worked with Hazel in the classroom. Encouraged by her teachers and by her peers, however, she had also had opportunities for working with a range of individuals and groups. Indeed, although Harriet and Hazel had shaped a playground and classroom identity that was distinct from the dominant girl's groups, that identity was also tempered and modified in the context of maintaining acceptability within a wider friendship group. In Year 6, however, as Sarah's and William's stories describe, working groups in the classroom increasingly centred round friendship choices. Where girls' groups were concerned especially, almost exclusive identification with a particular group became the norm. Some of the girls with whom Harriet had formerly had good working relationships were in the group of six girls, which as we have seen from William's and Sarah's stories became increasingly embroiled in its own difficulties and isolated from many of its peers. Harriet continued to be scathing about 'teacher's pets' – a term which encompassed most of the girls now that her former friend Sarah gravitated towards a less demanding set of working relationships clustered round Mrs Chard's table. This left

Thursday 17th March

<u>Victorian topic evaluation</u>

I enjoyed the topic on Victorians because I learnt alot about it. I have done this topic 3 times and I have learnt something new every time. I enjoyed going to the suspension bridge, the so great Britain and Clarks cottage in the woodspring museum. I was, most interested in the great exhibition and finding out all of those interesting facts about the rich and the poor. I also enjoyed this learning about all the acts that the Government passed. I coped with the research quite well but some of the weeks work sp I have has been to much for me so I mus concentrate. I enjoy working by myself because I can do it all my way but sometimes I chat more than I work. I don't find working this way dificult. I think I do manage my time well but some times i chat all and my timer plan goes down the plug-hole. If there is alot of work on the sheet sometimes I don't get it finished. I think that sometimes I don't use my time well if I'm researching in depth, but I can research very well if I to put my mind to it. There is one simple anser to my management of time I shouldn't chat. I can improve my presentation by keeping my handwriting neat and remembering my ruler to draw my borders with. My main aim when I get the sheet is to try and get it all finished so I don't have to take it home. I think that the great achievements were the public heath act and the mines act which forbid people to young children and women from going down to in the mines. I think that Queen Victoria was more than a great queen she was brilliant.

A very honest and fair evaluation.

Document 7.4 *Harriet, Year 6, 'Victorian Topic Evaluation' (March 1994)*

Harriet and Hazel together with Naomi, who was becoming increasingly unpopular with the two.

As we also described in William's story, as well as clustering around classroom strategies, group identification among the girls and the boys was also determined by association with the opposite sex. In William's story we described the way in which pupils employing the strategic response of *re-defining* were at the cutting edge of peer-group norms and expectations, and indulged in the most sophisticated and overtly flirtatious behaviour with regard to their peers of the opposite sex. In interview, some *re-defining* girls from the group of 'teacher's pets' illuminated some of these defining characteristics of the peer-group culture:

Hannah:	William has been out with the most people, with six girls and he's asked three out again.
Sally:	I said 'No', because I was one of them.
Hannah:	He's been out with Sarah, me, Sally, Charlotte and he's going out with Vicki now. Maurice likes Sally now.
Sally:	We've been going out for about fifteen, sixteen weeks now.
AF:	What does 'going out' with someone mean?
Hannah:	You can't exactly kiss them in school.
Sally:	In school it means . . .
Charlotte:	. . . fancy each other.
Hannah:	Sally doesn't talk to Maurice much in school.
Sally:	I have a Christmas card from Maurice saying 'To Sally Cute, love from Maurice' and he drew . . . [*Sally draws for AF the heart with 'kisses' in it and an arrow through that Maurice put on the card*]. I see Maurice at Easthampton Roller-Coaster but I skate around with Hannah or other girls.
AF:	So 'going out' is about understanding that a boy and a girl like each other rather than doing anything or even talking together much?
All:	(*this is agreed by the three girls*)
Charlotte:	Mary is depressed because she doesn't have a boyfriend.
Hannah:	Three boys have asked Mary out but she won't go out with them, then cries 'cos she doesn't have a boyfriend.
Sally:	She says 'They are not up to my standard'.
AF:	So what do you like doing in the playground?
Charlotte:	(*glancing meaningfully at Hannah*) Flirting with the boys.
Hannah:	Depends what everyone else is doing.
Sally:	Flirting. No I don't like flirting. Depends. I hang around with Hannah. She [Charlotte] likes flirting.
	(. . . . .)
AF:	What is your group like in class then?
Hannah:	(Meaningfully) I know who are teacher's pets.
Sally:	Vicki.
Charlotte:	And you.
Sally:	I'm not teacher's pet.
AF:	What about work?
Sally and Hannah:	(*in unison*) We're quite good.
Sally:	When I put my hair down Maurice says 'You look sexy like that' so I put my hairband back on.
Hannah:	We get on with most boys.
Charlotte:	You've got to be in the right crowd to get on with the boys.
Hannah:	If I went in with Vicki, Mary and Amanda it would be different, but if you went in with Hazel, Harriet and Naomi it would be

AF:	She's going to be a headteacher, isn't she.
Harriet:	Oh gawd! I'm glad I'm not going to be in her school. No one will like her except the girlie girls (. . .) She thinks I'm a pain in the neck 'cos she keeps calling me one. My chatting.

(. . . . .)

Harriet:	This is the worst year. And Mr Brown's class and Miss Scott's.
AF:	What were the best bits?
Harriet:	When I ran away from school but it wasn't good when Mrs Davison came to pick me up. I thought I was going home to lunch and Mum wasn't there so I went on my own and I thought, this is great because no-one can find me and pick me up and I hid in the garden. It's in my file. (*she laughs*) I expect it will be reported to Halberton [Grammar School] that I might run away.
AF:	Were there any good years?
Harriet:	Miss George's, Miss King's, Miss French's. I liked the teachers and they liked me.

(Pupil interview, June 1994, Year 6)

Within the context of the classroom, however, Harriet's resentment showed in a less directly challenging way than did William's and some of his group. Certainly Harriet's withdrawn indifference, though regarded by her teacher as in some respects regrettable, was not perceived as greatly problematic:

She's sort of friends with Hazel and Hazel is somewhat withdrawn from what is going on with the rest of us and I think Harriet has adopted some of that so she's not, she doesn't appear to be within the class (. . .) She can work in with a group (. . .) but she's just as happy with just the two of them. She enjoys life with Hazel.
(Mrs Chard, teacher interview, June 1994, Year 6)

It seems that in her view of Harriet as self-sufficient and leading a fulfilling life out of school, there was, in her perception of Harriet, again a sense that she was a 'loner by choice' in her withdrawal from classroom life. As we saw in Robert's story, Mrs Chard appreciated that pupils had different preferences in their working relationships which she was prepared to accommodate. However, it seems that Mrs Chard, perhaps because she had no experience of Harriet as a committed and enthusiastic participant in classroom life, did not appreciate Harriet's unhappiness that year or that her withdrawal was a symptom of it.

On the last day at Greenside School, when pupils' dresses and shirts were covered in inked messages of farewell, Harriet, Hazel and Ellen were the only Year 6 girls who asked no-one to sign their dresses. Amid the farewell celebrations, the hugs and the tears of their peers on that final afternoon, Harriet told Ann Filer 'I shan't be sorry to leave'. Despite successful and happy times in between, both Harriet and Hazel left Greenside as they began it in Reception and Year 1, with no clear point of identification with the school and with little sense of belonging to it.

Home and family relationships in Year 6

Harriet continued to enjoy a busy and active life out of school and, interviewing Mrs Morley towards the end of Harriet's Year 6 at Greenside, Ann Filer asked about her current involvement with horses:

Oh, she still very much enjoys that. We still keep a horse at Durcott and she helps up at the Riding for Disabled on Saturdays and they're all quite a lot older there. She's just eleven and most of them are at least fourteen and she gets on fine with them. They have prisoners up there as well. They go to help. She's ever so bossy with them. What else do we do? It's mostly out of doors. The flute she still enjoys, and swimming.
(Mrs Morley, parent interview, June 1994, Year 6)

In that interview, Mrs Morley also talked about Harriet's limited choice of friends at school contributing to her unhappiness that year:

From a friendship point of view which is so important, it has been absolutely hopeless. Every day she comes out of school totally black, honestly.
(Parent interview, June 1994, Year 6)

Mrs Morley was annoyed about the fact that Harriet had to cope with Naomi working with her, and as we have seen, Harriet and Hazel were not getting on well with Naomi. Mrs Morley felt that Mrs Chard should have been more pro-active in the organization of groups to remedy this:

She's had Hazel Farthing but I don't feel myself that Mrs Chard has managed to, or bothered to see any of the personality effects that kids have on one another. I've tried to say to Mrs Chard that she should not put Harriet next to this girl [Naomi].
(Parent interview, June 1994, Year 6)

Of course, during the year as we have seen from the various case stories, other friendship and inter-group rivalries were simultaneously commanding Mrs Chard's attention. Harriet, as we have seen, expressed her unhappiness through a degree of withdrawal from the life and work of the class and that simply looked like indifference and self-sufficiency to her teacher. On the other hand, as we saw in William's story, the high-profile resentment and challenge of other groups, together with the competitive rivalries within the group of six girls, did present a significant and obvious threat to classroom harmony and to the work of many pupils. If it was the case that Mrs Chard was at this time preoccupied with the necessity to resolve those issues, it would have been understandable. Nevertheless, from Mrs Morley's perspective as from Harriet's, this was one of the least happy years at Greenside:

I like to see a child coming out looking happy and ready to take on the rest of the evening in a happy way, and it hasn't been like that, not one day. I'd say that this has been by far the worst year that we've had. Over the past few years she's got on very well with the teachers. We've had a good report every year, but what does that mean? I'll bet they all get excellent reports.
(Parent interview, June 1994, Year 6)

Clearly Harriet's mother seemed as unhappy about Harriet's educational experience as she had been in some of the early years when home–school relationships had been difficult. She seemed as disenchanted with Harriet's experience at the end of her career at Greenside school as did Harriet.

Summary of Harriet's Year 6

In Year 6 the culture of the girls' peer group was one in which highly competitive, 'good' and largely stereotypically gendered behaviour overwhelmingly predominated.

Harriet's options for wider friendships and classroom contacts decreased as the girls' friendship groups became more sharply defined and inward looking. In a classroom context that for many pupils was academically stimulating, Harriet, with fewer friendship options in the classroom and feeling not liked by her teacher, adopted a position that looked like indifference and self-sufficiency but which masked some unhappiness and a fair degree of resentment. Despite her social and academic competence which, as always, meant that she was well accepted as a member of the class by her teacher and her peers, Harriet, unlike most of her classmates, was not sorry to leave Greenside School.

Harriet's identity and career in the later years at Greenside School

Through Years 4 and 5 Harriet again experienced the supportive relationships and rapport with her teachers that she had in Year 2. For Hazel as well as for Harriet these classroom contexts reduced their former close dependence on each other in the classroom. With the opportunity to incorporate her out-of-school identity into her life and work in the classroom in Year 4, Harriet experienced an increase in motivation and achievement and, mindful of the opinion of the wider peer group, began to modify some of the more extreme manifestations of her playground identity. In Year 5 Harriet was highly regarded and publicly recognized by her teacher for her personal as well as academic qualities in the classroom. She moved away from some of the pervasive and childlike expressions of identity and began to differentiate herself in more fundamental ways from the playground and classroom cultural and interaction styles of the dominant girls' groups.

Years 4 and 5 therefore were, like Year 2, happy and successful years for Harriet in which, in supportive classroom contexts she was able to grow towards a self-confident assertion of her distinct identity. In Year 6, however, Harriet reverted to a position in which she seemed to have no channel through which she felt able to give expression to her identity in the classroom and no-one replaced that channel that Hazel had formerly represented in the playground. At the end of her primary school career at Greenside, Harriet had reverted to the position she was in at the beginning, with no clear point of identification with the school and no sense of belonging.

HARRIET'S IDENTITY AND CAREER – CASE-STUDY OVERVIEW

As we have described in the introduction to the case studies, the triadic representation (Figure 7.1) depicts, in the outer triangle, the social context within which Harriet learned and developed and to which she could contribute and, in the inner star, the dynamic relationship between Harriet, her peers, her family and her teachers within which she shaped and maintained her identity. In very simple terms we can thus describe Harriet's predominant career interests of asserting and establishing an identity independent of teacher and peer norms and expectations.

Through Harriet's story we have tracked the similarities with Robert's career strategy of *non-conformity*. Hazel's story, which featured in *The Social World of Children's Learning* and was picked up again through the telling of Harriet's story,

Matrix 7.3   *Harriet, Years 4, 5 and 6, a summary matrix*

	Family relationships	Peer-group relationships	Teacher relationships	Identity	Career
Year 4: Miss King	Mrs Morley approves of the quiet classroom and attention to spelling and tables this year. Harriet's sister says she will have to 'go with the trends more' at her secondary school. Harriet continues active and busy with horses.	Miss King supportive of Harriet and Hazel and they eventually work more independently of each other. Harriet widens her friendship base and disengages from some of the more wildly imaginative aspects of her playground identity.	Structural position: age, 18/30, maths and science in top few, English in top quarter. Harriet's teacher likes her and recognizes her intelligence. Organization of learning in this class means horses are back as a source of inspiration for tasks.	Harriet sees herself as working harder and having more friends this year. 'Horse mad' identity at home, in classroom and playground.	The incorporation of Harriet's out-of-school identity into her pupil identity coincides with a reduction in extreme manifestations of it in play. Still outside mainstream culture, though careful to distance herself from the 'weird' identity of the group.
Year 5: Miss French	Mrs Morley continues to feel positive about the school this year. She believes they are not 'pushy' enough as parents for high academic success for their children. Parents concerned about Harriet's maths. Arrange private tuition.	Groups are designated. Harriet works with Sarah. Cooperates with peers, is not easily led, believes pupils get on by being 'teachers' pets'. Horses and dragons play dies out. Harriet articulates an identity distinct from peers' body and style consciousness.	Structural position: age, 6/28, English, maths and science in the top quarter. Harriet is publicly commended by her teacher for kindness and cheerfulness. Miss French says Harriet takes a pride in her work, is very creative in writing.	Seen by her teacher as 'kind', 'creative', independent. With a move away from the more child-like expressions of her identity, Harriet is now recognizing and confidently asserting her identity in terms of gendered behaviours and interests.	Harriet continues to enjoy high academic and social status this year in the classroom. This year, Year 4 and Year 2 are considered to be the best years by Harriet because 'I liked the teachers and they liked me.'
Year 6: Mrs Chard	Mrs Morley feels this to be a disastrous years for Harriet's friendships and considered Mrs Chard unresponsive to her concerns for Harriet.	Choice for working companions is limited as friendship groups become less fluid. Works with Hazel, though playground association dwindles. Competitive, 'good' and stereotypically gendered behaviour predominates among girls and is perceived by some to be disproportionately rewarded in class.	Structural position: age, 23/26, maths and science about one third of the way down, English, 'patchy and variable'. Mrs Chard sees Harriet as confident, 'bubbly' with a loving, fulfilled home life, not really part of the class, under-achieving, lacking enthusiasm. Harriet believes her teacher dislikes her.	Seen by her teacher as 'self confident', 'bubbly', 'sparky'. 'Fulfilled and loved at home', not identifying with the life of the class. As in some earlier years, no clear channel through which Harriet felt able to assert her identity in class. No one replaced the channel Hazel represented in the playground.	At the end of her primary school career Harriet has reverted to the position she was in at the beginning with no clear point of identification with the school and no sense of belonging.

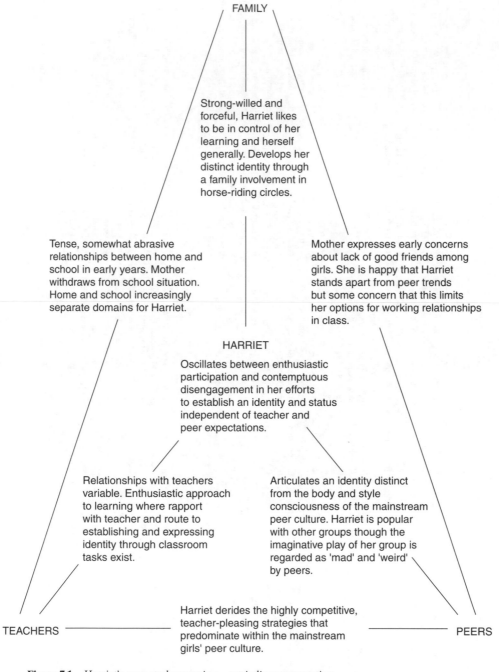

FAMILY

Strong-willed and
forceful, Harriet likes
to be in control of her
learning and herself
generally. Develops her
distinct identity through
a family involvement in
horse-riding circles.

Tense, somewhat abrasive
relationships between home and
school in early years. Mother
withdraws from school situation.
Home and school increasingly
separate domains for Harriet.

Mother expresses early concerns
about lack of good friends among
girls. She is happy that Harriet
stands apart from peer trends
but some concern that this limits
her options for working relationships
in class.

HARRIET

Oscillates between enthusiastic
participation and contemptuous
disengagement in her efforts
to establish an identity and status
independent of teacher and
peer expectations.

Relationships with teachers
variable. Enthusiastic approach
to learning where rapport
with teacher and route to
establishing and expressing
identity through classroom
tasks exist.

Articulates an identity distinct
from the body and style
consciousness of the mainstream
peer culture. Harriet is popular
with other groups though the
imaginative play of her group is
regarded as 'mad' and 'weird'
by peers.

TEACHERS

Harriet derides the highly competitive,
teacher-pleasing strategies that
predominate within the mainstream
girls' peer culture.

PEERS

Figure 7.1   *Harriet's case-study overview – a triadic representation*

gave us a further example of an independent stance of the children in relation to teacher, curricular and peer expectations.

Throughout each of these children's stories we see that they have a classroom identity associated with strong individual interests developed out of school and nurtured within their families. Their career patterns reflect fluctuations in their success as they strive to incorporate and express these interests and identities through their classroom learning and playground activities. Thus in Harriet's story we see she was capable of great enthusiasm and participation, high achievement and satisfactory relationships. She was as likely, however, to become demotivated and dispirited, privately holding a degree of mild contempt for the expectations and interests of both teachers and peers.

However, the ebb and flow of Harriet's and Hazel's engagement and disengagement with teacher expectations and the life of the classroom varied more than Robert's. For these girls, the incorporation of their out-of-school interests and identity into their learning was more difficult to achieve than it was for Robert. Although the process of pursuing his own agenda involved him in some struggle and negotiation with teachers, his interests in computers and technology were more relevant to the demands of the curriculum and also to the academic needs of his peers. Harriet's knowledge and skills related to horses were not so directly valued in classrooms and her strong positive sense of self – which continued to develop out of school – was only intermittently reflected in her identity as a pupil.

Robert's interests were also of more direct relevance to his success in establishing classroom status within the boys' peer group. Like Harriet, he had little interest in the mainstream, gender-related culture of the wider peer group. The promotion of Robert's academic identity by teachers, however, simultaneously conferred upon him an identity that was powerfully, if stereotypically, male and highly acceptable with other boys.

Enthusiasm and motivation for learning for Harriet, and indeed for Hazel, also rested more strongly than did Robert's on teacher appreciation of their identity in terms of personal qualities and on rapport established between teacher and pupil. For Harriet, happiness in class depended crucially on her awareness of being liked by her teacher and many of them viewed her with anything from mild incomprehension to antagonistic hostility. For Harriet, 'being liked' was strongly about being liked for her distinctive qualities and interactional style as opposed to the concern to be 'good' and the competitive concerns for being 'first and best' of the 'teacher's pets', which represented the more traditional route to pleasing teachers and classroom rewards. The girls within that cohort who were consistently highly regarded academically and socially across their careers had adopted that route and not diverted from it since their earliest days at Greenside School (see also *The Social World of Children's Learning*).

It was as a consequence of a range of curricular, classroom culture and gender-related issues, therefore, that Harriet found herself more often on the margins of mainstream life of the classroom through her career than did Robert. Throughout Harriet's story, we see her oscillating between motivated learning, and a fairly stubborn indifference to teacher approval or disapproval. When motivated, she benefited from a secure sense of identity, classroom status and belonging to the life of the class. On the other hand her indifference was marked by a fair degree of resentment, albeit well hidden.

Part Three

Reflecting

Chapter 8

Pupil Identity, Strategic Action and Career

8.1 INTRODUCTION

In Chapter 1 we presented a model of learning in social contexts (Figure 1.3) and our conception of pupil career as that model recursively spiralling through the years (Figure 1.4). We also described our conception of pupil career as being constituted from the *patterns* of strategic action and learning and social outcomes as pupils move through successive classroom and other school settings. As they move through these successive settings, pupils are continuously shaping and maintaining their identity and status as a pupil. They both draw on and develop their strategic biographies.

Such a model highlights the dynamic, recursive nature of pupil experience. In so doing it suggests a more holistic and less static understanding of pupils' learning and identities than is afforded by the limited range of academic and social outcomes which usually circumscribe thinking about school achievement.

If we look to the end of their final year at Greenside School, each of the four children, Sarah, William, Robert and Harriet, enjoyed a reasonably high degree of academic success, notwithstanding that each had areas of relative strength and weakness. Certainly all achieved well enough to go on to the (selective) secondary schools of their parents' choice; Sarah, William and Robert to independent schools, Harriet to a state-maintained grammar school.

As the last of the pre-national assessment cohorts, we have no way of measuring their academic successes against national outcomes. Nevertheless, in terms of both measurable achievement and access to independent schools, the pupils of Greenside School achieved highly compared with the majority of state primary schools. This was inevitably so, given the advantageous socio-economic conditions of the community served by the school.

Notwithstanding their undoubted successes, their Year 6 teacher felt that each had, to some degree, underachieved, having lacked motivation or application in some respect. Except in the case of Robert, this view was supported by the children's parents, though parents' views of to what, or whom, they attributed the cause could differ from those of their Year 6 teacher.

On the last day at primary school, Sarah, William Robert and Harriet carried away with them very different feelings about themselves as learners, about the sorts of relationships they could forge with teachers in pursuing learning goals, and the sorts of negotiations in which they could engage in defining those goals. They carried radically different experiences of the wider school beyond their classrooms as a place for learning, developing and enjoying a wide range of interests and skills, and as a place for participating, interacting and taking responsibilities within a wider social field of children and adults. They each had different perspectives on and stood in different relations to the various friendship groups within the broad peer culture of their class. They defined themselves and their place in the peer culture in terms of their particular sense of self as a girl or boy pupil, as clever or slow, as acceptable or different in some way, someone who led activities or was marginal by them; and so on. Finally, they left Greenside School with very different experiences and feelings with regard to the esteem in which they were held by the school. As individuals they felt differently valued through their place in school and classroom systems of rewards and recognition for their effort, participation, successes or simply their personality.

Thus, irrespective of *national* norms and expectations, these four children had come to define themselves as pupils within the cultural ethos of one particular school, through relations with seven or so classroom teachers, and, for the most part, against some thirty other children of both the same age and similar cultural and socio-economic backgrounds. Moreover, in following these children through their seven years at Greenside School, we perceive that there was little that was fixed about these outcomes. Although these children learnt, interacted and achieved in fairly patterned ways, those patterns were open to disruption. They moved through different teacher-created classroom contexts, were measured and measured them-selves against different groups of peers. In the process, learning and social strategies, relationships, statuses and achievements could be affected. The case-study stories document their strategic biographies. They tell us how the children saw themselves as learners and as pupils, and how others perceived them, and show that this was not a smooth, cumulative process towards the end-point of leaving the school. Rather, it was a dynamic, fluctuating process, to varying degrees appearing to be open to possibilities for change.

We set out in Chapter 2 a first level of analysis which enables us to get a handle on these many-faceted aspects of children's school experience. In Chapter 2, section 2.3, we described primary school pupils' careers as having three principal components. These are as follows:

- *patterns of outcomes*, related to the learning and social contexts of successive classrooms, together with those of the wider school and playground;
- *patterns of strategic action* developed in coping with, and acting within, these contexts;
- the *evolving sense of self* which pupils bring to, and derive from, school, playground and external contexts.

Looked at in this light, the *differences* between the four case-study children are potentially more revealing for telling us about learning and pupil careers than are their similarities at the end of the primary phase.

In this chapter therefore, we go on to make a comparison of the careers of the case-study pupils from the point of view of patterns of outcomes, patterns of strategic action and their evolving sense of self. Figures 8.1, 8.2 and 8.3 summarize the children's experience in these respects, enabling 'at a glance' access to some important similarities and differences across pupils' careers.

The tremendous influence of families, home environments and the wider community must not be forgotten in this analysis. We also include, therefore, a concise comparison of those influences (Figure 8.4) which helped shape pupils' wider sense of self and which in various ways they were able to draw on in elaborating their pupil identities.

Our analysis then moves to a further level of abstraction and we present *dimensions of strategic action* (Figure 8.5), a typology which was set out in a simplified form in Chapter 2 (Figure 2.3). In the case-study narratives we described the characteristic patterns of strategic action adopted by children in terms of *conformity, anti-conformity, non-conformity* and *redefining*. The typology in Figure 8.5 elaborates these four dimensions of conformity with respect to the characteristic orientations, adaptations and strategies which typify them. This typology enables us to see patterns in pupils' attitudes and responses to school as they shaped and maintained their pupil identities year on year across classroom, wider school and peer-group settings. Bearing in mind that these dimensions do not describe *pupils* but characteristic patterns of behaviour which they adopt, we illustrate the typology with respect to typical orientation, adaptation and strategic actions of Sarah, William, Robert and Harriet as they negotiated their careers.

Our emphasis throughout on the dynamics of perspectives, relationships and responses for shaping outcomes is explicated in the model and description of *the dynamics of strategic orientation and adaptation* (Figure 8.6). Children's dominant or preferred responses were liable to disruption or change as they became no longer viable or appropriate in particular teaching and classroom contexts. Year-on-year dynamic changes for each child are plotted on the model (Figure 8.7), together with representations of some of the ebb and flow of tensions within their classroom relations.

8.2   PATTERNS OF ACADEMIC AND SOCIAL CAREER OUTCOMES

First, let us briefly consider the outcomes which one would normally expect to see commented upon at the end of children's primary school careers. In the introduction to this chapter we have already established that, viewed in the context of national outcomes, there were broad similarities across the comparatively advantaged outcomes for these four children. Here we begin with those end-of-phase comparisons as a point from which to explore some of the more wide-ranging and significant differences. As we described in the introduction to this section, we then go on to show that these outcomes were not simply the end-points of cumulative processes of the children's primary education. Rather we see them as simply one point in a dynamic, constantly fluctuating process, to varying degrees constantly open to possibilities for different outcomes. To assist readers, the comparisons of children made in this section are summarized in the table in Figure 8.1 which relates to the children's longitudinal patterns of academic, social and status outcomes across school settings.

	Outcomes from learning and social contexts of classrooms	Outcomes from wider school learning and social contexts	Outcomes from learning and social contexts of peer culture
Sarah	Sarah maintained good attainment across the curriculum relative to her age and was regarded as quick-minded, articulate and well coordinated. Perceived failure to achieve her full potential was often seen by teachers in terms of an unwillingness to take some responsibility for her own learning. She was variously regarded as strong-willed or stubborn by some teachers.	Sarah was seen as a good and reliable pupil through helpfulness and taking on responsibilities. She participated enthusiastically in many sporting, musical and drama clubs and in school events generally. She did not achieve some of the outcomes she aspired to in terms of being chosen for teams, leading roles etc.	Sarah competently operated within the mainstream peer group and gender norms and expectations. She was well liked among her peers. She had friendly associations across all friendship groups except those of 'naughty boys', though she chose to associate strongly with groups of girls in classrooms and playground. Most peers saw her as one of the 'good' children.
William	William's attainment initially was well below chronological age, but quickly improved to attaining at, or well above it. His autonomous, fun-loving, communicative identity was experienced and interpreted differently by different teachers. For some it was a threat to teacher–pupil relationships, discipline and a hindrance to learning. With others it promoted rapport and was seen as integral to the learning process.	In the wider school context and from an early age William had friendly associations with other teachers and identified with older pupils. He outstripped the other pupils in the violin group, leaving it for private lessons and was allowed to join the school orchestra a year early. Failure to achieve sports teams (Year 5) was felt as placing him in a more marginal position to friends' and teacher's interests.	William was a leader of the mainstream peer cultures of classroom and playground and at the cutting edge of those children. There was some conflict and challenge to the validity of peers', usually girls', successes when his own was felt to be under threat. Belonging to high-status friendship groups, he was sometimes criticized by peers for exclusiveness in his associations.
Robert	Robert attained well above his chronological age. In early years his creativity was valued as inspirational; his self-direction, absorption in his own interests and volatility were indulged in terms of an 'oddball', 'odd professor' identity. In later years his independent slant on curriculum tasks was viewed more problematically, with increasing pressure to direct his time and energies towards teacher-specified outcomes.	While Robert made happy and confident contributions to class productions and school events as they were presented to him, he was not interested in taking on the usual roles and responsibilities of older pupils around the school. In later years he spasmodically attended chess club and in his final year he negotiated a role taking responsibility for school-wide computer support for teachers.	Most boys saw Robert as 'not like us' though where he gained some autonomy to develop a helping, explaining role in classrooms he won respect and status among his peers. Then, he was 'Einstein', and 'a genius'; 'too much in his own head' but accepted as 'OK'. Where teacher expectations did not support that role he could be ignored or rejected by many peers, and felt miserable.
Harriet	Harriet attained at or above her chronological age for English but less strongly in maths. In classrooms where she could incorporate her interests into tasks she was 'intelligent', 'creative' and 'cooperative'. Where not she was 'underachieving', 'stubborn', 'lacking enthusiasm' and viewed with incomprehension, even hostility.	Harriet was happy to attend choir practice and some occasional extra-curricular activities along with her friend Hazel. Harriet and her friends were not interested in roles and responsibilities around the school such as monitoring the younger children or visiting an elderly neighbour, which most of her peers enjoyed	In her early years, Harriet was on the margins of girls' groups, enjoying activities more traditionally associated with boys. Shared interests in writing stories, especially about horses and exotic creatures, brought her together with Hazel, the two later becoming a group of four. Tagged 'weird' and 'mad' by peers for the highly imaginative play developed out of those shared interests.

Figure 8.1 *Longitudinal patterns of academic, social and status outcomes across school settings*

Readers may recall that during her final year at Greenside School, Sarah achieved a fair degree of academic and extra-curricular success. Though her Year 6 teacher and her parents felt that she had not achieved all that she was capable of, she had fulfilled her parents' hopes for her, and gained confidence in her abilities, through passing the entrance exam for the independent school which her brother attended. During Year 6 Sarah had established working and playground relationships within a group against which she 'looked good' academically and which offered little challenge to her ideas in the classroom. She maintained good relationships with her teacher and peers generally, though she did not achieve the public rewards and recognition for achievements to which she aspired.

At that same point in his career William was enthusiastically looking forward to taking his place at an independent grammar school, though Mrs Chard and his parents felt he could have achieved more that year. From Mrs Chard's perspective, he had been something of a noisy nuisance in the classroom; William's response to the curbs on his exuberance was often expressed through withdrawal of cooperation and resentful opposition. Nevertheless, he achieved a satisfying end to the year. He communicated to Mrs Chard his goal of achieving a place in the weekly 'Parade of Excellence', which she ultimately felt able to grant him and he enthusiastically participated in a range of events that marked Year 6 leaving the school. After a year marked by inter-group rivalries and resentments among the high-status boys' and girls' groups, their departure from Greenside School was marked with celebrations and affirmations of mutual affection and friendship.

Robert had also secured a place at Easthampton Grammar School, though Mrs Chard felt she had failed to draw out the best from him that year. Mrs Chard was ambivalent regarding Robert's autonomous approach to learning, the way in which she felt he 'worked the system' for his own ends and interests and related to her on his own terms. She supported plentiful access to the computer for him, not least on account of the role he assumed in manoeuvring to secure it; that of a kind of tutor and facilitator to his classmates, offering tangible benefit in the structuring and production of computer-assisted work. This, together with the deployment of other computer-related knowledge and skills, was also supportive of the work of his teacher, as well as of his relationship with her. Robert achieved a lot of satisfaction from his classroom relationships that year, despite the lack of any special friends.

Harriet's academic achievements had secured for her a place at a local education authority grammar school. Mrs Chard's hopes for greater excellence in Harriet's academic performance that she showed early in the year had not materialized and, as the year progressed, Harriet was perceived to lapse increasingly into withdrawal and indifference. Harriet's social and academic competence meant that she was well accepted as a member of the class by her teacher and peers. However, her friendships and classroom contacts became fewer during the year as the girls' friendship groups became more sharply defined and inward looking. Apart from a trip to school camp for a week which she greatly enjoyed, the summer term activities for 'the leavers' left her unmoved. Unlike most of her classmates, Harriet was not sorry to leave Greenside School.

As described in the children's case studies, and set out in the matrices in those chapters, on any objective measure, these four children did not achieve academic outcomes that were so very different from each other. Though they achieved variably against their relative age in the class, all attained within the upper half of what we have suggested was a fairly highly attaining cohort of 26 children. Even on the basis of these 'snapshots' of outcomes, however, there are clearly differences between their learning, experience and perceptions of school that would appear to have considerable implications for their future careers as pupils, for their learning dispositions, for their school relationships, happiness and success in their different secondary schools. However significant these outcomes look, though, as the case studies tell us and as we have suggested above, it is important to consider career outcomes longitudinally in order to consider the possibility of other outcomes for these children.

Reviewing Sarah's case longitudinally, however, other possibilities seem few. Her end of Year 6 outcomes do indeed appear to represent resolutions of patterns of achievement and social relations which began to be generated quite early in her career. Apart from some upsets with a relatively inexperienced teacher, she fulfilled the academic and social *expectation* of teachers. In tension with this success, however, was a failure to achieve her academic *potential* as perceived by teachers and parents. She also began to experience over time a growing sense of disappointment on her own behalf that some of her extra-curricular aspirations and expectations had not been realized in school. At Greenside School, and in the context of highly competitive and able peers, Sarah's enthusiastic participation and competence were not, in themselves, sufficient qualities for achieving the sort of recognition and rewards that Sarah saw some of her high-profile 'into everything' friends achieving.

Across school and peer-group contexts William's patterns of success and relationships were much more varied than Sarah's. Some of his teachers viewed his communicative, interactive identity as a hindrance to classroom learning, other teachers viewed it as integral to the learning process. In some years, teacher organization and expectations led to his social skills being harnessed for the benefit of learning and his teachers found him lively, enthusiastic and full of ideas. He enjoyed an easy rapport with teachers, an image of himself as clever and successful with high playground as well as classroom status. In other years, failure to attract teacher esteem and rewards and recognition for his classroom efforts saw his relationships with them and with his peers flounder with a retreat into minimalism, conformity or withdrawal of effort in his approach to tasks.

As was the case for William, different teachers viewed Robert's approach to learning with different degrees of approval. Some were hugely impressed by his creative, autonomous approach. However, in later years especially, teachers expected more formal expressions of knowledge. In those years there were fewer opportunities for Robert to autonomously follow his own interests and his achievements were often something of a disappointment to his teachers. The extent to which Robert was able to develop satisfactory classroom relationships and status was variable across classroom contexts. He experienced some less happy and successful years in maintaining a satisfactory identity and good relationships with his peers as well as with his teachers.

Among the four children, perhaps Harriet was viewed most variably and had the most varied relationships with her teachers. Some developed a rapport with Harriet and structured tasks in ways that allowed her to incorporate her interests into her writing, her classroom talk and artwork and so on. Harriet felt liked and appreciated by those teachers and they perceived her as 'intelligent', 'creative' and 'cooperative'.

Others viewed her with incomprehension, even hostility, as 'stubborn', 'lacking enthusiasm' and 'underachieving'. Though always maintaining an identity on the margins of the mainstream interests of peers, Harriet was nevertheless well accepted as a classroom and playground companion, when she wished it.

Viewing the children's careers longitudinally, therefore, we see considerable variability in the ways in which they were viewed, and viewed themselves, as learners. Different teacher expectations, perceptions and different structural contexts brought about more, or less, positive academic learning outcomes. In parallel, and not surprisingly, they also brought about more, or less positive outcomes with regard to pupil relationships with teachers. What is also clear is that, along with those parallel outcomes were others: most distinctly, integration, cooperation and improved status with peers went hand in hand with being held in higher regard by a teacher. They also went hand in hand with opportunities for children to realize their personal learning goals and incorporate their individual identities in the learning process.

It is also clear from the children's case studies and matrices, that their experiences and responses to each teacher and classroom context were particular and variable. For instance, Year 4 was 'a good year' for Harriet and for William. They were viewed very positively by Miss King, their learning was supported by her expectations and peer relations and status were enhanced. However, for Sarah that year was less good in these respects, while for Robert it was probably the least happy and successful with regard to academic learning as well as social outcomes. The previous year, Year 3 with Mr Brown, had, conversely, been a very 'good' one for Robert's learning and relationships, as it was for William. It was rather less successful for Sarah and experienced fairly negatively all round by Harriet. What we also see, of course, is that what is good for the learning and relationships of individual children is clearly beneficial to their overall identity as a pupil. This is so with respect, not only to how they are perceived by others, but also to their own self-esteem.

8.3   PATTERNS OF STRATEGIC ACTION

Of course, outcomes for pupils and their evolving pupil identities did not come about simply as a result of different classroom structures, teacher expectations and perceptions. As we discussed in Chapter 2 and described above, pupils develop patterns of strategic actions in coping with these changing contexts. It is this second aspect of pupil careers, concerned with the patterning of their strategies, that we now explore in relation to each of the four children's cases. As with comparisons of longitudinal outcomes, comparisons of the children's patterns of strategic action across school settings are available in tabular form, in Figure 8.2.

Sarah's career was characteristic for the predominance of low-risk strategies, avoidance of challenge, conflict or 'going out on a limb' academically or socially. Across the social settings of classrooms, the wider school and the playground, she developed and maintained her identity as a pupil within given structures for success laid down by others. Her approach was one of competent adaptation to norms and expectations of teachers and the mainstream peer culture and a high awareness of social rules and regulations for behaviour, for play, and for general acceptability within the peer culture.

	Strategic action in classroom settings	Strategic action in wider school settings	Strategic action in relation to peers
Sarah	Adapted to academic, rules and relationship expectations. Through low-risk strategies and classroom peer alliances, evaded challenges to her ideas and exploration beyond teacher-given areas of curriculum and frameworks for success. She usually maintained good relationships with teachers while being quietly stubborn in maintaining her own interests which she felt were not recognized by some teachers.	Participated fully within the opportunities provided by the school. High-profile rewards of selections for teams and leading roles that Sarah aspired to required the highly competitive initiative-taking strategies displayed by some of her friends and which Sarah was not comfortable with.	Sarah used her physical and verbal skills to effect in playground games and interaction. Her friendship career was characterized by realignments as Sarah progressively disengaged from rivalrous, competitive friends, increasingly characterized by 'sophisticated', flirtatious behaviour and 'into everything' profiles. Sarah maintained a less challenging position within mainstream girls' groups.
William	William aspired to teacher esteem and academic status. Individuality and flair in academic tasks could switch to low-risk, minimalist conformity according to pedagogic expectations and his classroom academic status. Failure to attract high teacher esteem meant that his usual easy, negotiative relations with them could flounder or degenerate into critical opposition or withdrawal of effort.	The use of high-risk strategies and a highly interactive, competitive bid for status meant that William often operated on a knife edge of social approval. Thus, from time to time, he stepped over expected bounds of familiar exchange with teachers, was prepared to challenge the school reward systems to which he looked for prestige, and take a critical stance towards the management of school systems.	William was astute in maintaining popularity, making peers laugh and generally having fun in class while endeavouring to stay out of trouble with teachers. Scathing about girls and their achievements, he nevertheless was highly interactive, first in 'kiss chase' then later in the highly interactive, 'sophisticated' social and sexual behaviour associated with the higher status boys' and girls' groups.
Robert	Robert's strategies for learning involved the maintenance of a measure of autonomous self-direction, developing his own interests through classroom tasks. He adapted to increasing pressure to conform to teacher expectations by developing a supporting role towards peers and teachers, actively promoting his ideas and negotiating to create space for his own interests and slant on the curriculum.	School clubs and teams offered Robert little in the way of enhancing his interests or status. His scientific, technical and computer interests found expression in the home and classroom and, apart from negotiating a role supporting computer work, he had little strategic interest in voluntary involvement in school-wide activities.	While he possessed a good physique, Robert was not a physically active boy. He did not run well and was not interested in outdoor play. He thus stood outside the mainstream boys' peer culture.
Harriet	Harriet oscillated between enthusiastic participation and contemptuous disengagement in her efforts to establish a classroom identity and status independent of teacher and peer expectations. She liked to be appreciated by teachers, though maintaining her own distinctive qualities rather than adapting and pleasing through being 'good' 'first' or 'best'. She was scornful of teachers and pupils in 'teacher's pets' relationships.	Harriet's prime interest in animals and horses was developed at home and neither did she have interest in the rewards or recognition that some pupils sought in their wider school activities. As such, she had minimal points of contact and little strategic interest in them.	Despite her marginality to other girls' groups, her easygoing nature and competence as a classroom companion mean that she was popular and her friendship sought. She often walked a tightrope of loyalty, friendship and classroom support for Hazel while maintaining companionship and support within the mainstream girls' groups.

Figure 8.2 *Patterns of strategic action adopted across school settings*

If Sarah's strategies could be characterized in terms of adaptation, William's could be described in terms of negotiation and challenge. His main strategic approach was characterized by a socially astute and highly interactive bid for status. As we have seen though, this strategic approach was only manageable in some years. Where the rewards and status he sought were not forthcoming, positive challenge could degenerate into opposition, withdrawal of cooperation and conflictual relations with teachers or peers.

The dominant strategic approaches adopted by Harriet and Robert were rather more independent of changing classroom contexts than were those of Sarah or William. They were certainly far less dependent upon school systems of rewards and recognition for their self-esteem, success and enjoyment of school than were most others in the class cohort. Both were happiest where their particular interests and identities were accommodated and valued by teachers and peers. However, Robert's personal skills and knowledge with respect to computers were of greater potential value to teachers and peers than those of Harriet. Perhaps for this reason he was able to develop adaptive strategies in less accommodating classroom contexts. Over time he developed negotiative strategies which allowed him to pursue his own interests at the same time as maintaining a satisfactory identity and classroom status in the eyes of teachers and peers. Harriet was less adaptive, rather, she maintained and asserted her distinct identity and separateness more assertively where she did not feel valued by teachers.

In the above we have compared the pupils' strategies as they developed and changed in response to changing classroom contexts. As with a comparison of outcomes, different contexts brought forth different sorts of changes. In Year 6, for instance, the usually highly negotiative William developed *less* negotiative, *less* cooperative strategies in response to Mrs Chard's expectations. Within those same organizational structures and teacher expectations, Robert, usually less adaptive to changing contexts, developed a *more* strategic and negotiative stance. He manoeuvred satisfactory outcomes for himself in a way that he had not done, or perhaps had not been able to do, in any previous context.

As with our discussion of 'outcomes' above, it is also important to note the *coherence* of children's strategies. For example, if Sarah was adaptive to teacher expectations, though not overtly into teacher pleasing, so she was with peers. In that context she maintained acceptability within the mainstream culture but also maintained an independence with respect to those aspects of the culture she found distasteful. William pursued status in the eyes of teachers, at the same time as pushing at the boundaries of what was socially acceptable, and we see the same patterns in his peer relations; similarly with Harriet and Robert, both of whom maintained an independent stance with respect to teacher rewards and expectations and also with respect to peer culture and expectations. These children drew on resources beyond the school context – on their broader experiences, biographies and sense of self.

8.4   THE EVOLVING SENSE OF SELF

This section brings us on to considerations of the aspects of home experience and wider identity that pupils were able to draw on in school settings in elaborating their pupil identity. A summary of the comparisons can be found in Figure 8.3.

	Sense of self, brought to and derived from classroom learning and social contexts	Sense of self, brought to and derived from wider school learning and social contexts	Sense of self, brought to and derived from learning and social contexts of peer culture
Sarah	Sarah seemed satisfied with her pupil identity and status with regard to her not inconsiderable academic achievements. How she perceived herself as a learner was more doubtful. Relatively low confidence in her own ideas remained unchanged throughout her career and classroom learning for Sarah continued to be about other people's expectations and given structures.	Sarah gained much satisfaction through extra-curricular activities and elaborated her sense of her own artistic, dramatic and musical identity. However, her enthusiasm and self-esteem as a *pupil* diminished as she increasingly felt overlooked and undervalued by teachers, as rewards and recognition seemed consistently to go to a few, high-profile girls.	Sarah's early friendship group confirmed and elaborated her sense of herself as a pupil with traditional girls' interests in classroom and playground and as being 'good'. Progressively, Sarah sought less challenging classroom and playground alliances, maintaining these highly gendered peer norms, also giving her a more authoritative and leading role in relation to her immediate friends.
William	William strove to shape, and articulated, a positive self-image as a pupil. His drive for status and teacher esteem meant that he was strongly reliant on extrinsic rewards, recognition and grades. When they were not available to him, though disaffection followed, his close identification with the academic and social aims of schooling meant that adult pressure brought him back on track.	William's musical or sporting talents were not, in the long term, extensively developed during his primary school career. Certainly, an aspect of such interests was that they offered him an opportunity for transient identification with a variety of images which reflected the stylishly avant garde among popular young sporting or musical heroes.	William's closest friends shared and elaborated his clever, funny and entertaining image as self proclaimed 'Jesters', later as challenging 'Rebels'. The mainstream peer culture supported their status at the cutting edge of action and style, some with the begrudging 'Smart Guys' tag. His self-image as a pupil was most consistently threatened by high-achieving girls who were popular with teachers.
Robert	Measuring his achievements against peers, to please parents or teachers had never been a source of motivation for Robert. Classrooms satisfying to Robert's sense of self were those in which his helping, troubleshooter identity enabled him to shape positive relationships with peers and simultaneously develop his own learning. Without that, he failed to establish good classroom relationships or self-esteem.	Though Robert lacked interest in sporting achievement he could not be indifferent to it. The high status accorded to sporting prowess in the boys' peer group and in the school generally was a source of vulnerability. While involvement in physically tough activities could be avoided in the playground, sports days were often distressing events, Robert tearful and upset at home, fearful of coming last in races.	For Robert 'computer expert' was a powerful 'male' identity, crucial to his acceptance and status within the boys' culture. In the playground he was socially marginalized by his dislike of boys' games. There his identity was elaborated, and he developed close relationships only when he was able to find special friends with whom to play imaginative games and converse around shared interests.
Harriet	Harriet was relatively indifferent to teacher urging, and extrinsic rewards or measurements of achievement against peers did little to motivate her. She grew towards a self-confident assertion of her distinct identity in those years in which she was able to give expression to it and incorporate it into her learning. In other years she seemed to have no sense of identification or belonging in classrooms.	Harriet's self-esteem and identity as a pupil were neither enhanced nor threatened by schoolwide activities and she had minimal interest in them. A strong and energetic girl, happy at home with a hockey stick or kicking a ball, as well as on a horse, she did not relate to school activities as many in the girls' culture did, in terms of a bodily projection of self through dance, gymnastics, drama etc.	With Hazel and their group of friends she elaborated a high-profile playground identity through wildly imaginative 'horses' and 'dragons' play. As she got older this began to be replaced by less childlike expressions of self as she began with Hazel to articulate an identity distinct from the stereotypically gendered behaviour which predominated in the girls' peer groups.

Figure 8.3 *Evolving sense of self which children bring to and derive from school settings*

In Chapter 2 we identified as the third aspect of pupil careers *the evolving sense of self* which pupils bring to and derive from the learning and social contexts of school. We also discussed in that chapter the concept of 'pupil identity' shaped in relation to aspects of school experience that are evaluated and assessed by teachers, peers and parents. It is through these aspects of school therefore that pupils shape, maintain and *experience* their status and sense of self as a pupil. Pupil identity therefore is forged through those aspects of school through which pupils interact, work and compete (or not as the case may be) for what is valued by their significant others; their peers, parents and teachers, as well as by pupils themselves. This bears a very important relationship to the symbolic interactionist position as discussed in Chapter 1. It emphasizes the development of self-awareness and the construction of meaning through interpersonal relationships. As we have seen in the children's case studies, teachers, parents, peers and children themselves draw on any number of academic, social, physical, cultural or gender characteristics in construing a child as a pupil. Through the pupils' case studies, and summarized in the 'identity' columns in their matrices in their chapters, we have tracked the diverse and evolving perception of all these significant others, as well as children's perceptions of themselves.

As Figure 8.3 summarizes, children brought to and derived from classroom and playground experiences a sense of themselves as individuals, with distinctly personal expectations and purposes. That sense of themselves, though, reflected their strategic biography as a whole, and was about more than the construction and elaboration of a 'pupil identity'. We can also see (summarized in Figure 8.4) how much of that which the children brought to school learning and social contexts in terms of expectations, interests, talents and personal and social resources was derived from and shaped within a wider field of family, home and community relationships, activities and cultural expectations.

As described in the *The Social World of Children's Learning* and in Chapter 1 of this book, the wider sense of self which a pupil brings to school learning contexts is shaped within a particular political and cultural context and through the inter-relation of a range of biological, socio-cultural and relationship influences. As children experience and develop this sense of self, they are deeply influenced by their gender, social class and ethnicity, by their material, cultural and linguistic resources and by their physical and intellectual capability and potential. Through the case studies presented in this book, we have been able to track something of these experiences and strategic biographies, and to explore the relationship between the wider sense of self and more specific pupil identities. Indeed, we have highlighted how particular children draw on their wider experiences in quite different ways in school settings. Additionally, we have been able to identify where school contexts affirmed, celebrated, challenged or marginalized those children and the experiences they brought. Of course, the messages from school were of considerable significance for the sense of self of each child because, beyond the influence of home and community, primary school is the first major organization to be experienced in a sustained way.

In considering specific cases, we can begin by considering the sense of self which Sarah brought to the learning contexts of classrooms. First, in school, as in the home and community, she shaped her identity in relation to structures and patterns of success laid down and clearly available to her. Similarly both contexts reflected a dislike of conflict and unwillingness to put herself in a situation in which she would

	Learning in family and community relationships and setting	Learning in sibling relationships	Family perspectives on school learning and relationships
Sarah	Competence and independence were encouraged within traditionally structured family, church and community expectations. Sarah thus participated in many out-of-school activities and lessons; in most, patterns of success were already laid down by her brother. She was slow to develop a willingness to express opinions, be wrong or challenge her parents.	Sarah competed vigorously and conflicted with older, high-achieving brother. She was prepared to vociferously defend her opinions and status in the context of sibling rivalry in a way she was not prepared to in relation to school peers. Competition and assertive 'standing up' to her brother were encouraged by her mother.	There was a mismatch between parents' traditional leanings and the ethos of Greenside School. Sarah's parents felt that she did not achieve her potential at school due to lack of encouragement and recognition on the part of her teachers and pupils' lack of access to them in the classroom. They also believed that Sarah felt safer with a low pupil profile and average attainment.
William	William's parents wished him to develop in his own way, but with Christian principles. He pushed at parental boundaries; discipline requiring constant negotiation. He entertained his parents with verbal accounts and mimicry – a 'showman'. With high aspirations generally, he showed talent in music and sporting lessons, liked to win though was not highly competitive.	William's sister was three years younger. He enjoyed creative, imaginative play with his sister, got on well with her generally despite occasional 'flare ups' between them. He took an interest in her learning, sometimes belitting her where he felt threatened by her achievements. There was a tendency for the children to identify with their same-sex parent.	William's parents had no strong views about the methods used in school but were supportive of it generally, trying not to put pressure on him to succeed, his father finding this more difficult. They were ready to investigate concerns related to school, explaining teachers' perspectives and moods to William; working with teachers to influence his behaviour.
Robert	Robert was strong-willed in pursuing his interests in his own time. His parents were prepared to negotiate a compromise between his needs for autonomy and those of other family members with which they often conflicted. He liked to take on a 'showing', 'explaining' role at home and with strangers, though talk of 'cleverness' was discouraged.	Robert's structural position as oldest of three brothers meant he was in a powerful position to push through his own agenda, in imaginative play, in disputes and in the use of the computer and other resources. As in school, he took on an explaining and showing role in relation to his younger brothers.	There was a match between the childrearing cultures and learning in Robert's home and the predominant ethos at Greenside School. His parents had no strong views about teaching methods, but were pleased that his enthusiasm for learning was maintained. They were relaxed about his early difficulty learning tables and indifferent spelling. Robert told his parents little about his school experiences.
Harriet	Harriet came from a busy and active family with close associations with horse-riding communities. Her parents accepted, and to some extent encouraged Harriet's autonomy and strong-willed self-direction in her learning at home, though her mother's expectations for learning in school were different. Within her family, Harriet is perceived as 'interesting', 'funny to listen to', 'kind', 'sympathetic'.	Harriet had a brother five years older and a sister four years older. As with other family members, Harriet was powerful and quite stubborn in asserting her own interests with her older siblings. She was regarded as the noisiest and the bossiest of the three.	Harriet's mother regretted what she saw as a lack of emphasis upon formal learning and basic skills in primary schools generally. Her progressive withdrawal from the school situation followed some mutually antagonistic relations with teachers. This and her distance from school meant that they became increasingly separate domains for Harriet.

Figure 8.4 *Patterns of family and wider community influences on learning and mediation of school experience*

be challenged, either intellectually or socially. She elaborated her identity of 'goodness' and of competence in meeting the expectations of others across these settings. We see that this strategic identity was not inevitable, given the contentious relationship with her brother which was already part of her biography. However, it was rewarded in school, given the tendencies of many teachers there to support and reward 'good' and conforming strategies, especially among girls. It was also rewarded in terms of wide-ranging, supportive classroom and playground relationships.

At this point it is useful to draw comparisons with the sense of self which Harriet brought to those same classroom contexts. For Harriet, an early disposition towards autonomy and self-direction was powerful in asserting her will and gaining support for her learning in relation to parents and family. In some years she was able to draw on this identity in school. She was able to achieve a rapport with her teachers while asserting some autonomy over her learning, together with a self-confident assertion of her own distinct identity which supported her learning. In other years she was unable to draw in that same identity and seemed to have no sense of identification or belonging in classrooms. The culture of Greenside School more obviously and readily reflected and supported the expression of the more dominant culture among girls from Greenside families. Harriet's physical and cultural sense of self was at odds with the kinds of highly gendered style and body consciousness, as well as the competitive 'goodness', that were characteristic of that culture.

At home Robert, like Harriet, was a strongly autonomous learner. There he was in a powerful position to push forward his agenda and secure resources and support for learning and play. He drew on his computer knowledge and skills in shaping his pupil identity. Without that identity, his marginal position in relation to the dominant boys' culture of physical skills and toughness, meant that he failed to establish satisfying classroom relationships and self-esteem as a pupil and as a boy. Because of their marginality to the dominant socio-cultural concerns of Greenside children and the social and academic curriculum of their school, both Robert and Harriet were dependent on individual teachers for a measure of space and autonomy in learning. Given this, both were able to give expression to interests, forge successful pupil identities and, at the same time, achieve social integration with peers. Without them, their sense of self as different and marginal to the life and learning of the rest of the class was reinforced.

William's learning and social development in the home, as in school, were supported by an exuberant, communicative and negotiative identity, though in both contexts he was capable of offering a more forceful and contentious challenge where his sense of self and status became threatened. William held in tension his teacher, peer and his own strong autonomous expectations more easily in some years than others. In his more successful years, William displayed the level of competitive challenge which put him at the cutting edge of socio-cultural expectations for Greenside pupils. Where structural constraints or teacher perceptions denied him that status he from time to time stepped over the line of the social or principled expectations of teachers, parents and peers. However, at a deeper level his identification with those expectations, and his need for social approval, compelled astute retreat.

Thus we see that children were constantly active in shaping and maintaining their sense of self and their identities as pupils throughout their careers at Greenside

School. The case studies and summaries present some of the complexity of the origins of some of these wider outcomes for the children. We see through the biographical narratives how their sense of themselves as pupils is continuously being shaped at the dynamic intersection of important relationships, of socio-cultural expectations of their homes, of other Greenside families and children and of Greenside School. Certainly, successive and changing classroom contexts were crucial for influencing the range of children's social and academic outcomes. However, it is also clearly the case that these children themselves were constantly active in that process, in shaping and maintaining their identities as pupils, developing and adapting their strategic responses across the social and cultural contexts of school.

Our goal in this chapter has been to make sense of the complexity of influences from the perspectives of each child, to track patterns and coherence across social settings of home, playground and classroom for each, as well as across time. We have aimed to highlight pupil careers and their relationship to the strategic biographies within which they are nested. At the same time we aim to make comparisons and to analyse and explore what seemed to be important differences between those stories. In so doing, we have considered the concept of pupil career across a range of social as well as academic outcomes, regarding patterns of strategic action, and in terms of the evolving sense of self which pupils bring to and derive from their school experience.

We can now progress to a further level of analysis, focused on the dimensions and dynamics of strategic action.

8.5   DIMENSIONS OF STRATEGIC ACTION

In the process of tracking the careers of all nine Greenside children, as well as those in the parallel study (Filer and Pollard, forthcoming) we have further developed our analysis in terms of the dimensions of pupils' strategic action. In Chapter 2 we summarized some of the characteristics of the 'dimensions of strategic action', of *conformity*, *anti-conformity*, *non-conformity* and *redefining* (Figure 2.2). At this point we can use the case-study data of the four children in this book to illustrate those characteristic orientations, strategic and adaptive responses towards the career structures and expectations of school. A review of the case-study narratives in this book, as well as those in *The Social World of Children's Learning*, will offer further examples of individuals and friendship groups using the patterns of strategies illustrated here. The table of this fuller account, presented as a typology of the four dimensions, can be found in Figure 8.5.

Through her case-study narrative we have described Sarah's preferred strategic response to school expectations in terms of the dimension of *conformity* and in terms of an orientation of *reification* of academic, social and extra-curricular structures and expectation for success which are available to all pupils. We can perceive the reification of such structures and expectation in Sarah's steady year-on-year, almost dogged adaptation to *others' agendas* and in her expectation of the rewards and recognition by teachers which she felt should come to her through it.

William, on the other hand, with his preferred strategy of *redefining*, rather than working *within* such frameworks for success, operated at the cutting edge of

Orientation	CONFORMITY (Adaptation)	ANTI-CONFORMITY (Deviance)	NON-CONFORMITY (Independence)	REDEFINING (Negotiation/Challenge)
	Reification	*Rejection*	*Indifference*	*Identification*
Strategies in relation to school structures and expectations.	Low risk, works within given structures. Others' agendas.	Low concern for risk. Oppositional agenda.	Relatively low awareness of risk, stands outside structures. Own agenda.	High-risk negotiation and challenge to structures. Influencing the shared agenda.
Emotional and social adaptation to school structures and expectation.	Adaptation and response. Socially competent. General acceptance and upholding of boundaries and rules.	Anti-social or less competent socially. Breaking rules.	Slow or reluctant to adapt socially and emotionally. Personal evasion of boundaries and rules.	Cue consciousness. Socially adept. High-profile negotiation and testing of boundaries of rules.
Strategies and relations with teachers	Teacher–pupil relationships characterized by 'respect' (may be strategic), reasonable compliance.	Teacher–pupil relationships characterized by non-compliance, antagonism or conflict.	Variable teacher–pupil relationships characterized by empathy and rapport or incomprehension/exasperation.	Teacher–pupil relationships characterized by easy, informal rapport, negotiation, challenge.
Strategies and relations with peers.	Conforms to mainstream peer and gender norms. Most separation of sexes in classroom and playground. Integrated, competent, accepted by peers.	Most stereotypically gendered behaviour and attitudes. Gangs. Alternative status systems and pursuits.	Stands outside peer group and gender norms; 'weird'; 'mad'; 'oddball'; 'loner'. One-to-one or small group friendships, centring around special interests. Separate interests, non-competitive with peers.	Leaders of peer and gender norms, high status. 'Bossy'. 'Sophisticated' social/sexual behaviour. Most integration of sexes in classroom and playground. Highly competitive with peers.

Figure 8.5 *Dimensions of pupils' strategic action*

them. His orientation was one of personal *identification* with school structures and expectations for career success. His preferred strategy was to be interacting, challenging and negotiating ideas for shaping the *shared agenda*. Not all classroom social and academic structures supported this collection of strategies. Where they were viable, he was able to maintain good rapport with teachers, go beyond their expectations for pupils' academic responses and hold a leading and defining role within the mainstream peer culture.

Despite their very different patterns of career outcomes, Robert and Harriet to various degrees shared the basic strategic response that we have identified as *non-conformity*. They both demonstrated a measure of *indifference* to the social and academic structures and expectations of the school and, it follows, to the rewards which their peers looked to for meeting, or indeed going beyond them. They both had their own distinct agenda for classroom and for playground which might, or might not, be accommodated by the expectations of teachers and peers. Often variously characterized as 'mad' and 'oddballs', they operated, with their close friends, on the margins of the mainstream social and cultural life of classrooms and playground. Integration with other peers was very much on their own terms.

As described in Chapter 2, we do not have examples of *anti-conformity* among our nine Greenside sample. However, they were present in the wider year-group cohort, as well as at Albert Park School (see Filer and Pollard, forthcoming). Our anti-conformity dimension was therefore constructed from that wider sample, as well as from the numerous other ethnographies of pupil strategies such as those described in Chapter 1. However, as we have described in Chapter 2 and as the children's stories also tell us, the 'dimensions of strategic action' of *conformity*, *anti-conformity*, *non-conformity* and *redefining* do not describe children *per se*. Neither do they represent psychological 'types'. Rather, they are abstracted conceptualizations of potential strategic choices.

Although each of the children demonstrated characteristic or preferred stances, strategies and styles of interaction, we nevertheless see that these patterns of strategic actions were liable to disruption when they became more or less viable or appropriate within changing classroom contexts. In the following section we will track the broad movements of these changes for each of our four case-study children.

8.6   DYNAMICS OF STRATEGIC ACTION

The model in Figure 8.6 is designed to show the dynamic potential of pupils' strategic action and identity. Pupils may move towards greater or lesser *conformity* in response to a particular pedagogy or structural position in the learning context. For similar reasons, a switch from, for example, a *redefining* position of negotiation and challenge towards *anti-conformity* and deviance may occur. The model is also designed to depict the way in which the gaps between conformity and the other strategic approaches of *anti-conformity*, *non-conformity* and *redefining* are, potentially, sites of tension. Such tension may occur between an individual pupil and a teacher or between individual pupils and their peers as a result of a learning stance or expression of identity that contravenes norms and expectations.

The dynamics of change has been demonstrated in the children's case-study data, within the analysis above and in the supporting tables of Figures 8.1, 8.2 and 8.3.

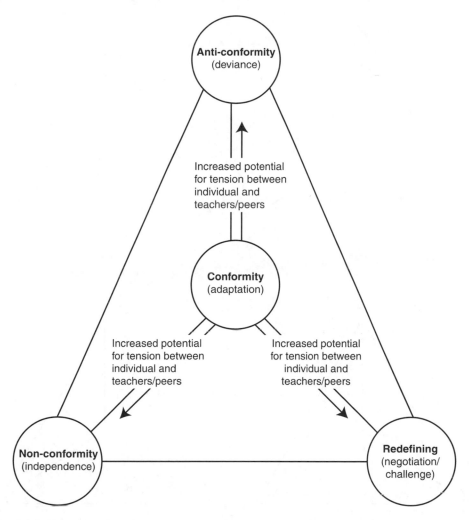

Figure 8.6 *Dynamics of pupil's strategic action*

Figure 8.7 provides a new way of plotting those annual changes for each of the children, together with an indication of their impact on pupil–teacher relationships. These are shown as 'high', 'medium' or 'low' tension (H, M, L). For example, we can see that, following her integration in Reception and apart from a degree of disenchantment in Year 2, Sarah provides a relatively stable case of conformity which generated little tension in her relationships with teachers. William's basic redefining stance is indicated, together with his reduction of risk in his learning in Year 5, and his more conflictual forays at particular points during several other years. Harriet's predominant non-conformity is represented, along with the varying degrees of tension experienced by her in relation to different teachers. We also see her more integrative adaptions in Years 4 and 5. For Robert, his movement between non-conformity and redefining strategies is shown to be extremely teacher- and context-dependent.

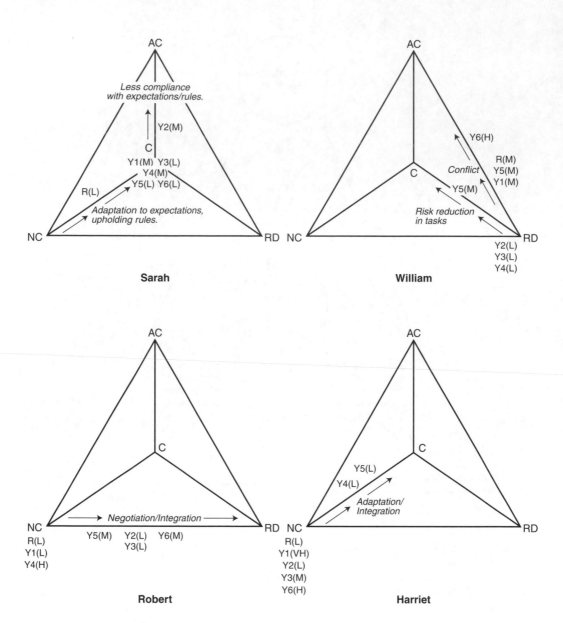

Representations of pupils' strategic adaptations by school year.
Brackets indicate (very) high, medium and low tension experienced in the pupil–teacher relationship.
Arrows and text indicate the dynamics and type of strategic change.

Figure 8.7 *Plotting the dynamics of pupils' strategic action*

Of course, these diagrams are another form of summary of our overall argument and, in order to avoid repetition, we present them without further substantive text. However, readers wishing to 'flesh out' the year-on-year dynamics and relationships can do so against the case-study matrices, or indeed, in relation to the narratives themselves.

8.7 CONCLUSION

The above analysis and models represent our major analytic insights regarding pupils' strategic responses to school and the interrelation of classroom, home and peer group contexts. Examples relating to these insights permeate the children's case studies and are readily accessible to readers through the case-study matrices and through the summary analyses in Figures 8.1 to 8.4. However, as we describe in Chapter 9, these analytic insights were developed in relation to wider pupil, school and research contexts than that of the four case studies presented here. They show, conclusively in our view, that children in English primary schools are extremely active in the construction and negotiation of their lives across home, playground and school settings. The models which show the dimensions and dynamics of pupils' strategic action are important reminders of differences between children in the sorts of relationships they were able to construct and the sorts of negotiations in which they were able to engage as they pursued important social as well as learning goals. They show also that pupils act in patterned and coherent ways within the structural and relationship constraints of the different classroom contexts in which they find themselves. Differences between pupils' patterns of strategic action remind us that they can only operate the strategies with which they feel comfortable, which they can manage socially and which are viable and appropriate for them within given structural contexts. They also show that they can develop new patterns of strategies or adapt familiar ones; and that they draw on identities developed in the home and wider community in elaborating and evolving their identities as pupils.

We set out the major theoretical conclusions of the study in the following chapter, together with the implications for policy and practice. At this point, it is sufficient to conclude that analysis and models presented in this chapter support one of the principal assertions of *The Identity and Learning Programme*: that children do not act passively in response to changing circumstances and different social contexts, enacting ascribed roles or accommodating to structural imperatives. Rather they respond actively and dynamically in protecting, shaping and maintaining their sense of self and identity as pupils. We believe that this has considerable implications for the policies and practices of teachers, parents and other adults.

Chapter 9

Social Processes and Pupil Learning

9.1 INTRODUCTION

In this final chapter, we begin by taking stock of the major elements of the *Identity and Learning Programme*, the series of cumulative studies and publications to which this book contributes. We then move to consider the implications of this overall analysis. We are particularly concerned with considering pupil experience developmentally using longitudinal analysis. James and Prout, in their book *Constructing and Reconstructing Childhood* (1990), emphasize not just pupil activity but also the temporal and developmental dimensions in studies of childhood. We see 'strategic biography' and 'pupil career' as important conceptual tools within this new paradigm, reflecting as they do the tracks which children develop, negotiate and accomplish as they progress through childhood. Throughout, we emphasize our fundamental concern with the agency, activity and rights of young people, as children or as pupils.

Of course, the normal qualifications associated with ethnographic research apply. We therefore recognize the need to be cautious about generalization beyond the cases which we have studied. In particular, we acknowledge that the analysis is rooted in studies of English children, families and state primary schooling, and reflects associated socio-historical and cultural contexts. On the other hand, we claim the capacity of ethnography to generate grounded, valid, holistic insights which may not be available in any other form of enquiry, and we are aware that many readers of previous work have found a resonance between our analysis and their own experiences and perceptions in other contexts. Further, we draw confidence from the comparative and longitudinal design of our work and the complementary studies of many other researchers. Overall then, while recognizing that *specific* substantive findings must be treated with particular caution, we feel that the accumulation of this work invites consideration of the wider application of the conceptual and analytic tools which have been generated. As a contribution to this, towards the end of this chapter we have suggested some implications for education policy and classroom practice.

9.2 CUMULATIVE ARGUMENTS IN THE IDENTITY AND LEARNING PROGRAMME

The *Identity and Learning Programme* is the name we have coined to describe the series of studies we have been engaged in on children's experience and perspectives of schooling. Some of this work is described in Chapters 1 and 2, but we review it briefly here to contextualize the results of the present book.

The Social World of the Primary School (Pollard, 1985) provided a sociological analysis of teacher and pupil perspectives, coping strategies, classroom relationships and processes of social differentiation. However, it did not directly address questions of children's learning, or the development of their identities as learners over time.

The Social World of Children's Learning (Pollard with Filer, 1996) extended that earlier analysis by holistically tracking the early learning experiences of five case-study children from age four to seven at Greenside Primary School. It explored the ways in which material, physical and intellectual resources, together with gender, socio-political and cultural circumstances, influenced the development and fulfilment of their learning potential. The major focus of the book was on the influence of inter-personal processes in home, classroom and playground.

The present book, *The Social World of Pupil Career*, represents a close develop-ment of these previous studies. The four case-study study children in this 'career' book were classmates with Mary, Hazel, Daniel, Sally and James who featured in the previous book, and other pupil cases could easily have been chosen to illustrate our analysis. Indeed, in developing the stories in this volume, we have revisited and interwoven the stories of the children from the earlier volume where appropriate.

The present book has focused on the development of the identities and learning dispositions of William, Robert, Sarah and Harriet through their primary school careers. Through accounts of their 'strategic biographies', we have documented continuity and change within cases, as well as variations across cases. We have thus been able to describe children's emergent sense of self as learners, and their changing conceptions of 'pupil identity'. More analytically, we formalized our understanding of how pupil identity is played out in terms of the *dimensions* and *dynamics* of strategic action (as described in Chapters 2 and 8).

By way of our major conclusions, we suggest the following:

1. Children's social development can be conceptualized in terms of 'strategic biog-raphy' and represented through narratives of influences, perspectives, actions and consequences in lives over time. 'Pupil career' is an aspect of strategic biography in specific relation to schooling. For analytical purposes, it is helpful to distinguish between four major dimensions of strategic action: conformity, anti-conformity, non-conformity and redefining.

2. As children get older and develop their pupil careers, strategic awareness of teacher requirements gradually increases and characteristic patterns of strategic action and orientation to learning tend to become established. These relative continuities articulate with patterns of action derived from the wider matrix of social relations and cultural expectations of home, community and playground and also reflect an emergent sense of identity. Parents, siblings and peers provide

particular mediating influences as new experiences are interpreted, and they are also themselves shaped by processes of challenge, negotiation and compromise.

3. On the other hand, the strategies deployed in a pupil career are also dynamic. Pupils negotiate their path through successive teacher and classroom settings and in so doing they create, maintain and shape their pupil identity. In particular, changing power-relations may act to enhance or threaten a pupil's established sense of self as a pupil, and may derive from factors such as discontinuity in a pupil's structural position in a class, different teacher expectations or organization for learning, or a new teacher's interpretations of a pupil's strategies. In such circumstances, existing strategies are liable to modification or change if they become no longer viable, appropriate or comfortable for a pupil to maintain.

4. The concept of 'pupil career' thus reflects the year-by-year interplay of previous orientations and contextually specific forms of strategic action in schools. It has particular consequences in terms of identity, self-confidence and learning disposi-ton and is a key element of each child's overall strategic biography.

We continue to work on further elements of the *Identity and Learning Programme*. Our study of children from Greenside Primary School has been complemented by a parallel study in a less affluent suburb of Easthampton. Albert Park Primary School was the context of Ann Filer's PhD study where, from 1989, she began tracking a cohort's classroom assessment experiences. Tracking the pupils through Key Stage 1 and into Key Stage 2, her thesis showed how teacher-created social and organisational factors could act to influence pupils' classroom language and responses to tasks. It highlighted the need for teacher assessments to be seen as context-related social accomplishments on the part of pupil, teachers and peers (Filer, 1993a, 1993b, 1993c, 1995, 1997). The study was then extended, with ESRC support (Pollard and Filer 1993), through to the end of Key Stage Two, and it was developed with respect to parental perspectives and as a comparative case study with Greenside. The result is an analysis, bridging the two case-study ethnographies, of the *Social World of Pupil Assessment*. A book of that title will follow this publication (Filer and Pollard, forthcoming), thus making a further contribution to the *Identity and Learning Programme* as a whole.

The latest phase of the *Identity and Learning Programme* tracks the secondary school careers of sixteen of the children who attended Greenside and Albert Park primary schools (Pollard, Filer and Furlong, 1995). They now attend nine contrasting secondary schools within Easthampton and their experiences will be studied to the end of their compulsory schooling at age 16. Considerable differences in the life experiences and trajectories of the children are already apparent and the analysis of this phase of the programme will unite our interest in processes of social differentia-tion and in social influences on learning. We are joined in this by Anne Malindine, studying for her PhD and bringing a particular focus on gender issues.

9.3   CHALLENGING 'CHILD' AND 'PUPIL' REPRESENTATIONS

Our brief review of the cumulative, analytic insights of the *Identity and Learning Programme*, as it has developed so far, shows that children are extremely active in the construction and negotiation of their lives both in home, playground and school settings. While they certainly respond to changing circumstances, they are by no means passive subjects enacting ascribed roles, fulfilling developmental models, or accommodating to structural or curricular imperatives. Additionally, through their actions, children also influence the lives of those with whom they interact. For parents, siblings, friends, peers and teachers, this influence is direct. For headteachers, governors, the community, local education authorities, employers, the media and national governments, it is progressively less direct. And yet, through the multiplication of patterns of action and response, children do shape the circumstances of others, as well as being shaped themselves.

Children act, however, within the particular historical, economic, political and cultural context of their society. This produces overt legal rights and obligations, discrepancies of resource and opportunity associated with social class, gender and ethnicity, and the particular priorities and structures which are expressed through the education system. It also brings social representations and forms of discourse through which commonsense understandings of key concepts such as: 'children', 'childhood', 'pupil', 'ability', 'effort', 'boy' and 'girl' are constructed.

In the Introduction of the present book, we discussed social representations of children and of childhood, drawing on Muscovici's work. He argued that social representations transform specialized, scientific knowledge into forms of culturally embedded commonsense knowledge: they become a taken-for-granted 'reality'. Regarding conceptions of children, we suggested that this has happened to some key ideas from social science. Deriving from sociology, the concept of 'socialization' has become anchored within pre-existing beliefs that children should be inducted into adult norms and had to 'grow up' and 'settle down'. The enduring conception of the child as 'uncivilized' and in need of control is not far away here. From psychology we have the key behaviourist idea that learning occurs through reinforcement, which articulates directly with historically established, traditional forms of didactic pedagogy. Thus, if we are to overcome the 'ignorance' and 'deficiencies' of childhood, more instruction, sequenced work and practice are needed. Additionally, the developmental psychology of Piaget offered a technical analysis of 'stages' in intellectual development which is now lodged as a scientific legitimation of commonsense understandings of child development.

There is a pattern in the way in which such ideas are anchored and objectified in common sense – it is consistently adult-centred. Thus children are conceptualized not in their own right, but in terms of how they impact on the lives of adults. The social representations which are embedded in our culture reflect both an imbalance of power and a failure to understand children's experience.

James, Jenks and Prout (1998) challenge us to break with these constrained and constraining images. They argue that the child should be understood in his or her own right 'as a person, a status, a course of action, a set of needs, rights or differences' (p. 207). An 'epistemological break' with the past is offered:

> New sociological approaches to the study of childhood ... move to study real children or the experiences of being a child. The socially developing model, by contrast, rarely addressed children at all. Traditional developmental psychology for example, was outstanding in its dedication to fitting the child to a 'stage' or 'level' of attainment, and socialisation theory, in its mimicry, searched childhood expressions for evidence of adult

interactional skills as steps towards the achievement of adulthood. Such approaches remain ignorant of the everyday, synchronic experience of the child actually living in the social world 'as a child'.
(James, Jenks and Prout, 1998, p. 208)

The *Identity and Learning Programme* is a contribution to this new paradigm, and we have a particular responsibility to attempt to link it to educational issues.

9.4   TEACHING *FOR* LEARNING

Throughout the *Identity and Learning Programme*, we have argued that children are active in constructing and negotiating their experiences in coherent and culturally patterned ways, and that in so doing, they shape the experiences of others. More specifically, we have described how classroom negotiation and interactive relationships between pupils and teachers tend to produce particular cycles of teaching and learning. These may be positive – such as when teachers show respect for pupil dignity, exercise authority fairly, and provide a stimulating, appropriate curriculum. On the other hand, they may also be negative – perhaps when teacher actions threaten pupil dignity, reflect the illegitimate use of power, and yield boring, routinized curricular activities.

Three major implications for classroom practice follow.

First, attempts to influence pupils as if they are passive objects to be controlled and instructed are crudely misconceived. Unfortunately, the fundamental needs of pupils *as active learners* have been inadequately understood or addressed by UK government policy in recent decades, with a consequential failure to fully support teachers in harnessing pupil motivation for educational purposes. This has contributed to disappointing levels of pupil performance in many schools, despite the scale and range of other educational 'reforms' and new requirements.

Second, teachers have a vital role in negotiating positive relationships as the moral foundation of positive learning cycles within classrooms. Indeed, if we wish to promote higher and higher standards of pupil attainment while also fostering children's self-confidence as lifelong learners, then we must create classroom climates within which *all* young people are able to manage the personal risk and ambiguity which are inherent in such an approach. The inclusivity which is implied here is particularly challenging, at a time when performance is measured and rewarded increasingly overtly.

Third, we believe that the *Identity and Learning Programme* demonstrates the importance of valuing and respecting children as individuals with unique identities and distinct approaches to learning. This is particularly significant for teachers who wish to develop mutual respect among their pupils and to minimize the damaging effects of classroom competition and rivalries. The children's case studies also show the significance of allowing individual children to incorporate and maintain distinct identities within and through their classroom learning. This is especially important where a child's identity is distinctly different from, or in tension with, those of the mainstream girls', boys' or other peer culture.

The case studies presented in this book have a lot to say about the active engagement of learners. Indeed, the aspiration was absolutely central to the espoused goals of Greenside Primary School and to the beliefs of the headteacher, Mrs Davison. Similarly, all of the teachers from Year 2 onwards subscribed to such a philosophy. So, in considering the longitudinal 'pupil careers' of our case-study children, perhaps through the summaries in Chapter 8, what can we learn about the ways in which successive teachers realized or fell short of such aspirations? Particular issues are highlighted by the most active, challenging or non-conforming strategies of learners. For such children, the perceptions of successive teachers can be crucial. For instance:

> William's autonomous, fun-loving, communicative classroom identity was experienced and interpreted very differently by his various teachers over the years. For some it was seen as contributing to rapport among the class as a whole, and was valued as integral to the learning process. For others it was variously seen as a threat to teacher–pupil relationships, as a source of ill-discipline and as a hindrance to William's own learning. In the latter cases, William might reduce his individuality and flair to a low-risk minimalist conformity, but his easy negotiative relationships could also be transformed into withdrawal of effort or even critical opposition.
>
> Harriet's distinctive identity and interests often did not conform to classroom and playground norms. However, in classrooms where she could incorporate her out-of-school interests and identity into tasks, she enjoyed school. In such classrooms her teachers viewed her as 'intelligent', 'creative' and 'cooperative'. Where her interests and individual identity could not be accommodated, she disliked school. She was then viewed by her teachers with incomprehension and even hostility, as 'underachieving' 'lacking enthusiasm' and 'stubborn'.
>
> In some teacher-created contexts, Robert's creativity, self-direction in learning, and absorption in his own learning were valued and positively incorporated into his classroom learning. In such settings, he developed a distinctive pupil identity that carried status with his peers. However, in the classrooms of some teachers, those qualities were viewed problematically. This gave rise to poor classroom relationships, unhappiness and some loss of motivation and self-esteem.

While active and challenging strategies can be variously perceived as problems to teachers, pupil conformity and the search for teacher approval are often more comfortable pupil strategies for teachers to live with. Pupil 'drift' may mesh with relatively routinized teaching. Indeed, if new targets for pupil attainment are to be achieved, it may be necessary that 'conformity' in the learning process should be a less comfortable, less viable strategic option for pupils – as Sarah's case study shows us:

> Teachers' perceptions that Sarah failed to achieve her full potential were often described in terms of an unwillingness to take some responsibility for her own learning. Through low-risk strategies and particular classroom peer alliances, she evaded challenges to her ideas and exploration beyond teacher-given areas of curriculum and frameworks for success. In a school that supported the notion of active, independent learners, her strategies certainly were often regretted by teachers as contributing to underachievement and safe mediocrity. However, such conformity, and that of other children using the same strategy, was never actively challenged by teachers. In fact, in some years it was encouraged by teachers through the often highly rewarded and teacher approved 'good girl' culture of mainstream girls' groups.

This mesh of teacher–pupil strategies and the nature of positive and negative learning cycles in classrooms were analysed in *The Social World of the Primary School* (Pollard, 1985), and examples for individuals and groups of children can also be found in the case-study chapters of *The Social World of Children's Learning*

(Pollard with Filer, 1996). However, with its longitudinal data-set, the present book highlights the implications of such learning relationships over the much longer period of seven years. In this context, 'pupil career' conceptualizes the strategic engagement of individuals with successive classrooms, curricula and teachers and with the development of identity through these settings. Can positive learning cycles be developed and sustained throughout pupil careers?

While established patterns of pupil strategies may be reinforced by new classroom experiences, they are also vulnerable to disruption if successive teachers interpret and respond to individual pupils' learning strategies in different ways. We analysed this by modelling major *dynamics of strategic action* (Figure 8.6). This depicts potential sites of tension between conformity to teacher expectations and pupil strategies of non-conformity, anti-conformity and redefining. Such tensions arise when pupils' previously viable strategies are challenged by the routines and expectations of a new teacher. In such circumstances, pupils may occupy positions of greater or lesser conformity, or may develop new coping strategies in response to a particular pedagogy or a changed structural position. Where their preferred approach to learning and identity is not accommodated, affirmed and valued, the change of strategy may become part of a negative cycle of deteriorating relationships and loss of motivation. Where pupils feel themselves to be valued and appropriately challenged intellectually, tensions are reduced and a positive cycle of relationships and learning is more likely to develop.

However, national education policies are of vital importance in supporting the development of such practices, and it is to such issues that we now turn.

9.5 POLICY IMPLICATIONS

As we have begun to argue in the present chapter, this analysis has significant implications for the development of any National Curriculum. In making this case, we draw additionally on some of the broad findings of the Primary Assessment, Curriculum and Experience (PACE) project (Pollard *et al.*, 1994; Croll, 1996; Pollard and Triggs, forthcoming; Osborn, McNess and Broadfoot, forthcoming; Broadfoot and Pollard, forthcoming). We have developed our argument in particular relation to English education policy and practice, but we believe that the principles may also apply elsewhere.

First, we would call for full recognition of the fundamental educational reality that primary education is concerned with the development of young children during a formative period of their lives. As they progressively acquire the skills, knowledge and understandings which are part of the formal curriculum, they also begin to develop unique identities, attitudes and values which will underpin their future development and lifelong learning. Additionally, their childhood lives and school experiences should be regarded as having intrinsic worth. Any national curriculum should thus be explicitly designed to complement, extend and enrich the basic process of learning.

Second, there is a strategic argument concerning how to maximize the long-term effectiveness of educational provision, if we accept that rapid social, economic, cultural and technological change is likely to continue in the 21st century and beyond.

It follows that an emphasis on transferable skills, conceptual knowledge and self-confidence in learning will be of particular importance for future citizens and for national competitiveness. For instance, the subject-based National Curriculum introduced to England and Wales in the early 1990s was traditional in structure, conservative in content and may unwittingly undermine forms of education which are necessary preparations for the future.

Third, a pragmatic, instrumental argument can be made about the effectiveness of the reforms to the national curricula of the 1990s. These were underpinned by a conception of education which focused on subject knowledge and its effective delivery in classrooms. Systemic curricular specification, assessment, inspection and accountability systems, combined with professional training and support, should certainly increase the quality and consistency of teaching across schools. However, this reflects a partial and ultimately invalid model of learning itself. We would argue that, to maximize standards of learning attainment over the long term, teachers must complement appropriate subject knowledge with knowledge and skill concerning pupil motivation, and awareness of the physical, intellectual, emotional, social, cultural, linguistic and economic factors which affect all learners.

Finally, there is a contextual argument about the differential impact of national curricula. We have to recognize that poverty, insecurity and social exclusion are a reality for many families, and that social differentiation has increased in recent decades. Despite considerable knowledge of inequalities associated with social class, ethnicity, gender and disability, systemic education reforms of the 1990s were not designed responsively. For instance, in the case of England and Wales we would suggest that the breadth and subject focus of the National Curriculum of the 1990s have favoured children whose self-confidence has been established at home and who are able to draw both on secure and enriching family backgrounds and significant amounts of cultural capital. Moves, however tentative, to set children by 'ability' are likely to make matters worse. A more enduring strategy should include serious recognition of the role of personal and social education and the development of lifelong learning dispositions and skills.

So what does this add up to regarding the future of primary and elementary school education?

We believe that the commitment to curricular 'breadth and balance', when couched in terms of an extensive range of subject knowledge, should be reconceptualized (Pollard, 1997). While maintaining a focus on literacy, numeracy, science and information technology, the curriculum should also be addressed in relation to:

- lifelong learning skills, understanding and capability;
- personal, social and moral education.

In the UK, 1998 brought moves in this direction, with a significant reduction in subject-based curricular requirements, and this will probably lead to some clustering of subjects in the future. Such change is the inevitable consequence of recognition that the curriculum of the 1990s was overloaded and over-constrained. Outside the core curriculum, it is to be hoped that it may be possible to build on the progress made in analysing key concepts in other subjects, while being less prescriptive about specific content. Teachers need appropriate scope to exercise professional judgement in response to local circumstances and pupil needs.

Complementing a reduction in curricular prescription, our work suggests a new emphasis on both lifelong learning and personal, social and moral education. Lifelong learning requires the development of positive self-confidence as a learner; judgement and skill in deploying learning strategies appropriately; and the capacity to reflect on learning in openminded and self-critical ways. These capabilities and attributes can certainly be taught and nurtured from a very young age, through processes such as planning, review, self-assessment and conferencing. Personal, social and moral education provides fundamental links between developmental processes, the agency of children, and the priorities of our society. It is crucial to the development of the quality of individual lives, and of responsible and self-critical citizens.

In such circumstances, national requirements would be more consistent with the flow of developmental learning processes, teachers and parents would derive more satisfaction as pupil careers became more fulfilled, and 'society' could gain from realizing the potential of more of its members as skilled, flexible, highly motivated and socially responsible citizens.

References

Aggleton, P. (1987) *Rebels Without a Cause*. London: Falmer.

Alexander, R., Rose, J. and Woodhead, C. (1992) *Curriculum Organisation and Classroom Practice in Primary Schools*. London: DES.

Althusser, L. (1971) Ideology and the ideological state apparatus. In B. R. Cosin (ed.) *Education, Structure and Society*. Harmondsworth: Penguin.

Ball, S. (1981) *Beachside Comprehensive*. Cambridge: Cambridge University Press.

Ball, S. J. (1980) Initial encounters in the classroom and the progress of establishment. In P. Woods (ed.) *Pupil Strategies*. Beckenham: Croom Helm.

Berger, P. and Berger, B. (1976) *Sociology: A Biographical Approach*. London: Penguin.

Berger, P. L. and Luckman, T. (1967) *The Social Construction of Reality*. London: Allen Lane.

Blunkett, D. (1998) Press statement announcing curriculum review, *Times Educational Supplement*, June.

Bowles, S. and Gintis, H. (1976) *Schooling in Capitalist America*. London: Routledge.

Breakwell, G. M. (1986) *Coping With Threatened Identities*. London: Methuen.

Broadfoot, P. and Pollard, A. (1996) Continuity and Change in English Primary Education. In P. Croll (ed.) (1996) *Teachers, Pupils and Primary Schooling*. London: Cassell.

Broadfoot, P. and Pollard, A. (forthcoming) *The Assessment Society: Changing the Discourse of Primary Education*. London: Cassell.

Bruner, J. (1990) *Acts of Meaning*. Cambridge, MA: Harvard University Press.

Bruner, J. S. (1986) *Actual Minds: Possible Worlds*. Cambridge, MA: Harvard University Press.

Central Advisory Council for Education (CACE) (1967) *Children and Their Primary Schools*. London: HMSO.

Caldwell, B. J. and Spinks, J. M. (1988) *The Self-Managing School*. London: Falmer.

Clandinin, D. J. (1986) *Classroom Practice: Teacher Images in Action*. London: Falmer.

Cortazzi, M. (1990) *Primary Teaching, How It Is: A Narrative Account*. London: Fulton.

Croll, P. (ed.) (1996) *Teachers, Pupils and Primary Schooling*. London: Cassell.

Davies, B. (1982) *Life in Classroom and Playground*. London: Routledge.

Dearing, R. (1993) *The National Curriculum and its Assessment: A Final Report*. London: SCAA.

Department of Education and Science (1992) *The Parent's Charter*. London: DES.

Donaldson, M. (1978) *Children's Minds*. Glasgow: Collins/Fontana.

Durkheim, E. (1956) *Education and Society*. Glencoe, Illinois: The Free Press

Filer, A. (1993a) Contexts of assessment in a primary classroom. *British Education Research Journal*, **19** (1), 95–108.

Filer, A. (1993b) The assessment of classroom language: challenging the rhetoric of 'objectivity'. *International Studies in Sociology of Education*, **3** (2), 193–212.

Filer, A. (1993c) *Classroom Contexts of Assessment in a Primary School*, Unpublished PhD, University of the West of England.

Filer, A. (1995) Teacher assessment: social process and social product. *Assessment in Education*. **2** (1), 23–38.

Filer, A. (1997) 'At least they were laughing': Assessment and the functions of children's language in their news session. In A. Pollard, D. Thiessen and A. Filer, *Children and Their Curriculum: The Perspectives of Primary and Elementary School Children*. London, Falmer.

Filer, A. and Pollard, A. (forthcoming) *The Social World of Pupil Assessment*. London: Cassell.

Filer, A. with Pollard, A. (1998) 'Principles and pragmatism in a longitudinal ethnography of pupil careers. In G. Walford (ed.) *Doing Research about Education*. London: Falmer.

Giddens, A. (1991) *Modernity and Self Identity*. Cambridge: Polity.

Hargreaves, A. (1978) The significance of classroom coping strategies. In L. Barton and R. Meighan (ed.) *Sociological Interpretations of Schooling and Classrooms*. Driffield: Nafferton.

Hargreaves, D. (1967) *Social Relations in a Secondary School*. London: Routledge.

Hargreaves, D. (1972) *Interpersonal Relationships and Education*. London: Routledge.

Hargreaves, D. and Hopkins, D. (1989) *Planning for School Development*. London: DES.

Hartley, D. (1985) *Understanding the Primary School*. London: Croom Helm.

HMI (1986) *The Curriculum from 5 to 16*. London: HMSO.

Jackson, P. W. (1968) *Life in Classrooms*. New York: Holt, Rinehart and Winston.

James, A. and Prout, A. (eds) (1990) *Constructing and Reconstructing Childhood*. London: Falmer.

James, A., Jenks, C. and Prout, A. (1998) *Theorising Childhood*. Cambridge: Polity.

Jenkins, R. (1996) *Social Identity*. London: Routledge.

King, R. (1978) *All Things Bright and Beautiful?* Chichester: Wiley.

Lloyd, B. and Duveen, G. (1990) A semiotic analysis of the development of social representations of gender. In G. Duveen and B. Lloyd (eds) *Social Representations and the Development of Knowledge*. Cambridge: Cambridge University Press.

Lortie, D. (1975) *Schoolteacher: A Sociological Study*. Chicago: University of Chicago Press.

Mac an Ghaill, M. (1988) *Young, Gifted and Black*. Buckingham: Open University Press.

Maitland, S. (1991) *Three Times Table*. London: Virago.

Mead, G. H. (1934) *Mind, Self and Society*. Chicago: Chicago University Press.

Muscovici, S. (1976) *Social Influence and Social Change*. London: Academic Press.

Muscovici, S. (1981) On social representations. In J. P. Forgas (ed.) *Social Cognition: Perspectives on Everyday Understanding*. London: Academic Press.

Muscovici, S. (1984) The phenomenon of social representations. In R. M. Farr and S. Muscovici (eds) *Social Representations*. Cambridge: Cambridge University Press.

Nash, R. (1976) *Teacher Expectations and Pupil Learning*. London: Routledge.

OFSTED (1997) *The Annual Report of Her Majesty's Inspector of Schools*. London: OFSTED.

Osborn, M., McNess, E. and Broadfoot, P. (forthcoming) *Policy, Practice and Teacher Experience: Changing English Primary Education*. London: Cassell

Parsons, T. (1951) *The Social System*. London: Routledge.

Pollard, A. (1979) Negotiating deviance and 'getting done' in primary school classrooms. In L. Barton, and R. Meighan (eds) *Schools, Pupils and Deviance*. Driffield: Nafferton.

Pollard, A. (1982) Towards a model of coping strategies, *British Journal of Sociology of Education*, **3** (1), 19–37.

Pollard, A. (1985) *The Social World of the Primary School*. London: Cassell

Pollard, A. (1987) *Children and Their Primary Schools*. London: Falmer.

Pollard, A. (1990) Towards a Sociology of Learning in Primary Schools, *British Journal of Sociology of Education*, **11** (3), 241–56.

Pollard, A. (1997) Learning and a new educational curriculum for primary education. In *Developing the Primary School Curriculum: The Next Steps*. London: SCAA.

Pollard, A. and Filer, A. (1993) *Assessment and Career in a Primary School: A Longitudinal Ethnography*. Application to ESRC (Grant R000234719).

Pollard, A., Filer, A. and Furlong, J. (1995) *Identity and Secondary Schooling: A Longitudinal Ethnography of Pupil Career*, Application to ESRC (Grant R000236687).

Pollard, A. and Triggs, P. (1999) *Policy, Practice and Pupil Experience: Changing English Primary Education*. London: Cassell.

Pollard, A. with Filer, A. (1996) *The Social World of Children's Learning*. London: Cassell.

Pollard, A., Broadfoot, P., Croll, P., Osborn, M. and Abbott, D. (1994) *Changing English Primary Schools?* London: Cassell.

Pollard, A., Thiessen, D. and Filer, A. (1997) *Children and Their Curriculum*. London: Falmer.

Prout, A. and James, A. (1990) *Reconstructing the Sociology of Childhood*. London: Falmer.

Rogoff, B. (1990) *Apprenticeship in Thinking*. New York: Oxford University Press.

Rowland, S. (1985) *The Enquiring School*. London: Falmer.

Sharp, R. and Green, A. (1975) *Education and Social Control*. London: Routledge.

Shibutani, T. (1955) 'Reference Groups as Perspectives', *American Journal of Sociology*, **60** (6), 562–9.

Stenhouse, L. (1975) *An Introduction to Curriculum Research and Development*. London: Heinemann

Styan, D. (1990) *Developing School Management: The Way Forward*. London: HMSO.

Tattum, D. P. and Lane, D. A. (1989) *Bullying in Schools*. Stoke on Trent: Trentham Books.

Task Group on Assessment and Testing (1988) *National Curriculum, Report*. London: DES.

Tharp, R. and Gallimore, R. (1988) *Rousing Minds to Life: Teaching, Learning and Schooling in Social Context*. New York: Cambridge University Press.

Tizard, B. and Hughes, M. (1984) *Young Children Learning*. London: Fontana.

Turner, G. (1985) *The Social World of the Comprehensive School*. London: Croom Helm.

Vygotsky, L. S. (1962) *Thought and Language*. Cambridge, MA: Massachusetts Institute of Technology.

Vygotsky, L. S. (1978) *Mind in Society: The Development of Higher Psychological Processes*. Cambridge, MA: Harvard University Press.

Walkerdine, V. (1983) It's only natural: rethinking child-centred pedagogy. In A. M. Wolpe and J. Donald (eds) *Is There Anybody There from Education?* London: Pluto Press.

Wallace, M. (1991) Coping with multiple innovations in schools, *School Organisation*, **11** (2), 187–209.

Wallace, M. (1994) School development planning in turbulent times. In D. Hargraves and D. Hopkins (eds) *Development Planning for School Improvement*. London: Cassell.

Waller, W. (1932) *The Sociology of Teaching*. New York: Russell and Russell

Willes, M. (1983) *Children into Pupils*. London: Routledge.

Willis, P. (1977) *Learning to Labour*. London: Saxon House.

Woods, P. (1977) Teaching for survival. In P. Woods and M. Hammersley (eds), *School Experience*. London: Croom Helm.

Woods, P. (1979) *The Divided School*. London: Routledge.

Wrong, D. (1961) The oversocialised conception of man in modern sociology. *American Sociological Review*, **26**, 183–93.

Author Index

Case-study Index of Children and Teachers

This is an index of case-study narrative chapters. It has been constructed to:

• facilitate cross referencing to children who feature in this book and in other *Social World* books;

• support readers in tracking the teachers and classroom contexts across the cases.

Analytic Subject Index

This index highlights some of the key issues within the analytic chapters of this book. It has been constructed to:

- assist engagement with the concepts and theoretical models;
- direct readers to the research design, data gathering methods and forms of analysis;
- highlight issues of policy relevance.